A STOIC BREVIARY

Classical wisdom in daily practice

Liam Milburn

Oh dear Pan, and all the other gods of this place,
Grant that I may be beautiful inside.
Let all my external possessions
Be in friendly harmony with what is within.
May I consider the wise man to be rich.

As for gold,
Let me have as much as a moderate man could bear
And carry with him.

—Socrates' Prayer, Plato, *Phaedrus* 279c, tr Jowett

❖ ❖ ❖ ❖ ❖

If you work at that which is before you, following right reason seriously, vigorously, calmly, without allowing anything else to distract you, but keeping your divine part pure, as if you should be bound to give it back immediately; if you hold to this, expecting nothing, fearing nothing, but satisfied with your present activity according to Nature, and with heroic truth in every word and sound which you utter, you will live happy.
And there is no man who is able to prevent this.

—Marcus Aurelius, *Meditations* Book 3, tr Long

❖ ❖ ❖ ❖ ❖

FOR ICS,
WITHOUT WHOM THIS BOOK WOULD NEVER HAVE BEEN POSSIBLE.
YOU ARE ALWAYS LOVED.

❖ ❖ ❖ ❖ ❖

Preface

I think it important to say exactly what this book on Stoicism isn't, before explaining what it is.

Though I am by vocation and profession a teacher of philosophy and the humanities, this is not a scholarly text. It is not intended as a tool for academic research, and it makes no claims to advancing scholarship on the study of the Stoic philosophers.

Over the years I have learned exactly how little I know about even the things I am supposed to know, so I would not dare to presume such a role.

While never intending to "dumb down" the content of Stoicism, I try to present the material in a way that any thoughtful and curious reader can hopefully appreciate.

I also do not wish to ignore some of the more precise, complex, technical questions of logic, metaphysics, or cosmology considered by many of the Stoics, but I do believe this book should first and foremost be an introduction to the basic ethical approach of the Stoic school.

A text on other necessary and more advanced topics may be for another time and place, and most likely for a writer more skilled than myself.

This is also most certainly not a book in psychology, and I would dissuade you from using it in place of proper psychological care. Though I study and teach on many matters relating to the field of psychology, I am not qualified to tell you anything about your own mental health. I refer you to esteemed professionals in the field for such assistance.

Likewise, though I will reference my own health in this text, don't confuse anything here with sound medical advice. When you want your taxes done, you don't go to an auto mechanic, and if you need medical advice, you certainly don't go to a philosophy professor.

It is also not a book arguing for a certain type of new–fangled therapy, or any type of simplistic self–help model. Our world is sadly too full of the sound and fury of trendy advice, most of it signifying nothing.

I have no desire to join in the clamor of diet plans, get-rich-quick schemes, or formulas for instant happiness. Only you are the source of your own happiness, and there is no quick, or even easy, solution.

And by no means am I preaching about religion or social matters. We have enough clerics and politicians to do that for us, a very few who are noble, most who are rotten. They already have their reward. It usually involves our money finding its way into their pockets.

Where does that leave us? If this book won't make you a better philosopher, cure your neuroses or your acne, won't make you happy in the next sixty days, or send you to straight to heaven, why should you bother reading it?

I can only offer one, and one seemingly insignificant, answer. I am a human being, a person like you. Despite all the differences we may have, of class, race, creed, religion, or politics, every one of us shares that same nature. It is our common bond.

What I have written isn't a formal treatise, or a work of research, or a handbook, or a set of instructions. It's just the honest reflection of a single human being, facing the obstacles, the pains, and the doubts that I suspect each and every one of us faces each and every day. This book simply asks you to consider your humanity, and what that may mean.

And I do this in light of a tradition in philosophy, very ancient, but also completely timeless, called Stoicism. It is a way of thinking, and more importantly, a way of living that saved my life. That is what this book is about.

❖ ❖ ❖ ❖ ❖

Introduction

"Stoic" is one of those unfortunate words that has changed its meaning over the years, and consequently gets a bum rap. Whenever I hear it used these days, it almost invariably signifies a person who is cold, emotionless, or willing to heartlessly suffer without complaint. It is seen as an attitude of toughness, the stiff upper lip, the get-over-it mentality, and an approach that stresses strength over sympathy.

This is sadly something of a misunderstanding. The true Stoic, Classically understood, is a person who looks to a love of the natural order of all things as a first guide. He seeks to live with Nature, and never against it. He recognizes how his own happiness is a part of the whole order of things, and he understands that his reason and freedom exist within that whole.

He doesn't merely meet suffering and misfortune with denial, but sees the opportunity for the good in all things. He knows that he chooses how to live, and that his environment does not rule him. He does not allow his life to depend upon his circumstances, but bases his well being upon his own wisdom and moral character.

Finally, and I think most importantly, he never closes himself off to others. Knowing that his practice of virtue and excellence are the very purpose for his existence, he loves and cares for his fellows without condition.

It is only by his concern for the good of others, that he becomes good himself. Far from being cold and emotionless, he finds the greatest and deepest joy in the love of all things.

These things are easy to say. They are also hard to do. And I would suggest that the most important things in life are precisely the things that are most difficult. Whatever is worthwhile requires effort to achieve.

These are attitudes and ideas that have been present throughout all of human history, in both the East and the West. And I claim, with no apology, that this is because they are true. A Christian, a Buddhist, a Muslim, a Hindu, and even an Atheist can all agree on many of these principles, precisely because they speak to our shared humanity.

❖ ❖ ❖ ❖ ❖

The formal school of Stoicism was founded by Zeno of Citium (c 334–262 BC), and takes its name from the public space in Athens where he taught. He was, in turn, succeeded by Cleanthes of Assos (c 330–c 230 BC), and Chrysippus of Soli (c 279–206 BC) as heads of the school.

Sadly, no complete texts from this Early Period or the Middle Period of Stoicism survive. We know only of their teachings from fragments and the accounts of others, most importantly the 3rd century AD work *The lives and opinions of eminent philosophers* by Diogenes Laertius.

Thankfully, we have richer resources available in the writings of the Roman Late Period of Stoicism, including the great figures of Seneca the Younger (c 4 BC–65 AD), Musonius Rufus (c 20 AD–c.100 AD), Epictetus (50 AD–135 AD), and Emperor Marcus Aurelius (121 AD–180 AD). Though eclectic in his philosophy, many of the ideas and values of Cicero (106 BC–43 BC) also have a markedly Stoic character.

While a dominant philosophical movement in the Roman period, often in tension with Skepticism and its chief rival, Epicureanism, Stoicism gradually faded from fashion in the Christian era. Even so, its influence is profound and perennial.

Though traditional scholarship stresses Neo-Platonic influences as primary in the early Christian philosopher Boethius, I would argue that his Stoic roots are equally important. Accordingly, I always consider his wonderful *Consolation of Philosophy* to be an honorary Stoic text. That is why I include his excerpts in this book, with no apology.

The Stoics studied a wide range of topics, and divided their work into three disciplines: logic, physics, and ethics. As this book primarily concerns the search for the good life, my stress is on their model of ethics, though related elements on the nature of human reason and order of the natural world will obviously come into play as well.

In recent years one can discern a slightly renewed interest in Stoicism, and not merely as an academic exercise, but as a practice of daily living. I believe this to be its great and unique appeal, as it speaks not only to our abstract reflection but also to our immediate choices and actions.

This is, I think, all the more important in our own time, where there is an urgent need to find meaning and purpose in a world where people are more closely connected through industry and technology, but often seem more separated from one another morally and spiritually.

Many of us know the experience of feeling completely alone in a city of a million, or even of many millions, of being surrounded by people with whom we have no real connections. And our contemporary world, so full of noise, images and so much that is artificial, has never been more removed from Nature.

❖ ❖ ❖ ❖ ❖

I came to Stoicism fairly late in my own philosophical wanderings. My first love was for the philosophy of St Thomas Aquinas. Always able to distinguish the different senses of the meaning and depth of a wide scope of traditions, he was a master at integrating a variety of insights into a greater and harmonious whole, discerning how all things proceed from and return to their Divine source.

St Thomas is still the philosopher who speaks most to my intellect. Over time, Blaise Pascal became the philosopher who spoke most deeply to my heart. But in the end, it has been the Stoics, and particularly the *Meditations* of Marcus Aurelius, that help me most in how to live.

I suspect that if I had been groomed in Stoic thinking and practice earlier in my life, I would probably have become a much better, and therefore happier, person than I now am. And even so, what little sense of character I may now have is certainly much due to even this late influence.

My first indirect introduction to the Stoic values of self-reliance in the face of Fortune came through Boethius' *Consolation*, and this planted the seeds for my slow but certain embrace of this way of life.

It is because Stoicism has had such a positive and profound effect on my way of thinking and living that I feel called to share it, in however humble and insufficient a way, with others.

❖ ❖ ❖ ❖ ❖

My own journey has had many twists and turns.

I will refer to a few of them as examples in this book, as Stoic practice has helped me in so many different ways.

But most importantly, and so central to my own life, has been how it has been an aid in fighting what I refer to, with a nod to two of my heroes, Samuel Johnson and Winston Churchill, as the "Black Dog".

Call it what you will, melancholy, dejection, a sadness of life, existential despair, or by its medical name, clinical depression. Those who have not been cursed to suffer the Black Dog may find it hard to understand or relate to, but it is a state of heart and mind that goes far beyond feeling down or low. The sufferer often rightly feels frustrated when others refer to a simple bad mood as being "depressed".

It is a type of sadness, a severe hopelessness, a misery that seems to consume the possibility of any joy. The extreme pain even takes on a powerful physical form. And it cannot simply be wished away when one is advised to "get over it" or "move on".

I again wish to remind the reader that I do not suggest the practice of Stoicism as any sort of replacement for medical, or psychological, or spiritual help where it is truly needed. But it can be a philosophical supplement, an aid, a potent weapon in a varied arsenal to help restore a sense of joy.

❖ ❖ ❖ ❖ ❖

The Black Dog only really showed himself fully to me in early adulthood. I had always been a quiet, shy, and reflective child, and, having unusual likes and interests, I was often alone. I was awkward, ungainly, unattractive, and never really liked by my peers. Books and daydreaming were often my best friends. But at that time I still had a firm hope that, one day, everything would somehow work out fine.

When I went to college, I was immediately surprised by love. And I fell very hard. I hadn't been expecting it, and I honestly didn't think I had any right to it. But my bond with another person, slowly but surely, became the glue that bound my life together. All my thoughts, feelings, dreams and plans revolved around this single star. I didn't know what the future would hold, but I could not imagine it without my truest and dearest friend.

It wasn't all roses. She struggled to suffer my insecurities and my foul temper. I struggled to bear her problems with honesty and fidelity. We were an odd pair, but we became seemingly inseparable.

As the years passed, I sensed malaise. For some reason, I was becoming bitter, lazy, cynical, and intemperate.

I started drinking far too much, and found myself in the company of toxic friends. We were both increasingly adrift, and losing the direction given by a moral compass. Being the sadly reflective person I am (my parents had already jokingly called me "the little philosopher" when I was an infant) I struggled to take a personal inventory.

I made an immediate and firm decision to do some major rebuilding, to commit to living a more healthy and virtuous life, and to rededicate myself to my vocation as a teacher. And the central part of the effort was that I would confirm my devotion to the love of my life.

I hatched the big romantic plan. I intended to meet her at Church on a Sunday morning, and then surprise her with the usual falling to one knee. I had nothing better or fancier to offer than my unconditional love, an empty wallet, and my grandmother's old engagement ring.

Here is where things went tragically wrong. Only a few weeks earlier she had told me she wanted nothing more than for us to spend our lives together, and I still believed her.

Nevertheless, always the insecure pessimist, I had prepared myself for the very likely possibility of a refusal, and I steeled myself to accept this if it came to pass. I would, at least, have given it my best. I loved her for her sake, and I always will, regardless of whether she fancied me.

But I had not prepared myself for something much darker. She wasn't at Church as expected, and when I walked the few blocks to her new apartment I found that she wouldn't answer her door, even as she peeked through the blinds.

She had spent the night with another man, someone I at the time considered a friend.
The romantic loss was far outweighed by the sense of being deceived and abandoned by the friend I loved beyond all else.

The pain was overwhelming, and compounded threefold: the emptiness of losing the person dearest to me, the shame of having allowed myself be so foolishly deceived for so long, and the agony of rejection and betrayal.

Always the hopeless romantic at heart, I would often think of Bogart from *In a Lonely Place*: 'I was born when she kissed me. I died when she left me. I lived a few weeks while she loved me.'

This is when the Black Dog started to walk by my side. It was the trigger, the occasion for most of what followed. He's been there ever since.

❖ ❖ ❖ ❖ ❖ ❖

From that point on, there always seemed to be something broken in me. It was like a physical wound or injury that never heals quite right, and always causes crippling pain.

A psychiatrist I deeply respect surprised me by diagnosing me, many years later, with Post-Traumatic Stress Disorder, something I assumed was for soldiers, not jilted and cuckolded lovers.

And every other occurrence, every good or bad fortune, always seemed to link back to that defining event. It was never a deliberate choice, but an immediate and seemingly uncontrollable instinct.
It often became so severe that any memory, any place, any person or life event would end up leading me straight to that pain. At times my temperament would improve, but the overall direction became one of a gradual decline.

The reader who is already familiar with Stoicism will perhaps recognize where the problem lay, though I did not see it at the time. My own thinking was on some days rooted in deep resentment, and a sense that I had been wronged. At other times it also took a form where I felt that I inevitably deserved the pain as a penance for my sins.

Whatever the case, the common theme was simply that I had unwittingly made my happiness or misery entirely dependent on things that were outside of me.

I had already started that early on, when I made the value of my own life contingent only upon the support of another person.

The love I felt turned out not to be enough of a love of giving, and too much of a love of needing; the problem wasn't that I was living according to love, but in that I was requiring the love of another for living. And when I lost that person, I was also lost, and I moved between being tossed and swayed by anger or guilt.

There were far too many times when I put a noose around my neck, or a .45 in my mouth. I will never be so vain as to claim that I defeated those instincts out of any virtue. I only avoided taking my own life out of fear, and the pain it would cause my family.

This destructive habit of thinking spread out and attached itself to most every other aspect of my life. If I faced conflict in my work, I was immediately moved to resentment or despair. When I tried to form relationships with others, I would assume insincerity by default. When I later suffered problems with my health, I could think of nothing good to struggle onward for.

When my wife and I lost our first child, that same pattern seemed to impose itself. The loss must either be a grave injustice or a deserved punishment, and I allowed that pain alone to determine my life. I cried for hours sitting alone in my car, and broke many parts of that poor vehicle when I lashed out in anger.

If Stoicism has a cardinal sin, this is it, as we will soon see. If I choose to make my life depend upon things that are beyond my control, I become not the master of my life, but a slave to my circumstances.

The daily practice of Stoicism has been a necessary part of my ability not only to survive, but also to live well. I still stumble and fall, all of the time, but now I get up again. And I know this is worth doing, because Nature has given me all the tools that I need to be happy. That is a joyous, wondrous, and beautiful thing.

❖ ❖ ❖ ❖ ❖

A few words are in order on the format and structure of this book.

I call it a breviary, not in the specific sense of a book of prayers, but in the broader sense of the Latin word *breviarium*, a collection, abridgment, anthology, or compendium.

It is like an old-school primer.

I have chosen brief passages from Stoic thought that have been of great assistance in my own philosophical recovery.

That there are 365 such passages in this book is of no deeper significance than that it allows the reader to meditate on them over a complete year.

I then follow the passage with a brief reflection, based on my own thoughts and experiences.

They may or may not appeal to you, and you may or may not agree with them, but the good to be gained here, is I think, your own willingness to wrestle with these same questions, and in your own way.

Don't fight me, or the original author, but fight yourself.

In some cases, I imagine that the reflection may be very specific to my own situation, and for that I do apologize.

Simply skip the ones that don't speak to you, and embark upon your own reflection.

At times you may see a repetition of concepts and values.

I may repeat something to help myself and build my habits.

Pass over it, if it's not your thing.

As is often said at a variety of self-help meetings, "Take what you need, and leave the rest."

They can be read in order or out of order, though in some cases I assume that the content of an earlier passage will help with the comprehension of a later one.

You can also read this book quickly or slowly, though I have personally found that Stoicism, like any strong medicine, is best taken in small doses.

Finally, your interest may be one of simple curiosity, or perhaps, as it was for me, out of an urgent need for comfort.

The depth and completeness with which you read the book, whether it be browsing or deep meditation, should follow your own situation.

In my later years, my own habits have involved sitting down every morning, right after rising, and well before dawn, but before the work of the day begins, to read a Stoic passage.

I try to keep it to a single primary theme, and then I use that theme to help me during the day when I find conflict, sadness, anger, or loneliness.

Almost invariably, in ways I could not have predicted, the Stoic wisdom for that day has a profound effect.

By changing my thinking, I can change my living.

The direct sections from Epictetus are usually right to the point, and while profound, present Stoic wisdom in a very immediate form.

I turn to Marcus Aurelius, whose writing I find more personal and reflective, when I sense the day will be especially challenging.

And I turn to Seneca when I have the luxury or the need for a more extended and closely reasoned train of thought.

I find Musonius Rufus the most emotionally comforting, as I see him as a very sympathetic writer.

The short fragments, sadly small in number, of the Early and Middle Period can serve like a quick energy shot, and on the fringes of the Stoic tradition Boethius is my guide when I'm feeling more metaphysical, and certain passages from Cicero when I long for soaring rhetoric.

❖ ❖ ❖ ❖ ❖

Finally, I offer a few words on sources.

The original texts are, of course, in Greek and Latin.

Different English translations are available, all with their own distinct merits.

In this book, I draw from older, classic translations, mainly from the late 19th and early 20th centuries.

I do this for two reasons.

First, aesthetically—and I am eccentric in this regard—I prefer the dignity of such an older style, which I find is especially suitable for Stoic thought.

Second, on a purely practical level, this project began as an informal way to distribute Stoic texts to friends and colleagues at little or no cost, and using works now in the public domain avoided any entanglements or expenses associated with copyright law.

I choose to continue that tradition in this version.

Wherever the English seems too archaic, I will sometimes very slightly alter the wording, but never the meaning, of the text, to speak most directly to a modern reader.

This is, again, not a work of formal scholarship, but one of personal reflection.

If you are inspired by Stoic wisdom, I encourage you to pursue a more in–depth interest in the tradition, and consult the wide variety of secondary sources available.

Yet I suggest that, most of all, Stoicism only really matters if you use it in your own life.

Think of this Stoic Breviary more as a primer, or a set of readings to get your feet wet.

If it is to your liking, I hope to soon find you swimming in the deep end.

Because I am a Stoic, you are my fellow citizen of the world, and my friend, even if I have never met you.

❖ ❖ ❖ ❖ ❖

16

D a y 1

Of all existing things some are in our power, and others are not in our power. In our power are thought, impulse, will to get and will to avoid, and, in a word, everything which is our own doing.

Things not in our power include the body, property, reputation, office, and, in a word, everything which is not our own doing.

Things in our power are by Nature free, unhindered, and untrammeled; things not in our power are weak, servile, subject to hindrance, dependent on others.

Remember then that if you imagine that what is naturally slavish is free, and what is naturally another's is your own, you will be hampered, you will mourn, you will be put to confusion, you will blame gods and men.

But if you think that only your own belongs to you, and that what is another's is indeed another's, no one will ever put compulsion or hindrance on you, you will blame none, you will accuse none, you will do nothing against your will, no one will hurt you, you will have no enemy, for no harm can touch you.

—Epictetus, *Enchiridion* 1, tr Matheson

If there was ever a single, concise mission statement for Stoicism, I think this would have to be it. It's not a terribly difficult concept to understand, at least in theory, but it can be a very difficult set of values to live in practice.

It certainly felt difficult, if not impossible, to me, since so many of us are so completely bound up with the conditions and circumstances of our lives.

Our families, or careers, our education, our friends and social standing, our health, our wealth and property, even our appearance, are seen as defining us.

Though we may feel ashamed to acknowledge it, these are the standards we are given to accept as a default.

It is hard to think without them.

The distinction is clear enough.

We are in control of some things, our thoughts, our choices, and our own actions.

These things are free of outside limitations, if we only so decide.

We are not in control of other things, the circumstances of our world, wealth, power, honor, the actions of others, even our own bodies.

By relying on such things, we become enslaved to them, ironically by that same power of decision.

Now would it ever make sense to have happiness to depend on something uncontrollable?

This is why we become miserable, complain, blame others, and even blame God for our state of affairs.

Yet if we rely only on what belongs to us, we will be in want of nothing.

It isn't that the things outside of us have no value in themselves, but they have value in relation to our happiness only if we learn to use them to aid us in wisdom and virtue, and never as a hindrance to them.

❖ ❖ ❖ ❖ ❖

Begin the morning by saying to yourself, I shall meet with the busy-body, the ungrateful, arrogant, deceitful, envious, unsocial. All these things happen to them by reason of their ignorance of what is good and evil.

But I who have seen the nature of the good that it is beautiful, and of the bad that it is ugly, and the nature of him who does wrong, that it is akin to me, not only of the same blood or seed, but that it participates in the same intelligence and the same portion of the divinity, I can neither be injured by any of them, for no one can fix on me what is ugly, nor can I be angry with my kinsman, nor hate him,

For we are made for cooperation, like feet, like hands, like eyelids, like the rows of the upper and lower teeth. To act against one another then is contrary to Nature; and it is acting against one another to be vexed and to turn away.

—Marcus Aurelius, *Meditations* Book 2, tr Long

Most of us don't wake up and face the day like an advertisement for a brand of coffee.
  We already recognize that we will face hardships, some extremely severe, and that many of the people we will encounter will act very poorly toward us.

But if my happiness does indeed rest in my own actions, and does not come from the actions of others, I have found a new freedom.
  It allows me to dedicate myself to my own thoughts, decisions, and character.

How others treat me is up to them, and I can only react to their actions, good or evil, as a means to becoming better myself.
  Perhaps by acting with wisdom and virtue I may also encourage them to recognize and experience what is truly good about life.
  But that can only be their choice, however noble the example that is given.

I cannot directly control the actions of others.
  But why would others act this way?
  Do not necessarily presume malice.
  People seek false goods out of degrees of ignorance, for whatever reason, voluntary or involuntary, and this deserves my sympathy, not my hatred.

Even if my neighbor does evil to me, he is a person like me, sharing in the exact same humanity, with the exact same dignity.
  Though he may not recognize it, he and I weren't made to be enemies.

As beings of reason and will, and not only of feeling and instinct, we can consciously recognize that we share that same purpose.

The analogy of organs and members of the body is a beautiful one.

Participating in the same purpose of Nature, to live with excellence and joy, we are made to work together.

I turn away from Nature when I act out of anger or hatred.

It is the nature of rational animals to be cooperative, not competitive.

When I meet hatred with hatred, I simply compound it.

When I meet hatred with love, I defeat it.

❖ ❖ ❖ ❖ ❖

'The wise man is self-sufficient.' This phrase, my dear Lucilius, is incorrectly explained by many; for they withdraw the wise man from the world, and force him to dwell within his own skin.

But we must mark with care what this sentence signifies and how far it applies; the wise man is sufficient unto himself for a happy existence, but not for mere existence. For he needs many helps towards mere existence; but for a happy existence he needs only a sound and upright soul, one that despises Fortune.

—Seneca the Younger, *Moral Letters to Lucilius* 9, tr Gummere

Seneca reminds us not to misunderstand the central concept of self-reliance.
It is not a rejection of or separation from the world.
It has much in common, I think, with St Paul's advice to be in the world, but not of the world.

To exist, in the sense of survival, requires many externals, such as air, water, food, warmth, or shelter.
To survive with greater security may add friends, family, wealth, employment, leisure, or planning for the future.

But the mere existence of survival isn't why we're here.
Anyone who has existed in misery knows this.
The good life isn't just living, it's living well, and living well isn't measured in proportion to the degree of externals we possess.
Anyone who has been rich in fortune but poor in spirit understands.

In other words, the quality of our living, which depends on our choices and actions, is not the same thing as the quantity of how much we have, or how long we live.
A happy life can be a short one in poverty.
A long life can be a miserable one rolling in riches.

Since this means I should care more for the quality than the quantity of life, the higher over the lower, it also requires that I don't treat my circumstances as good or bad in themselves.

Good fortune can help me or hurt me, depending entirely on my estimation and use of it.
Bad fortune can help me or hurt me, depending entirely on my estimation and use of it.
A blessing or a curse can both be opportunities for improvement or failure.
To "despise" fortune is to never love it for its own sake.

I believe deeply that a person who cherishes virtue, who makes love and compassion the measure of his merit, will gladly give up the quantities of his life for the quality of his character.
He may give up his riches, his reputation, or his health.
He may even offer up his very life.

He may surrender his existence for a happy existence.
Once I understood that, I had taken an important step in reforming my life.

❖   ❖   ❖   ❖   ❖

Day 4

Aiming then at these high matters, you must remember that to attain them requires more than ordinary effort; you will have to give up some things entirely, and put off others for the moment.

And if you would have these also—office and wealth—it may be that you will fail to get them, just because your desire is set on the former, and you will certainly fail to attain those things which alone bring freedom and happiness.

—Epictetus, *Enchiridion* 1

Epictetus is not just saying that the Stoic life is going to be difficult.
It isn't just that it will require work, or that it may sometimes hurt, at least at first.

He means that we are going to have to make decisions about what is more or less important to us, and that those decisions will make us recognize that we can't have it both ways.
We can't serve two masters, or have our cake and eat it too.

Again, the key is remembering the goods of our wisdom and virtues are greater than the goods of our fortune and circumstances.
This means I may have to realign my priorities.
I may have to defer some things and abandon others.

The helping hand offered to a neighbor in need may make me late for work, or even mean that I need to delay my vacation.
I may want that high-paying job that will make me the envy of the community, but I can never take it if it means I need to deceive, steal, or abuse others in order to keep it.

If I want to build my moral worth, the highest good that is mine alone, I can't go around compromising it for fame and fortune, things that really have nothing to do with me at all.
I can easily lose the fame and fortune in any event, and I will certainly have lost the freedom of happiness.

Many years ago, when I was working in social services, a superior pressured me to disclose things that had been said to me by a client in the strictest confidence.
I very firmly, but as politely as possible, refused.
He raised the stakes by suggesting that my own position would benefit if I agreed.
I sadly lost my temper, and I offered my resignation.
It wasn't accepted, but it could well have been, and I never moved up in any way at that job.

I haven't usually been that consistent.
In high school, a Headmaster once asked me to speak honestly about something I had witnessed, and that had caused another person great harm.
I lied, justifying it in my own mind by the rule that nobody likes a snitch.

There's the rub.
I cared about my reputation first, and I squirmed inside when the bully I was protecting gave me a sinister wink and thumbs up.

❖ ❖ ❖ ❖ ❖

21

Nothing, therefore, is more important than that we should not, like sheep, follow the flock that has gone before us, and thus proceed not whither we ought, but whither the rest are going.

Now nothing gets us into greater troubles than our subservience to common rumor, and our habit of thinking that those things are best which are most generally received as such, of taking many counterfeits for truly good things, and of living not by reason but by imitation of others.

This is the cause of those great heaps into which men rush till they are piled one upon another. In a great crush of people, when the crowd presses upon itself, no one can fall without drawing some one else down upon him, and those who go before cause the destruction of those who follow them.

—Seneca the Younger, *On a Happy Life* 1, tr Stewart

Our mothers may have scolded us by asking, "If everyone else jumped off a bridge, would you do it, too?"
We sheepishly said "no", but something within us still resisted.
That something is the pull of honor, the feeling that we need to be respected, to be liked as fully and by as many people as possible.

The love of honor, position, and status is a perfect example of casting our happiness in with our external circumstances, the things outside of our power.

First, how we are liked or disliked has nothing to do with us, and everything to do with the judgment of others.

Second, as it depends upon others, it will come and go with their whims.

Third, while one should certainly respect what is virtuous, an action does not become virtuous because it is respected. If we think the latter, we have our wires crossed.

It may seem snobbish or elitist not to follow what is popular, but arrogance can arise just as readily, if not even more readily, through the conformity of the majority.
As we follow, blindly and moved only by passion, we are subsumed into the crowd, and are all drawn down together.

The field of education may seem a far cry from the world of business, but over the last few years I've noticed the increasing appeal to "best practice" as a guide for policy and curriculum.
At first, I naively assumed this meant doing something in the best possible way.

It was only gradually that I realized the best possible way meant, in effect, doing what everyone else did.
This shocked my admittedly unpopular sensibilities, but instead of being offered a reasoned argument, I was told this was the only way to operate.

G.K. Chesterton once said *Dead things swim with the current, living ones against it.*
Don't surrender your ability to make your own decisions.

❖ ❖ ❖ ❖ ❖

Day 6

All that is from the gods is full of Providence. That which is from Fortune is not separated from Nature or without an interweaving and involution with the things that are ordered by Providence.

From thence all things flow; and there is besides necessity, and that which is for the advantage of the whole universe, of which you art a part. But that is good for every part of Nature, which the Nature of the whole brings, and what serves to maintain this Nature.

Now the universe is preserved, as by the changes of the elements so by the changes of things compounded of the elements. Let these principles be enough for you, let them always be fixed opinions. But cast away the thirst after books, that you may not die murmuring, but cheerfully, truly, and from thy heart thankful to the gods.

—Marcus Aurelius, *Meditations* Book 2

The Stoic model rests upon certain first principles about the order of Nature.
  These principles, I have found, can be an aid to all, whether they might be religious or not.

The term "Providence" here refers to the fact that Nature is intrinsically ordered, that every effect has a cause, and that the state of all individual things is necessarily connected within the harmony of the whole.

Where there is a change in one thing, there will be a change in another, and so on.
  Young people understand this well enough when they are taught about an ecosystem, for example.
  Now simply understand that this order rules the whole universe.

Defer, if you will, for the moment the question of the origin of this plan of order.
  Attribute it to God, the gods, or just the Cosmos itself.
  However we discern its origin, its presence is clearly felt in our daily living.

We might think, however, that many things in Nature are random or chaotic.
  Fortune, for example, seems to come and go for no reason.
  They may only appear to be so because of our particular ignorance of the causes.
  Something cannot logically come from nothing.
  What may appear without purpose often has a purpose only later revealed to us.

The things of fortune, contingent and changeable things, are not outside Providence, but are rather within the order of the whole, just as much as necessary and determined things are.

Consider that everything, however mysterious or obscure, must happen for a reason, and that no event exists separate from the unity of all things.

Now start reflecting about what that may mean about the events and circumstances of our own lives, however small, as well the as the crucial role of our own choices and responses to those events.

❖ ❖ ❖ ❖ ❖

D a y   7

It is not possible to live well today unless one thinks of it as his last.

—Musonius Rufus, *Fragments* 22, tr Lutz

Short and sweet, but it may taste bitter to many of us at first.

We've been so habituated in thinking our existence alone, our survival, is our greatest good.
 But as Seneca reminded us, what matters more is living well.
 If that's true, remember, the quality of life is more important than the quantity.

Is that quality measured by our accumulation of externals, or the development of our internal character?

If it's the latter, does it matter if I am rich or poor?
 Honored or reviled?
 Healthy or sick?
 Live a long life or short life?
 To even ask this question rubs us the wrong way.

The following thought exercise might be fruitful.
 Why might I want to live a longer life?
 Why would I be afraid of dying today?
 That may sound morbid, so I could reword the question.
 What can tomorrow give me that I cannot, by my own judgment and choice, find contentment and joy with today?

Right here and now, I can find happiness in appreciating the truth and beauty in each and every circumstance of my existence. I can love others, and recognize their dignity, whether or not they may love me.
 I can act with fairness and mercy, in even the smallest of things.

If I, for example, love my wife or my child, will that love become better or greater by having more wives and children?
 More isn't better.
 Better is better.

So, too, with a long or short life.
 Why do I seek more opportunities if only one is necessary?
 If I depend on the possibilities of the future to become better, that can easily just become an excuse to not be better at all.
 That would be depending on the external fortune of what could be to avoid what can be right now.

It is part of Nature for things to come into being, to grow and change, and then to cease to be.
  That is not an evil.
  A fruit fly lives for a few weeks, while a man may live for eighty years.
  If those times were reversed, would it be any less fair?

The past doesn't exist anymore, and the future doesn't exist yet.
  Only the now is real.
  Live it with all your might, and don't depend on days passed, or days yet to come.

❖   ❖   ❖   ❖   ❖

Day 8

What disturbs men's minds is not events but their judgments on events. For instance, death is nothing dreadful, or else Socrates would have thought it so.

No, the only dreadful thing about it is men's judgment that it is dreadful. And so when we are hindered, or disturbed, or distressed, let us never lay the blame on others, but on ourselves, that is on our own judgments.

To accuse others for one's own misfortunes is a sign of want of education; to accuse oneself shows that one's education has begun; to accuse neither oneself nor others shows that one's education is complete.

—Epictetus, *Enchiridion* 5

Here is yet another one of those basic principles of Stoicism that's easier to understand than practice.

As with all actions, they are perfected by habit.

In the simplest of terms, things are what they are in themselves, each sharing in a portion of the good of the whole.

What makes something horrible, frightening, or sorrowful is only that I choose to make that thing horrible, frightening, or sorrowful in relation to me.

Imagine this first with a more trivial matter.

I once had a friend who had an extremely annoying nervous habit.

I found it frustrating to the point of distraction.

At times I wanted to yell profanities at him to simply stop.

But the nervous habit wasn't the problem.

My evaluation of it was the problem.

It was what it was, and may surely have been so for a good reason, but I chose to make it something for me.

It was my annoyance that was dreadful.

In my younger years, I used to take the subway every day to go to school.

I was often disappointed that dozens of people were packed into a small metal tube, but none of us acknowledged one another.

I was also disappointed when people who did know one another, usually from work or a shared social group, would meet and spend their entire conversation complaining about others, their bosses, their colleagues, their friends, none of whom were, of course, there to hear it.

Whether their behavior was right or wrong really had nothing to do with me, and my disappointment was once again mine and mine alone.

It would, however, have been in my power to offer a friendly smile or greeting to a stranger, or say a kind word about an absent friend.

But I never did that. I complained about the complainers later when I got to school.

I would sometimes feel guilty about complaining, without recognizing I just had to change my thinking, and therefore how I acted, to stop blaming even myself.

Whether the blame is for others or for oneself, resentment or guilt, there's no need for it.

Fix the judgment, and you fix the disturbance.

Is it any different with the big things?

Death? Taxes? Loss? Despair? Betrayal?

The difference is only in degree, not in kind.

❖ ❖ ❖ ❖ ❖

One man, when he has done a service to another, is ready to set it down to his account as a
   favor conferred.
Another is not ready to do this, but still in his own mind he thinks of the man as his debtor,
   and he knows what he has done.
A third in a manner does not even know what he has done, but he is like a vine that has
   produced grapes, and seeks for nothing more after it has once produced its proper fruit.
As a horse when he has run, a dog when he has tracked the game, a bee when it has made
   the honey, so a man when he has done a good act, does not call out for others to come and
   see, but he goes on to another act, as a vine goes on to produce again the grapes in season.

—Marcus Aurelius, *Meditations* Book 5

When we do good for others, but demand a return for it, it isn't doing good at all, but the want of a
   reward.

Even when we do good, but harbor only within us a sense of being owed, there is little difference.
   That love of fortune has just been internalized.

Is it possible to do good without any concern at all for the debits and credits being content only
   with acting as is right according to Nature?

Of course.
   We see it in Nature all the time.
   The examples offered by Marcus Aurelius reveal the beauty of something done for its own sake,
   and for nothing else.
   If plants and animals, beings that by their nature lack reason, can do so, all the more right that a
   human being, endowed with reason, can consciously and freely choose what is right, and find
   peace and joy in this alone.

We are all prone to confusing ends and means.
   Should I simply acquire learning to get a job?
   Should I produce art for a commission?
   Should I seek office for the fame?
   Or could it be that the greatest reward is simply the action itself, done for the sake of doing it
   well?

I might learn for the sake of truth.
   I might create for the sake of beauty.
   I might work for the sake of the good.
   If I ask for more, my heart was never in the right place.

❖ ❖ ❖ ❖ ❖

If you consider any man a friend whom you do not trust as you trust yourself, you are mightily mistaken and you do not sufficiently understand what true friendship means.

Indeed, I would have you discuss everything with a friend; but first of all discuss the man himself. When friendship is settled, you must trust; before friendship is formed, you must pass judgment.

Those persons indeed put last first and confound their duties, who, violating the rules of Theophrastus, judge a man after they have made him their friend, instead of making him their friend after they have judged him.

Ponder for a long time whether you shall admit a given person to your friendship; but when you have decided to admit him, welcome him with all your heart and soul. Speak as boldly with him as with yourself.

—Seneca the Younger, *Moral Letters to Lucilius* 3

Few things seem to cause such extremes of joy and grief than friendship.
It appears odd that one thing can be so good and so bad at the same time.
Perhaps it is because we aren't actually talking about the same thing at all?

There may be no shame in having affection for someone, but recognizing that the liking depends upon the pleasure or usefulness received, for where the benefit ceases, the relationship ceases.
Affection is relative and conditional.

The love of friendship is a different matter.
The true friend is a second self.
The love is absolute and unconditional.

Love is not love which alters when it alteration finds.

But why would the Stoic need friends?
Isn't he self-sufficient?

When I was first drawn into the vast world of St Thomas Aquinas, I would follow the example of Flannery O'Connor, and read an article of the *Summa Theologica* every night.

As I grew familiar with his method, I would challenge myself to answer his question before reading the response.
One evening I came across the question (ST I II q. 4. art. 8), *Whether the fellowship of friends is necessary for happiness?*

I was sure I already knew this.
No, I thought, since happiness is in what we do, and not merely in what happens to us, we don't need the benefits that friends give us, however pleasant they might be.

How mistaken, and selfish, my answer was.

St Thomas, like a Stoic, turns this around.

We don't need friends because of what they do for us, we need them because of what we can do for them.

It is the loving that perfects us, not just the being loved.

Choose your friends wisely.

But once we have made a person a second self, there can be no conditions or terms.

People are not disposable.

❖ ❖ ❖ ❖ ❖

Do not be elated at an excellence which is not your own. If the horse in his pride were to say, 'I am handsome', we could bear with it. But when you say with pride, 'I have a handsome horse', know that the good horse is the ground of your pride.

You ask then what you can call your own. 'The answer is—the way you deal with your impressions.' Therefore when you deal with your impressions in accord with Nature, then you may be proud indeed, for your pride will be in a good which is your own.

—Epictetus, *Enchiridion* 6

My great-grandfather used to quite regularly say to me: "A pig wearing lipstick is still just a pig." As a good Irishman, he also had more profane versions of the same idea.

Things, by their distinct nature, all have their own beauty and goodness, all of them in their own way and in their own place.

If this is the case, how does my act of possessing something reflect upon me?

Am I any better or worse because I have or don't have wealth, popularity, or fine possessions?

The shallow answer, the one so common today, is that those things make all the difference.

The Stoic recognizes that, apart from our own estimation of them, they make no difference whatsoever.

Whatever sort of external good it may be, a horse, car, house, career, the act of "adding" such a thing to me doesn't make me any more of a person.

In fact, it could easily become a distraction from my true self, as cosmetics or clothes can so easily distract from natural beauty.

Saying "mine" about something else makes me no better, but recognizing what is truly mine, my judgment and character, is something to be proud of.

❖ ❖ ❖ ❖ ❖

Day 12

Most men ebb and flow in wretchedness between the fear of death and the hardships of life; they are unwilling to live, and yet they do not know how to die. For this reason, make life as a whole agreeable to yourself by banishing all worry about it.

No good thing renders its possessor happy, unless his mind is reconciled to the possibility of loss; nothing, however, is lost with less discomfort than that which, when lost, cannot be missed. Therefore, encourage and toughen your spirit against the mishaps that afflict even the most powerful.

—Seneca the Younger, *Moral Letters to Lucilius* 4

The ghostly half-life, half-death that Seneca describes can be sensed daily, in so many of those around us, and probably also within ourselves.
We run from death, because we blindly cling to existence.

Yet we also flinch from the opportunities to live well, for they might demand effort and the taking of risks, a commitment to giving up shallow, easy, and empty things.

It may sound trite to suggest that happiness is simply giving up worry, and if we meant this in the blasé form of a three-minute pop song, that would be true.

There is a deeper standard here, a test that can never fail, as long as we are honest in our answer:

"Am I basing my happiness on something that would make me deeply unhappy if I were to lose it?"

Its presence or absence can't be what my happiness is about.
The worry will not preserve the pleasure or remove the pain.

One can easily fill in the blank.
If I am happy because of my money, my home, my job, my friends, my lover, will I then be miserable if I lose those things?
And if happiness or misery is so conditional and relative, is that really happiness at all?

To "toughen the spirit" is not to be heartless, cold, or unfeeling.
All of us, at one time or another, and in one way or another, will suffer tremendously.
The externals, the goods of fortune, must indeed be a part of how I actively choose to live, but am I going to let them passively define my very blessedness or misery?

❖ ❖ ❖ ❖ ❖

Day 13

In one respect man is the nearest thing to me, so far as I must do good to men and endure them. But so far as some men make themselves obstacles to my proper acts, man becomes to me one of the things which are indifferent, no less than the sun or wind or a wild beast.

Now it is true that these may impede my action, but they are no impediments to my affects and disposition, which have the power of acting conditionally and changing: for the mind converts and changes every hindrance to its activity into an aid; and so that which is a hindrance is made a furtherance to an act; and that which is an obstacle on the road helps us on this road.

Marcus Aurelius, *Meditations* Book 5

I have known too many people who love those who are useful to them, and simply ignore anyone else.

That's selfishness, not Stoicism.

Unlike the rival Epicureans, who often argued for distancing oneself from others to find contentment, the Stoics demand a real commitment to all persons.

Any man, friend or stranger, even my enemy, is near and dear to me because he is like me in nature.

I must therefore act for his good as much as for my own.

This becomes difficult, of course, when someone does evil, harms me, stands against me.

In Stoicism, those things that are "indifferent" are not things we neglect, but rather things where their value to us depends entirely upon how we judge them and make use of them.

So it must also be with people who do evil.

I should not treat their actions as bad in themselves, but rather ask how I can take that evil done to me and turn it into something good.

The actions of another may do harm to me externally, and may even block my own actions.

How can this possibly be good?

My judgment is still under my control, and that allows me to transform anything and everything done to me into a benefit.

Where I see injustice, it simply gives another chance to be more just, where I see hatred it simply lets me love more fully, where I see sadness I can respond with greater joy.

That is within my power. I don't simply take the bad as bad.

Lead becomes gold, in a sort of moral alchemy.

❖ ❖ ❖ ❖ ❖

Day 14

In order to support more easily and more cheerfully those hardships which we may expect to suffer in behalf of virtue and goodness, it is useful to recall what hardships people will endure for unworthy ends.

Thus for example consider what intemperate lovers undergo for the sake of evil desires, and how much exertion others expend for the sake of making profit, and how much suffering those who are pursuing fame endure, and bear in mind that all of these people submit to all kinds of toil and hardship voluntarily.

Is it not then monstrous that they for no honorable reward endure such things, while we for the sake of the ideal good—that is not only the avoidance of evil such as wrecks our lives, but also the acquisition of virtue, which we may call the provider of all goods—are not ready to bear every hardship?

—Musonius Rufus, *Lectures* 7, tr Lutz

"This all sounds too hard, and I want nothing to do with it. I want things to be easy, and it just seems that I'm going to suffer all the more if I take this path. It sounds too hard to be a good person."

The reader cannot be blamed for such a reaction.

But if we think of this in another way, we just can't help but laugh.
 To what ridiculous ends do we go to get the most pathetic things, and yet while doing so we may not even realize how difficult and painful those efforts were?

Back in High School, I once spent a good amount of hours, each and every day for some six months, seeking to get even the slightest attention from a girl, not out of any sense of love, but simply out of desire.
 I recognize the waste and futility now, but at the time it seemed effortless.

Most of us in our secular, consumer society run the daily rat race of money, power, and fame.
 Observe how much time and energy, almost our entire lives, we expend in their pursuit.
 In the end, after years and years, many of us don't even get what we want, and those who do inevitably find it empty of meaning.

I have, on occasion, met happy people who are rich, powerful, or popular.
 But I have never met anyone who is happy *because* he is rich, powerful or popular.

If I'm willing to go to such extremes looking for the lower things that can never fully satisfy me, shouldn't I be inspired to work even harder, suffer and sacrifice even more, for the higher things that will truly set me free?

Once the blessing of genuine virtue and happiness is recognized, we will, like the lover in pursuit of the beloved, face any obstacle to acquire it.
 And we will do so gladly, and without complaint, because we know the reward is priceless.

❖　❖　❖　❖　❖

Day 15

Try how the life of the good man suits you, the life of him who is satisfied with his portion out of the whole, and satisfied with his own just acts and benevolent disposition.

—Marcus Aurelius, *Meditations* Book 4

"This may all sound good in theory? But will it do in practice? How can I know if this way of thinking and of living will work?"

The answer is fairly simple.
Try doing it to find out.
Just do it for a week, even a day, maybe even just for an hour here and there.

It isn't rocket science.
Practice small acts of being grateful for what Nature gives you, doing simple good deeds only for their own sake, with no seeking of reward beyond itself, and exercising even the slightest good will and cheerfulness.

At first, those three things may seem incredibly hard, like that first regimen of physical exercise.
If that is so, bite off a smaller chunk.
Work up to it slowly.

I can assure you, if you do this with sincerity, you will notice a difference, small at first, but more perceptible with repetition.
Like all good things, a good habit makes us better and stronger.
You will discover slight and brief moments of peace, and the more you practice living well, the more that peace will become the norm, not the exception.

Again, there is no need to start big.
The beginning runner who attempts a marathon will be sorely disappointed.
If you miss your bus, then take a walk, or enjoy watching the world while you wait.
If a person says a mean word, respond with a kind one.
Do something helpful for someone and never tell him you did it.
You will find that you enjoy doing things that way, simply for their own sake.

The only hindrance to such a life is our own attitudes, judgments, or impressions that try to tell us our happiness is outside of us, not within us.

These thoughts may be the result of many years of habitual frustration, resentment, and disappointment.
They may be deeply engrained.
Replace those old habits, piece by piece, with completely new ones.
Nothing stops us from being happy but ourselves.

❖ ❖ ❖ ❖ ❖

Day 16

Ask not that events should happen as you will, but let your will be that events should happen as they do, and you shall have peace.

—Epictetus, *Enchiridion* 8

Here Stoicism has much in common with the Taoist conception of *wu wei*.
Do not act against Nature, act with Nature.
Why should I assume that reality is inherently competitive, defined merely by conflict?
Insofar as Nature always acts out of meaning and order, can I not understand it as cooperative and harmonious?
Whatever the form this distinction may take, could we not see it as the ultimate distinction between war and peace as guiding principles of life?

A sailing ship that tries to travel directly against the wind does so in vain.
This does not mean the captain allows himself to be tossed aimlessly by the weather; by beating to windward, for example, he wisely uses the force of the elements to his advantage.

So too, the wise and happy man does not force himself on the order of things, but instead brings his will into balance with things.
It is much like the ethical version of rolling with the punches.

In practice, we surely recognize that reality does not change simply because we wish it to.
Even with the noblest and bravest of efforts, we can often barely even nudge the world.

Most of our circumstances are well beyond our power, or fleeting when we do grasp a tenuous hold upon them.
But I can change my own judgment and choice.
If I can learn to accept the things that are beyond my power in tranquility, I have in turn become the master of myself.

The *Serenity Prayer* of Reinhold Niebuhr, later popularized by 12 Step Programs, is also a wonderful parallel to this principle: If I can use my wisdom to distinguish between the things I cannot change (fortune) and the things I can (my own thinking), I am embracing this virtue of acceptance.

> *God, grant me the serenity to accept the things I cannot change,*
> *Courage to change the things I can,*
> *And wisdom to know the difference.*

This is hardly defeatism, but rather a humbling recognition of what is real, and a willingness to find the good I can do in each and every circumstance.

❖ ❖ ❖ ❖ ❖

Day 17

I have always been of the opinion that infamy earned by doing what is right is not infamy at all, but glory.

—Cicero. *Against Cataline* 1, tr Blakiston

I am well advised to worry more about what is good than what is popular.
Cicero was first and foremost a statesman and orator, and surely well versed in the reality of politics.
He can hardly be accused of being merely an abstract philosopher with his head in the clouds; perhaps the very story of his exploits, the high points and the low, is an indication that philosophy is about living, not just about thinking.

Cicero hardly limited himself to a single school of thought because, like anyone practiced in prudence, he recognized the truth wherever he found it.
The guiding force of Stoicism in his words and deeds is, however, immediately apparent.

When Cataline sought to control the Roman Republic through deception and violence, Cicero opposed him at great danger to himself.
Years later, when he stood against Mark Antony, that same courage cost him his life.

To simply agree with what is popular, convenient, or expedient is hardly even agreement.
It is surrender.
What is right may sometimes be popular, and sometimes not.
The key lies in recognizing that what we must reconsider our very measure of what we consider glorious.

The standard of trends and fashions is fleeting and relative, while the standard of morality and of Nature is eternal and absolute.
We should not expect the two to necessarily conform, and when they do not do so, our calling is clear.

The bravery necessary to live a good life is not just physical, but moral.

When Socrates was asked by the Thirty Tyrants of Athens to bring them Leon of Salamis to be executed, he simply ignored them by returning home.
Had the Thirty not been overthrown shortly thereafter, Socrates would likely have shared Leon's fate.
He knew it was wrong to harm an innocent man, and refused to allow himself to be caught up in the fervor of the popular oppression of the moment.
The fickle conditions of opinion and circumstance saved his life on that day.

Years, later, of course, the mood was once again different, and Socrates found himself put to death for corruption and impiety. He did not play to popular emotions, but stuck to his principles.

I am always immediately wary when I see any argument based only upon conformity.
Words like "offensive", "inappropriate", "unacceptable", "anti-social", "politically incorrect", or "unprofessional" can sometimes just be synonyms for "unpopular".
One must judge such standards with great care.

❖ ❖ ❖ ❖ ❖

Of this one thing make sure against your dying day—let your faults die before you die. Away with those disordered pleasures, which must be dearly paid for; it is not only those that are to come that harm me, but also those that have come and gone.

Just as crimes, even if they have not been detected when they were committed, do not allow anxiety to end with them; so with guilty pleasures, regret remains even after the pleasures are over. They are not substantial, they are not trustworthy; even if they do not harm us, and they are fleeting.

Cast about rather for some good which will abide. But there can be no such good except as the soul discovers it for itself within itself. Virtue alone affords everlasting and peace-giving joy; even if some obstacle arise, it is but like an intervening cloud, which floats beneath the sun but never prevails against it.

—Seneca the Younger, *Moral letters to Lucilius 27*

I have often vainly hoped that I could ignore, skip over, or turn a blind eye to certain of my vices.
  I see others getting away with them all the time, of course, so I assume I can get away with them as well.
  After all, it would seem that so many evils are never even punished.

I've seen holy men preaching chastity while engaged in affairs with their flock, and everyone turns a blind eye.
  I've seen self-styled socially conscious businessmen milk others dry for their own profit, and the world calls them heroes.
  I've seen politicians praise honesty from one side of the mouth and tell lies from the other.
  We re-elect them.
  Can't I overlook my own vices in much the same manner?

The punishment for a misdeed doesn't depend merely on whether we are caught out.
  We already pay the price by disturbing our own Nature.
  Nor does the passage of time remove this anxiety and misery; without care, the wound will fester instead of heal.
  Ignoring a vice won't make it go away.

The argument is fundamental.
  Happiness can only be found in complete and lasting goods.
  Selfish pleasures, fleeting and unreliable, are never complete goods.
  This is why the grasping man is also never happy.
  He has everything he wants, but he exudes discontent.

The practical proof of this rests in a simple human observation: we may find greedy and self-absorbed men who are rich, powerful, or who constantly gratify their passions, but we need only note that these are the same people who invariably live in anxiety, confusion, and misery.

Only a reliance on our own virtue and character brings peace and joy, because only these things can never fail us.

I have always been inspired by Seneca's final image.

Circumstances may rise up against this highest of human goods, but they can never defeat it.

It is a light that cannot be fully obscured or extinguished.

❖   ❖   ❖   ❖   ❖

Day 19

Do not be ashamed to be helped; for it is your business to do your duty like a soldier in the assault on a town. How then, if being lame you cannot mount up on the battlements alone, but with the help of another it is possible?

—Marcus Aurelius. *Meditations* Book 7

Self-reliance is neither arrogance nor isolation.
 It is right and natural for us to help one another.
 On the one hand, some people will refuse to offer help, while on the other hand some people will refuse to accept it.
 Both extremes come from the same kind of foolish pride.

The former is much more readily recognized, and criticized.
 It is easy to resent a favor withheld, but often far more difficult to accept a favor offered.
 If I feel wronged and slighted, my indignation is itself a reflection of my self-importance, as it revolves around a sense of my own entitlement.
 I assume that kindness from another is something I deserve.

Ironically, when I actually do receive this kindness, the same pride rears its ugly head.
 By being offered the assistance, it seems an insult to my own ability and strength.
 In the end, I'm angered by not being helped, and also angered by being helped.

In reality, shouldn't both the offering and the acceptance of assistance be both humbling and joyful?
 It is humbling, because it allows us to recognize ourselves as part of humanity, not above humanity.
 It is joyful, because in this very recognition I know that I have a part to play in the order of all things.

Amidst all the turmoil and horror that is war, good soldiers know to help one another.
 They will turn aside to help a fallen comrade, they will cooperate to overcome the greatest obstacles, and they will even give their own lives so that others may live.

Perhaps this is because battle removes all that is trivial and unnecessary, leaving only the core of who we are?
 When everything else has fallen away, and even our very existence is on the line, then only character remains.
 There is no reason that lesson cannot be practiced each and every day, even in the most mundane of circumstances.

About a decade ago, a truck struck me while I was walking back to my old family home.
 The driver sped off.
 It was bitterly cold and late at night, I was two blocks from the house, and I found I couldn't use my mangled right leg.
 I must have been a fine sight, blood running down my face, spitting out pieces of my teeth, dragging myself along inch by inch.

I was suddenly excited to see a neighbor walking at the end of the road.
 As I called out for some help, I noticed him quickly turning away in a different direction, conveniently averting his eyes.
 He did a wonderful job of pretending not to see me.

I knew exactly who he was, and I knew exactly why he ignored me.
 I knew why he looked away, but that in no way justified my rage.

The resentment I felt for that neglect seemed to compete with the pain I felt over the months of physical recovery.
 The anger only left me when I recognized something shamefully equivalent in myself.

My poor family was constantly suffering my stubbornness in refusing their help.
 I was angry at both the neglect and the assistance.
 And the latter was far worse, because it was a situation that I could actually have done something about.

❖ ❖ ❖ ❖ ❖

Day 20

Of things some are good, some are bad, and others are indifferent. The good then are the virtues and the things which partake of the virtues; the bad are the vices, and the things which partake of them; and the indifferent are the things which lie between the virtues and the vices, wealth, health, life, death, pleasure, pain.

—Epictetus, *Discourses* 1.19, tr Long

These words are helpful on two levels.
First, they are a reminder of what is truly good and bad in our lives.
Second, they are a reminder to not merely parrot words, but to comprehend their purpose and practice them in daily living.

By the time of Epictetus, the formula above, attributed with slight variations to diverse early Stoics, would have been well known to any student of philosophy.
One can imagine the teacher quizzing the student on the Stoic meaning of the terms "good", "bad" and, "indifferent", and the student dutifully presenting these definitions from memory.

How many of us have done the same?
We memorize Euclid's Theorems, Newton's Laws of Motion, the poetry of Shakespeare, the words of the Preamble to the Declaration of Independence.
But do we actually understand and apply these truths?

In this particular discourse, Epictetus berates the student for simply knowing the words and not reflecting on the meaning.
He wonders whether many who label themselves as Stoics are, in fact, veiled Epicureans, pleasure-seekers.
The proof of conviction is not in the mouthing of words, but in comprehension and action.

The test is a simple one: do my actions conform to my words?
Am I practicing what I preach?
If I am to live according to Stoic values, this would be readily apparent in my life, and there could be no confusion.
I would look to the good, completely and without condition, in the dignity and value of my own character.
Nothing would intervene.

Conversely, I would discern evil as the result of my own ignorance and vice.
Everything else in my life, my wealth and possessions, my power, my popularity, my body, only become good or evil for me in how I relate to them and make use of them.
I should be indifferent to them, not in a sense of neglect or carelessness, but insofar as I should never value them for their own sake, but only as they can be of assistance in living well.

The words are easy, but the practice is a complete shift of values.
If I am to compromise the higher for the sake of the lower, I may be talking like a Stoic, but I'm certainly not living like one.

Have I ever made my love of what is true, good, and beautiful conditional on my job, my reputation, my comfort, or my convenience?
Then I'm not a Stoic.
I'm just a hypocrite.

St Ignatius of Loyola established his *Principle and Foundation* as the guiding rule of the Jesuit order. The specific context here is Christian, but the first principle is the same.

Order all things toward the highest end:

> *Man is created to praise, reverence, and serve God Our Lord, and by doing so, to save his soul. All other things on the face of the earth are created for man in order to help him pursue the end for which he is created.*
>
> *It follows from this that one must use other created things, in so far as they help towards one's end, and free oneself from them, in so far as they are obstacles to one's end.*
>
> *To do this, we need to make ourselves indifferent to all created things, provided the matter is subject to our free choice and there is no other prohibition.*
>
> *Thus, as far as we are concerned, we should not want health more than illness, wealth more than poverty, fame more than disgrace, a long life more than a short one, and similarly for all the rest, but we should desire and choose only what helps us more towards the end for which we are created.*

A friend once asked me how it was possible for the Stoics, for the Buddha, for St Ignatius to all say such amazingly similar things.

My answer was simply that it was because whatever time, place, or tradition we may come from, the wise always recognize a universal, shared truth.

❖ ❖ ❖ ❖ ❖

Day 21

This is the reason why we have two ears and only one mouth, that we may hear more and speak less.

—Zeno of Citium ex Diogenes Laertius,
Lives and opinions of eminent philosophers 7.1.19, tr Yonge

This may seem to be a platitude or truism.
  It is still good advice, if we only attend to the meaning.

I have always been both shy and an introvert, and I often find it difficult to relate to others without deep anxiety.
  Though I am usually rather quiet in company, I can become pointlessly talkative when I feel pressured.
  A wave of words might spew forth simply because I am disturbed by awkward silence.
  I will have the instinct that something said, whatever it may be, is less painful than nothing said at all.

At other times I may find myself excited by something I've seen, read, or have been thinking through, and I fail to realize that others might not be nearly as interested as I am.

In both cases, whether out of nerves or enthusiasm, the implicit drive is to speak out.
  There are two root causes here: a thinly veiled vanity, and an assumption that sound is better than silence, that speaking trumps listening.

As noble as the intent may be, there is certain egoism in thinking that my own words will make things better.
  In fact, unless I've thought through what I need to say, I often find that the words I want to say will only make things worse.

There is a reason the wise used to say that silence is golden.
  By just listening, I open myself to the world, to other persons, to the true, the good, and the beautiful, simply for its own sake.
  Silence can, rightly understood, be the greatest sign of respect.

Words must be carefully chosen, and for those of us not regularly inspired by the Muses, this means speaking far less and listening more.

I try to ask myself: is what I intend to say going to help someone else understand?
  Will it help them feel joy?
  Will it make others and myself better, and therefore happier?
  If the answer is in the negative, it was just noise.

Do not confuse sound and noise.
  Noise is just a distraction and diversion from Nature.

❖ ❖ ❖ ❖ ❖

For this reason a wise man should never complain, whenever he is brought into strife with Fortune; just as a brave man cannot properly be disgusted whenever the noise of battle is heard, since for both of them their very difficulty is their opportunity, for the brave man of increasing his glory, for the wise man of confirming and strengthening his wisdom.

From this is virtue itself so named, because it is so supported by its strength that it is not overcome by adversity. And you who were set in the advance of virtue have not come to this pass of being dissipated by delights, or enervated by pleasure; but you fight too bitterly against all Fortune.

Keep the middle path of strength and virtue, lest you be overwhelmed by misfortune or corrupted by pleasant Fortune.

All that falls short or goes too far ahead, has contempt for happiness, and gains not the reward for labor done. It rests in your own hands what shall be the nature of the Fortune which you choose to form for yourself. For all Fortune which seems difficult, either exercises virtue, or corrects or punishes vice.

—Boethius, *The consolation of Philosophy* Book 4 Prose 7,

tr Cooper

Though Boethius was a Christian philosopher strongly guided by Neo–Platonism, the Stoic influence is also unmistakable.
I have a special personal affection for his writing, as he was the first to more closely introduce me to these values.
Hence I include him in the broader grouping of Stoic thinkers.

We assume that some luck is good, and some is bad.
For the Stoic, there are two problems here.

First, what we call luck or fortune is hardly random.
Everything does happen for a reason within the whole, even if its purpose is not immediately apparent.

Second, fortune, being indifferent, is only good or bad depending on what we choose to make of it.
Winning the lottery can be good or bad.
Losing one's job can be good or bad.
Loneliness can be good or bad.
The difference between a blessing and curse lies only in our judgment and the use of our circumstances.

Misfortune can be seen as an opportunity.
We can choose to be wiser, braver, kinder, and calmer in the face of difficulties.
This can thereby make us better and happier, for there is joy in the achievement of character and self-control.

Pleasures can be just as destructive for us as pains, contentment just as much an impediment as suffering.

The Ancients often stressed the importance of the balanced middle ground, the moderation or mean.

Too much or too little becomes a burden.

Only our own wisdom can point out the middle path.

Think of any fortune as a means to self-improvement.

If we face a hardship, this can give us the chance to practice goodness, to fix our mistakes, or to pay the debt of our misdeeds.

All these things are good.

What I had always assumed was the greatest misfortune of my life has, in a beautiful irony, become my greatest blessing.

The loss of my dearest friend was first met with despair.

I seemed to have wasted many years of my life trusting someone I should never have trusted, and many years more in a state of loneliness and shellshock.

But one can employ what I like to call the "Stoic Turn".

That another person acted with dishonesty and disloyalty deserves my compassion, not my anger; that I allowed myself to make my own bad choices is what I can freely choose to change.

Without these things having happened, I would not have been able to learn or improve myself in the way that I did.

I would not have learned the nature of genuine love, and how it differs from merely self-serving lust.

It doesn't necessarily make the pain go away, but it can give it the deepest transformative purpose.

Pain can always be used as a means to strengthen our joy.

Hatred can always be used as a means to strengthen our love.

❖ ❖ ❖ ❖ ❖

Day 23

Sickness is a hindrance to the body, but not to the will, unless the will consent. Lameness is a hindrance to the leg, but not to the will. Say this to yourself at each event that happens, for you shall find that though it hinders something else it will not hinder you.

—Epictetus, *Enchiridion* 9

The philosophical problem of evil and suffering is also a deeply personal problem.
  The Stoic solution is fairly direct: things only become as good or evil to us as we choose to make them.
  That pain is a burden is not in question; whether it must be a burden to my will is another matter.

In my own experience, I have always found emotional pain far more severe than physical pain.
  But each, in its own way, can seem to consume us.
  On the one hand, we are tempted to surrender to suffering, thinking it unbearable.
  On the other hand, we may close our eyes to it, choose to deny it, suppress it.
  People often think the Stoic does the latter.

I have found the middle ground to be what Epictetus describes.
  Do not deny that disease and suffering are real.
  They are a hindrance indeed, at times incredibly powerful.
  But what do they hinder?
  As long as I live, physical suffering hinders the body, and emotional suffering hinders my feelings.

But whether they hinder my mind and will, my ability and willingness to know and love, the very core of what makes me human, is another matter.
  As long as I live, I may choose to live well.
  And if injury, pain or disease completely destroys my body, then all the more important to have lived well in the time that Nature has given me.

When I was younger, I often suffered from severe emotional pain, even while I was still physically healthy.
  As I grew older, the body also began to decay.
  I have often thought of the deep connection between these two levels of human existence, and I began to visualize myself as a set of concentric spheres, much like the layers of an onion.

While the outer layers of the body and the inner layers of the passions were subject to constant change and suffering, I began to see that at the core, the self that was still fully me could rise above being ruled by such conditions.

The story of Maximilian Kolbe was always a vivid and profound example of such values for me.
  Hinder the outside of me, and I can choose to strengthen the inside of me.

❖ ❖ ❖ ❖ ❖

Day 24

How ridiculous and what a stranger he is who is surprised at anything which happens in life.

—Marcus Aurelius, *Meditations* Book 12

I'm shocked, shocked to find that gambling is going on in here!

Like Captain Renault in *Casablanca*, I wonder how often we feign surprise, and when our confusion is genuine.

I would humbly suggest that *Casablanca* is a wonderful instance of Stoicism in classic cinema.
  I hardly know if that was a deliberate intent or a wonderful accident, but if you view it with the values of Stoicism in mind, you will never see the film, or perhaps even life, in the same way again.

The true philosopher, with Heraclitus, recognizes that there is nothing new under the sun.
  He has seen the very good, the very bad, and all that is in between.
  Nothing in the breadth of human greatness and depravity surprises him, because he understands the human condition.

And he understands that as chaotic as it may at first appear, there is a profound order to all things.
  There can be no effect without a cause, and all causes are connected.

The naïve pessimist is surprised by good.
  The naïve optimist is surprised by evil.
  The realist will expect to encounter both, and will always make the most of these conditions.

❖ ❖ ❖ ❖ ❖

Day 25

Does a man get angry? Do you, on the contrary, challenge him with kindness? Animosity, if abandoned by one side, forthwith dies; it takes two to make a fight. But if anger shall be rife on both sides, if the conflict comes, he is the better man who first withdraws; the vanquished is the one who wins.

If some one strikes you, step back; for by striking back you will give him both the opportunity and the excuse to repeat his blow; when you later wish to extricate yourself, it will be impossible.

—Seneca the Younger, *On anger* 2.24, tr Basore

Anger for anger simply breeds more anger, and it can only be overcome through love.
Do not respond in kind, as tempting as it may seem.
While I cannot always control my instincts and feelings, I most certainly can determine how I judge and act upon those feelings.
As with all good things, self-restraint is perfected through the habit of practice.

Recall that justice and vengeance are hardly the same thing.
While one seeks to defend the good of others, the other intends to do harm out of anger.
However much I try to make excuses, in my own heart and mind the difference is immediately clear out of the motivation.
I just have to be honest with myself to make sense of the feeling.

When I was younger, my anger was often immediate and usually brutal, either physically or emotionally.
With age, my anger has become slow and creeping, and it can now scheme with great subtlety.
I have only been able to overcome either form through careful and deliberate choice.

❖ ❖ ❖ ❖ ❖

Day 26

If one were to measure what is agreeable by the standard of pleasure, nothing would be pleasanter than self-control; and if one were to measure what is to be avoided by pain, nothing would be more painful than lack of self-control.

—Musonius Rufus, *Fragments* 24

Musonius, the "Roman Socrates", is having a bit of fun here.
  While the Epicureans, who often debated endlessly with the Stoics on such matters, followed the pleasure principle of life, the Stoic recognizes that pleasure can be a good, but never the absolute or highest good.

The choice of pleasure as the measure of the good is nothing new for our modern world.
  We readily assume that if something feels good, it is good.
  This is the most simple and base selfishness, because it assumes the value of anything and everything in the world is relative to how it makes me feel.

Dressing the idea up in fancier language does not change the meaning.
  I once knew someone who liked to say "I'm happy because I do what I love, and I am passionate about life. I seize every opportunity."
  That may even sound downright noble at first.
  But one had simply to attend to what this person meant by "love" to see that it meant the desire to possess, not the love of things for their own sake.
  And being "passionate" didn't mean virtue in this case, it meant just having strong feelings.
  The tyrant, murderer, robber, or rapist also takes what he likes, seizes every opportunity, and does so passionately.

Even if the selfishness of such a rule were not an impediment to living, the pleasure principle is itself inconsistent, as Musonius here cleverly points out.
  We know that not all pleasures are good, especially when we pursue them in excess.
  Therefore pleasure must be tempered by self-control, and is itself relative, not absolute.

Since self-control, temperance grounded in reason, must rule our desire for pleasure, pleasure itself is conditional, and cannot be the highest good.
  The Epicurean can't even follow the pleasure principle, because it wouldn't even give him the pleasure he wanted.

❖ ❖ ❖ ❖ ❖

…How great You are,The Lord supreme
  for ever and for ever!
No work is wrought apart from You, O God,
Or in the world, or in the heaven above,

Or on the deep, save only what is done
By sinners in their folly.
No, You can
Make the rough smooth, bring wondrous order forth
From chaos; in Your sight unloveliness

Seems beautiful; for so You have fitted things
Together, good and evil, that there reigns
One everlasting Reason in them all.
The wicked heed not this, but suffer it
To slip, to their undoing; these are they
Who, yearning ever to secure the good,

Mark not nor hear the law of God, by wise
Obedience unto which they might attain
A nobler life, with Reason harmonized.

But now, unbid, they pass on divers paths
Each his own way, yet knowing not the truth,—
Some in unlovely striving for renown,
Some bent on lawless gains, on pleasure some,
Working their own undoing, self-deceived.

O You most bounteous God that sits enthroned
In clouds, the Lord of lightning, save mankind
From grievous ignorance!

Oh, scatter it
Far from their souls, and grant them to achieve
True knowledge, on whose might You do rely
To govern all the world in righteousness…

—Cleanthes of Assos
from *The hymn to Zeus*, tr Blakeney

Stoicism was never a religion, in the sense that it in no way relied upon articles of faith or revelation.
As a philosophy, it's knowledge of the true, the good, and the beautiful derived from reason alone.
This hardly means philosophy is contrary to theology; I would argue that, in fact, they are deeply complementary.

But when reading the *Hymn to Zeus* by Cleanthes, we should not assume that this is only the language of faith, or devotional "God talk".
Zeus here is far more than the immortal ruler of the Olympians; his image represents a much deeper ruling principle of reason that orders and directs all things.

The Divine is not merely great and mighty.
That greatness is active and manifest clearly in the balance and harmony that Providence gives to the whole world.
Not only good things are subject to God.
Even those who are evil, the selfish ones who lust for power, wealth, or pleasure, come to serve the higher good.

We may be ignorant of our place, but we fulfill our role nonetheless.
When we choose evil, the design of reason will make certain that these things, too, will serve what is right.

There's a beautiful irony in understanding that even when I turn away from what is good, I still unwittingly return right back to it.

❖   ❖   ❖   ❖   ❖

Day 28

Never say of anything, ' I lost it', but say, 'I gave it back'. Has your child died? It was
given back. Has your wife died? She was given back. Has your estate been taken from you?
Was not this also given back?

But you say, 'He who took it from me is wicked'. What does it matter to you through whom
the giver asked it back? As long as he gives it you, take care of it, but not as your own;
treat it as passers-by treat an inn.

—Epictetus, *Enchridion* 11

This passage may at first seem heartless, indicative of how most people identify Stoicism.
I have rather found it, with the benefit of time, reflection, and some hard knocks, to be one of the
most helpful and compassionate statements I have ever read.

Over the years, I have dealt with many of the losses we all dread: the death of family and friends,
especially the death of a child, conflict with and separation from loved ones, the loss of jobs,
homes, health, wealth, and property.

In each and every case I thought I was getting the short end of the stick, and I envied those who
seemed to be on Easy Street.
The vain self-pity of resentment or guilt has an unhealthy way of numbing such feelings.

The solution was far, deeper than just avoiding resentment or guilt.
The solution lay in recognizing that not one of those things was ever a loss.

To lose something means that it was mine to begin with.
My mind and will are my own.
But my body, family, friends, position, reputation, wealth, or property don't belong to me at all.
They have their goodness and beauty all to themselves, and my relationship with them changes
nothing of their nature, or of mine.

It was Nature that had lent these things to me, and it is within the order and right of Nature that
they be returned.
I am given care for them to use for the good, but I cannot begrudge it when Nature asks for them
back, in whatever way or at whatever time. I was given a privilege, a gift, a blessing.
They were never rights.

Such an insight can allow us to do two things.
First, it can help us rightly distinguish Nature and Fortune, what is within our power and what is
not in our power.

Second, it can help us show genuine joy and gratitude for our gifts, and return them gladly when
the time is right.
We own nothing but ourselves.
The circumstances of my life are not my property.
I am a steward, a caretaker, for whatever I am given.
Therein lies freedom and thankfulness.
That is the real Stoicism.

❖ ❖ ❖ ❖ ❖

Day 29

Reverence the faculty which produces right opinion. On this faculty it entirely depends whether there shall exist in thy ruling part any opinion inconsistent with Nature and the constitution of the rational animal. And this faculty promises freedom from hasty judgment, and friendship towards men, and obedience to the gods.

—Marcus Aurelius, *Meditations* Book3

Whenever and wherever I have taught philosophy, I deliberately steer students to a question of human nature.
Does anything make us different from other living things?

Almost invariably, students will at first answer with something like this: "We're different from animals because we have feelings."
I have, over the years, learned to accept this odd characteristic of the modern world with a kindness and patience, for it defines us as sensitive and appetitive animals.

We are indeed animals.
But I can perceive that, just like myself, any animal feels pleasure and pain, fear and contentment, anger and affection.
In that way, I'm not sure I'm different from any other animal.

"We use tools and language, and we have society."
But I observe the use of tools, communication and social order in many other living things.
The difference there seems only one of degree, not one of kind.

What remains?
The power of reason, and the proof of it lies in the very fact that you and I are even now thinking about this question.
We can apprehend our world not only through the sensation and instinct, but also through the intellect.
In this way, we not only feel something, but can know what it is, universally and necessarily.

As one of my favorite college professors liked to say, 'Dogs don't do mathematics, and they don't write poetry.'

It is the right use of reason that allows us to live well, to make free choices from our own judgments, and to thereby love others for their own sake, not merely for our own.

❖ ❖ ❖ ❖ ❖

Day 30

Toward good men God has the mind of a father, he cherishes for them a manly love, and he says, 'Let them be harassed by toil, by suffering, by losses, in order that they may gather true strength.'

Bodies grown fat through sloth are weak, and not only labor, but even movement and their very weight cause them to break down. Unimpaired prosperity cannot withstand a single blow; but he who has struggled constantly with his ills becomes hardened through suffering; and yields to no misfortune; nay, even if he falls, he still fights upon his knees.

—Seneca the Younger, *On Providence* 2, tr Basore

Why would Nature, or Nature's God, treat us with such tough love?

Why be hard when you can be kind?

Most of us, of course, are usually hard, and very rarely kind, but we are appealing to Nature and God here, not ourselves.

We expect better standards from our betters.

It is because hardship can make us better and stronger.

This isn't just a matter of physical strength, but more importantly one of moral strength.

Just as a body grows weak through sloth and luxury, so, too, the mind and will, the capacity to know and to love, grow weak without the struggle to overcome hardship.

We would never expect an athlete to compete without the difficulty of training, and we should never expect any human being to face life without the need to overcome obstacles.

This isn't about appearing or feeling tough.

All of that is a charade.

It's about learning to be just.

Though we each follow our own distinct path, and we all have the opportunity to live well if we but so choose, a life of entitlement stacks the odds against us.

I went to college with many fine young folks, most of them gifted with intelligence, inherited wealth, and opportunities handed to them on a silver platter.

Sadly, very few of them became good people.

Being spoiled often very literally means being spoiled.

I often now, many years after the fact, thank my parents for being tough on me.

So too, I now thank Nature for her love in teaching me a few good habits through hardship.

❖　❖　❖　❖　❖

In the first place, be not hurried away by the rapidity of the appearance, but say, 'Appearances, wait for me a little: let me see who you are, and what you are about: let me put you to the test.'

And then do not allow the appearance to lead you on and draw lively pictures of the things which will follow; for if you do, it will carry you off wherever it pleases. But rather bring in to oppose it some other beautiful and noble appearance and cast out this base appearance.

—Epictetus, *Discourses* 2.18

Our modern world is one ruled by appearance and image.
 It seems to matter far less what something is, than what it appears to be.
 A very successful advertising agent once told me that the most important thing young people should learn in school is that 'appearance is reality'.
 I almost cried right there and then.

Stoicism sees through such illusions, because it looks to the order of Nature itself.
 Appearances, taken simply as they are, can be tricky things.
 If we only look or feel without attending to the truth behind the image, we easily deceive ourselves.

An impression or feeling shouldn't be accepted hastily.
 Judge it with care.
 Look behind it.
 Don't just ask what it looks like, ask yourself what it means.

We might not be able to control all the images that confront us, but we can certainly challenge them and meet the ugly with the beautiful.
 The feeling of sexual desire can, for example, be a powerful one.
 Contrast the image of lust with the image of the true beauty of a person, and you can now reorder you actions.
 You can treat a person with respect, and not as a mere object.

Advertising, which rules so much of our media-driven society, can so easily corrupt us because it can appeal to appearance over reality.
 A certain car, alcohol, or credit card won't make you rich, handsome, or popular. It will only move you around, get you drunk, or make you poorer.
 See something for what it is in itself, not what someone else tells you it is.

❖ ❖ ❖ ❖ ❖

Day 32

When a man enters the foot race, it is his duty to put forth all his strength and strive with all his might to win; but he ought never with his foot to trip, or with his hand to foul a competitor. Thus in the stadium of life, it is not unfair for anyone to seek to obtain what is needful for his own advantage, but he has no right to wrest it from his neighbor.

—Chrysippus ex Cicero, *On Duties*, 3.10, tr Miller

I was teaching at a Catholic high school a decade ago, and I had most of our men's basketball team in my Classical Literature class.
  I usually taught them right after their practice, which is why they were also usually late, and very sweaty.
  One day, they arrived in a foul mood. "We're just a terrible team. We always lose."

The iconic light bulb went on in my head.
  Here was a possible teaching moment.

'If you think that winning alone makes you a good athlete? Would you cheat to win?'

'No, of course not.'

'Then winning isn't the thing you're aiming at.
  There's a higher standard. We used to call it sportsmanship.
  First and foremost, play the game with effort, skill, and character.
  The rest is secondary.'

They sighed, rolled their eyes, and smirked at me.
  That's just fine, because they were teenage boys.
  I knew it had somehow sunk in later when one of them sent me a message.
  'I didn't get that job you wrote me a letter for.
  But I did my best, like you told us years ago, and that's what counts.'

On that very day in class, we were reading Book 6 of the *Iliad*. Hector returns to Troy from battle.
  He berates his lazy and lustful brother, Paris.
  He then sees his wife, Andromache, and their infant son, Astyanax.

Andromache begs and pleads with him.
  The war is lost, and prophecy has made clear there can be no chance of victory.
  She asks him to stay with her, for what little time they have left.
  Why fight any more?

Hector knows very well that Troy will fall.
  But he will live only to defend his kin.
  He will not see them reduced to ruin.
  He will fight, not for victory in war, not to win, but to live and die with character above all else.

  May I be dead, and the earth piled above me, before I hear your cries as they drag you away.

Hector falls to Achilles, who then desecrates his corpse.

Andromache is made a slave.

Astyanax is dashed upon the rocks, so no heir can avenge Troy.

The story is deeply tragic, but it is also deeply beautiful, because it embodies the very values championed by the Stoic.

Much of life is indeed conflict and struggle.

Fight the good fight, but fight fair.

There can never be honor in lying, cheating, or slandering.

We were not made to destroy one another at any cost.

We were made to love one another.

❖ ❖ ❖ ❖ ❖

Day 33

If you wish to make progress, you must be content in external matters to seem a fool and a simpleton; do not wish men to think you know anything, and if any should think you to be somebody, distrust yourself. For know that it is not easy to keep your will in accord with Nature and at the same time keep outward things; if you attend to one you must needs neglect the other.

—Epictetus, *Enchiridion* 13

Let us be brutally honest with one another.

We like to be liked.

Consider how much effort during our day is spent in pursuit of this goal.

The Stoic will kindly advise us that we are wasting our time.

At the most basic level, we might hope that we are liked because we are good, not good because we are liked.

In other words, we sadly reverse the value of merit and reputation.

The former can't depend upon the latter.

Plato and Aristotle had argued no less.

But Epictetus is upping the ante.

It is a grave danger to even care about our reputations at all, because once we care, we are tempted to start dividing our loyalties.

Be happy to not care for your popularity in any manner.

It is a fickle and unreliable thing.

In fact, it might be a good idea to deliberately work at seeming dull, ignorant, or unworthy of honor, especially to the sort of people who are quick to deal in praise and blame.

They are often empty within themselves, so they fill themselves with such externals. And perhaps when such people heap praise upon you, it's time to worry.

Look at the sort of things they care about. Is that what you wish to be liked for?

If the wrong people are telling you you're doing it right, it turns out you're probably doing it wrong.

Epictetus asks quite a bit of us here, but I suggest the key insight is once again that we can't compromise higher things for lower things.

I find myself very rarely praised, but at the times when I do, it can become worrying.

It's easy to become puffed-up, and then the good characteristics I might actually have can disappear into pride.

I know that there are things worthy of praise and honor, but honor itself is not one of them.

Once I begin to care at all what others think of me, I can end up making myself less free and more dependent.

It isn't that we shouldn't love others; it's that we don't define ourselves by whether they admire us.

❖ ❖ ❖ ❖ ❖

Day 34

It is equally faulty to trust everyone and to trust no one. Yet the former fault is, I should say, the more ingenuous, the latter the more safe. In like manner you should rebuke these two kinds of men—both those who always lack repose, and those who are always in repose.

For love of bustle is not industry—it is only the restlessness of a hunted mind. And true repose does not consist in condemning all motion as merely vexation; that kind of repose is slackness and inertia.

Therefore, you should note the following saying, taken from my reading in Pomponius: 'Some men shrink into dark corners, to such a degree that they see darkly by day.'

No, men should combine these tendencies, and he who reposes should act and he who acts should take repose. Discuss the problem with Nature; she will tell you that she has created both day and night.

—Seneca the Younger. *Moral letters to Lucilius* 3

The Ancient doctrine of the mean can be found in many forms, and the Stoics put their own particular spin on it.
  Broadly speaking, it recognizes that moderation and balance are the keys to happiness and virtue, and such a mean rests between two extremes of excess and deficiency.

I sometimes wonder if we Moderns need to do some extra-credit work on this.
  We often aim too far on either side, too much or too little, and miss the mark in the middle.

It's a mistake, Seneca, tells us to trust without question and to never trust at all.
  So too, avoid following the example of those who are too busy and those who are too lazy.
  The right balance of work and leisure is made clear when we look to the needs of Nature.

I find both extremes equally common, though we often admire the over-achiever, and seem to far prefer being critical of the lazy.
  Following Seneca's pattern, however, we should be equally concerned about both the busybody and the slothful; while the first flaw is the more motivated and clever, the second is just safer and easier.

Being overly busy and constantly occupied is not always a good thing.
  It can become an external distraction, a diversion from those goods within our souls that we too often neglect.
  Your work will just be aimless noise and posturing if it isn't ordered toward those most basic human needs: love, peace, harmony, tranquility, reflection, appreciation.

Like light and dark, day and night, work and leisure were meant to complement one another, not conflict.
  Neither "I'm too busy" nor "It's too much work" are ever an excuse for not being human, first and foremost.

❖ ❖ ❖ ❖ ❖

Day 35

If you find in human life anything better than justice, truth, temperance, fortitude, and, in a word, anything better than your own mind's self-satisfaction in the things which it enables thee to do according to right reason, and in the condition that is assigned to you without thy own choice; if, I say, you see anything better than this, turn to it with all your soul, and enjoy that which you have found to be the best.

But if nothing appears to be better than the deity which is planted in you, which has subjected to itself all your appetites, and carefully examines all the impressions, and, as Socrates said, has detached itself from the persuasions of sense, and has submitted itself to the gods, and cares for mankind.

If you find everything else smaller and of less value than this, give place to nothing else, for if you do once diverge and incline to it, you will no longer without distraction be able to give the preference to that good thing which is your proper possession and your own.

For it is not right that anything of any other kind, such as praise from the many, or power, or enjoyment of pleasure, should come into competition with that which is rationally and politically or practically good.

All these things, even though they may seem to adapt themselves to the better things in a small degree, obtain the superiority all at once, and carry us away. But do you, I say, simply and freely choose the better, and hold to it. But that which is useful is the better.

Well then, if it is useful to you as a rational being, keep to it; but if it is only useful to you as an animal, say so, and maintain your judgment without arrogance: only take care that you make the inquiry by a sure method.

—Marcus Aurelius, *Meditations* Book 3

The Stoics, like many other Ancient philosophers, stressed four Cardinal Virtues, the four habits that will help us to live well and happy.

Prudence is the wisdom to grasp the truth.

Fortitude is the strength to face fear for the sake of what is good.

Temperance is the self-control to seek moderation in pleasure.

Justice is the act of fairness, of treating our fellows with equal and proper respect.

They derive from Plato's timeless analysis of society and the human soul in the *Republic*.

Don't just accept these virtues blindly and without question. Marcus Aurelius reminds us that if we find a model that seems to do a better job of making us happy, by all means, we should choose that path.

If we honestly think that money, power, image, and pleasure are best, we should commit to these in life.

The Stoic is hardly a pushy or autocratic fellow, and he will let us live as we see fit.
He is a bit of a philosophical libertarian.

If, however, we become convinced that wisdom trumps wealth, that moral courage bests popularity, that temperance is greater than greed, and that justice matters more than power, then we need to act on that commitment.

We should hold to what we most dearly value.
 On the one hand lies the danger of hypocrisy.
 On the other hand lies the danger of equivocation over our priorities.
 The reader has already seen many warnings against both vices many times in this book, and that is because the Stoic recognizes the fruitlessness of valuing something without doing it with all our hearts.

Whatever path in life I may choose, I need to do so with complete commitment.
 If I am going to be an animal, then I should do that all the way.
 But If I am going to be a man, I need to fully embrace something very different.

I found that many of the obstacles I have faced in grappling with the Black Dog rested on my own sloppy thinking.
 I intellectually thought I wanted one thing, but I was still using a different standard in my feelings and actions. If the standards practiced by the greedy, deceitful, vain, lustful, and power-hungry aren't the things I want, I can't keep expecting to be disappointed when I fail to get those things.

Marcus Aurelius' passage made me a little angry when I first read it, probably because I knew how right he was for calling me out.

❖ ❖ ❖ ❖ ❖

Day 36

What indictment can we make against tyrants when we ourselves are much worse than they? For we have the same impulses as theirs but not the same opportunity to indulge them.

—Musonius Rufus, *Fragments* 23

It would hardly be reasonable of me to accuse others of this, because the whole point of the passage is to learn to indict ourselves.

In practice, I find it easy to blame others and to praise myself, and a very hard thing to praise others and blame myself.

And often that has little to do with whether I or another are better or worse.

It usually has far more to do with the circumstances, conditions, and burdens we're working under.

So it's easy to criticize someone else's vices, when I would most likely commit precisely the same ones if I just had the chance.

The real test would be whether, even under the same opportunities, I acted differently, because of what I knew was right, not just because of what I could get away with.

It is sadly a platitude to say that we should walk in someone else's shoes, to see as they see, to feel as they feel.

Maybe we should say it less and practice it more.

I've seen this problem in so many different forms, both in myself and in others.

I can hardly criticize promiscuity just because I'm not as handsome, charming or as wealthy as someone else, I can't judge someone who abuses power just because I'm not powerful enough to put myself in his situation, and I certainly can't condemn a liar because he's smart enough not to be caught out.

I'm perhaps far better served not to be cast judgment on others at all.

If I worry more about the virtue of my own actions under similar conditions, this might be an effort better spent.

❖ ❖ ❖ ❖ ❖

There is a true law, a right reason, conformable to Nature, universal, unchangeable, eternal, whose commands urge us to duty, and whose prohibitions restrain us from evil. Whether it enjoins or forbids, the good respect its injunctions, and the wicked treat them with indifference.

This law cannot be contradicted by any other law, and is not liable either to derogation or abrogation. Neither the senate nor the people can give us any dispensation for not obeying this universal law of justice.

It needs no other expositor and interpreter than our own conscience. It is not one thing at Rome and another at Athens; one thing to–day and another to–morrow; but in all times and nations this universal law must for ever reign, eternal and imperishable. It is the sovereign master and emperor of all beings. God himself is its author, its promulgator, its enforcer.

He who obeys it not, flies from himself, and does violence to the very nature of man. For his crime he must endure the severest penalties hereafter, even if he avoid the usual misfortunes of the present life.

—Cicero, *Of the Republic* 3, tr Barham

Cicero is here referring to the Classical distinction between Natural Law and Human Law.

Whereas the human law depends upon particular convention, the natural law rests upon the universal order of things themselves.

In the most basic terms, we can understand the difference using the old Socratic question: Is a thing good because it is desired, or should it be desired because it is good?

The Ancients understand that specific times, circumstances and needs often required different solutions.

But if we make everything totally relative, then the good becomes merely a matter of the fad of popularity, which is the rule of the mob, or brute power, which is the rule of tyrant.

Such relativism is very much the trend of our day, and it requires a more solid foundation.

Convention becomes meaningless without being grounded in Nature.

I often use two different examples to explain this, which can be helpful for students of any age.

When the "Founding Fathers" wrote the Declaration of Independence, they understood the need for a reasoned argument to explain their actions, and they understood that power and popularity did not make right.

Their appeal was to the very natural law Cicero describes:

> *We hold these truths to be self-evident, that all men are created equal, that they are endowed by their Creator with certain unalienable Rights, that among these are Life, Liberty and the pursuit of Happiness.*

When Martin Luther King sat in a Birmingham Jail, and sought to defend civil disobedience against racial discrimination, he made a very similar appeal:

> *One may want to ask: 'How can you advocate breaking some laws and obeying others?' The answer lies in the fact that there are two types of laws: just and unjust. I would be the first to advocate obeying just laws. One has not only a legal but a moral responsibility to obey just laws. Conversely, one has a moral responsibility to disobey unjust laws. I would agree with St Augustine that 'An unjust law is no law at all.'*
>
> *Now, what is the difference between the two? How does one determine whether a law is just or unjust? A just law is a man-made code that squares with the moral law or the law of God. An unjust law is a code that is out of harmony with the moral law. To put it in the terms of St Thomas Aquinas: An unjust law is a human law that is not rooted in eternal law and natural law. Any law that uplifts human personality is just. Any law that degrades human personality is unjust.*

Cicero, Jefferson, and King, along with Augustine and Aquinas, are reminding us of something crucially important: We shouldn't treat another person with respect and decency simply because it suits us, because it is convenient or popular at the moment, or because it gives us some specific benefit.

That isn't respect at all.

We should treat another person with respect because of their innate dignity as human beings, given to them by Nature.

The Stoics understood this at the root of their sense of justice and law.

❖ ❖ ❖ ❖ ❖

Day 38

Remember that you must behave in life as you would at a banquet. A dish is handed round and comes to you; put out your hand and take it politely. It passes you; do not stop it. It has not reached you; do not be impatient to get it, but wait till your turn comes. bear yourself thus towards children, wife, office, wealth, and one day you will be worthy to banquet with the gods.

But if when they are set before you, you do not take them but despise them, then you shall not only share the gods' banquet, but shall share their rule. For by so doing Diogenes and Heraclitus and men like them were called divine and deserved the name.

—Epictetus, *Enchiridion* 15

The emotional pain of loss or resentment doesn't go away overnight.

But once I can begin to think rightly about what is truly mine, about what I deserve or don't deserve, about the dignity of my own nature, then my feelings, my impressions, as the Stoics liked to say, can be tempered by judgment.

And with time, an impression can begin to lose its sting, if I recognize that the poison need not be fatal.

We've sadly lost most of our sense of etiquette and table manners these days, but the image remains a powerful one.

I shouldn't grab greedily for everything around me, and not be that person that defines himself by getting whatever he wants.

My will is not the center of the universe.

I can be patient, grateful for what Nature gives me, accepting when she passes something by.

I am given all I need, because all I really need is to rule myself.

Now imagine if I could not only be grateful and accepting of good circumstances, but not care for them at all either way, and be totally indifferent to them.

Epictetus says this is God–like.

I've struggled greatly with the first step, and look in awe at the second.

But there is absolutely no reason I shouldn't be able to live in such a manner, except my own choices and habits.

I believe he intends to encourage us, not to discourage us.

❖ ❖ ❖ ❖ ❖

Day 39

As physicians have always their instruments and knives ready for cases which suddenly require their skill, so do you have principles ready for the understanding of things divine and human, and for doing everything, even the smallest, with a recollection of the bond which unites the divine and human to one another. For neither will you do anything well which pertains to man without at the same time having a reference to things divine; nor the contrary.

—Marcus Aurelius, *Meditations* Book 3

We would think it ridiculous if the doctor, the mechanic, the lawyer, or the teacher did not know how to do their jobs, or neglected the tools of their trade.
Now what skills and tools do we need to simply be human?
Do we have them ready at hand?

These tools are, of course, the tools of philosophy, the means by which we discern true from false, the good from evil, the beautiful from the ugly.
And since being human is our very core, and being happy our highest good, surely these are the most important tools we'll ever need?

A University Dean once told me that our students really didn't need too much philosophy or humanities, because they were all going into professional careers.
They needed just enough to impress their future employers.
And that is exactly the ignorant attitude that causes us to neglect our humanity.

By all means, learn the tools of your trade with great skill.
Now learn to be a good person with even greater skill, because that is a far more important purpose for your existence.

To be a true philosopher, not just a stuffy academic, is to see all things in order and harmony, the higher and the lower, heaven and earth, the divine and human.
I can't get to my destination without a map, and I can't be human without knowing my place among all other things.

❖ ❖ ❖ ❖ ❖

Of all the propositions which I have advanced, the most difficult seems to be the one stated first, that those things which we all shudder and tremble at are for the good of the persons themselves to whom they come.

'Is it,' you ask, 'for their own good that men are driven into exile, reduced to want, that they bear to the grave wife or children, that they suffer public disgrace, and are broken in health?' If you are surprised that these things are for any man's good, you must also be surprised that by means of surgery and cautery, and also by fasting and thirst, the sick are sometimes made well.

But if you will reflect that for the sake of being cured the sick sometimes have their bones scraped and removed, and their veins pulled out, and that sometimes members are amputated which could not be left without causing destruction to the whole body, you will allow yourself to be convinced of this as well, that ills are sometimes for the good of those to whom they come; just as much so, my word for it, as that things which are lauded and sought after are sometimes to the hurt of those who delight in them, being very much like over-eating, drunkenness, and the other indulgences which kill by giving pleasure.

—Seneca the Younger , *On Providence* 3

I always had an intellectual attraction to Stoicism.
 For many years, I also had a personal and emotional revulsion to it.
 Like anyone else, I enjoy pleasure, and I don't like feeling pain.
 It seemed I was being asked to deny what was enjoyable, and then just suffer without complaint.

That view was the fault of my own ignorance, not of Stoic philosophy.
 The Stoic neither denies pleasure, nor encourages pain.
 He recognizes both as necessary aspects of life, but he sees that the human good is above and beyond these shallow measures.

Seneca reminds us that, in all of Nature, pain and suffering serve a purpose.
 For the body, they can be the necessary means to healing.
 Why should it be any different for the soul?
 Pain is always telling us something, and we harm ourselves all the more for denying, numbing, or repressing it.

I have often wished to be relieved of the pain and memory of a certain loss.
 But that is deeply selfish and narrow-minded.
 I must admit that, prior that event, I was a person who was far too cynical and dismissive.
 I was very quick to judge and dispose of others, perhaps because it was easier and less painful to be cold.

Once I felt rejection and dismissal myself, however, something changed.
  I found myself able to feel not only sympathy, but also empathy for the pain of others.
  And that changed everything about how I now understand my own life and the unique dignity of every person.
  I can no longer easily dispose of others, and I cannot bear to see pain in others, especially those who have been abused and treated unfairly.

Perhaps some other event, at some other time, could have served as the means for this change.
  But I'm not sure what it could have been.
  A few years in either direction would most likely have been too early, or too late.
  Professional disappointments would have hardly have held the same weight, and would perhaps have only encouraged a greater hardness of heart.

What could have been, I'll never know, but I do know that I needed the sorrow to heal.
  The only thing good about me came from this, and I would be far worse without it.

❖   ❖   ❖   ❖   ❖

'But now,' said she, 'is the time for the physician's art, rather than for complaining.' Then fixing her eyes wholly on me, she said, 'Are you the man who was nourished upon the milk of my learning, brought up with my food until you had won your way to the power of a manly soul? Surely I had given you such weapons as would keep you safe, and your strength unconquered; if you had not thrown them away. Do you know me? Why do you keep silence? Are you dumb from shame or from dull amazement? I would it were from shame, but I see that amazement has overwhelmed you.'

When she saw that I was not only silent, but utterly tongue-tied and dumb, she put her hand gently upon my breast, and said, 'There is no danger: he is suffering from drowsiness, that disease which attacks so many minds which have been deceived. He has forgotten himself for a moment and will quickly remember, as soon as he recognizes me. That he may do so, let me brush away from his eyes the darkening cloud of thoughts of matters perishable.' So saying, she gathered her robe into a fold and dried my swimming eyes.

—Boethius, *The consolation of Philosophy*, Book 1 Prose 2

Boethius did not merely write the Consolation as an exercise in thought.
He had been an old-school Roman gentleman, wealthy, powerful, educated, with the love of family and friends.
He came into the service of the new Gothic King of Italy, Theodoric.

As is so often the case, life has a way of running away from us.
Boethius, always a man who defended justice, was outraged when a fellow civil servant was accused of treason.
Boethius, knowing him to be innocent, rose to his defense, and fell with him.
He found himself in prison, also accused of treason, and awaiting his execution.

All had been lost, and lost, at that, for doing what was right.
Boethius wrote the *Consolation* during his imprisonment, considering the all-too-real problem of life's ultimate meaning.
Why did life punish the innocent, and reward the guilty?
His musings take on the form of a symbolic conversation with Lady Philosophy, the personification of Wisdom.
She first finds Boethius feeling sorry for himself, and writing melancholic poetry.
She chases away the Muses.
He doesn't need to coddle his feelings right now, she insists, he needs to consult with reason.

It is said that the Oracle at Delphi had the following inscription at its entrance: *Know Thyself.*
Despite all of his learning, Boethius has forgotten who he was, what it means to be human.
He has confused his nature with the empty promises of fame, wealth, and power.
He need only recollect, and it is the work of philosophy to help us remember.

❖ ❖ ❖ ❖ ❖

Day 42

Through this kinship with the flesh, some of us inclining to it become like wolves, faithless and treacherous and mischievous: some become like lions, savage and untamed; but the greater part of us become foxes and other worse animals.

For what else is a slanderer and a malignant man than a fox, or some other more wretched and meaner animal? See, then, and take care that you do not become some one of these miserable things.

—Epictetus, *Discourses* 1.3

Epictetus is, of course, speaking figuratively, but symbols can be just as powerful truths as literal facts.

In a sense, when we forget our humanity, as Boethius did, we begin to transform ourselves into something different.

The outward appearance may remain the same, but the inward character becomes twisted, distorted.

We find similar themes in the writings of Plato and Ovid, or in the theory of reincarnation in Hinduism and Buddhism.

How we think, what we love, how we live have real consequences.

We become how we behave.

I must always remind myself that there is no shame in a lion being a lion, or a fox being a fox.

But when a man is consumed by savagery or cunning, he falls from the station given to him by Nature.

❖ ❖ ❖ ❖ ❖

'It is difficult, however,' you say, 'to bring the mind to a point where it can scorn life.' But do you not see what trifling reasons impel men to scorn life? One hangs himself before the door of his mistress; another hurls himself from the house-top that he may no longer be compelled to bear the taunts of a bad- tempered master; a third, to be saved from arrest after running away, drives a sword into his vitals.

Do you not suppose that virtue will be as efficacious as excessive fear? No man can have a peaceful life who thinks too much about lengthening it, or believes that living through many consulships is a great blessing.

—Seneca the Younger, *Moral letters to Lucilius* 4

We often have an odd view of the value of life.

On the one hand, we are willing to give up anything and everything to extend the quantity of our lives, but we will give very little to improve their quality.

Likewise, we worry very much about our own lives, which we believe deserve special care, but will readily neglect those of others.

People are often confused, even offended, when they see the Stoic telling us to scorn life.

It's not about desiring death, it's about understanding what is truly good about any life.

Epictetus reminds us how readily, through loss, despair, or fear, we are ready to give up this life.

If fear is so powerful a motivator, wouldn't virtue be an even more powerful one?

Neither a long life, nor one of power and fame, wealth, pleasure, will make that life any better.

We need to learn where the true riches lie.

❖   ❖   ❖   ❖   ❖

Day 44

Though you could be going to live three thousand years, and as many times ten thousand years, still remember that no man loses any other life than this which he now lives, nor lives any other than this which he now loses. The longest and shortest are thus brought to the same. For the present is the same to all, though that which perishes is not the same; and so that which is lost appears to be a mere moment.

For a man cannot lose either the past or the future: for what a man has not, how can any one take this from him? These two things then you must bear in mind:

The one, that all things from eternity are of like forms and come round in a circle, and that it makes no difference whether a man shall see the same things during a hundred years or two hundred, or an infinite time.

And the second, that the longest liver and he who will die soonest lose just the same. For the present is the only thing of which a man can be deprived, if it is true that this is the only thing which he has, and that a man cannot lose a thing if he has it not.

—Marcus Aurelius, *Meditations* Book 2

On a recent sleepless night, I watched a typical cable TV science show.

Though often high on the melodrama, light on the actual science, I was fascinated to hear of all the recent attempts to effectively make human beings immortal.

From cures for various diseases, to cloning, to cybernetics, to genetic engineering, I was told all about how this would change everything.

We could all live forever, and everything would be better.

René Descartes expressed much the same idea in his philosophy, the hope that science could conquer death and make us masters of nature.

The Stoic looks at all of this with suspicion, not out of an aversion to science, but out of a question of human values.

First, is it even helpful or necessary to conquer death?

Second, why would I wish to dominate nature?

I am part of it, not above it.

I wonder if this is our modern day Tower of Babel.

Living longer isn't better.

Living better is better.

More chances at doing it right become a burden just as easily as they could be a gift.

Nature is intended to follow an order and cycle.

I prefer to embrace that harmony than vainly struggle against it.

Most importantly, we deceive ourselves if we define our existence through the past and the future.

Now is now, and everyone has the same now.

Past and future are gone, or will be.

All of our "nows" are equally finite, and yet, in another sense, equally infinite.

No one is winning or losing by living more or less. I own my present being, and nothing else, as my past and future are entirely beyond my power.

This passage is, I think, a great help in understanding why the Stoic does not fear death.

❖ ❖ ❖ ❖ ❖

Musonius said that there was no more shameful inconsistency than to recall the weakness of the body under stress of pain, but to forget it in the enjoyment of pleasure.
—Musonius Rufus, *Fragments* 25

Of course, we forget the important things when they are inconvenient, and remember them when we suddenly need them.

The flesh is weak.

Yet we elevate the glory of our bodies when we enjoy the pleasures of food, drink, or sex, but then we denigrate the body only when it causes us suffering through hunger, thirst, or want.

Not only would it be best to be consistent, but it would also be best for us to reconsider the whole equation.

The body is weak in either case, with pleasure and with pain.

Without judgment, the ability to make a good decision on what matters, either extreme will destroy us.

When we are gratified, or when we hurt, the only thing that matters at all is to make good sense of that impression.

Once I succumb to it alone, I am ruled by the flesh alone, and that is what makes me weak.

❖ ❖ ❖ ❖ ❖

Day 46

Remember that you are an actor in a play, and the Playwright chooses the manner of it: if he wants it short, it is short if long, it is long. If he wants you to act a poor man you must act the part with all your powers and so if your part be a cripple or a magistrate or a plain man. For your business is to act the character that is given you and act it well; the choice of the cast is Another's.

—Epictetus, *Enchiridion* 17

I'm not a scholar by any measure, and to be honest, I'm very glad that I'm not.
Contemporary scholarship seems to be far too tied up with honor and status for my taste.
I prefer to teach in a classroom, however humble.

Over the years, I've really only pursued three topics for any deeper "research".
The first was my dissertation on Thomas Aquinas and Thomas Reid.
I'm not sure anyone actually read it, but I'm fine with that.

The second, of course, is Stoicism.
In that case, I learned quickly that the living mattered far more than the publishing, so I stuck with the former. I do not regret that one bit.
I even wonder if a contemporary scholarly reflection on Stoicism might even defeat the very purpose of the discipline.

The third is a rather sweeping idea I've had in my head since my first year in college.
It is something inspired by Fulton Sheen, Catholic philosopher, priest, bishop, writer, and TV celebrity.
It's all about measures.

What do we consider to be the measure, the standard, the absolute, of our lives?
Where does the center lie?
We either make ourselves the absolute, or we look to that which transcends ourselves.

Now I promised that there would be no religious pontificating in this book, and I try to stick to my promises.
I will gladly bracket the question of what, or who, this Absolute may be.
That is a matter for a different time.

But the basic decision remains the same:
Will I decide that I am the center and measure of all things, or will I recognize that the universe is bigger than me?
That I am a creature, not the Creator?
That I am incomplete, made perfect by sharing in what is complete?

In my own thinking, I relate this to astronomy.
The old Ptolemaic model of astronomy was geocentric.
Earth was the center.
The modern Copernican model is heliocentric.
The sun is the center.

Ironically, in modern philosophy, we have gone in the reverse direction.
 For the Ancients, the Divine was the center.
 But for us, the self is the center.
 As we grow less self–centered in astronomy, we grow more self–centered in philosophy.

Epictetus is simply reminding us that we are the actors, not the playwrights.
 We don't determine the parts.
 We determine how well we play the parts.
 A humility we have all lost is necessary to understand any of this.

❖ ❖ ❖ ❖ ❖

From my grandfather, Verus, I learned good morals and the government of my temper. From the reputation and remembrance of my father, modesty and a manly character. From my mother, piety and beneficence, and abstinence, not only from evil deeds, but even from evil thoughts; and further, simplicity in my way of living, far removed from the habits of the rich.

—Marcus Aurelius, *Meditations* Book 1

The entire first book of Marcus Aurelius' *Meditations* is a dedication.
Many readers, therefore, skip it.
He refers to dozens of people, and offers how and why they helped him to become the man that he was.

We expect a dedication to be something merely formal.
An author will thank his wife and children, an actor or musician will thank his producer or manager, and any celebrity at an awards ceremony will thank God.
It matters little that few of them believe in God; the appearance is what matters.

When looking at Homer's *Iliad*, the Catalogue of the ships from Book 2, or in the genealogies of the Old Testament, we fuss and complain about how boring these sections are.
Why should we care who came over on a ship for a war, or who begat whom?

Because individual people really matter.
Each and every human being, in every time and place, is important; families matter, connections matter, relationships matter.
History is not just about facts and figures.
It is all about real lives, each lived with the same depth that you and I do.
Marcus Aurelius often tells us that to be sociable is a very part of our nature, and that we should have genuine and lasting relationships with others.

When Marcus Aurelius, the virtuous Emperor of Rome and Stoic philosopher, writes a whole chapter dedicated to the people he admired and those who inspired him, it might be a time to listen.

This little book I've written is dedicated to one person, and it isn't even my wife or one of my children, certainly not my manager or producer, and not even the Almighty.
It is not meant lightly.
It is meant with the deepest love.
No human being should ever be thrown away.
The only way I can change that is by starting with myself, and to show love and gratitude whenever I can.

❖ ❖ ❖ ❖ ❖

Day 48

Withdraw into yourself, as far as you can. Associate with those who will make a better man of you. Welcome those whom you yourself can improve. The process is mutual; for men learn while they teach.

—Seneca the Younger, *Moral letters to Lucilius 7*

Withdrawing into oneself is not isolation or any sort of hiding away.
Seneca's second sentence makes that clear.
To withdraw means here to depend upon oneself first and foremost, to tend to our own character, and to rely as little as possible on anything external, including making our value contingent merely upon social status.
There is no shame in solitude, no harm in practicing self-reliance.

And while it does not mean removing oneself from society, it does mean choosing our friends very carefully, and very sparingly.
As with the number of years of our lives, the number of our friends means very little.
In fact, I often suspect we spread ourselves far too thin with all the people in our lives, the ones we call friends.
Really, they are just acquaintances, people we associate with.
They are not our second selves.

I suppose I can easily say that, having always had very few friends.
With only a very few exceptions, my dearest friends, those whom I love as I love myself, have been family.
I include my parents, my wife, and my children, and only a small handful more.

Have I ever wanted more friends?
The only time I found myself popular, at the center of a social circle for about a year, I enjoyed the companionship and attention, but I found it far too easily distracted me.
I became a worse person, because I did not withdraw enough to care for the state of my own judgments.

A friend is someone you help become better, and someone who helps you become better in turn.
I have learned through hard experience that morally corrupt people not only make bad friends, but really aren't even capable of being friends at all.
Their friendships are nothing but alliances of convenience.

❖ ❖ ❖ ❖ ❖

Day 49

There is no sweeter delight than that the soul should be charged through and through with justice, exercising itself in her eternal principles and doctrines and leaving no vacant place into which injustice can make its way.

—Philo of Alexandria, *On the special laws* 97, tr Colson

Philo of Alexandria was a Jewish-Hellenist philosopher, and his writings, especially those on law and virtue, are deeply inspired by and in harmony with the entire Stoic tradition.

It's not only right and good that we be fair and just.
It is, I think, quite literally the greatest joy that Philo describes.
I can point to my own experience, certainly. I have never felt more complete, more delighted than when I can do good for another, simply for its own sake.
Likewise, I find the deepest emptiness when I act with greed or malice.

I can also point to philosophy itself here.
What greater fulfillment could there be for man, a being made to know and to love, than to understand the good in itself and to act upon it, with no concern for any other reward?

To be just is, quite simply, to love fully, to respect another without condition, to give and to receive what is rightly and naturally owed.

My own bad experiences with being hurt over the years have made it difficult for me to recognize that there are indeed fair and decent people in this world.
Perhaps there are few of them, or perhaps we just don't always see them because their purpose is not to draw attention to themselves.

My unwillingness to love or trust arose from allowing myself to be ruled by my impressions, to be dragged around by my feelings without sound judgment.

When I first met the woman who would one day become my wife, I was suspicious.
Surely, this can't be right, I thought.
While she is an emotional firebrand, and can be as stubborn as a mule, she has never once deceived me, she has never attempted to manipulate me for her own ends, and she has never once been disloyal.

The desire for money, or power, or status has no place in her priorities.
She genuinely sees love and truth as the highest goods.
I know that she has a soul charged through and through with justice, and that was a gift I needed to experience at just that time.
Nature never acts in vain.

❖ ❖ ❖ ❖ ❖

If I had engaged in politics, I should have perished long ago and done no good to either you or to myself...for the truth is that no man who goes to war with you or any other multitude, honestly struggling against the commission of unrighteousness and wrong in the State, will save his life; he who will really fight for right, if he would live even for a little while, must have a private station and not a public one.

—Socrates, ex Plato, *Apology* 31e, tr Jowett

Socrates was, of course, not a Stoic philosopher.
 But I include a handful of quotes from Plato about Socrates, because his influence upon Stoicism is abundant.
 I find the *Apology* alone to be a wellspring of true Stoicism in spirit.

There is an unfortunate reason that the political life is reviled by so many.
 It isn't because politics is about serving the common good, which is its very purpose in the natural order.
 It is because so many politicians pervert service to others into service of self.

I suspect this is precisely because of the implicit dangers and temptations of power and public life.
 To gain the support of the many, it becomes too easy to pander to the many.
 Honesty, fairness, or humility do not win support as readily as deception, favoritism, or arrogance.
 By appealing to the lowest wants of the human condition, the public figure may take the easiest way to power, but not the right way.

Socrates understands this all too well, and his advice is a warning to be heeded.
 Avoid the trappings of public life, with all its false appearances and fineries.
 Be first and foremost a person of character, a man of private station.
 An honest man will not live long to do any good in that sordid world.
 Be that same person in whatever you do, and never compromise your principles for the fickle approval of public opinion.

❖ ❖ ❖ ❖ ❖

The mind at times fashions for itself false shapes of evil when there are no signs that point to any evil; it twists into the worst construction some word of doubtful meaning; or it fancies some personal grudge to be more serious than it really is, considering not how angry the enemy is, but to what lengths he may go if he is angry.

But life is not worth living, and there is no limit to our sorrows, if we indulge our fears to the greatest possible extent; in this matter, let prudence help you, and condemn with a resolute spirit even when it is in plain sight.

—Seneca the Younger, *Moral letters to Lucilius* 13

The Stoic always warns against being ruled by our impressions, surrendering our power of judgment over to our feeling alone.
 Things are not always what they originally seem to be, and a hasty leap often precedes a fatal fall.
 Look to the reality behind the appearance.

Unbridled fear is surely one of these false imaginings.
 We easily see the worst in everything and find the good in nothing.
 We rightly comfort a child who sees things in the dark that are not there, and is filled with horror at these vivid impressions.
 Let us also defend ourselves against these illusions.

My own experience of the Black Dog has involved many such instances.
 The negativity inherent in an attitude of sadness or dejection either monstrously exaggerates evils that do exist, or even creates entirely new ones.

I often find that the most insignificant obstacle becomes insurmountable in my feelings, and by extension every other occurrence seems to fall in line with this perception.
 I see one thing that appears bad to me, I magnify it, and then I see it in everything else.
 It's a horrible cycle.

There are many tools we can use in life to combat such false impressions.
 On the philosophical side, the Stoic suggests encouraging my thinking to order my feelings.
 By deliberately and consciously deciding to "turn" a certain impression, or contrast one bad aspect of an appearance with a good one, I've made the first steps.

I'm not letting myself be enslaved to my impressions, but I'm asking myself how I can discover the true and the good behind my feelings.

❖ ❖ ❖ ❖ ❖

Whatever this is that I am, it is a little flesh and breath, and the ruling part. Throw away
your books; no longer distract yourself: it is not allowed; but as if you were now dying,
despise the flesh; it is blood and bones and a network, a contexture of nerves, veins, and
arteries.

See the breath also, what kind of a thing it is, air, and not always the same, but every
moment sent out and again sucked in.

The third then is the ruling part: consider thus: You are an old man; no longer let this be a
slave, no longer be pulled by the strings like a puppet to unsocial movements, no longer
either be dissatisfied with your present lot, or shrink from the future.

—Marcus Aurelius, *Meditations* Book 2

I am always in awe that while Marcus Aurelius was a Roman Emperor, Epictetus was a slave.
It tells us something very important when two of the great proponents of a school could come
from such totally different backgrounds, while sharing exactly the same values.

It is precisely because they gave no weight or merit to the successes of this world that they could
both find equal joy and humility in their stations of life.
They recognized what it meant to be truly human, and that all the rest was just vanity.

The body is just matter, is pushed and scattered, as with so many of the trappings of the flesh we
are so keen on worshipping.
Marcus Aurelius even includes the earthly vanity of learning.
Books are just books, and of themselves will make us none the wiser.

Even breath, the fact that the body is animate and not inanimate, is fragile and weak of itself.
We are more than just bodies, or even living bodies.
It is our minds that allow us to rule ourselves, to be free, to be happy.

As we grow older, we may learn this far more readily, because we see the weakness of the flesh all
the more clearly.
But wisdom need not wait for old age, and it is beautiful whenever we are called to this
recognition.

❖ ❖ ❖ ❖ ❖

Day 53

One begins to lose his hesitation to do unseemly things when one loses his hesitation to speak of them.

—Musonius Rufus, *Fragments* 26

To the modern reader, such a statement may see horribly prudish.
Many of us believe, after all, that we have learned to liberate ourselves from such restrictions.

But I hardly think that Musonius has any political or social censorship agenda in mind here, whether it might be of the right or of the left.
He is making a deeper point about the relationship between our thinking and our language.

Words are signs that point to real things, and it only makes sense to recognize that when we use our words with greater or lesser care, this directly influences whether we make judgments with greater or lesser care.
Just as images and impressions can profoundly affect our thinking, so language also moves the soul.

If I speak of something with carelessness, neglect, or moral ambiguity, I am tempting myself and others to think and act with carelessness, neglect, or moral ambiguity concerning the realities those words represent.

When I was younger, I assumed I was above such niceties.
The words I spoke or listened too surely had no effect on my inner character.
It was only when my son overheard me referring to a certain politician as a "dirtbag" that I realized the power of my words.

A few weeks later, he was using the exact same term to describe a schoolmate.
When I called him out, he rightly pointed straight back to the source.
And I would be sorely mistaken if I thought that an adult mind is any less susceptible to the sloppy thinking that can come from sloppy speaking.

❖ ❖ ❖ ❖ ❖

Day 54

It is the mind that is wounded, and all this external imbecility, despair, and languishing, spring from this fountain, that the mind is thus prostrated and cast down. The principal and sovereign part has let the scepter fall and is become so vile and abject that it willingly serves its own servants. Tell me, what can any place or peregrination work in this case?
—Justus Lipsius, *On constancy* 1.2, tr Stradling

Justus Lipsius was not an ancient Stoic, but a Renaissance thinker who sought a revival of Stoicism for his own time.

His writings are a wonderful reminder that, despite all the passing trends of the ages, a solid truth can always be good and inspiring, whatever the time, place, or circumstance.

I wonder how much we could use this same wisdom here and now, at a time when the pursuit of success and possessions, along with the accompanying despair and human loss, are so very prevalent.

Lipsius is here writing about people who think they can fix their problems simply by fixing their surroundings, specifically with travel and moving about.

It's the subject of many a good pop song about the salvation that will come from "moving to a new town and changing my name."

And as appealing as that may seem, it doesn't get to the root of pain, which is my own thinking about my surroundings.

Changing the outside of me won't change the inside of me.

It will not give me constancy, however much it may distract, hide, or numb.

I am terribly guilty of this sin.

I've done it three times over the years, for whenever I add new worries, I foolishly figure it will all be fine if I just buy new luggage to carry them all in.

My grandmother had a wonderful phrase expressing the same idea: "Time to move house, the ashtrays are full."

By all means, travel and move around.

Life often puts us in unexpected places.

But don't do it and think that it will be a cure for having let your scepter fall, or having dropped the ball.

❖ ❖ ❖ ❖ ❖

Day 55

When a raven croaks with an evil omen, let not the impression carry you away, but straightway distinguish in your own mind and say:

'These portents mean nothing to me; but only to my bit of a body or my bit of property or name, or my children or my wife. But for me all omens are favorable if I will, for, whatever the issue may be, it is in my power to get benefit from them.'

—Epictetus, *Enchiridion* 18

We have already seen the danger of allowing ourselves to be ruled by impressions, and the destructive cycle of false imaginings that can carry us away.
Whether or not we believe in the supernatural, we are also equally susceptible to signs and portents.
We readily assume a sign, however slight, signifies good luck or bad luck, glory or doom, in our future.

While the causality of Providence rules all, it is vanity to assume we can interpret the meaning of more than a handful of its signs; the vastness and greatness of Nature far exceeds our power.
But let us, for the sake of argument, assume that a portent of bad luck is as clear as day.
It tells me, like it told Hector, that I will suffer, lose my wealth or reputation, that I will soon die.

This need only worry me if I care about those things as the measure of the good.
All "luck" is good, if we only so choose to let it help us become better.
We don't control all that is around us, but we do control ourselves.

I have had quite a few instances where the signs and portent were indeed crystal clear, croaking raven or not.
I once moved to a new job, only to find upon my arrival that no one there even knew who I was.
All those who had hired me a few months earlier had either quit or been fired.
This was not going to end well.

I could have run away then and there and hid my head in the sand, bemoaning the cruelty of fate.
I didn't.
I stuck it out, for once, and did my best with what little fortune had given me.
It was a painful, lonely, and frustrating time, but I became a better man because of it.
Our perspective and choices make or break the toss of the dice.

❖ ❖ ❖ ❖ ❖

Day 56

Remember how long you have been putting off these things, and how often you have received an opportunity from the gods, and yet do not use it. You must now at last perceive of what universe you are a part, and of what ruler of the universe your existence is an efflux, and that a limit of time is fixed for you, which if you do not use for clearing away the clouds from your mind, it will go and you will go, and it will never return.

—Marcus Aurelius, *Meditations* Book 2

They say that youth is wasted on the young, and as I pass well into what they call "middle age", I'm beginning to understand that. I never felt quite right in my skin when I was young, but I maintained a sense of hope that some time in the future, somewhere around the bend, it would all work itself out. I would pass the buck.

It will get better, next month, next year, when I finish my degree, when I get this new job, when that perfect friend falls into my life.

I often had the sense to start over with a clean sweep, but I missed the most necessary ingredient.

I assumed something would come to me later, forgetting that I had to do something for myself.

Not the success of riches or fame, which have absolutely nothing to do with me, but the success of virtue and self-control.

Though hardly a paragon of manly strength or beauty, I had always been in good health.

When the Black Dog trotted alongside, I slowly began to experience physical symptoms that, I assumed, were just part of the emotional pain.

My heart pounded and hurt, I became weak and tired very easily, I was out of breath even many years after having given up many bad habits.

When I started gritting my teeth from chest pains, losing my balance, and eventually passing out upon coming home, I realized these weren't just the physical outliers of depression.

I dragged myself to a doctor for the first time in years.

I was told I was suffering from advanced heart failure, and I was told I should get my affairs in order.

I had always assumed I would break into a panic, or uncontrollable tears, if and when I was told such a thing.

Instead, I felt a wonderful inner peace, not because I wanted to die, but because suddenly life was beautiful, stripped of all the extraneous nonsense we pile upon it.

As I write this passage, I am five months beyond my originally predicted expiration date.
Medical science, like all human knowledge, isn't always precise.
I know most likely what will kill me, how it will happen, and that it will be sooner rather than later.
But whether I live for a few more years, months, weeks, days, hours, or even minutes, this has taught me something so essential that I can only show the greatest gratitude.

My opportunity to live well is now, not tomorrow.
I need to stop putting things off, and caring about shallow things.
I must make my peace now, not later.
I need to tell people that I love them, even if they hate me.
The suffering of the body has helped me clear my heart and mind.

❖ ❖ ❖ ❖ ❖

Day 57

Why is it that God afflicts the best men with ill health, or sorrow, or some other misfortune?
For the same reason that in the army the bravest men are assigned to the hazardous tasks; it
is the picked soldier that a general sends to surprise the enemy by a night attack, or to
reconnoiter the road, or to dislodge a garrison.

Not a man of these will say as he goes, 'My commander has done me an ill turn', but
instead, 'He has paid me a compliment.' In like manner, all those who are called to suffer
what would make cowards and poltroons weep may say, 'God has deemed us worthy
instruments of his purpose to discover how much human nature can endure.'

Flee luxury, flee enfeebling good fortune, from which men's minds grow sodden, and if
nothing intervenes to remind them of the common lot, they sink, as it were, into the stupor
of unending drunkenness. The man who has always had glazed windows to shield him
from a drought, whose feet have been kept warm by hot applications renewed from time to
time, whose dining- halls have been tempered by hot air passing beneath the floor and
circulating round the walls—this man will run great risk if he is brushed by a gentle
breeze.

—Seneca the Younger, *On Providence* 4.8

We are pleased as punch when we receive a promotion in our careers, even as we know that it
requires more work, greater responsibility, and heightened risk.
It's going to hurt to do it well.
After all, we rise to the challenge, and we are honored by it, because it is the road to the worldly
success, of climbing the proverbial ladder.

At the same time, we complain about the bigger, and the far more important, picture.
When life gives us misfortunes that challenge our inner happiness we are angered and indignant.

Why should this be?
We rise to the challenge with the lesser things, but cringe in horror when put to the test with the
greater things.
I believe it is because we have our priorities flipped.
We think that the success of worldly fortune depends upon our struggle and hard work.
We assume that the goods of the soul are then an entitlement.

Something quite different is true.
Worldly fortune comes and goes, and often has little to do with my own efforts.
I should feel honored, on the other hand, when Nature and Providence make it difficult for me,
ask more of me, and give me a moral promotion.
What will the man coddled and spoiled by good fortune do when his character is challenged?
He will fold under the pressure.

❖ ❖ ❖ ❖ ❖

Can we call the person truly chaste, who abstains from adultery merely for the fear of public exposure, and that disgrace which is only one of its many evil consequences? For what can be praised or blamed with reason, if you depart from that great law and rule of Nature, which makes the difference between right and wrong?

Shall bodily defects, if they are remarkable, shock our sensibilities, and shall of the soul make no impression on us? Of the soul, I say, whose turpitude is so evidently proved by its vices. For what is there more hideous than avarice, more brutal than lust, more contemptible than cowardice, more base than stupidity and folly?

—Cicero, *On the laws* 1.51, tr Yonge

I both laugh and cringe when I think of all the people I have known who are sinners in secret, and saints in public.

I have sometimes been guilty of it myself.

We do this under the assumption that what is right and wrong is determined by the approval or disdain of others.

It's not about our being, it's about our being seen.

Instead of recognizing the natural good of virtue within us, we defer our value to the opinions of others.

The difference, of course, corresponds to those things within our power, and those things outside of our power, and this is why the person who seeks honor is a slave.

What Cicero describes is a form of the cardinal sin of Stoicism, seeking happiness in the very things that can never provide it.

Years ago, a friend I had gone to both high school and college with sent me a newspaper interview with one of our classmates.

He marked it only with a large question mark, knowing full well I would catch his meaning.

In it, the classmate described how a trip to Rome had been a spiritual transformation, and how deeply she was touched by the holiness of John Paul II.

Sadly, we both knew this was far from the truth.

She had spent the entire trip binge drinking and sleeping with a series of men.

The appearance, given to gain approval, masked the reality, hidden to avoid shame.

We are all tempted to such a false security, and we may even come to believe our own delusions.

What truly makes an ugly person?

Not someone with a deformed or diseased body, but with a deformed and diseased soul.

Again, we sadly reverse the order of goods in our lives.

We praise those who are physically strong and sexually attractive, and ridicule the weak and awkward.

And we rarely look within, at the hearts and minds that truly define us and give us our genuine worth.

Stoicism reveals that we live in an upside down world.

❖ ❖ ❖ ❖ ❖

Day 59

Now there are two kinds of hardening, one of the understanding, the other of the sense of shame, when a man is resolved not to assent to what is manifest nor to desist from contradictions. Most of us are afraid of mortification of the body, and would contrive all means to avoid such a thing, but we care not about the soul's mortification.

And indeed with regard to the soul, if a man be in such a state as not to apprehend anything, or understand at all, we think that he is in a bad condition; but if the sense of shame and modesty are deadened, this we even call power.

—Epictetus, *Discourses* 1.5

It is one thing to be ignorant, quite another to be shameless.
One is like a stubbornness of a mind that refuses to learn, the other like an obstinacy of a heart that refuses to follow conscience.
We are easily ashamed of our bodies, rarely ashamed of our souls.
We squint, look the other way, and awkwardly avoid meeting the gaze of our own sense of right.

We are right to consider ignorance a defect, but it is interesting how many people don't feel the same way about shamelessness.
It is almost as if virtue and conscience are seen as a hindrance to success and achievement, as if being ruled by love and is a weakness, as if justice is an inconvenience.
As Epictetus says, we love power so much that we will smother and silence conscience.

We may call such people strong, effective, go-getters, successful folks who always know what they want and just go take it.
They aren't robber barons, they are simply business savvy.
They aren't abusers, but are now achievers.

We turn a vice into a virtue.
Coldness and indifference become admirable qualities.
The only cure for the hardening of the heart is love, and we can only love when we understand and embrace what is truly good and dignified about both ourselves and about others.

❖ ❖ ❖ ❖ ❖

Day 60

'We have to be angry', you say, 'in order to punish.' What? Think you the law is angry with men it does not know, whom it has never seen, who it hopes will never be? The spirit of the law, therefore, we should make our own—the law which shows not anger but determination. For if it is right for a good man to be angry at the crimes of wicked men, it will also be right for him to be envious of their prosperity.

And what, indeed, seems more unjust than that certain reprobates should prosper and become the pets of fortune—men for whom there could be found no fortune bad enough? But the good man will no more view their blessings with envy than he views their crimes with anger. A good judge condemns wrongful deeds, but he does not hate them.

—Seneca the Younger, *On anger* 1.16

Just as we confuse vengeance and justice, we assume that punishment requires anger.

By all means let us be firm in our aversion to vice, unwavering in our rejection of evil deeds.

But this never means hostility toward the person, for we correct to improve and correct, not to destroy.

A later form of this same wisdom may be to hate the sin, but love the sinner.

A misguided anger is indeed very similar to envy, and I have often experienced the two in immediate partnership.

I may see another commit an injustice, and then I see the apparent benefits he receives.

If he cheats he becomes richer, if he lies he becomes more popular, if he slanders he becomes more powerful.

That simply doesn't seem fair, and I become jealous that he has what he doesn't deserve while I am left with nothing.

I find this very challenging.

How many times have I seen the most dedicated people abused, while the abusers live in luxury?

I need to remember that ill-gotten gains are not a reward.

They become a prison for the man who loves all the wrong things.

Perhaps Nature actually gives us everything we want, which means we should be careful what we wish for?

❖ ❖ ❖ ❖ ❖

Day 61

Do wrong to yourself, do wrong to yourself, my soul; but you will no longer have the opportunity of honoring yourself. Every man's life is sufficient. But yours is nearly finished, though your soul reverences not itself but places your felicity in the souls of others.

—Marcus Aurelius, *Meditations* Book 2

In the *Confessions* St Augustine asked God to save him, but not quite yet.
I may think I know very well that something is good, but I'd rather have something else instead, at least for the moment.
Then I'm afraid I never fully knew it, and I certainly didn't really believe it.
I'm putting a lesser good above a higher good.
Where there is no action, there is no genuine commitment. I tell myself that I believe my life alone is sufficient, while my deeds follow the same old trust in what is external.

Commitment isn't a matter of force or strength.
Remember, Stoicism isn't a brutal philosophy.
Commitment involves replacing old habits with new ones, humbly opening the mind to what is really true, and reaching out the heart to what is really good.
Once again, thinking and living go hand in hand.

I catch myself daily slipping into the pursuit of false goods, and I only correct myself when sound judgment redirects my choices and habits.
I increasingly see the importance of not wasting each and every of these precious opportunities.

❖ ❖ ❖ ❖ ❖

And if you choose to hold fast to what is right, do not be irked by difficult circumstances, but reflect on how many things have already happened to you in life in ways that you did not wish, and yet they have turned out for the best.

—Musonius Rufus, *Fragments* 27

I am in ever-increasing awe at the beauty of Providence.
Call the source and origin whatever you will, but with time and open-minded reflection I perceive more and more how everything rightly connects with the order of everything else.
The universe admits of deeper and deeper meaning and purpose.
Nothing happens in vain, however seemingly insignificant.

Some of the most painful and frightening events of life have a way of putting us right where we need to be.
Even if the externals don't seem ideal, each and every occurrence offers us the opportunity to learn, to improve, and to practice virtue.
This isn't just helpful in theory.
It is a powerful comfort when nothing seems to be going right.

If my father hadn't had a colleague that sent her children to a certain Liberal Arts school, I would never have ended up there.
It was perhaps the most challenging time of my life.
I wasn't the sharpest tool in the shed, and the demands of the work were brutal.
I suffered doubts and insecurities I can now barely fathom.
I swayed between being timid and scared on the one hand, and frantically clinging to wild instincts of anger on the other.

But after all these years, I know that was exactly where I needed to be.
I learned to think clearly for myself for the first time; I found that there were others just like me, and I had the rare experience of finding a few real friends amid the chaos.
What there is that is good in me now needed all that back then.

❖ ❖ ❖ ❖ ❖

Day 63

From everything which is or happens in the world, it is easy to praise Providence, if a man possesses these two qualities, the faculty of seeing what belongs and happens to all persons and things, and a grateful disposition. If he does not possess these two qualities, one man will not see the use of things that are and which happen; another will not be thankful for them, even if he does know them.

If God had made colors, but had not made the faculty of seeing them, what would have been their use? None at all. On the other hand, if He had made the faculty of vision, but had not made objects such as to fall under the faculty, what in that case also would have been the use of it? None at all.

Well, suppose that He had made both, but had not made light? In that case, also, they would have been of no use. Who is it, then, who has fitted this to that and that to this? And who is it that has fitted the knife to the case and the case to the knife? Is it no one? And, indeed, from the very structure of things that have attained their completion, we are accustomed to show that the work is certainly the act of some artificer, and that it has not been constructed without a purpose. Does then each of these things demonstrate the workman, and do not visible things and the faculty of seeing and light demonstrate Him?

—Epictetus, *Discourses* 1.6

Awareness, gratitude, and the power of Nature's design; no single one of these can exist without the others.

I could be conscious without showing any appreciation, I could show appreciation without consciousness, but this would be a dead end.

No improvement or action can proceed without both.

And perhaps most fundamentally, if Nature had no meaning and order, none of it would make any sense at all.

I adore the analogy Epictetus employs: It reminds me very much of the use of the image of light in Plato and Augustine.

There must be the ability to see, actual things to be seen, and the medium of light to make this relationship possible.

I think of the light as the necessary condition for all else, for warmth, for life, for all perception.

If I stand in the grandeur and beauty of a Gothic cathedral, I have both myself and the beauty around me.

But without that light streaming through those vast multi-speckled windows, I would be unable to appreciate either.

It isn't just about me, and it isn't just about the things outside of me.

It's about how the relationship between us, made possible only through the illumination cast upon all things.

❖　❖　❖　❖　❖

Day 64

Do the things external which fall upon you distract you? Give yourself time to learn something new and good, and cease to be whirled around. But then you must also avoid being carried about the other way. For those, too, are triflers who have wearied themselves in life by their activity, and yet have no object to which to direct every movement, and, in a word, all their thoughts.

—Marcus Aurelius, *Meditations* Book 2

From the beginning, I think I have always known what I must do to live well and be happy.
It has been the fullness of knowing, the practice of that very theory, which has tripped me up, time and time again.

I had often considered it a curse that I was born into this world shy, socially awkward, and physically ungainly.
I had a family, a few teachers, and a small handful of friends who always encouraged me.
Yet I still kept foolishly falling for the usual lies and gimmicks.
I assumed there was some way I could make it all work, where I could find the comfort in success that I craved.
I desired it because everyone else around me, both the bullies and the drones, told me that was the only way to go.

No circumstance given to any one of us is a curse.
Anything and everything is a blessing, rightly understood.

Please, don't buy into the lies; we are not defined essentially by shallow values.
I wasted far too much time playing it one way, and then, when I got burned, I went to the other extreme.
It took my poor future wife three months to get me to even speak to her.

Like so many, I swayed from an extreme of dependence, to an extreme of isolation.
Self-reliance is neither social arrogance nor total retirement.
It is the confidence and peace from finding that precious middle way.

❖ ❖ ❖ ❖ ❖

Prove your words by your deeds. Far different is the purpose of those who are speech-making and trying to win the approbation of a throng of hearers, far different that of those who allure the ears of young men and idlers by many-sided or fluent argumentation; philosophy teaches us to act, not to speak; it exacts of every man that he should live according to his own standards, that his life should not be out of harmony with his words, and that, further, his inner life should be of one hue and not out of harmony with all his activities.

This, I say, is the highest duty and the highest proof of wisdom, that deed and word should be in accord, that a man should be equal to himself under all conditions, and always the same.

—Seneca the Younger, *Moral letters to Lucilius* 20

Back when I was, quite ridiculously, the Chairman of an Academic Department, I put myself on the line to insist that we hire a specific candidate.
 Others were opposed to his application since he simply didn't have the right credentials.
 I argued that he was the right fellow, not because of any fancy achievements, but because he had genuine character.
 He expressed, with great eloquence, his commitment to Liberal Arts learning, to collegiality, and to true justice above all things.
 He was an eccentric, like myself, and argued that his love of what was right came before anything else.

Within a few weeks of his hiring, I discovered that he had privately sidestepped solidarity with his colleagues to arrange a better salary with the administration.
 He now earned far more than any of the rest of us.
 When I directly asked him about this, his answer was simply that he needed to find "leverage" to insure his own "security."

I now saw my fatal mistake.
 I had listened to his fine words, and not really considered his actions.
 I had, in a sense, been seduced, not romantically, but intellectually and morally.
 And the fault was entirely my own.

The fellow in question knows how to play a game.
 He's now Provost at the same institution.
 He didn't get there through honesty or character.
 He got there through submission to power and popularity.
 I was angry at first, but quickly turned it into a simple life lesson: don't be like that, at any cost.
 I have been learning to redirect the frustration.

❖ ❖ ❖ ❖ ❖

While I grieved thus in long-drawn prating, Philosophy looked on with a calm countenance, not one whit moved by my complaints. Then said she, 'When I saw you in grief and in tears I knew thereby that you were unhappy and in exile, but I knew not how distant was your exile until your speech declared it.

'But you have not been driven so far from your home; you have wandered there yourself: or if you would rather hold that you have been driven, you have been driven by yourself rather than by any other. No other could have done so to you.

'For if you recall your true native country, you know that it is not under the rule of the many-headed people, as was Athens of old, but there is one Lord, one King, who rejoices in the greater number of his subjects, not in their banishment. To be guided by his reins, to bow to his justice, is the highest liberty.

'Know you not that sacred and ancient law of your own state by which it is enacted that no man, who would establish a dwelling-place for himself therein, may lawfully be put forth? For there is no fear that any man should merit exile, if he be kept safe therein by its protecting walls.

'But any man that may no longer wish to dwell there, does equally no longer deserve to be there. Wherefore it is your looks rather than the aspect of this place which disturb me. It is not the walls of your library, decked with ivory and glass, that I need, but rather the resting-place in your heart, wherein I have not stored books, but I have of old put that which gives value to books, a store of thoughts from books of mine.'

—Boethius , *The consolation of Philosophy* Book 1 Prose 5

Where is home?
Some say that home is the place where you have your roots.
If that's true I'm an exile from my two homes.
I was born in Graz, Austria, and then in later years grew up in Boston, Massachusetts.
All of my thoughts, loves, and memories are tied to those two places.
My family in Austria was the center of my being, and living just outside of Boston was the backdrop for twenty-five years of my life, through good and bad, thick and thin.

As I am sadly a person very deeply moved by the power of memory, I have the greatest difficulty in ever setting foot in Austria again, because some of the best, and yet now desperately lost, memories of my life are so deeply tied to it.
Most everything I loved there is now gone.

My parents still live in my old family home in Boston, while at the same time the lost love of my life later decided to buy a house a block away.
It had nothing to do with me, I know, as I had long ago ceased to be of use or interest, and it was surely all about the school system and the social status that went with the particular neighborhood.
I attribute this to thoughtlessness, not malice.
But I can't attempt to sleep in my old childhood bedroom without now seeing her front yard.

Stronger and better people than myself might be able to handle such things, but I haven't acquired that strength yet.

I can do my best to withstand pain, but I see no point, at least not right now, in deliberately putting myself in its path. So that is another exile.

So where is home?

Perhaps another common answer, perhaps even another platitude, is the best.

Home is where the heart lies.

Home is wherever and whenever I can know what is true and love what is good.

It is where I can do my best to live well, to serve others without any demand for reward, to practice character, however poorly, in whatever time Providence has chosen to give me.

It isn't a place.

No true person is really an exile, because one cannot be exiled from oneself, or from the True, the Good, and the Beautiful.

❖   ❖   ❖   ❖   ❖

I would rather die having spoken in my manner, than speak in your manner and live. For neither in war nor yet in law ought any man use every way of escaping death. For often in battle there is no doubt that if a man will throw away his arms, and fall on his knees before his pursuers, he may escape death, if a man is willing to say or do anything. The difficulty, my friends, is not in avoiding death, but in avoiding unrighteousness; for that runs deeper than death.

—Socrates ex Plato, *Apology*, 38e-39a, tr Jowett

I often feel like Socrates personified so much of what defines Stoicism, well before the Stoic School even existed.

Indeed, for many Stoics, he is the archetype to follow.

It is vice, not death, which is the greatest danger for man.

My father would quote Shakespeare to me from as early as I can remember:

> *Cowards die many times before their deaths;*
> *the valiant never taste of death but once.*
> *Of all the wonders that I yet have heard,*
> *it seems to me most strange that men should fear;*
> *seeing that death, a necessary end,*
> *will come when it will come.*

I wish I had reflected on this more carefully when I was young. The true death is not that of the body, but of a soul that turns away from what is right.

That I must die is a necessity; whether I will be a good or an evil man is a matter of my choice alone.

❖ ❖ ❖ ❖ ❖

Day 68

> *You can be invincible, if you never enter on a contest where victory is not in your power. Beware then that when you see a man raised to honor or great power or high repute you do not let your impression carry you away. For if the reality of good lies in what is in our power, there is no room for envy or jealousy. And you will not wish to be praetor, or prefect or consul, but to be free; and there is but one way to freedom—to despise what is not in our power.*
>
> —Epictetus, *Enchiridion* 19

This passage requires a classic double take.

It may sound like Epictetus is telling us to never take a risk, to only fight the easy fights we can win.

That sounds more like a bully than a brave man.

But of course he means something rather different.

The greatest victory isn't the easiest one at all, but rather the one that can never be taken from us once we have won it.

Only my own efforts will bring me happiness.

It is a battle I can win if only I wish to do so, and the struggle will never be with anything outside my power, but only with myself.

All worldly gains are a gamble, easily won and lost, but my character is fully my own.

Rudyard Kipling, like so many things of his age, is out of fashion these days.

I believe he deserves far better.

His brand of Victorian Stoicism can certainly be seen as a tough, cold, heartless, "stiff upper lip" sort of creed.

I choose to read him very differently, informed by the Classics that surely inspired Kipling himself.

Whenever I read Epictetus, I immediately associate it with the poem "If—."

For me, this is deeply moving, filled with all the beauty and goodness of human dignity.

If you can keep your head when all about you
*   are losing theirs and blaming it on you,*
if you can trust yourself when all men doubt you,
*   but make allowance for their doubting too;*
if you can wait and not be tired by waiting,
*   or being lied about, don't deal in lies,*
or being hated, don't give way to hating,
*   and yet don't look too good, nor talk too wise:*

If you can dream—and not make dreams your master;
*   if you can think—and not make thoughts your aim;*
if you can meet with Triumph and Disaster
*   and treat those two impostors just the same;*
if you can bear to hear the truth you've spoken
*   twisted by knaves to make a trap for fools,*
or watch the things you gave your life to, broken,
*   and stoop and build 'em up with worn-out tools:*

If you can make one heap of all your winnings
*   and risk it on one turn of pitch-and-toss,*
and lose, and start again at your beginnings
*   and never breathe a word about your loss;*
if you can force your heart and nerve and sinew
*   to serve your turn long after they are gone,*
and so hold on when there is nothing in you
*   except the Will which says to them: "Hold on!"*

If you can talk with crowds and keep your virtue,
*   or walk with Kings—nor lose the common touch,*
if neither foes nor loving friends can hurt you,
*   if all men count with you, but none too much;*
if you can fill the unforgiving minute
*   with sixty seconds' worth of distance run,*
yours is the Earth and everything that's in it,
*   and—which is more—you'll be a Man, my son.*

❖ ❖ ❖ ❖ ❖

Choose to die well while it is possible, lest shortly it may become necessary for you to die,
but it will no longer be possible to die well.

—Musonius Rufus, *Fragments* 28

Musonius here reiterates a common first principle of Stoicism, though this very brief and direct version was one that had a very powerful effect on me the moment I first read it, and opened up a wonderful avenue of reflection.

It was a great aid in seeing something about myself I had previously not quite understood.

My self-evaluation had always been that, at a certain point in my life, I became unable to find hope. I started calling this the Black Dog, and though deeply painful, it seemed simple enough to understand.

Hope and joy were once there, and now they were gone.

That failed, of course, to address what was really happening in my thinking, and why it was happening.

What Musonius warns us against, of course, is putting off until tomorrow what we could do today, because tomorrow may well be too late.

What I realized was that I had overshot the mean, that middle ground, by flipping from one extreme view to the other.

I had started out suffering from uncertainty, loneliness, and restlessness, but I had always assumed I could find hope later.

As time passed, I suffered the same things, but now assumed that hope could never be found.

I had missed the mark because I was moved by the force of impressions alone, and not by my judgment about those impressions.

At one point, I could always get it later, so that would be fine.

At another point, I was sure I had lost it forever.

Both, of course, were wrong. I could still have it, and I could, and needed to, have it right here and now.

That hope wasn't from outside, but it could come from the inside, at this very moment.

It was always there, present, and never something to come or something lost.

❖ ❖ ❖ ❖ ❖

Day 70

Through not observing what is in the mind of another a man has seldom been seen to be unhappy; but those who do not observe the movements of their own minds must of necessity be unhappy.

—Marcus Aurelius, *Meditations* Book 2

One of the saddest things I have ever experienced is a person I cared for very deeply, full of promise and with a brilliant soul, slip slowly but surely from caring about self-knowledge to only caring about the opinions of others.

This is a temptation we all must bear, and one of the greatest obstacles to a good life.
Consider how much time and effort we spend concerned about what other people are thinking, why they might be thinking it, and how much this is going to affect us?

Now consider the other side of the coin.
How much time and effort do we spend concerned with the working of our own minds and hearts, why we are moved as we are, and how this is going to affect us?

As a wonderful teacher of mine used to repeat over and over, "You pays your money, and you makes your choice."
Worrying about what others think is both futile and fruitless.
Worrying about what I think is necessary and always of benefit.
As usual, the Stoic flips the priorities, the beauty of the Stoic Turn.

❖ ❖ ❖ ❖ ❖

In short, enjoy the blessing of strength while you have it and do not bewail it when it is gone, unless you believe that youth must lament the loss of infancy, or early manhood the passing of youth.

Life's race-course is fixed; Nature has only a single path and that path is run but once, and to each stage of existence has been allotted its own appropriate quality; so that the weakness of childhood, the impetuosity of youth, the seriousness of middle life, the maturity of old age-each bears some of Nature's fruit, which must be garnered in its own season.

—Cicero, *On old age* 33, tr Falconer

I used to tell myself I'd never have a mid-life crisis.
  Instead, as I was finishing college, I would wryly joke that I was having a pre–life crisis.
  Once I figured out what I was going to do, and what my place in the world was going to be, the rest would take care of itself.
  People rightly found this amusing, but not for the reason I thought.

It was, of course, foolish and naïve.
  What I called my pre–life crisis was itself a sense of loss, though I didn't recognize it at the time.
  I feared the loss of being young and carefree, and of becoming a real adult.

Did I ever have that mid-life crisis?
  Of course I did, because once again, I feared for something, the loss of my times of strength and success, however humble they were.
  I was growing weaker, in both body and mind, and my flickering star was beginning to fade.
  I didn't buy a red convertible or find a mistress to compensate, but I felt it nonetheless.

Being someone so moved by the power of memory, I often feel as if my life is like a Marcel Proust novel.
  I deeply regret not having lived my youth as fully as I could have, and I deeply regret the failures of my adult years.
  Now, in whatever time I have left, I'm entering the home stretch, and it sometimes seems like such a waste.

All of that is bad thinking, and it is allowing myself to be ruled by my impressions.
  If I had known in my youth what I knew in my middle age, well then, I wouldn't have been young, and if I had known what I know now when I was middle-aged, then I wouldn't have been middle-aged.
  It is ridiculous to apply the measure of the now to the past, because the measure of the now is only possible through the learning from the past.

I have been learning, with great difficulty, that life is a wonderful unfolding.
  What once was, was meant to be what it was, and what is now, is meant to be what it is now.

When my future wife and I first met, we were little more than adult versions of children, bright, foolish, and full of energy.

We look at one another now, and while the glow of youth is quite muted, the love is stronger, and it is better.

We are worse for wear, but better for wisdom.

It is now what it was meant to grow into.

I am not proud of many things in my life, but I am proud of that.

I finally learned to give my heart to a real, honest, and loving woman, and together we gave our lives to our children.

There were never any lies, deceptions, or games.

We have always lived with the ideal of love first, and never the pursuit of the vanities that distracted us along the way. We have both learned never to seek wealth, power, or honor.

The children, too, are now on that same path of growth.

They will quite soon make lives of their own, and I will feel sadness for that loss.

But I will smile with that sadness, because Nature has unfolded, as it rightly should.

True love never fails.

❖　❖　❖　❖　❖

If you set your desire on philosophy you must at once prepare to meet with ridicule and the jeers of many who will say, 'Here he come again, turned philosopher. Where has he gotten these proud looks?'

No, put on no proud looks, but hold fast to what seems best to you, in confidence that God has set you at this post. And remember that if you abide where you are, those who first laugh at you will one day admire you, and that if you give way to them, you will get doubly laughed at.

—Epictetus, *Enchiridion* 22

I had attended an eccentric high school, where students lounged about the hallways discussing Dostoyevsky, Fermat's Last Theorem, and the relative merits of The Talking Heads vs. The Smiths.

When I went to college, I was pleasantly surprised to find so many other philosophy majors, people I assumed shared the same loves and concerns that I did.

It was oddly interesting that so many of them were double Philosophy and English majors.
Well, I thought, those two go together like toast and jam for the lover of truth and beauty.

Yet it was also a bit troubling that there was no lounging about the hallways talking about philosophy, art, or literature.
There was rather much more drinking, fornicating, and boasting.
The courses and readings I loved so dearly were seen by many simply as a job, a task to be completed.
To be completed well, of course, but with no passion whatsoever.

I remember very vividly the day the scales were lifted from my eyes.
I was asked, in my sophomore year, which law schools I was going to apply to.

"Not a one," was my answer.
I also said something far too rude about lawyers.

"Well, then why are you a philosophy major?"

It turned out that the very year we had all applied to college, a major news magazine had said that Philosophy and English majors were statistically the most likely to be accepted to the most prestigious law schools.
That explained everything.

I took a different path.
Philosophy was never a stepping-stone to fame and fortune.
I always knew I needed to be a philosopher in daily life, and not of the sort that is an academic blowhard, to live well and rightly.
And I finally learned this would make me an unpopular fellow.
That is a cross I will bear gladly for the rewards philosophy, rightly understood, has given me.

❖ ❖ ❖ ❖ ❖

From business, however, my dear Lucilius, it is easy to escape, if only you will despise the rewards of business. We are held back and kept from escaping by thoughts like these: 'What then? Shall I leave behind me these great prospects? Shall I depart at the very time of harvest? Shall I have no slaves at my side? No retinue for my litter? No crowd in my reception room?'

Hence men leave such advantages as these with reluctance; they love the reward of their hardships, but curse the hardships themselves. Men complain about their ambitions as they complain about their mistresses; in other words, if you penetrate their real feelings, you will find, not hatred, but bickering.

Search the minds of those who cry down what they have desired, who talk about escaping from things which they are unable to do without; you will comprehend that they are lingering of their own free will in a situation which they declare they find it hard and wretched to endure.

It is so, my dear Lucilius: there are a few men whom slavery holds fast, but there are many more who hold fast to slavery.

—Seneca the Younger, *Moral letters to Lucilius* 22

When money itself becomes a god, it seems like blasphemy to criticize the love of money.
We feel uncomfortable, even offended, when the life of money is criticized.
Seneca has no such inhibitions, so his words may make us squirm.
Perhaps they should.

The very world you and I live in seems so often to be ruled by "business".
What matters the most is the making and spending of money, and most of us devote almost all of our time toward that pursuit.

We pay our lip service to justice, to compassion, to service.
But let us please be brutally honest.
We love the big buck first and foremost.
We desire the security of wealth, and only then speak of all the rest.

It is absolutely of no credit to any of us when we give freely while we are filthy rich; charity most reveals itself when we are piss-poor.
I see little merit in the rich and powerful showing their apparent care for the sake of the praise they then receive.
They are losing nothing at all, and are gaining only pride and status.

And this is exactly one reason why we are a twisted society.
I prefer to call it all "busyness".
I have no illusions that the thrust of modern life will change in an instant.
But I will make the effort to change myself, as that is all that I can do.
Perhaps this will encourage my son and daughter to love rightly, or maybe even a student or two, and perhaps they may inspire others in turn.
One day at a time, one step at a time.

Seneca understands the rat race all too well.

He sees how we all love the results of our efforts, yet we despise and complain about the effort itself.

I spent a very brief time working in financial software, quite simply because I needed money, that apparent cure for all of our ills.

I hated every minute of it, and every co-worker I had hated it just as much.

But we sure loved that Christmas bonus.

And that is a reason why the world of business becomes so petty and shallow.

Wisdom and love are the only currencies that count.

We wouldn't even need the rule of money if we had life in proper order.

We have contorted all things, such that people are now seen as a means to make money, and we rarely see money as a means to serve people.

We have freely chosen to make ourselves slaves to the most brutal of masters.

❖ ❖ ❖ ❖ ❖

Day 74

This you must always bear in mind, what is the nature of the whole, and what is my nature, and how this is related to that, and what kind of a part it is of what kind of a whole; and that there is no one who hinders you from always doing and saying the things which are according to the nature of which you are a part.

—Marcus Aurelius, *Meditations* Book 2

My mother often spoke of the generation I had been born into as the "Me Generation", an entire swarm of young people raised to believe that nothing was more important than their own self-fulfillment.

The entire world, she would say, was now seen as something that revolved around, and even existed for, the self.

My father observed something similar when he said that, at around the same time, the church hymns we sang began suddenly to speak of God in the first person.

I have seen some people view Stoicism as a means for such egocentric living.

They use the concept of self-reliance as a vehicle for selfishness, and assume that since happiness comes out of our own actions, we are also the center and measure of all things.

What such a perversion of philosophy misses is that we live within, and are ruled by, the whole of Nature.

We neither live in isolation from the world, nor does the world exist for us.

There can be no place for the subjectivism of modernity here, no place for Ayn Rand.

We become good and happy by living for Nature, and understanding ourselves in relation to that whole.

We are very good at talking about ourselves, and looking to ourselves first.

I once had a teacher who discouraged us from starting a phrase with "I think" so that we would avoid the temptation of making the truth depend on us.

"If it's true, say it like it's true for itself. Don't bring yourself into it."

By all means reflect upon the self, but always understand the self in relation to other things, as but one thread in the whole tapestry.

❖ ❖ ❖ ❖ ❖

The end may be defined as life in accordance with Nature or, in other words, in accordance with our own human nature as well as that of the universe.

—Zeno of Citium ex Diogenes Laertius,
Lives and opinions of eminent philosophers 7.87

An episode of the sitcom *Friends* had Phoebe challenge the group to commit a genuinely selfless good deed.

Hilarity, of course, ensues as all of them realize that anything they try to do well simply for its own sake seems to end up giving a selfish reward.

Philosophy classes have ever since used this as a helpful teaching tool in ethics.

From the Stoic perspective, the amusing dilemma is a false dichotomy.

This isn't matter of an either/or, but rather of a both/and.

By living well, a man does well for himself and for others.

Let the external consequences of action be pleasure or pain, fame or infamy, wealth or poverty, for the joy of virtue is simply having done right.

Zeno expresses this beautifully when he reminds us that the good of own individual nature is within that of the whole universe.

A kind word to a friend in pain, or a helping hand at a time of need should fulfillment and joy to be the giver and receiver, one because he has lived rightly, the other because it also helps him live rightly.

Any remaining circumstances are indifferent.

❖ ❖ ❖ ❖ ❖

If the things are true which are said by the philosophers about the kinship between God and man, what else remains for men to do then what Socrates did?

Never in reply to the question, to what country you belong, say that you are an Athenian or a Corinthian, but that you are a citizen of the world. For why do you say that you are an Athenian, and why do you not say that you belong to the small nook only into which your poor body was cast at birth? Is it not plain that you call yourself an Athenian or Corinthian from the place which has a greater authority and comprises not only that small nook itself and all your family, but even the whole country from which the stock of your progenitors is derived down to you?

He then who has observed with intelligence the administration of the world, and has learned that the greatest and supreme and the most comprehensive community is that which is composed of men and God, and that from God have descended the seeds not only to my father and grandfather, but to all beings which are generated on the earth and are produced, and particularly to rational beings — for these only are by their nature formed to have communion with God, being by means of reason conjoined with Him — why should not such a man call himself a citizen of the world, why not a son of God, and why should he be afraid of anything which happens among men?

Is kinship with Caesar or with any other of the powerful in Rome sufficient to enable us to live in safety, and above contempt and without any fear at all? And to have God for your maker and father and guardian, shall not this release us from sorrows and fears?

—Epictetus, *Discourses* 1.9

The Stoics were remarkably cosmopolitan in their views, and not only preached constant social concern and action, in contrast to the Epicureans, but also stressed that it is our common humanity within Nature, under the authority of the Divine, that fully defines us.

It is no exaggeration, then, to say that we should view ourselves first as citizens of the world, and as children of God.

This doesn't mean our local and personal bonds are meaningless, but rather that they can only be rightly understood within our human unity.

I often discern how we miss the mark with the tribal bonds of patriotism or ethnic pride, for we stress the difference over what is common.

I have seen this is on the political "right", in various forms and degrees of racial or ethnic superiority, and I have seen it in a very similar form on the "left", where a love of diversity moves in the other direction, but ends up at exactly the same place, stressing divisions and relativism.

Having myself grown up in a rather traditional European household, I was still of mixed heritage, a quirky blend of Irish and Austrian.

I found that while we recognized all the differences of our backgrounds, and were even able to laugh about it together, this was itself only possible because the unspoken rule was still fairly simple.

Always respect another person simply for having the dignity of being human, and not for the accidents that we add later, or because of our own preferences.

Though attributed variously to St Augustine, Richard Baxter, Peter Meiderlin, or Marco Antonio de Dominis, the following splendid saying always comes to mind when I read Epictetus' passage:

Unity in necessary things;
liberty in doubtful things;
charity in all things

❖ ❖ ❖ ❖ ❖

How quickly all things disappear, in the universe the bodies themselves, but in time the remembrance of them; what is the nature of all sensible things, and particularly those which attract with the bait of pleasure or terrify by pain, or are noised abroad by vapory fame; how worthless, and contemptible, and sordid, and perishable, and dead they are—all this it is the part of the intellectual faculty to observe.

To observe too who these are whose opinions and voices give reputation; what death is, and the fact that, if a man looks at it in itself, and by the abstractive power of reflection resolves into their parts all the things which present themselves to the imagination in it, he will then consider it to be nothing else than an operation of Nature; and if any one is afraid of an operation of Nature, he is a child. This, however, is not only an operation of Nature, but it is also a thing that conduces to the purposes of Nature. To observe too how man comes near to the deity, and by what part of him, and when this part of man is so disposed.

—Marcus Aurelius, *Meditations* Book 2

The vanity and weakness of worldly things is a common theme throughout the philosophy, religion, and literature of countless cultures.

I have never taken this as a hatred of the flesh, but rather as a yardstick by which to judge the most important aspects of life.

If I can remember how transient pleasure, fame, or power are, I will be less easily distracted by them, and I can then keep my attention on what truly matters.

Even these lesser things are a part of Nature, but can only be understood within the greater and higher purpose of Nature.

The impressions of memory, and the consequent burden of nostalgia and melancholy, have the most powerful effect upon my awareness.

Even those impressions, when turned rightly, can be used for seeing the bigger picture.

I recently happened across a photograph of a dormitory on my old college campus being torn down.

Only the steel frame was still barely standing.

I had spent two years with that building at the center of my life, and for many years later it was always still standing there as a reminder.

It's gone now, as are so many other things from past years.

My first ever office is now abandoned, and that building, too, will apparently soon be demolished.

Of all my old teachers, many are now dead, and the rest are retiring.

What little good I achieved in my studies and my early work years is now long forgotten.

No one remembers any of my petty achievements.

Some friends, too, have already died, and I share little in common with many others.

Our lives have sadly split.

And as powerful as impressions can be on the imagination, I can just as easily turn that power into something of great value.

I can remember that however fine and good the temporary things of this world can be, their dignity is as nothing compared to the greater part.

They serve their place in Nature not to be dwelled upon for their own sake, but in how they can lead me to happiness.

I think of the Parable of the Pearl in the Gospel of Matthew, or the Golden Fleece, or the Fisher King.

❖ ❖ ❖ ❖ ❖

Day 78

Remember, however, before all else, to strip things of all that disturbs and confuses, and to see what each is at bottom; you will then comprehend that they contain nothing fearful except the actual fear.

That which you see happening to boys happens also to ourselves, who are only slightly bigger boys: when those whom they love, with whom they daily associate, with whom they play, appear with masks on, the boys are frightened out of their wits. We should strip the mask, not only from men, but from things, and restore to each object its own aspect.

—Seneca the Younger, *Moral letters to Lucilius* 24

My own clinical depression has been what the experts apparently call treatment–resistant.
From the perspective of my personal experience, this means that the Black Dog doesn't back away for much of anything, and he is hard to shake off once he's bitten.
He will come and go, sometimes without warning, and sometimes, because of the effect of some impression or circumstance, I've already been expecting him.

This means that, however certain medical treatments may or may not have helped in ways I couldn't directly perceive, my only conscious way of facing the Black Dog is to adjust my thinking about my feelings.
The pain I feel is largely one of sadness, loneliness, dejection, hopelessness, and loss, but it is usually also accompanied by certain physical symptoms such as crippling headaches, trembling, fevers, or chest pains.
These feelings are in themselves entirely instinctive, and I can't just wish them away.

The only aid left to me is taking a mental deep breath.
Describe the feeling. How does it feel?
Now try to explain it. Why might I be feeling it?
Next discern if anything in the impression is in and of itself disturbing.
I see a scene in a film, and it reminds me of something painful.
It isn't the scene, but the association of the scene.
In fact, it isn't even the memory associated, but rather how I perceive that memory.
The memory is of an event, but the pain is from a perception.

As Seneca says, the thing itself is neither good nor bad for me, only my perception of it.
It wears a mask.
Mentally remove the mask, and perceive the reality.

The last time I was in Boston I walked by an Irish pub I used to go to for many years, for the fine company, the stout, and the music.
It was, quite unusually for that part of town, completely unchanged, and I could feel the old anxiety coming along.

Now why was that memory painful?

I flipped the memory, and found something within it that was pleasant, my first time playing the mandolin in front of a real audience.

That replaced the loss, and then I took it a step further.

I turned the painful part away completely by reminding myself how I had employed those circumstances to be become better and happier.

The odd result of this Stoic self-evaluation, for lack of a better term, is that it will sometimes leave me crying and smiling at the same time.

The crying is from the instincts, and the smiling is from the thinking.

And as odd as that may seem to someone else, I've grown used to that process.

As unpleasant as it might be, I have accepted that the pain, mental and physical, will most likely never disappear. It is only Stoic thinking and living that has made that bearable.

❖ ❖ ❖ ❖ ❖

Those who require proofs at every point, even where the matter is perfectly clear, or demand to have demonstrated at length things which could be explained briefly are completely inept and dull-witted.

—Musonius Rufus, *Lectures* 1

Pardon the bluntness, but few things are more annoying than a wiseass, the sort of person who argues simply for the sake of arguing and not to find the truth, who bickers but does not debate, who emotes but does not reason.

A family friend described a visit to France during his youth, when he was sitting in a café with a bohemian university student tackling some important life question.
Frustrated by the circular nature of the discussion, our friend decided to simply agree with the opposing position, at which point the other student now began arguing for the very position he had been criticizing for hours.
That's the pleasure some get from being difficult.

During my graduate years another friend quite similarly made a point of denying any and every statement of truth or fact.
His attitude was one of pure academic skepticism.

I once suggested to him that his doubt did not come from a desire for finding certainty, but rather a deliberate desire to avoid it.
In other words, I wondered out loud if his Pilate–like rejection of truth was a way of shirking any degree of moral responsibility.
It simply allowed him to wash his hands.

Immediately realizing that what I had said had come across as very rude, I opened my mouth to apologize.

"No," he said, "you're right, and you're the only person who ever saw through it."

Discerning what is real and true certainly isn't always easy, but it need not deliberately be made difficult.
Being intellectually obtuse may be dull-witted, and it may also be a stubborn way to reject the possibility of commitment.
There is no shame in accepting what is self-evident, and no merit in seeking to prove what is apparent.

❖ ❖ ❖ ❖ ❖

Remembering, then, this disposition of things we ought to go to be instructed, not that we may change the constitution of things—for we have not the power to do it, nor is it better that we should have the power— but in order that, as the things around us are what they are and by Nature exist, we may maintain our minds in harmony with them things which happen.

For can we escape from men? And how is it possible? And if we associate with them, can we change them? Who gives us the power? What then remains, or what method is discovered of holding commerce with them? Is there such a method by which they shall do what seems fit to them, and we not the less shall be in a mood which is conformable to Nature?

But you are unwilling to endure and are discontented: and if you are alone, you call it solitude; and of you are with men, you call them knaves and robbers; and you find fault with your own parents and children, and brothers and neighbors.

But you ought when you are alone to call this condition by the name of tranquility and freedom, and to think yourself like to the gods; and when you are with many, you ought not to call it crowd, nor trouble, nor uneasiness, but festival and assembly, and so accept all contentedly.

—Epictetus, *Discourses* 1.12

I deeply admire the confidence and exuberance of many young people, especially their faith that the world will fall into their hands simply through their own diligence.

It is hard to suggest to them that one of two things will happen.
Either the world will be to their liking, or it will not.
If it is the former, they are sorely tempted to define their own success and failure by things beyond their power, while living under the dangerous illusion that is somehow within their power.

If it is the latter, they will be deeply disappointed, and they will think that all their efforts are in vain.

The effort, the diligence, the hard work is not in vain.
But the vanity lies in where it is directed.
What am I seeking to change?
The belief that we can rule the world will be our downfall with either of the above results.
This is not cynical, negative, or gloomy at all.
It simply recognizes the classic Stoic distinction between those things within our power, and those outside of our power.

I can only be certain to change myself.
Nature cannot, and should not, be subject to my whims and desires.

Perhaps we can think of this in a more positive light: it is best to allow persons, things, and circumstances to be what they are, and to limit our responsibility to what is rightly ours, our own judgments and actions.
Assist others, inspire them, motivate them with hope and love, but never embrace the arrogance of being their master.

Otherwise, we will become weak and complacent when things go our way, or we will grumble when they don't.

Neither will do.

It is tempting to grumble and to be discontent with the world, and to never see the source of comfort.

I think it no accident that Tolkien's Gandalf often sounds very Stoic in his wisdom.

Even when I was very young, these words resonated with me:

> 'I wish it need not have happened in my time,' said Frodo.
> 'So do I,' said Gandalf, 'and so do all who live to see such times.
> But that is not for them to decide.
> All we have to decide is what to do with the time that is given us.'

And especially this:

> Many that live deserve death.
> And some that die deserve life.
> Can you give it to them?
> Then do not be too eager to deal out death in judgment.
> For even the very wise cannot see all ends.

❖ ❖ ❖ ❖ ❖

Day 81

Remember that all is opinion. For what was said by the Cynic Monimus is manifest: and manifest too is the use of what was said, if a man receives what may be got out of it as far as it is true.

—Marcus Aurelius, *Meditations* Book 2

I believe this to be the must misunderstood, and the most abused, passage in all of Stoic philosophy, if not all of philosophy in general.

We Moderns, like the Ancient Academics and Pyrrhonians, have become shackled by excessive skepticism, subjectivism, and relativism.
We are so befuddled by doubt that we deny that anything can ever be known with certainty.
Consequently, we assume that something can only be true because we believe it, and that nothing can be true in itself.
Finally, without an objective measure, this means that anything and everything is true, depending only on our opinions.

The Stoics were not skeptics, subjectivists, or relativists.
They believed the mind could, with right effort, come to know the truth, that this truth was grounded in the very Nature of things themselves, and that there were inherent standards of right and wrong within that Nature.

Marcus Aurelius is not, like a relativist, saying that anything becomes true or good because we believe it.
In the whole context of his philosophy, he is simply reminding us that the manner in which we choose to perceive the meaning or value of our circumstances is what determines our own virtue and happiness.
These are not the same thing.
The relativist thinks he creates the good; the Stoic says he discovers it.

"Opinion" here is perhaps better understood as judgment, estimation, or perspective.
If I choose to judge things only relative to my own subjective impressions and inclinations, this will bring me misery.
If I see them in a proper objective relation to myself, I will approach blessedness.
This is, in fact, quite the opposite of relativism, and a condemnation of the claim that my feelings determine reality.

Hearing a phrase like this misrepresented used to make me clench my teeth.
I am thankfully now much more patient, because I know precisely that the value of my "opinion", of my sound judgment, doesn't just depend upon my interior passions. What a wonderful irony!

❖ ❖ ❖ ❖ ❖

'Now,' said she, 'I know the cause, or the chief cause, of your sickness. You have forgotten what you are. Now therefore I have found out to the full the manner of your sickness, and how to attempt the restoring of your health. You are overwhelmed by this forgetfulness of yourself: hence you have been thus sorrowing that you are exiled and robbed of all your possessions.

'You do not know the aim and end of all things; hence you think that if men are worthless and wicked, they are powerful and fortunate. You have forgotten by what methods the universe is guided; hence you think that the chances of good and bad fortune are tossed about with no ruling hand. These things may lead not to disease only, but even to death as well.

'But let us thank the Giver of all health, that your Nature has not altogether left you. We have yet the chief spark for your health's fire, for you have a true knowledge of the hand that guides the universe: you do believe that its government is not subject to random chance, but to divine reason.

'Therefore have no fear. From this tiny spark the fire of life shall forthwith shine upon you. But it is not time to use severer remedies, and since we know that it is the way of all minds to clothe themselves ever in false opinions as they throw off the true, and these false ones breed a dark distraction which confuses the true insight, therefore will I try to lessen this darkness for a while with gentle applications of easy remedies, that so the shadows of deceiving passions may be dissipated, and you may have power to perceive the brightness of true light.'

—Boethius, *The consolation of Philosophy* Book 1 Prose 6

We have already seen Boethius suggest that a root of our misery is forgetting who we are, not our names or memories, but our very human nature. He expands upon this point here.

Far from being a forced or stale routine, I have found that whenever and wherever I teach philosophy, literature, history, or art, I instinctively challenge my poor students on one, most basic question.

I find I do this with my long-suffering friends as well, in a far different way, of course, far removed from the classroom.

What do you want?

Why are you here?

What is our shared purpose as human beings, the end for which we exist?

So many sigh and roll their eyes, and that's just fine.

It's a part of the whole journey, I now think.

But this does not remove the priority of the question.

Without a goal, there can be no action.

I go to school to get into a better school, I go to the better school to get a job, I get the job to make money and acquire power, I make money to buy things I want and get power to rule over others, and I get better and better jobs to buy nicer and nicer things and boss around more people... and then?

That's the part we forget, the most important part. Boethius apparently forgot that as well.

Lady Philosophy reminds him, in kindness, and not in anger, that there is still a faintly glowing ember.

He does not yet believe that the universe is all chance and chaos.

He still believes in reason and order, and the existence of the Absolute.

He still craves justice, and he may yet still find it by looking to something beyond and above himself.

❖ ❖ ❖ ❖ ❖

What, then, is the punishment of those who do not accept? It is to be what they are. Is any person dissatisfied with being alone, let him be alone. Is a man dissatisfied with his parents? Let him be a bad son, and lament. Is he dissatisfied with his children? Let him be a bad father. 'Cast him into prison.' What prison? Where he is already, for he is there against his will; and where a man is against his will, there he is in prison. So Socrates was not in prison, for he was there willingly.

'Must my leg then be lamed?' Wretch, do you then on account of one poor leg find fault with the world? Will you not willingly surrender it for the whole? Will you not withdraw from it? Will you not gladly part with it to him who gave it? And will you be vexed and discontented with the things established by Zeus, which he with the Fates who were present and spinning the thread of your generation, defined and put in order?

Know you not how small a part you are compared with the whole? I mean with respect to the body, for as to intelligence you are not inferior to the gods nor less; for the magnitude of intelligence is not measured by length nor yet by height, but by thoughts.

—Epictetus, *Discourses* 1.12

Virtue is its own reward.
  Vice is its own punishment.
  This makes no sense to the utilitarian, for whom the most useful, pleasant and convenient results are the only measure of action.
  For such a person, the ends justify the means.

My own experience has been that consequences can sway me one way or the other, but that in the end, I must bake my cake, and eat it too.
  A bad choice, judgment, or action will harm my very soul, regardless of whether the worldly consequences reward or punish me.

Dostoyevsky's *Crime and Punishment* had a great impact on me the very first time I read it.
  Of the many complex and connected themes, the fact that Raskolnikov's inner sense of guilt has far more power over him than any public shame or penalty speaks to the same idea.

Poe's 'The Tell-Tale Heart' addresses this as well.
  An angry, resentful, vengeful, or ungrateful person doesn't ultimately need to go to prison.
  He's already there, by having allowed himself to become a slave to his passions.

Acceptance and gratitude to the whole of Nature does indeed require us to feel small.
  But it is only the small part of us that needs to feel small, the weakness of the flesh and of fortune.
  By humbly accepting our place within the whole, our minds and hearts, the greater parts, are made more noble and divine.

❖   ❖   ❖   ❖   ❖

The soul of man does violence to itself, first of all, when it becomes an abscess and, as it were, a tumor on the universe, so far as it can. For to be vexed at anything which happens is a separation of ourselves from Nature, in some part of which the natures of all other things are contained.

In the next place, the soul does violence to itself when it turns away from any man, or even moves towards him with the intention of injuring, such as are the souls of those who are angry.

In the third place, the soul does violence to itself when it is overpowered by pleasure or by pain.

Fourthly, when it plays a part, and does or says anything insincerely and untruly.

Fifthly, when it allows any act of its own and any movement to be without an aim, and does anything thoughtlessly and without considering what it is, it being right that even the smallest things be done with reference to an end; and the end of rational animals is to follow the reason and the law of the most ancient city and polity.

—Marcus Aurelius, *Meditations* Book 2

What a wonderfully penetrating, yet direct and concise, summation of Stoic ethics.
Respect Nature.
Love your fellows.
Rise above your passions.
Practice integrity.
Act with judgment and purpose toward those very ends.

One can present the moral law in a number of beautiful ways, but what strikes me the most here are the two binding principles of this approach.
First, by doing evil we do harm to our own nature, and second, by harming our own nature we do harm to the whole universe of which we are a part.

I need not think of the moral law as something imposed from without, or merely as relative to external rewards and punishments, or as a laundry list of prohibitions.
I can live it from within, understanding how it is that I fulfill both my own being, and in my intimate relationship with Nature, the being of all other things.
The good should rightly be a joy, not just a chore.

❖ ❖ ❖ ❖ ❖

Day 85

'What,' say you, 'are you giving me advice? Indeed, have you already advised yourself, already corrected your own faults? Is this the reason why you have leisure to reform ether men?'

No, I am not so shameless as to undertake to cure my fellow men when I am ill myself. I am, however, discussing with you troubles which concern us both, and sharing the remedy with you, just as if we were lying ill in the same hospital. Listen to me, therefore, as you would if I were talking to myself.

—Seneca the Younger, *Moral letters to Lucilius* 27

We like to take offense when others offer guidance. We perhaps feel inferior, and we assume that we are being judged.

All of this rests on the premise that human lives must live in competition.

Once again, Stoicism exposes a false dichotomy.

Men are not made to be in conflict and opposition with one another, and the fact that another may be wiser or better than me in one way or another, need not make me see myself as less worthy.

We were made to be in harmony and agreement with each other.

Seneca reminds us that our human purpose is shared, and that we are on this journey together.

It isn't a race.

One of my own terrible weaknesses is an unwillingness to accept assistance or guidance because it runs against my sense of self-reliance.

This is, of course, a twisted version of Stoic self-sufficiency.

It took the seeming misfortune of serious illness to make me accept my wife's kindness and suggestions.

Advice, correction, or a helping hand, are rightly given out of love, not condemnation.

Learning to say "yes" to such love, to be willing to cooperate and not conflict is a liberating joy.

❖ ❖ ❖ ❖ ❖

All of us, he used to say, are so fashioned by Nature that we can live our lives free from error and nobly; not that one can and another cannot, but all. The clearest evidence of this is the fact that lawgivers lay down for all alike what may be done and forbid what may not be done, exempting from punishment no one who disobeys or does wrong, not the young nor the old, not the strong nor the weak, not anyone whomsoever.

And yet if the whole notion of virtue were something that came to us from without, and we shared no part of it by birth, just as in activities pertaining to the other arts no one who has not learned the art is expected to be free from error, so in like manner in things pertaining to the conduct of life it would not be reasonable to expect anyone to be free from error who had not learned virtue, seeing that virtue is the only thing that saves us from error in daily living.

—Musonius Rufus, *Lectures* 2

Our human conventions often have one standard for the privileged, another for the everyman. The rich and the poor, the powerful and the weak, the attractive and the awkward, are often held to very different rules.

My family still laughs, with just a little grumbling, about the time I saw a police car, without its lights on, swerve past me on a two–lane road well above the speed limit. A minute or so later and a mile down the road I saw the same car in the drive-through at a coffee shop. No emergency, no need, just privilege. If I behaved as many of our businessmen, politicians, or lawyers do, I would long be behind bars.

There is no need to be resentful, because these aren't the measure of right and wrong that really matter, and the Stoic is not impressed with such perks. They are the inventions only of our own vanity. The true law, the law of Nature, admits of no exceptions, and treats all without prejudice, regardless of their status and position. It is grounded in our very being, not in the world of impressions.

And the fact that true justice makes us all equal before Nature tells us also that the ability to distinguish right from wrong is not something that is a gift or a privilege for the few. Moral snobs may like to think only they have access to the good, but that reflects only their sense of own self-importance. The knowledge of what is right is not reserved for the few, but available to all, simply by reflecting on what it means to be human. It isn't something we create or grant, it is something each and every one of is free to discover within us, if only we so choose.

❖ ❖ ❖ ❖ ❖

Day 87

If it ever happen to you to be diverted to things outside, so that you desire to please another, know that you have lost your life's plan. Be content then always to be a philosopher; if you wish to be regarded as one too, show yourself that you are one and you will be able to achieve it.

—Epictetus, *Enchiridion* 23

I always took philosophy to be a grand and noble thing, perhaps because I was raised to love learning simply for its own sake.
It never occurred to me when I was younger that one could frown upon such a vocation.

There are, however, at least two reasons why philosophy has fallen upon hard times, and has become a laughing stock for many.

First, the goals of genuine philosophy, the love of truth, are diametrically opposed to the rules of a society ordered by the love of money, power, and fame.
"If you're so smart, why aren't you rich?" is the watchword of the times.
I hear variations on this theme most every day.
The Stoic shakes his head and moves on, as there's no common ground to build on.

Second, philosophers themselves are hardly making a good case for themselves.
Philosophy has become just another worldly career, and it looks ridiculous in this guise, with supposed scholars jostling to be published, go to conferences, and fight for the best jobs.

In a world where the measure of our externals is prized first, even by supposed philosophers, it should come as no surprise that philosophy is an outlier.
Take it as a compliment.
If you feel the calling to be, and to be seen, as a philosopher, worry about your actions over your reputation.

❖ ❖ ❖ ❖ ❖

That is why we give to children a proverb, or that which the Greeks call Chreia to be learned by heart; that sort of thing can be comprehended by the young mind, which cannot as yet hold more.

For a man, however, whose progress is definite, to chase after choice extracts and to prop his weakness by the best known and the briefest sayings and to depend upon his memory, is disgraceful; it is time for him to lean on himself. He should make such maxims and not memorize them.

For it is disgraceful even for an old man, or one who has sighted old age, to have a note-book knowledge. 'This is what Zeno said.' But what have you yourself said? 'This is the opinion of Cleanthes.' But what is your own opinion? How long shall you march under another man's orders?

—Seneca the Younger, *Moral letters to Lucilius* 33

Perhaps we don't like thinking for ourselves, because it is easier to have others do our thinking for us.

As slothful as I can sometimes be, I've never felt comfortable having someone else do my laundry, mow my lawn, or clean my house.

I firmly draw the line at outsourcing my own judgment.

Academics have their own version of this, when the name-dropping of acceptable sources becomes the measure of sound thinking.

In graduate school, frustrated by the sheepish conformity to trendy hipster authorities, I lightheartedly invented a fake German 20th century phenomenological philosopher, Ignatz Schmukenheimer, and began casually and impishly referring to him in class, or mentioning his obscure work, *The unity of ontical consideration*, off-hand during a conversation.

It started as a bit of good fun.

At first my fellow students looked confused, but didn't want to admit that they didn't know who I was talking about.

Slowly but surely, some of them would say "Yes, I think I remember reading that part and finding it very helpful", and I began to be seen as the local authority on Schmukenheimer's work.

I was once asked if I'd be writing my dissertation on him.

No, I am not joking.

This is precisely how pathetic my trade is.

The rest of us are really no different.

We turn to politicians, actors, athletes, musicians, film directors and color–by–numbers writers to tell us how to live.

I am reminded of Aldous Huxley's words:

People will come to love their oppression, to adore the technologies that undo their capacities to think.

By all means, humbly listen and learn from others, but do not sell yourself to them.

❖ ❖ ❖ ❖ ❖

D a y   8 9

We ought to observe also that even the things which follow after the things which are produced according to Nature contain something pleasing and attractive.

For instance, when bread is baked some parts are split at the surface, and these parts which thus open, and have a certain fashion contrary to the purpose of the baker's art, are beautiful in a manner, and in a peculiar way excite a desire for eating.

And again, figs, when they are quite ripe, gape open; and in the ripe olives the very circumstance of their being near to rottenness adds a peculiar beauty to the fruit.

And the ears of corn bending down, and the lion's eyebrows, and the foam which flows from the mouth of wild boars, and many other things — though they are far from being beautiful, if a man should examine them severally — still, because they are consequent upon the things which are formed by Nature, help to adorn them, and they please the mind; so that if a man should have a feeling and deeper insight with respect to the things which are produced in the universe, there is hardly one of those which follow by way of consequence which will not seem to him to be in a manner disposed so as to give pleasure.

And so he will see even the real gaping jaws of wild beasts with no less pleasure than those which painters and sculptors show by imitation; and in an old woman and an old man he will be able to see a certain maturity and comeliness; and the attractive loveliness of young persons he will be able to look on with chaste eyes; and many such things will present themselves, not pleasing to every man, but to him only who has become truly familiar with Nature and her works.

—Marcus Aurelius, *Meditations* Book 3

This is so poetic and delicate a passage that I find myself reading it over and over.
 Nature is itself so full of beauty, and it can be perceived in all of her manifestations and effects, however humble or obscure.
 The oddest detail becomes so wonderful, not merely in itself, but because of how it exists in harmony with and as an expression of the whole.

I remember how when I was a child, there was an oak tree in front of our house.
 It sadly came down during a very bad storm years later.
 A light green moss grew on the bark, and it somehow smelled like my grandmother's perfume.
 Can you see a six-year old boy hugging a tree to remember his grandmother?
 That is one of my experiences of how one of the odd consequences of Nature, a green moss on a tree, has such beauty.

Even the things others see as ugly can be perceived as gorgeous as a result.
 I had been doing something like for years before I discovered Stoicism, so it comes more easily to me.
 I find it almost impossible now, for example, to see a person as being physically unattractive anymore, because even wrinkles, or scars, or the marks of disease or suffering point to humanity itself all the more for me.

Even the ugliest of man-made monstrosities, like smokestacks, garbage dumps, diesel fumes, or IRS forms, can be appreciated when seen in this way.

When I worked in social services, I often accompanied a caseworker to a local prison to offer care to some of the inmates.

I dreaded the trip more and more every week, because I saw only loss and despair.

But on one day, I had an epiphany. I was sitting with an older man, who had spent more of his life in prison than he had on the outside.

He had only half his teeth, he was gaunt and pale like a corpse, and he stank of sweat and urine. Quite honestly, I felt disgusted by him.

And then he simply stopped and looked at me in a certain way. I can only describe it by saying that everything about him became beautiful, and I saw in all his qualities both sadness and dignity.

He was a person so different from me yet so very much like me.

I am deeply grateful for the Stoic's appreciation of the beautiful in anything and everything.

One of the only things I still find ugly is a heart filled with indifference and neglect, and I cannot bear to see any person, even my worst enemy, laid low or passed over.

That, for me, is still deeply disgusting.

❖ ❖ ❖ ❖ ❖

Day 90

It is no mean manifestation of Nature and Reason that man is the only animal that has a feeling for order, for propriety, for moderation in word and deed. And so no other animal has a sense of beauty, loveliness, harmony in the visible world; and Nature and Reason, extending the analogy of this from the world of sense to the world of spirit, find that beauty, consistency, order are far more to be maintained in thought and deed, and the same Nature and Reason are careful to do nothing in an improper or unmanly fashion, and in every thought and deed to do or think nothing capriciously.

—Cicero, *On duties* 1.4, tr Miller

As Dante asked us:
Consider your origins. You were not made to live as brutes, but to follow virtue and knowledge.

It is precisely our ability to reason, and to choose to act according to meaning and purpose, that makes us so distinct from all the rest of the living things known to us.
We share with other animals our bodies, our feelings, and our instincts.
We share in something more when we reflect and understand patterns of order and design.

Nature itself reveals order, purpose, and design, and in this way we have the wonderful gift of being able to share and participate in this greater harmony.
We not only live and act, but we are able to understand how and why we live and act.
To understand something is not only to describe it, but also to explain it.

Just as I can intend a conscious goal, and direct my actions toward it, Nature itself acts in the same manner.
Just as I can choose to live well, Nature also orders all things for the sake of the good, each and every part and aspect a part of the harmonious whole.

Any small, or seemingly insignificant, action is actually a necessary part of this whole.
There was once a time, quite a while ago, when I tried to think big, to make big plans, to expand the horizon as far as I could.
This did not last long, first because it simply isn't in my temperament to be a special person, and second, because I started to see that a nail can be just as important as a kingdom.

I consider my day a success not when I have scored the big deal, or won a noble victory, but when I have simply managed something as simple as a few kind words, a small action of encouragement, or helped someone else deal with the drudgery of the moment.
This, too, shares, in the order of Nature, as much, and perhaps even more so, than the sweeping gestures of the special people.

❖ ❖ ❖ ❖ ❖

Day 91

It is in our power to discover the will of Nature from those matters on which we have no difference of opinion. For instance, when another man's slave has broken the wine-cup we are very ready to say at once, 'Such things must happen'. Know then that when your own cup is broken, you ought to behave in the same way as when your neighbor's was broken.

Apply the same principle to higher matters. Is another's child or wife dead? Not one of us but would say, ' Such is the lot of man'; but when one's own dies, straightway one cries, 'Alas! Miserable am I!' But we ought to remember what our feelings are when we hear it of another.

—Epictetus, *Enchiridion* 26

The Golden Rule, Stoic style.

So caught up in our individual lives, and torn by the stresses of our differences, we forget that as sharing in a common humanity, we participate in the same nature, and therefore in precisely the same good.

The moral law is universal, applying fully and equally to all of us.

You can immediately recognize the Stoic in spirit because he does not apply different standards to himself and to others.

He can think and feel with, and through, another person, as if that person were himself.

I was not always able to manage this, because I would scoff at a quality in another that I took very seriously in my self.

It is only through daily practice that I've gotten better at seeing myself in others, and my experiences have bred a type of empathy in my character.

At first one may have to deliberately make every step in respecting another, but with time it can become habitual.

The Stoic Turn, where we look at an impression from a different angle or perspective is, I think, at the root of genuine love.

When I flip the annoying appearance in another into myself, I am doing precisely that.

See the other in a new light, not as different but the same, and I have lifted the double standard.

❖ ❖ ❖ ❖ ❖

Labor not unwillingly, nor without regard to the common interest, nor without due consideration, nor with distraction; nor let studied ornament set off your thoughts, and be not either a man of many words, or busy about too many things.

And further, let the Deity which is in you be the guardian of a living being, manly and of ripe age, and engaged in matter political, and a Roman, and a ruler, who has taken his post like a man waiting for the signal which summons him from life, and ready to go, having need neither of oath nor of any man's testimony. Be cheerful also, and seek not external help nor the tranquility that others give. A man then must stand erect, not be kept erect by others.

—Marcus Aurelius, *Meditations* Book 3

As cynical and bitter as we often are, we can be easily dismissive of the values of the Victorian gentleman, the chivalry of the medieval knight, or the noble demeanor of the Roman patrician. It may seem stuffy, trite, or fake.

I am admittedly a hopeless romantic, and I recognize that this colors my perspective, for both good and ill.

But I am still convinced that there is something deeply beautiful about a view of life where character, gratitude, respect, and humility, joined with strength of conviction alone can conquer all adversity.

It must admittedly be sincere, and not merely a show.

I know it exists because I have seen others live quietly and humbly this way, seeking no reward but the knowledge of a life lived well, and at the rare times when I can rise to such heights, I am in awe at the peace and joy that comes from knowing that a man can stand in the company of greatness by simply loving what is good and decent.

The version that speaks most deeply to my heart is Robert E. Lee's definition of a gentleman:

> *The forbearing use of power does not only form a touchstone, but the manner in which an individual enjoys certain advantages over others is a test of a true gentleman.*
>
> *The power which the strong have over the weak, the employer over the employed, the educated over the unlettered, the experienced over the confiding, even the clever over the silly—the forbearing or inoffensive use of all this power or authority, or a total abstinence from it when the case admits it, will show the gentleman in a plain light.*
>
> *The gentleman does not needlessly and unnecessarily remind an offender of a wrong he may have committed against him. He cannot only forgive, he can forget; and he strives for that nobleness of self and mildness of character which impart sufficient strength to let the past be but the past. A true man of honor feels humbled himself when he cannot help humbling others.*

❖ ❖ ❖ ❖ ❖

Day 93

Kindly remember that he whom you call your slave sprang from the same stock, is smiled upon by the same skies, and on equal terms with yourself breathes, lives, and dies. It is just as possible for you to see in him a free-born man as for him to see in you a slave.

—Seneca the Younger, *Moral letters to Lucilius 47*

Snobbery and the love of status have always rubbed me the wrong way, perhaps because I saw so much of it as a child and teenager.

My family was always deeply cultured and refined in their taste, but we were never wealthy.

We certainly had champagne taste on a beer budget, but all the fine things I was exposed to while young came not from wastefulness, but long, hard, and patient saving.

Quality came before quantity, and less was definitely more.

Many of those I went to school with were quick to remind me of my low position.

There seemed to be a sort of malicious joy in putting others down.

I still shake my head at listening to the many hours of bickering by some of my peers as to which family had the best car, the biggest house, or the most elaborate vacations.

I have a distinct memory of a group of 11 year olds at my elementary school boasting about the fine colleges they apparently already knew they would attend.

The blame lay less with them, than the corrupt parents who had fed them such nonsense.

Privilege adds nothing to character; in fact, it can quite often be the occasion of the death of character.

Show me a corporate lawyer and a stock boy, and four times out of five I can guess right away who is the better and more decent man.

I can also tell you who is likely the real slave.

Poverty, dejection, and worldly subservience will never make you as much of a slave as the love of power and wealth.

We are not defined by such vanities.

❖ ❖ ❖ ❖ ❖

Day 94

Theory, which teaches how one should act, is related to application, and comes first, since it is not possible to do anything really well unless its practical execution be in harmony with theory. In effectiveness, however, practice takes precedence over theory as being more influential in leading men to action.

—Musonius Rufus, *Lectures* 5

The great divide between theory and practice, between thinking and doing, has, I think, very much to do with the tragic skepticism and relativism of our times.
We falsely deny that anything can be universal or necessary.
Shunting the mind into its own dusty corner, and elevating the passions alone to a place of honor, we've ripped apart our very nature, and then wonder why we are all so puzzled and despairing.
We are told to be practical, and since reason can apparently offer no firm foundation in truth, we follow only our subjective impressions.

It's too simple, and too easy, and so completely destructive, to lose thought from things.
The Stoics understood that we must rather grasp that all our actions inform our thinking, and all our thinking informs our actions.
Each moves the other and needs the other, and each has its own strength and priority.
A man who tries to reflect without living, or to live without reflecting, is like a bird trying to fly with one wing.

I suspect this crippling aimlessness is one of the reasons Walker Percy said:
You live in a deranged age—more deranged than usual, because despite great scientific and technological advances, man has not the faintest idea of who he is or what he is doing.

❖ ❖ ❖ ❖ ❖

When a man was consulting him how he should persuade his brother to cease being angry with him, Epictetus replied: Philosophy does not propose to secure for a man any external thing. If it did, philosophy would be allowing something which is not within its province. For as the carpenter's material is wood, and that of the statuary is copper, so the matter of the art of living is each man's life.

'What then is my brother's?' That again belongs to his own art; but with respect to yours, it is one of the external things, like a piece of land, like health, like reputation. But Philosophy promises none of these. 'In every circumstance I will maintain,' she says, 'the governing part conformable to Nature.' Whose governing part? 'His in whom I am,' she says.

—Epictetus, *Discourses* 1.15

Drawn so to what is outside of us while we are empty within, we assume that any art or science serves us when it produces external results.

So what will philosophy "get" us, what profit or what benefit can it provide?

Will it make me rich, popular, powerful, give me sensual pleasure or convenient circumstances?

Will it, as we now say, give me "opportunities for advancement" in the world?

It will give me none of these things.

By the standards of our world, it is useless.

Then dispose of it, we are told.

Will it, as Epictetus, asks, help me to make my brother lose his anger?

No, but it can help me lose my anger.

And that makes all the difference.

The Buddha said:

Greater in battle than the man who would conquer a thousand–thousand men, is he who would conquer just one—himself.

If we wish to change our world, philosophy won't do that.

It is what it is, and we can only learn of it and love it, not alter it by our whims.

If, however, we wish to change ourselves, and therefore how we relate to that world, philosophy is the tool we are looking for.

Philosophy is only of any "use'" once I have rightly understood what it can do, and why I so desperately need that conquest of self as the key to my happiness.

❖ ❖ ❖ ❖ ❖

Virtue is free, inviolable, unmoved, unshaken, so steeled against the blows of chance that she cannot be bent, much less broken. Facing the instruments of torture she holds her gaze unflinching, her expression changes not at all, whether a hard or a happy lot is shown her. Therefore the wise man will lose nothing which he will be able to regard as loss; for the only possession he has is virtue, and of this he can never be robbed.

—Seneca the Younger, *On firmness* 5.9, tr Basore

I am reminded of a passage by Theodore Roosevelt, often perceived as a mere expression of brute manliness, but when, I think, read rightly, a prime example of Stoicism:

It is not the critic who counts; not the man who points out how the strong man stumbles, or where the doer of deeds could have done them better.

The credit belongs to the man who is actually in the arena, whose face is marred by dust and sweat and blood; who strives valiantly; who errs, who comes short again and again, because there is no effort without error and shortcoming; but who does actually strive to do the deeds; who knows great enthusiasms, the great devotions; who spends himself in a worthy cause; who at the best knows in the end the triumph of high achievement, and who at the worst, if he fails, at least fails while daring greatly, so that his place shall never be with those cold and timid souls who neither know victory nor defeat.

I have rarely known high achievement in external things; that is the hand that God has dealt me. But as time has passed, though I have failed in the world time and time again, I have been learning to dare greatly.

As Seneca says, no one can rob me of that.

I am growing more comfortable with the fact that not another soul will ever recognize this.

This does not matter, because it isn't a loss.

I aim to possess virtue, and I know it cannot be budged, bullied, or smothered.

❖ ❖ ❖ ❖ ❖

Day 97

Never value anything as profitable to yourself which shall compel you to break your promise, to lose your self-respect, to hate any man, to suspect, to curse, to act the hypocrite, to desire anything which needs walls and curtains: for he who has preferred to everything intelligence and spirit and the worship of its excellence, acts no tragic part, does not groan, will not need either solitude or much company.

And, what is chief of all, he will live without either pursuing or flying from death; but whether for a longer or a shorter time he shall have the soul enclosed in the body, he cares not at all: for even if he must depart immediately, he will go as readily as if he were going to do anything else which can be done with decency and order; taking care of this only all through life, that his thoughts turn not away from anything which belongs to a rational animal and a member of a civil community.

—Marcus Aurelius, *Meditations* 3

On a certain day, before going in to teach a string of classes, this passage revealed itself to me as part of my Stoic early morning reading.
 Usually I will just grab the closest of my Stoic texts, and open to a random page.
 But being a student of Stoicism, I have always known that nothing is random.

I cannot claim to know what cause or force provides me with a passage for that day, but almost without fail what I read works and helps me with the trials I will face.
 Perhaps it is Providence, perhaps it is that any passage can help me in a certain way, though, that too, is a form of Providence.

On this day, my first students were far more stubborn than usual. I did not understand exactly why, nor is it my place to judge them.
 It is my place to listen to them, and to help as best I can.
 They were questioning and challenging, as they rightly should, all the tenets of the Classical and Liberal Arts education I hold so dear.

"What's the use of all this?
 How will this help me have fun?
 Will it get me a job?"

I wasn't angry, but was able to be patient, because Marcus Aurelius was still in my head.
 I smiled and simply said: "You aren't just an animal, you are a rational animal. That's why."

I don't know if it convinced them at all, but they became very quiet, almost ashamed.
 I departed from my plan for the class, found this passage again, and read it to them.

It turned into one of the best class discussions I have ever had the privilege of being part of.
 The Stoic learns to show gratitude for anything and everything.

❖ ❖ ❖ ❖ ❖

What is it, mortal man, that has cast you down into grief and mourning? You have seen something unwonted, it would seem, something strange to you. But if you think that Fortune has changed towards you, you are wrong. These are ever her ways: this is her very nature. She has with you preserved her own constancy by her very change.

She was ever changeable at the time when she smiled upon you, when she was mocking you with the allurements of false good fortune. You have discovered both the different faces of the blind goddess. To the eyes of others she is veiled in part: to you she has made herself wholly known. If you find her welcome, make use of her ways, and so make no complaining. If she fills you with horror by her treachery, treat her with despite; thrust her away from you, for she tempts you to your ruin.

For though she is the cause of this great trouble for you, she ought to have been the subject of calmness and peace. For no man can ever make himself sure that she will never desert him, and thus has she deserted you. Do you reckon such happiness to be prized, which is sure to pass away? Is good fortune dear to you, which is with you for a time and is not sure to stay, and which is sure to bring you unhappiness when it is gone?

But seeing that it cannot be stayed at will, and that when it flees away it leaves misery behind, what is such a fleeting thing but a sign of coming misery? Nor should it ever satisfy any man to look only at that which is placed before his eyes. Prudence takes measure of the results to come from all things.

The very changeableness of good and bad makes Fortune's threats no more fearful, nor her smiles to be desired. And lastly, when you have once put your neck beneath the yoke of Fortune, you must with steadfast heart bear whatever comes to pass within her realm.

But if you would dictate the law by which she whom you have freely chosen to be your mistress must stay or go, surely you will be acting without justification; and your very impatience will make more bitter a lot which you cannot change.

If you set your sails before the wind, will you not move forward whither the wind drives you, not whither your will may choose to go? If you entrust your seed to the furrow, will you not weigh the rich years and the barren against each other? You have given yourself over to Fortune's rule, and you must bow yourself to your mistress's ways.

Are you trying to stay the force of her turning wheel? Ah! dull-witted mortal, if Fortune begin to stay still, she is no longer Fortune.

—Boethius, *The consolation of Philosophy* Book 2 Prose 1

Boethius' problem was that he had considered something to be reliable that wasn't reliable at all. He was seduced by the impression of comfort and stability that the world of circumstances offers us, only to find that he had enslaved himself to things beyond his power.

Was this the fault of the world, the fault of Fortune?

No. It was his choice, his free assent that placed him in shackles.

Let's not blame the world when we really need to examine ourselves first and foremost.

I have spent far too much of my life seeking the hows and the whys necessary to blame the world, to blame others.

First, I needed to learn not to blame, only to understand.

There is no place for resentment in the Stoic life.

Then, I needed to see that most everything that has haunted me, that has caused me loss and pain, was my own choice, and invariably a choice ruled by appearances alone, not by a grasp of the real.

I have, for example, repeatedly chosen work that seems noble on the outside, only to often find the people pulling the strings to be abusers and exploiters.

They use the appearance of noble ideology, for which a romantic has a weakness, to exercise power.

I need not blame them, I need not beat myself up over it; I need to recognize my weak judgment, to simply stop choosing and acting as I do.

When I lost someone I thought was my everything, it was easy to blame her.

That is, I now see, quite ridiculous. I had everything I needed right there in front of me, from the first moment we met, to know full well that we were working from a totally different moral map, from radically opposing values about life.

Yet I followed the impression of attraction and need, not the judgment about the impression, which would have revealed the true nature of love.

I failed, and the Black Dog that followed was self-inflicted.

I have paid a great price, but like Boethius, that can be the means for me to turn myself around.

❖   ❖   ❖   ❖   ❖

Day 99

'Ought not then this robber and this adulterer to be destroyed?' By no means say so, but speak rather in this way: 'This man who has been mistaken and deceived about the most important things, and blinded, not in the faculty of vision which distinguishes white and black, but in the faculty which distinguishes good and bad, should we not destroy him?'

If you speak thus, you will see how inhuman this is which you say, and that it is just as if you would say, 'Ought we not to destroy this blind and deaf man?' But if the greatest harm is the privation of the greatest things, and the greatest thing in every man is the will or choice such as it ought to be, and a man is deprived of this will, why are you also angry with him?

Man, you ought not to be affected contrary to Nature by the bad things of another. Pity him rather: drop this readiness to be offended and to hate, and these words which the many utter: 'These accursed and odious fellows.'

—Epictctus, *Discourses* 1.18

St Ambrose of Milan tells us that *No one heals himself by wounding another.*
Though I was far more ready to be a supporter of the firm hand of punishment and a cold justice when I was younger, age and experience have mellowed me.

From being a bit of a conservative poster-child in college, though an admittedly eccentric one, I am now regularly accused of being a hippie.
I thank people for the compliment without a bit of shame, because I understand that to mean that I think love comes first, without conditions, and that there is never room for hate or vengeance in this world.

It is loss and dejection that has taught me this, so I cannot bear to see loss and dejection in others.
Must we punish?
Of course, but punishment is not a means to hurt, but a means to help others, both the victim and the offender.
Hate the sin, but love the sinner.
Learn to be like a doctor who finds joy in healing, not like an executioner who delivers only agony and death.

❖ ❖ ❖ ❖ ❖

Throwing away then all things, hold to these only which are few; and besides bear in mind that every man lives only this present time, which is an indivisible point, and that all the rest of his life is either past or it is uncertain.

Short then is the time which every man lives, and small the nook of the earth where he lives; and short too the longest posthumous fame, and even this only continued by a succession of poor human beings, who will very soon die, and who know not even themselves, much less him who died long ago.

—Marcus Aurelius, *Meditations* Book 3

So much of my happiness seems to hinge upon how big or small I am, and the different senses in which I can understand that distinction.

It is when I make myself bigger in my estimation that I become arrogant and self-centered, and then I become more and more miserable, because I believe I deserve things that are not a part of me and are not my right.
It is through the humility of making myself smaller that I can recognize the true place, however weak and low, that I have within the whole.
This, in turn, is the root of my happiness.

In a sort of irony, I become bigger in one sense in that I am truly participating in Nature, when I make myself smaller in another sense, in recognizing that I am not the center of everything.

I don't at all think it morbid or dreary to ponder the weakness of my body, the fact that I am here for just a brief moment, that no power or fame will make me immortal or invincible.
It can be comforting to recognize that all worldly things pass, and are like straw, but it reminds us what is truly precious.

I have watched many people trying to be the Big Fish, desperately grasping for recognition and status as a means to importance and immortality.
I have always tried to avoid this myself, but occasionally I catch myself slipping into such thinking.
Recently I found I was feeling jealous of someone else's position, and I had to remind myself that absolutely none of that makes any difference whatsoever.

I like to observe this with musicians, actors, and other celebrities.
Inevitably, their fame gives them little peace, oftentimes great suffering, and it must eventually pass into nothingness.

There is always that sort of person who boasts in every single issue of the alumni class notes, or in a lengthy Christmas letter, how great his achievements are, how far he has come, and how deeply blessed he is.

Don't be too quick to believe it.

It is often a mask that hides things that aren't so pretty, and it can be a desperate way of trying to avoid being small.

Instead, I should be happy to embrace smallness and humility, casting away false delusions of grandeur.

It is Nature, and the Divine, that are great, and I can only find peace when I see my modest place within it.

❖ ❖ ❖ ❖ ❖

Day 101

If you mark them carefully, all acts are always significant, and you can gauge character by even the most trifling signs.

The lecherous man is revealed by his gait, by a movement of the hand, sometimes by a single answer, by his touching his head with a finger or by the shifting of his eye. The scamp is shown up by his laugh; the madman by his face and general appearance. These qualities become known by certain marks; but you can tell the character of every man when you see how he gives and receives praise.

—Seneca the Younger, *Moral letters to Lucilius* 52

It is deeply dangerous and unjust to make quick and hasty judgments based upon first appearances.

When we look with care and discernment, however, we can often see how the smallest qualities and behaviors can reveal quite a bit about a person's character.

The haughty look, the disdainful toss of the head, the angry clenched shoulders, the prideful walk, can be signs of our vices.

Honest eyes, a kind tilt of the head, a gentle stance can indicate our virtues.

I suspect the ability to discern such indicators comes with experience and a willingness to simply observe with care and concern.

I have always enjoyed simply observing people, because I find their demeanor and distinct qualities intriguing.

Being a quiet person who easily slips into the woodwork, I have had much opportunity to do so.

It is difficult, of course, to observe oneself. I recently looked at some pictures of myself I had never seen before, and I was a little taken aback.

In two of them, my thoughts and feelings, and their moral worth, were immediately apparent.

In one, I was simply listening to another person, and my genuine concern and interest were apparent in my expression and posture.

In another, I was clearly anxious and disturbed, though trying very hard to hide it.

The contrast between the peace of one and the tension of the other was obvious to me, even though I do not remember the times the pictures were taken.

The soul within, the good and the bad, is seen through the nuances of the body without.

❖ ❖ ❖ ❖ ❖

Day 102

One who by living is of use to many has not the right to choose to die unless by dying he may be of use to more.

—Musonius Rufus, *Fragments* 29

The Stoic position on death can be confusing and frustrating.

I rarely use it as an opener in describing Stoicism, because it just seems so contrary to the standards of our day.

Quite honestly, it feels like a turn-off and a deal-breaker.

We are told that our biological purpose is to survive and to reproduce, to pass our genes to our offspring.

On the level of instinct, this is indeed true. But man is not just an animal.

He is gifted with reason, with choice, the ability to know the truth and to love the good.

There is a greater purpose for our being here.

The Stoic does not desire death, nor is he not concerned about his survival.

He simply recognizes that death is itself a very part of life, and he views it with indifference.

That doesn't mean that he doesn't care, but rather that he knows that how long he lives has nothing to do with how well he lives.

All of the circumstances of life can be used for good or for evil, depending on our estimation and use of them.

This includes our existence and demise.

Musonius says this so beautifully. Life and death are not the measures of our purpose in this world.

Our purpose is to do good, to love, and to help others on this path.

Should I ever freely offer my life?

Yes, but only if by doing so I have served the true and the good more fully than if I were to live.

The death of our first child was a crippling event.

The realization that I was mortally ill was a great shock. Yet both events reminded me of something deeply moving.

We are all only here for a brief time, some a bit more, some a bit less.

However long that time may be, show love whenever and wherever you can.

Nothing else really matters. And if the act of complete and selfless love for others requires facing death, I do believe it is possible to do so with character and with joy.

❖ ❖ ❖ ❖ ❖

Day 103

'But the tyrant will chain.' What? The leg. 'He will take away.' What? The neck. What then will he not chain and not take away? The will. This is why the ancients taught the maxim, 'Know thyself.'

—Epictetus, *Discourses* 1.18

I have always had a deep respect and admiration for the work of Viktor Frankl, and his psychological model of logotherapy.

In the most basic terms, Frankl argues that it is our search for meaning, and not merely pleasure or power, that defines our humanity, and it is our ability to make our own meaningful choices, despite even the most crippling of circumstances, that is the key to our happiness.

I consider him, in many ways, to be an honorary Stoic.

Everything can be taken from a man but one thing: the last of the human freedom—to choose one's attitude in any given set of circumstances, to choose one's own way.

Or Frankl tells us
Between stimulus and response there is a space. In that space is our power to choose our response. In our response lies our growth and our freedom.
It seems to me like he is channeling Epictetus.

And the man wasn't just talking theory.
He lived it.
He lost his wife, mother, and brother to the Holocaust, and himself suffered the horrors of Auschwitz and Dachau.

I recommend that anyone and everyone read his book *Man's search for meaning*.
While the first half documents his personal struggle, the second explores his model of therapy.

As a child, I heard so many stories from my family about my great–uncle Josef, a Jesuit priest who was sent to Dachau for preaching against National Socialism from the pulpit.
The deep inspiration this always gave me was, I think, something that prepared me for the love of Stoicism.

You can take everything from me, but as long as I am still able to think, you cannot rob me of my thoughts and choices.

I think of the old German song, *Die Gedanken sind frei* (Thoughts are free):

And if I am thrown into the darkest dungeon,
all these are futile works,
because my thoughts tear all gates
and walls apart: Thoughts are free!

❖　❖　❖　❖　❖

Day 104

Let no act be done without a purpose, nor otherwise than according to the perfect principles of art.

—Marcus Aurelius, *Meditations* Book 4

I am a lover of all sorts of film, from the works of high art to the cheesiest B flicks, and quite often a phrase from a movie will creep into my daily thinking, helping me at the oddest of times to manage a real life problem.

One of these is a line from Mel Gibson's *The patriot*, a fine but rather over-the-top historical action drama that actually manages to address many wonderful moral and personal questions.

"Aim small, miss small" has become one of my mantras.

Many people seem puzzled by the phrase, but perhaps because I was already thinking along these lines, I was drawn to it immediately.
Don't aim at your opponent in battle, but aim rather at his tunic button.
You may miss the button, but you will still hit him.

Focus on the specific goal, without distraction, direct and clear, and practice the skill of intent and dedication.
As it is in marksmanship, so it is also in life.

All action is for the sake of an end, yet we seem more concerned with the means, and everything else that surrounds us, and often forget the ultimate purpose of our lives.

A wonderful story from the great Hindu epic, the *Mahabharata*, tells of how the Pandavas and Kauravas, two groups of brothers, are asked by their teacher, Drona, to line up to practice archery.
Drona instructs them to aim at a bird in a tree.
As they take aim, he asks them what they see.
One by one they say that they see the bird, the tree, the sky.
He turns them away.
But asked what he sees, Arjuna simply responds: "the bird's eye."

What else does he see?
"I see nothing but the eye."
Arjuna is told to release his arrow, which goes straight to the mark.
This is why Arjuna is the greatest of warriors.

And so it is in life.
It is the commitment to our purpose, constant, disciplined, and aimed as precisely as an arrow, and sharp as a blade, that brings us the great reward of victory.

❖ ❖ ❖ ❖ ❖

Day 105

It is in the power of any man to despise all things, but of no man to possess all things. The shortest cut to riches is to despise riches.

—Seneca the Younger, *Moral letters to Lucilius* 62

One of my heroes, G.K. Chesterton, observed that
There are two ways to get enough. One is to continue to accumulate more and more. The other is to desire less.
It is so deeply Stoic to recognize that it is my estimation that determines what I think I need.

My family has always been good with sayings and aphorisms.
My grandmother on one side would remind me that my eyes shouldn't be bigger than my stomach.
My grandmother on the other would advise me not to bite off more than I could chew.

It is a humbling and uplifting realization that I don't need much at all to be happy, far less than I had ever thought.
Many things I had assumed were necessities eventually appeared as luxuries, then finally even revealed themselves as burdens and limitations.

It at first seems so unfair that "good" things in life seem to slip from our grasp the more we scramble for them.

Then when we recognize them as false goods, and seek them no longer, the true good whispers kindly, "I was here all along. Welcome, old friend!"

I had long sought love as something to possess, something that when it came to me from without would make me whole.
I finally saw the vanity of such false idols, and then I was, without want or expectation, able to love, not as a need, but as a gift.

❖ ❖ ❖ ❖ ❖

There are certain duties that we owe even to those who have wronged us. For there is a limit to retribution and to punishment; or rather, I am inclined to think, it is sufficient that the aggressor should be brought to repent of his wrong- doing, in order that he may not repeat the offence and that others may be deterred from doing wrong.

Then, too, in the case of a state in its external relations, the rights of war must be strictly observed. For since there are two ways of settling a dispute: first, by discussion; second; by physical force; and since the former is characteristic of man, the latter of the brute, we must resort to force only in case we may not avail ourselves of discussion.

The only excuse, therefore, for going to war is that we may live in peace unharmed; and when the victory is won, we should spare those who have not been blood-thirsty and barbarous in their warfare.

—Cicero, *On duties* 1.11

We have already seen that justice comes from love, while vengeance comes out of hatred.
 And this is because no person is merely a means for our own pleasure or convenience.
 There can be no reason why we should deliberately wish to do harm; even punishment is for the improvement of all.

And as Cicero explains that, as it is with us individually, so it should be with us communally.
 Nations are not exempt from the requirements of justice.

War, like self-defense or punishment, is the last resort to retain the balance of what is right, and only after all other options are exhausted.
 Even then, the victors must act with mercy and compassion, never with hatred.

There are some things that only get better with age and repetition, like a good book, a piece of beautiful music, or a true friend. I think a film like Darabont's *The green mile* fits into this category.
 It can be a truly disturbing piece, because it so bluntly reveals the hatred and brutality of men, individually and politically.

The centerpiece of the film, however, John Coffey's words as he faces his death, remind us what is truly right, and why indifference, hatred and vengeance are so disturbing to any good man:

> *I'm tired, boss. Tired of being on the road, lonely as a sparrow in the rain. I'm tired of never having a buddy to be with, to tell me where we's going to, coming from, or why. Mostly, I'm tired of people being ugly to each other. I'm tired of all the pain I feel and hear in the world every day. There's too much of it. It's like pieces of glass in my head, all the time. Can you understand?*

❖ ❖ ❖ ❖ ❖

It is circumstances which show what men are. Therefore when a difficulty falls upon you, remember that God, like a trainer of wrestlers, has matched you with a strong young man. 'For what purpose?' you may say. Why, that you may become an Olympic conqueror; but it is not accomplished without sweat. In my opinion no man has had a more profitable difficulty than you have had, if you choose to make use of it as an athlete would deal with a young antagonist.

—Epictetus, *Discourses* 1.24

The Roman poet Ovid encouraged us: *Endure and persist, this pain will be useful to you.*

I suspect I was once reading his meaning only in part.
 I recognized the encouragement to be strong, but it was never quite clear to me why I should so. How would it be useful?

I assumed the reward was simply the toughness itself, the virtue of being immovable, and that is indeed the half of it.
 The other half is the true nature of the goal of toughness, and the fact that the pain is not simply to be suffered with a grimace, but to be embraced as a privilege and an opportunity.

When I suffer I can become stronger for the goal of giving comfort, when I am in pain I can respond with more joy, the more I am hated the more I can love.
 The Stoic Turn means flipping the force of circumstances, just as the wrestler takes advantage of force and momentum of his stronger opponent.

I often tried to be strong, believe me, but I fell flat each and every time.
 It is simply because I was trying to suffer well, and not to live well.
 I knew what I should do, but not why I should do it.
 I still saw pain as an evil in itself, simply to be tolerated in silence.

It did not occur to me that pain, being something indifferent, can be a positive means, a tool for my improvement.
 And that improvement isn't just strength, but the ability to use that strength to love, to serve, to live with excellence.

I can look at pain, and instead of gritting my teeth, I can be grateful for it—I can take it as an honor that Nature and the Divine think me worthy of this opportunity.
 If you were given the chance to be a star athlete or attend the most prestigious school, you would know full well that it was going to hurt.

Yet the glory of the victory puts all the pain into perspective, and I become thankful for such circumstances put in my way.
 If this is even beginning to make sense, there is a Stoic within you.

❖ ❖ ❖ ❖ ❖

Day 108

No man is able to rule unless he can also submit to be ruled.

—Seneca the Younger, *On anger* 2.15

Here is yet another variation of the Stoic Turn.

If I wish to be able to have authority, I must first submit to authority.

I had a very bright but very confident student a few years back who immediately said "Yes, yes, I get it: If I want to be the boss, I'm going to have to let myself be bossed around, until I impress the boss enough to get a promotion."

She said that very well, I think, and she understands the world of business and politics, but I think Seneca meant something slightly more.

It isn't, according the Stoic perspective, that I will temporarily allow myself to be ruled, so that I can later become the ruler; it's not a servant now, ruler later proposition.

Rather, it's that my very attitude and estimation must always, at all times and in all ways, reflect humility and submission, because I can only do good when I serve others.

I must always think of everything I do as for the sake of my fellows, and never for my own sake alone.

The school and model of Greenleaf's 'servant leadership' has, I believe, much in common with this ideal.

I only gain any real authority, which is moral authority, when I lay myself down fully and completely for those I would claim to rule.

This has a very pragmatic side, as well.

Like a dog that can sense your fear, as much as you try to hide it, a subject, employee, student, or any follower, can often instinctively tell when you are just a bully, or whether you care for them.

That is the voice of Nature working right there.

❖ ❖ ❖ ❖ ❖

Men seek retreats for themselves, houses in the country, sea-shores, and mountains; and you too are wont to desire such things very much. But this is altogether a mark of the most common sort of men, for it is in your power whenever you shall choose to retire into yourself.

For nowhere either with more quiet or more freedom from trouble does a man retire than into his own soul, particularly when he has within him such thoughts that by looking into them he is immediately in perfect tranquility; and I affirm that tranquility is nothing else than the good ordering of the mind.

Constantly then give to yourself this retreat, and renew yourself; and let your principles be brief and fundamental, which, as soon as you shall return to them, will be sufficient to cleanse the soul completely, and to send you back free from all discontent with the things to which you return. For with what are you discontented? With the evil of men?

Recall to your mind this conclusion, that rational animals exist for one another, and that to endure is a part of justice, and that men do wrong involuntarily; and consider how many already, after mutual enmity, suspicion, hatred, and fighting, have been stretched dead, reduced to ashes; and be quiet at last."

—Marcus Aurelius, *Meditations* Book 4

The important people use their vacations and second homes as one of the many badges of their achievements.

But Marcus Aurelius is not merely saying that these are status symbols, but also that they become a misguided reflection of our desire to escape.

Faced with the stresses of life, and the dreariness of the condition of our hearts, we think that running away, for even a brief time, may offer some respite.

It is the fatal error of the person ruled by what is outside of him to try to fill the human need for happiness with pieces that simply don't fit our nature.

Square peg, round hole.

We become aware, that at some level, things aren't quite right, and we then turn to another diversion.

We take flight from ourselves in the world, and then take flight from the world when it doesn't help us to fulfill ourselves.

I need only retreat within my own heart and mind to find that dream vacation, because that is where all peace and joy are to be found.

Likewise, I need not be ruled by, or alternately run away from, the world of those around me.

I am especially inspired by Aurelius' repeated insistence that as beings of reason, we were made for one another.

Wherever I am, in whatever conditions, I can take refuge in myself, and draw upon the wellspring of peace within me to give to others.

I feel saddened to see how many of us turn someone away when we feel sadness or anger at another.
That's really much the same thing as running away to the country house.
It doesn't have to be that way if we just choose to love both others and ourselves rightly.

❖ ❖ ❖ ❖ ❖

You will earn the respect of all men if you begin by earning the respect of yourself.
—Musonius Rufus, *Fragments* 30

Yet another subtle misreading might occur if we don't interpret this in light of the Stoic Turn.
  Once again, this doesn't mean I should respect myself in order that I can achieve the goal of others respecting me; it means rather that once I learn to respect myself, and become entirely indifferent to the respect of others, only then am I worthy of being respected.

It is by not caring for something at all that I might receive it, but the beautiful irony is that I now have no need for it.

They say true love only comes your way when you're not looking for it.
  I believe that is, in a sense, quite true, because the person desperately busy wanting to be loved isn't truly capable of giving love at all.
  I think it is much the same with broader category of respect.

Though I have never been a seeker of grand fame, not to my credit but simply because it isn't in my temperament, I have often let myself be swayed by worrying about what those around me think, and desiring to please them.

This has always been a millstone around my neck.
  It was quite liberating when I found that people actually started respecting me a little bit more when I became indifferent to their respect.
  I know I certainly respect other people who are sincere, selfless, and don't care for their status.

With the many changes in my health, both of body and mind, recently, I didn't necessarily need a change of place, but a change in how I was choosing to live.
  So I went back to teaching in a small, private, Liberal Arts secondary school, in the trenches right where I started, where I think the real work is done.
  My son is a student at the same school, and one day on the drive home started to say "the other students think you are…"

I cut him off right there. "I don't want to know what they think or say, unless they choose to share it with me."

"But don't you care about them?"

"Very much so, more than they will ever realize.
  And that's exactly why I don't care what they think of me."

He had a puzzled look for a moment, but then smiled and nodded.
  He is, after all, the son of a Stoic.

❖ ❖ ❖ ❖ ❖

Day 111

As Epictetus was saying that man is formed for fidelity, and that he who subverts fidelity subverts the peculiar characteristic of men, there entered one of those who are considered to be men of letters, who had once been detected in adultery in the city.

"hen Epictetus continued: But if we lay aside this fidelity for which we are formed and make designs against our neighbor's wife, what are we are we doing? What else but destroying and overthrowing? Whom? The man of fidelity, the man of modesty, the man of sanctity.

Is this all? And are we not overthrowing neighborhood, and friendship, and the community; and in what place are we putting ourselves? How shall I consider you, man? As a neighbor, as a friend? What kind of one? As a citizen? Wherein shall I trust you? So if you were a utensil so worthless that a man could not use you, you would be pitched out on the dung heaps, and no man would pick you up."

—Epictetus, *Discourses* 2.4

Another one of my great–grandfather's many sayings was that "In the end, the only thing a man has is his word."
That puzzled me back then, because it seemed like a man could also have many other things.
It would only be long after he was gone that it began to make sense, and I realized the scrappy Irish carpenter had been a Stoic at heart all along.

He was completely right.
The only things I control, that are really mine, are my own thoughts and actions, and the values I use to direct those thoughts and actions.
And this means it is not within my power to rule the world, but it is within my power to decide if I will be honest, sincere, and faithful.

I need not repeat why I personally have what my wife and I jokingly call "betrayal issues".
Yet on a more universal level, we can see why Epictetus is so harsh on the smart, successful man who could spout all kinds of fancy truths, but couldn't be faithful to his wife.

Fidelity and trust are at the very basis of all human relationships.
I don't just hurt my friend when I break faith, I also do great harm to my own nature.
I do evil and injustice to all of society, for it is only trust and fidelity that are the foundation of any and all association.
The liar, the fraud, the adulterer break their word and their promises, and by doing so break the whole community.
I know what Epictetus means. I have rarely felt more like human garbage than when I have broken a sacred bond of trust, and rarely felt as horrible as when that has been done to me.

❖ ❖ ❖ ❖ ❖

Day 112

If our intellectual part is common, the reason also, in respect of which we are rational beings, is common: if this is so, common also is the reason which commands us what to do, and what not to do; if this is so, there is a common law also; if this is so, we are fellow-citizens; if this is so, we are members of some political community; if this is so, the world is in a manner a state. For of what other common political community will any one say that the whole human race are members?

And from there, from this common political community comes also our very intellectual faculty and reasoning faculty and our capacity for law; or from where do they come? For as my earthly part is a portion given to me from certain earth, and that which is watery from another element, and that which is hot and fiery from some peculiar source (for nothing comes out of that which is nothing, as nothing also returns to non-existence), so also the intellectual part comes from some source.

—Marcus Aurelius, *Meditations* Book 4

I adore the beautiful progression of the argument here, and the stress on the necessary bond between our individual and social natures.

Aurelius regularly makes this emphasis.

Despite all of our differences, if we share in the power of reason, we are the same.

It is this shared nature that permits us to see our common good, to know right from wrong, and to participate in a community with one another.

The highest and most universal community, the one that defines us most fully, is simply our membership in humanity.

As all things have their origins, our shared ability to know and to love has a common source.

Call it what you will, but recognize it as the measure of all that we are.

Through all this, our divisions and differences still seem to define us.

We stare at out shoes while we should be gazing at the heavens.

Race, gender, nation and creed are used as barriers and not as bridges.

I know of too many people who feed off of, and even make a handsome living from, drawing constant attention to divisions, yet never once refer to our shared humanity, our common moral law, or the Divine Intelligence as our measure.

❖ ❖ ❖ ❖ ❖

The man who covets everybody's wife and considers the mere fact that she belongs to another an ample and just excuse for loving her, this same man will not have his own wife looked at; the strictest enforcer of loyalty is the traitor, the punisher of falsehood is himself a perjurer, and the trickster lawyer deeply resents an indictment being brought against himself; the man who has no regard for his own chastity will permit no tampering with that of his slaves.

The vices of others we keep before our eyes, our own behind our back; hence it happens that a father who is even worse than his son rebukes his son's untimely revels, that a man does not pardon another's excesses who sets no bound to his own, that the murderer stirs a tyrant's wrath, and the temple-robber punishes theft.

—Seneca the Younger, *On anger* 2.28

The Golden Rule is perhaps the most cited, and also the most neglected, principle of all time.
 We are all so familiar with its words, that we brush it off as self-evident whenever it is raised.
 At the same time, we seem to have absolutely no idea what it means.

The proof of this is not in our words, but in our actions.
 We expect to receive things entirely different than what we give.
 A friend who happens to be a divorce lawyer, for whom I am still a tolerable gadfly, told me just recently that the results of a case were "successful" for his client.
 I wondered out loud how successful they were for the other side.

The look on his face made it clear that such a concept, rooted in love and not in conflict, had never even occurred to him.
 While his client's success mattered, because it furthered his own profit, the life of the opponent was entirely disposable.

It is useless to rant about the evils of hypocrisy.
 Show me that you can live better.
 Then I will be convinced.

❖ ❖ ❖ ❖ ❖

Day 114

Wise people are in want of nothing, and yet need many things. On the other hand, nothing is needed by fools, for they do not understand how to use anything, but are in want of everything.

—Chrysippus ex Seneca the Younger, *Moral letters to Lucilius* 10

Want and need are in inverse proportions.
This isn't actually as obvious as it seems: We might think that the person who wants more needs more, and the person who wants less needs less.
Isn't the Stoic, after all, the person who doesn't need much?
It's the particular sense in which the term "need" is used here that makes all the difference.

The Stoic actually "needs" quite a bit.
He needs far more wisdom to prosper, far more love to provide, far more occasions for virtue.
These are the necessities of his life, and he wants no more.

Yet the vain and grasping man wants anything and everything except those necessities.
He doesn't need anything to live, because even if these noble and necessary goods were given to him, he would have no idea what to make of them.
He needs nothing to live, because he doesn't know how to live.
True goods would be extraneous to him, completely wasted.

Imagine giving a brush, paint, and canvas to Rembrandt, and then to a cat.
There's the difference.

❖ ❖ ❖ ❖ ❖

While Fortune then favored you, it seems you flaunted her, though she cherished you as her own darling. You carried off a bounty which she had never granted to any citizen before. Will you then balance accounts with Fortune? This is the first time that she has looked upon you with a grudging eye. If you think of your happy and unhappy circumstances both in number and in kind, you will not be able to say that you have not been fortunate until now.

And if you think that you were not fortunate because these things have passed away which then seemed to bring happiness, these things too are passing away, which you now hold to be miserable, wherefore you cannot think that you are wretched now. Is this your first entrance upon the stage of life? Are you come here unprepared and a stranger to the scene? Think you that there is any certainty in the affairs of mankind, when you know that often one swift hour can utterly destroy a man?

For though the chances of life may seldom be depended upon, yet the last day of a lifetime seems to be the end of Fortune's power, though it perhaps would stay. What, think you, should we therefore say; that you desert her by dying, or that she deserts you by leaving you?

—Boethius, *The consolation of Philosophy* Book 2 Prose 3

We give ourselves credit when things go well, and blame the world when they go wrong.
Lady Philosophy tells Boethius that he has been inconsistent, a hypocrite when it comes to his circumstances.
He took his many gifts for granted, and now complains when they are gone.
A gift can never been seen as an entitlement, and in the balance sheets of life he still came out safely in the black.

Fortune is fickle: She gives and takes away in equal measures.
If you bemoan that the good is temporary, remember also that the bad is temporary.
We wish to have it both ways.
We want her blessings, but bemoan that they are temporary.
At one moment we wish them to be permanent, at another we ask that they pass from us.

I often think of Tennyson's immortal lines when I consider all that has been given and all that has been taken away.

I hold it true, whate'er befall;
I feel it when I sorrow most;
'Tis better to have loved and lost
than never to have loved at all.

I used to violently disagree with this statement years ago, and I did so because I blamed the world for my pain.

I was sure I would have been happier had I never known love, because I would not now be suffering.

That is a foolish and selfish view.

Losing the beloved was in my circumstances, but the giving of love was always mine, and still remains mine.

And it is only the latter that makes any difference.

I will never take it back, because it was a promise.

❖ ❖ ❖ ❖ ❖

Day 116

Things themselves are indifferent; but the use of them is not indifferent. How then shall a man preserve firmness and tranquility, and at the same time be careful and neither rash nor negligent? If he imitates those who play at dice. The counters are indifferent; the dice are indifferent. How do I know what the cast will be? But to use carefully and dexterously the cast of the dice, this is my business.

—Epictetus, *Discourses* 2.5

It is at the core of the Stoic Turn that the good or evil of my world depends upon what I choose to make of it.

It becomes good or bad for me by whether I make it good or bad for my own character.

Nothing is a curse, and everything can be a blessing, if I just make it so.

I have never been a gambling man.

I have been familiar with most every vice, but never that one.

Epictetus, however, isn't talking about the vice here, but rather the wisdom of the man who knows how to relate himself to conditions over which he has no direct control.

With apologies to Kenny Rogers, but *You've got to know when to hold 'em, know when to fold 'em, know when to walk away, and know when to run….*

What makes a good gambler is precisely that his skill does not let him succumb to vice, and not to let himself be ruled by the dice or the cards.

He doesn't know what will come up, but he knows how to best manage, whatever the numbers.

I am pondering if it might be possible to fashion a whole school of playing poker based upon Stoic values.

Don't depend upon the cards you are dealt, but depend rather on your own ability to use those cards, and all your gifts, to your advantage.

❖   ❖   ❖   ❖   ❖

The archer must know what he is seeking to hit; then he must aim and control the weapon by his skill. Our plans miscarry because they have no aim. When a man does not know what harbor he is making for, no wind is the right wind.

—Seneca the Younger, *Moral letters to Lucilius* 71

We already know that Stoic values demand focus and a clear sense of purpose to guide our way.
We keep our eyes on the prize at all times, and seek to avoid distraction by the petty and shallow.
This demands that we know who we are, why we are here, and where we are going.
Every decision and action, however small, depends directly on those measures.
What is it that we are truly aiming at?
Can we honestly say that we genuinely know what we want?
An ambiguous answer will make for an ambiguous life.

I am a great admirer of the films of M. Night Shyamalan, even, and sometimes especially, the ones that are less than popular.
I don't see him as a writer and director of thrillers or twist-ending stories, but as a filmmaker who uses allegory to reflect on questions of spirituality and the depths of the human heart.
The words "Swing away!" from *Signs*, still have a powerful meaning for me, since they remind me that this universe is ruled by Providence and purpose.
And in the film *Unbreakable*, the words of Mr Glass echo Seneca's wisdom:

You know what the scariest thing is? To not know your place in this world, to not know why you're here.

❖ ❖ ❖ ❖ ❖

Day 118

Take away your opinion, and then there is taken away the complaint, 'I have been harmed.'
Take away the complaint, 'I have been harmed,' and the harm is taken away.
 —Marcus Aurelius, *Meditations* Book 4

I was once trying to comfort a friend with Stoic values, and I clearly must have expressed them
 poorly.
 She became very angry.
 "Stop telling me to think or wish away my pain. That won't make it go away!"

She was quite right, and I was glad when the confusion was finally resolved.
 No, the pain, in the body or in the soul, may not go away.
 I should certainly not expect that it would do so.
 Stoicism doesn't erase pain, but manages it, and helps us to make it a means for good.

My own Black Dog has felt different over the years.
 The pain was actually more bearable, a dull, throbbing ache in the soul, in the early days.
 For a reason I do not entirely understand, it changed shape a few years ago.
 It became sharp, far more intense, with sudden bursts of powerful grief.
 The intensity of my feelings of loss is sometimes indescribable in its horror.

I can only speculate that as I actually became more confident and hopeful in my thinking over the
 years, the Black Dog was somehow fighting back.

Though I would gladly have it lifted from me, I don't anticipate it ever disappearing.
 And Stoic thinking has now so completely permeated my life that while I feel the pain, I do not
 estimate it as a harm or a burden.
 I see it as an opportunity.
 I am grateful to be the man I now am, and I would not be that man without my burdens.
 They have not harmed me.

❖ ❖ ❖ ❖ ❖

Day 119

There seems to be sound advice, therefore, in this word of warning: 'The higher we are placed, the more humbly should we walk.' Panaetius tells us that Africanus, his pupil and friend, used to say: 'As, when horses have become mettlesome and unmanageable on account of their frequent participation in battles, their owners put them in the hands of trainers to make them more tractable; so men, who through prosperity have become restive and over self-confident, ought to be put into the training-ring, so to speak, of reason and learning, that they may be brought to comprehend the frailty of human affairs and the fickleness of fortune.'

—Cicero, *On duties* 1.27

I have often noted that when offered advice or correction, it is those innocent of the offense who often feel shame, while the guilty continue unaware.
So too, it is often those who need the benefits of philosophy the most who often fail to acknowledge her.

The temptations of worldly power and success can all to easily draw us away from recognizing the truth about ourselves and our world.
The love of truth is sadly most reviled where it is most needed.
Plato suggested that kings should become philosophers and philosophers should become kings.
That our society finds this ridiculous is only a sign of our corruption.

While working in AIDS and Prison ministry, I was asked to attend a fancy dinner and speech by a bigwig from the Department of Health and Human Services.
I attended obediently.
Though I had seen time and time again how the policies of this deeply corrupt state agency did great harm to our clients, I promised myself I would behave.

The entire affair was simply an exercise in ego boosting.
The important man preaching to us used each and every opportunity to blow his own horn, to praise all his great achievements.
Perhaps he was looking for a promotion from the Governor.
I bit my tongue, but perhaps my disgust showed on my face.

After his talk, he approached me and asked me what I did, and if I wanted a photo with him.
He shook my hand, and said, "I want to thank you for all the assistance you give the State in our noble pursuit of public service."

I lost it and, while I deeply regret allowing my Irish temper to get the better of me, I do not regret one bit the truth I spoke.
"Let's be clear," I responded.
"Please don't ever claim that what you do is public service.
What you do is self–service.
You are, sir, an expert in bureaucratic masturbation."

I imagine no one had ever spoken to him in that way.
Here was a man that needed the training-ring of truth and love.
His prosperity had spoiled him, though he had no clue how lost he was.

❖ ❖ ❖ ❖ ❖

Observe, this is the beginning of philosophy, a perception of the disagreement of men with one another, and an inquiry into the cause of the disagreement, and a condemnation and distrust of that which only 'seems,' and a certain investigation of that which 'seems' whether it 'seems' rightly, and a discovery of some rule, just as we have discovered a balance in the determination of weights, and a carpenter's rule in the case of straight and crooked things. This is the beginning of philosophy.

—Epictetus, *Discourses* 2.11

Weights and measures are such a wonderful analogy here.
Without an objective standard by which to judge, there can be no judgment.
Most often we observe that we disagree, and then either simply agree to disagree if we are of a gentle persuasion, or fight it out tooth and nail if we are driven.
Neither is good enough, because neither looks beyond the subjective appearances, our own biased slant, to what is real and shared underneath.

I find that I only dwell upon the disagreement, not when I am being charitable and tolerant, but when I'm simply being arrogant and lazy.
If I bother to respect another person or point of view, I should be bothered to understand it, to distinguish between the true and the false.
It is the attitude of philosophy that can make this possible.

❖　❖　❖　❖　❖

Consider that everything which happens, happens justly, and if you observe carefully, you will find it to be so. I do not say only with respect to the continuity of the series of things, but with respect to what is just, and as if it were done by one who assigns to each thing its value.

Observe then as you have begun; and whatever you do, do it in conjunction with this, the being good, and in the sense in which a man is properly understood to be good. Keep to this in every action.

—Marcus Aurelius, *Meditations* Book 4

I don't think this only means something as simplistic as that everything that happens is a deserved reward or punishment.
I believe it means that any and all circumstances are good and just, because each and every circumstance is a means by which we can become better.
This only makes sense when we understand the true Stoic measure of what is good, bad, and indifferent.

When I was still a Teaching Fellow in graduate school, someone I cared for very much, but who had hurt me by ignoring my past requests for help, suddenly showed at my office after three years.
My initial hopes, that this could be the rebuilding of a cherished friendship, were quickly dashed.
The visit seemed to serve no other purpose than a bragging session about a series of successes.
We parted far worse than we met, and we have sadly never spoken since.

Within a matter of days, the grave disappointment had opened many old wounds, and after three years of struggling with improving myself, I found myself in a state of total breakdown.
I was reduced to being curled up in bed, bawling uncontrollably.
I was forced to leave my school and my work, only to rebuild all over again, a process that took almost another year of painful recovery.

Now that hardly seemed just and fair.
It took me some time to recognize that it was indeed beautifully just and fair, because it was something I truly needed.
Nature had done right by me.

Simply ignoring a wound, turning away from a wrong, is deeply unhealthy and destructive.
I learned that if I simply suppressed pain and resentment, it would explode uncontrollably whenever I was prodded in the wrong way.
My thinking was still distorted, and needed a wake-up call.
So by my estimation of my true good, I needed to learn that it had been right and proper.
I needed to make it better, not compound it.

❖ ❖ ❖ ❖ ❖

164

Day 122

A happy life, therefore, is one which is in accordance with its own nature, and cannot be brought about unless in the first place the mind be sound and remain so without interruption, and next, be bold and vigorous, enduring all things with most admirable courage, suited to the times in which it lives, careful of the body and its appurtenances, yet not troublesomely careful. It must also set due value upon all the things which adorn our lives, without over-estimating any one of them, and must be able to enjoy the bounty of Fortune without becoming her slave.

You understand without my mentioning it that an unbroken calm and freedom ensue, when we have driven away all those things which either excite us or alarm us: for in the place of sensual pleasures and those slight perishable matters which are connected with the basest crimes, we thus gain an immense, unchangeable, equable joy, together with peace, calmness and greatness of mind, and kindliness: for all savageness is a sign of weakness.

—Seneca the Younger, *On a happy life* 3

There is quite the difference between a shallow pleasure and a deep, lasting joy of our being.
  While the pursuit of the first, which depends upon the conditions of fortune, is grasping and slavish, the search for the second arises out of a love of balance, and the liberation of a soul that rises above what is beneath its dignity.

Those who are truly happy, whether they be saints, sages, or the salt of the earth, can be known by their signs, if we just know how to look.
  They seek no attention, but often seem to draw it for that very reason.
  They are calm, content with what is simple, slow to anger.
  They will most often show cheerfulness and kindness, the outward reflection of inner love, for all persons.
  They radiate joy.

I do not know that I will ever be that person, though I would very much like to be.
  I still struggle with a foul temperament, and the temptation to succumb to sadness or hopelessness.
  My health does not improve these tendencies.

I seek to practice joy with the very simple things first.
  I have learned that I often appear somber to others, and so I now make a point of smiling when I can, or simply offering a kind word or gesture.
  I know such things have helped me find fragments of joy, and I attempt to pass this along.
  I have a little saying to remind myself of this that I use almost every day: "Too quick to judge, not enough love".

❖ ❖ ❖ ❖ ❖

Day 123

How, indeed, could a person immediately become temperate if he only knew that one must not be overcome by pleasures, but was quite unpracticed in withstanding pleasures?

How could one become just when he had learned that one must love fairness but had never exercised himself in avoidance of selfishness and greed?

How could we acquire courage if we had merely learned that the things which seem dreadful to the average person are not to be feared, but had no experience in showing courage in the face of such things?

How could we become prudent if we had come to recognize what things are truly good and what evil, but had never had practice in despising things which only seem good?

—Musonius Rufus, *Lectures* 6

We see again the Stoic insistence upon the unity of theory and practice, of thinking and doing.
Here it is in the context of the Cardinal Virtues, and with the recognition that we become good at these virtues through their exercise, and not merely by learning about them.

I have long pondered why I am able to accept and overcome certain wrongs more easily than others, and I have slowly discovered that I am most especially hurt not merely by an offense, but rather by an offense ignored or compounded by not being made right.
I believe the ability to correct a wrong, to make it good, is a crucial aspect of practicing virtue, and not merely by reflecting upon it.

When I recently learned that health was fading, I took a page from 12 Step Programs by doing my best to make amends to people I had harmed.
I could not bear the thought of leaving this world without having done all in my power to right my wrongs, wherever possible.
I wrote letters to three or four dozen people, expressing my regrets.

I did not expect anyone to respond, but I was so happy to see almost all of these people return a kind word, an appreciation, or good wishes.
I even rekindled some friendships I thought were long lost because of my past foolishness.
The one I needed to fix the most I heard nothing from, but I had expected that, and I understood why it had to be that way.

I now wish I had attempted something like that many years ago, because it was one of the most liberating and fulfilling things I have ever done.
The point wasn't to convince anyone else of anything, or earn anyone's respect.
It was to earn my own self-respect, knowing I had done all I could to right my wrongs.

I started thinking of this as "following through", not merely thinking good thoughts but putting those thoughts into concrete action.
And this also helped me to see why a hurt unresolved is the worst sort of hurt.

We all fail, and that can be humbly understood and easily forgiven.
It is in not correcting our failings, in not fixing what we have broken, that we truly abandon the virtues.

❖ ❖ ❖ ❖ ❖

Day 124

The road that leads to pleasure is downhill and very easy, with the result that one does not walk but is dragged along; the other which leads to self-control is uphill, toilsome no doubt but profitable exceedingly.

The one carries us away, forced lower and lower as it drives us down its steep incline, until it flings us off on to the level ground at its foot; the other leads heavenwards the immortal who have not fainted on the way and have had the strength to endure the roughness of the hard ascent.

—Philo of Alexandria, *On the special laws 77*

The laws of physics often mirror the laws of the soul, for while matter and spirit are very different modes of the natural world, they are still part of that one Nature.
It takes an opposite force to resists gravity, or to reach an escape velocity.

When I do nothing, when I choose not to act, I will be drawn downward, and the force that pulls me is the instinct of my lower nature, the desire for pleasure.
I come, by inaction, to be ruled by what is beneath.
It is when I use the power of my own action, of my own judgment, that I rise.

As a child I never properly learned to swim, and barely scraped my way through Boy Scouts as a consequence.
I was anxious about the water, and would panic, thrashing and flailing, out of the terror of drowning.
I was letting myself be consumed by my fear, and as a consequence could not choose to accept my own natural buoyancy.
And my own estimation was the difference between sinking and swimming.
All analogies are, of course, more or less weak, but I have found this one helpful when being drawn down by my passions.

❖ ❖ ❖ ❖ ❖

Day 125

When I see a man anxious, I say, 'What does this man want? If he did not want something which is not in his power, how could he be anxious?' For this reason a lute player when he is singing by himself has no anxiety, but when he enters the theatre, he is anxious even if he has a good voice and plays well on the lute; for he not only wishes to sing well, but also to obtain applause: but this is not in his power.

—Epictetus, *Discourses* 2.13

I often find enjoyment in coming across other people who aren't aware that someone else can see them, not in the manner of some sick voyeur, or so that I may mock or ridicule them in their privacy, but because there can be something deeply beautiful in people simply as they are, and for themselves.

The affectations, barriers, defenses, and masks are gone.

Sometimes one may see a person driving down the road, singing wildly and passionately to himself, oblivious to the fact that he is in a glass box.

Sometimes one stumbles across a person in a grocery store staring at a product with a quivering lip and moist eyes, dwelling upon some inner memory triggered by an image of pasta or crackers.

I think this is what Epictetus means here.

The anxiety comes from outside of us, and it falls away when we are unobserved.

That leaves our true selves, our own choices and values, for good or for ill, exposed and in the open.

To remember this can be a great aid in distinguishing what matters, and what we can control, from what is entirely outside of our grasp.

Perform the music of your life, so to speak, as if no one were listening.

Then you will be the virtuoso.

❖ ❖ ❖ ❖ ❖

Day 126

My master Attalus used to say: 'Evil herself drinks the largest portion of her own poison.' The poison which serpents carry for the destruction of others, and secrete without harm to themselves, is not like this poison; for this sort is ruinous to the possessor.

The ungrateful man tortures and torments himself; he hates the gifts which he has accepted, because he must make a return for them, and he tries to belittle their value, but he really enlarges and exaggerates the injuries which he has received. And what is more wretched than a man who forgets his benefits and clings to his injuries?

—Seneca the Younger, *Moral letters to Lucilius* 81

Even after over thirty years of studying philosophy, and over ten years of practicing Stoicism, I still get that twinge, that sense that life is unfair, that others are luckier, or more blessed, that I am.

Seneca helps me correct myself on two levels, both regarding my own sense of myself, and in my estimation of others.

I'm only poisoning myself with my own ungratefulness.

And the other person, of whom I am jealous because he flaunts fame, power, and riches, is also poisoning himself by clutching at straws.

I could certainly be happy and powerful and successful, but if I were truly happy, I would not care whether I was powerful or successful to begin with.

Therefore, when I care about the riches of the world, I'm already poisoning the well of my own happiness.

❖ ❖ ❖ ❖ ❖

Day 127

A man should always have these two rules in readiness: the one, to do only whatever the reason of the ruling and legislating faculty may suggest for the use of men; the other, to change your opinion, if there is any one at hand who sets you right and moves you from any opinion. But this change of opinion must proceed only from a certain persuasion, as of what is just or of common advantage, and the like, not because it appears pleasant or brings reputation.

—Marcus Aurelius, *Meditations* Book 4

St Thomas Aquinas said that a man must always follow his own conscience, but at the same time he must be certain that his conscience is correct, that it is rightly informed.

Readers often assume a stubbornness of conscience, because they neglect the equally necessary second part.

So Marcus Aurelius reminds us that we must allow ourselves to be steadfast in our thinking, but also that we should alter our thinking when we see our error or stand corrected.

Commitment only works paired with humility.

A good litmus test of character is whether someone will gladly, cheerfully, and gratefully admit that he is wrong.

Avoid the person who never changes his mind.

It isn't the truth that's changing, but the depth of our perception of it.

❖ ❖ ❖ ❖ ❖

Day 128

Drunkenness kindles and discloses every kind of vice, and removes the sense of shame that veils our evil undertakings. For more men abstain from forbidden actions because they are ashamed of sinning than because their inclinations are good. When the strength of wine has become too great and has gained control over the mind, every lurking evil comes forth from its hiding place.

Drunkenness does not create vice, it merely brings it into view; at such times the lustful man does not wait even for the privacy of a bedroom, but without postponement gives free play to the demands of his passions; at such times the unchaste man proclaims and publishes his malady; at such times your cross- grained fellow does not restrain his tongue or his hand. The haughty man increases his arrogance, the ruthless man his cruelty, the slanderer his spitefulness. Every vice is given free play and comes to the front.

—Seneca the Younger, *Moral letters to Lucilius* 83

I know that many of us bitten by the Black Dog also suffer from the temptations of drink and drugs.

I understand this from my time in social services, and, most importantly, from my own personal experience.

I have not suffered it quite as seriously as many I know or have known, but the power of intemperance and addiction has always been a great burden for me.

I do not speak of it lightly.

I also don't speak of it readily or often, even in a book as confessional as this one, simply because the horrific outweighs the redemptive in so much of my memory of these demons.

I could write a whole book about the relation of Stoicism to the suffering of addiction.

That may be for another time.

I was always a sensitive soul, and always rather melancholic.

So attending a college where alcohol abuse and sexual promiscuity were the institutional norm did not help me one bit.

By my senior year I was, sadly, a very heavy drinker.

After the personal losses I suffered, I spent four whole years in almost complete isolation, what I now call my "Wilderness Years", and alcohol and drugs were a misguided means to numb my pain.

I foolishly called it self-medication.

Little did I know that it only made everything worse.

Instead of erasing my weaknesses, it only magnified them.

Working to help others with those same demons helped me to help myself.

I can speak only for myself, but I found out many years later that Seneca was right.

Drink and drugs don't make us fail, but they are an opportunity to help us fail ourselves.

They encourage all of our vices.

The condition that can make us addicts is the material cause, the occasions that tempt us.
That in and of itself is not a moral flaw, but an issue of our circumstances.
We fail only, as an efficient cause, the agents of our actions, when we freely choose to succumb to those temptations.

It is only my commitment to the right ends, practiced daily, without any compromise, that has helped me avoid, prisons, asylums, or morgues.
My fellowship with true friends has been a means to this end.
To be a Stoic does not mean doing anything alone.

❖ ❖ ❖ ❖ ❖

Day 129

If someone gave away your body to the first man he met, you would be indignant, but yet you trust your mind to the chance comer, and allow it to be disturbed and confounded if he reviles you; are you not ashamed to do so?

—Epictetus, *Enchiridion* 28

What a wonderful observation!

It can reveal so precisely what it is that we care about the most.

When I was in middle school, at a place where many of the students were far from gentle or kind, another fellow once teasingly swiped my new eraser from my desk as he walked by.

It triggered something in me, probably the pent-up tension of constant bullying and ridicule, so I stood up and tackled him right there in geometry class.

We both got two days of in-school suspension, and thankfully became good friends by being locked in the library together.

So I was more worried about losing my eraser, and my social standing, than I was about giving away the dignity of my own choices and action.

I insisted on the former at the expense of the latter.

Now look at social media, law, politics, business, and the professional world, and tell me it is any different.

❖ ❖ ❖ ❖ ❖

Day 130

You have existed as a part. You shall disappear into that which produced you; but rather you shall be received back into its seminal principle by transmutation.

—Marcus Aurelius, *Meditations* Book 4

My religious faith, and the trust I hold in it, tells me that I will not only survive this life, but that I will become more fully myself in the next.

Religion, however, is not our concern here, so I leave that question to the reader's own judgment.

My study of so much philosophy convinces me of the argument that the mind is not merely reducible to matter, and that consequently my consciousness is an indication of my spiritual and immortal nature.

But I can respect that such an argument is not for everyone.

I have always suggested that one and the same good life, one of truth and love, should be lived regardless of whether I am given an eternal reward.

Those who have understood my point have invariably become kindred spirits.

The Stoics held a range of views on the definition of matter and spirit, and had some different perspectives on human immortality.

Yet whatever future awaits us, we must face with humility the recognition that we do not know precisely what it will be.

Our individual consciousness may continue in some form, or it may not.

But know that whatever may happen, what you are will return into what was and what will be, and nothing about you will cease.

You continue, transformed.

You remain, however you are changed, a part of the Nature that produced you.

One of my favorite musical groups, a progressive rock band from Philadelphia named Echolyn, sang a few words that always stay with me:

After the song is over,
the dance goes on, so dance away.
When all has been said and done,
remember what's been given, not taken away.
Remember all the life you shared every day.
There's never any endings,
...but I'll never be the same.

❖ ❖ ❖ ❖ ❖

Day 131

Vengeance consumes much time, and it exposes the doer to many injuries while he smarts from one; our anger always lasts longer than the hurt.

How much better it is to take the opposite course, and not to match fault with fault. Would any one think that he was well balanced if he repaid a mule with kicks and a dog with biting?

—Seneca the Younger, *On anger* 3.27

I greatly regret the times the younger me lashed out with anger, malice, or violence against someone who hurt me.
 I can never justify myself, or even consider their actions as the cause of my decision.

I once, in the rage of desperation, slapped a person I loved dearly.
 It was probably the very lowest moment of my entire life.
 Whatever pain either of us deserved is entirely beyond the pale.
 A second wrong makes two wrongs, not just one.

I realized I had become a slightly different person when, during the Wilderness Years, a fellow at an Irish music *seisiun* clearly didn't like the look of my face or the cut of my jib.
 He found every possible way to irritate and challenge me.
 Drink did not help his foul mood, and he became more aggressive the friendlier I tried to be.

He finally just stood up and punched me in the face.
 I took a deep breath, said a little prayer, got back up on my feet and simply said, as I wiped a bit of blood from my split lip, "Feel better?"

Much to my surprise, his head drooped, and he walked away, mumbling "Sorry."
 A few of my mates were deeply disappointed, quite eager to "have my back" when the fists started swinging.

If I am defending what I know to be just and right, I will fight like a lion.
 If I'm just angry, it's only about my pride.
 Walk away, or turn the other cheek.

❖ ❖ ❖ ❖ ❖

Out of all these possessions, then, which you reckon as your wealth, not one can really be shown to be your own. For if they have no beauty for you to acquire, what have they for which you should grieve if you lose them, or in keeping which you should rejoice? And if they are beautiful by their own nature, how are you the richer thereby?

For these would have been pleasing of themselves, though cut out from your possessions. They do not become valuable by reason that they have come into your wealth; but you have desired to count them among your wealth, because they seemed valuable. Why then do you long for them with such railing against Fortune?

You seek, I believe, to put want to flight by means of plenty. But you find that the opposite results. The more various is the beauty of furniture, the more helps are needed to keep it beautiful; and it is ever true that they who have much, need much; and on the other hand, they need least who measure their wealth by the needs of Nature, not by excess of display.

Is there then no good which belongs to you and is implanted within you, that you seek your good things elsewhere, in things without you and separate from you? Have things taken such a turn that the animal, whose reason gives it a claim to divinity, cannot seem beautiful to itself except by the possession of lifeless trappings?

Other classes of things are satisfied by their intrinsic possessions; but men, though made like God in understanding, seek to find among the lowest things adornment for their higher nature: and you do not understand that you do a great wrong thereby to your Creator. He intended that the human race should be above all other earthly beings; yet you thrust down your honorable place below the lowest.

For if every good thing is allowed to be more valuable than that to which it belongs, surely you are putting yourselves lower than them in your estimation, since you think precious the most worthless of things; and this is indeed a just result.

Since, then, this is the condition of human nature, that it surpasses other classes only when it realizes what is in itself; as soon as it ceases to know itself, it must be reduced to a lower rank than the beasts. To other animals ignorance of themselves is natural; in men it is a fault. How plainly and how widely do you err by thinking that anything can be adorned by ornaments that belong to others! Surely that cannot be. For if anything becomes brilliant by additions thereto, the praise for the brilliance belongs to the additions. But the subject remains in its own vileness, though hidden and covered by these externals.

Again, I say that naught can be a good thing which does harm to its possessor. Am I wrong? "No," you will say. Yet many a time do riches harm their possessors, since all base men, who are therefore the most covetous, think that they themselves alone are worthy to possess all gold and precious stones. You therefore, who now go in fear of the cudgel and sword of the robber, could laugh in his face if you had entered upon this path with empty pockets. How wonderful is the surpassing blessing of mortal wealth! As soon as you have acquired it, your cares begin!

—Boethius, *The consolation of Philosophy* Book 2 Prose 5

I'm sorry the Boethius passages are often the longest, but I am hesitant to chop them into pieces.
 The flow of his argument, and the grace of his language are part of their very beauty.
 I will often read these passages in smaller parts during the day, divided by the paragraphing I've
 added.

I'll try to compensate by limiting my comments on long Boethius passages.

Owning something external doesn't make us better; it is simply a testimony to the goodness of the
 things we love, not to ourselves.
 So if we define ourselves by what we own, we become subservient to those things.

And then, in some ridiculous and perverse caricature of the natural order, we complain when we
 are so deeply miserable.

❖ ❖ ❖ ❖ ❖

Day 133

What is the first business of him who philosophizes? To throw away all self-conceit. For it is impossible for a man to begin to learn that which he thinks that he knows.

—Epictetus, *Discourses* 2.17

Recall that philosophy is not a career.
No money can be made from it, and to pursue it for fame is contrary to its purpose.
It can never exist for the sake of pride or presumption.

It is a vocation and way of living, not something written about or bragged about, not a means to worldly gain, but rather the end in itself.
There is no reason for knowing than simply to know, there is no purpose for love than simply to love, no reason to appreciate beauty than simply for the sake of beauty.

This is obviously a question of the specific translation, but I reflect on the use of the term "business".
I have always, informed by my Classical upbringing, understood business to be my responsibilities, the sum of what I must do, the actions that virtue demands of me.

Business for the anti-Stoic is about entitlement, not responsibility.
It is about profit, not service.
It is about self, not about others.
I taught Business Ethics for quite a few years, and seemed to be wasting my efforts suggesting that the best business is the best service of the customer.
I still hope a student or two walked away with the seed of a different attitude.

In this sense, the terms "business" and "philosophy" are equally misunderstood in our time.

❖ ❖ ❖ ❖ ❖

Day 134

You do not have ears only for the purpose of listening to melodious sounds, soft and sweetly drawn and all in harmony; you should also lend ear to laughter and weeping, to soft words and bitter, to happiness and sorrow, to the voices of men and the roars and barking of animals.

Poor fellow! Why do you shudder at the shouting of a slave, at the rattling of bronze, or the banging of a door? Although you are so sensitive, you have to listen to thunder.

—Seneca the Younger, *On anger* 3.25

We live in a world where words and images are constantly filtered and censored to ensure ideological conformity, where students who feel threatened by another's thinking can run to a "safe-space" to avoid trigger words, where whatever is considered ugly or unacceptable is self-righteously shunned.

We seem to think that the uncomfortable will simply disappear if we ignore it.

But there is good reason ugliness exists alongside beauty, the uncomfortable with the pleasing, pain with joy.

The Stoic sees the purpose and place of all things, not merely those that are gratifying to us.

I find myself feeling offended many, many times in a day.

"Following through" means I must understand, first, that the offense is in my estimation.

Most often it is my own fault that is at the heart of the objection.

It also means, second, that I must employ the offense to do good for myself and for others, and not to grumble.

The grumbling will simply compound the frustration, and never resolve it.

❖ ❖ ❖ ❖ ❖

He who has a vehement desire for posthumous fame does not consider that every one of those who remember him will himself also die very soon; then again also they who have succeeded them, until the whole remembrance shall have been extinguished as it is transmitted through men who foolishly admire and perish.

But suppose that those who will remember are even immortal, and that the remembrance will be immortal, what then is this to you? And I say not what is it to the dead, but what is it to the living? What is praise except indeed so far as it has a certain utility? For you now reject unseasonably the gift of Nature, clinging to something else.

—Marcus Aurelius , *Meditations* Book 4

Marcus Aurelius here delivers a one–two punch.
Honor is fleeting, and even if it were lasting, it wouldn't make any difference at all.

Though far from being one of the esteemed elderly, I have been around long enough to begin viewing things from a broader perspective.
Time takes on a different context and flow when one has circled the block a few times.
I have now seen, over a few cycles of fashion, how those people who were once the talk of the town are now completely forgotten.
And I have also seen how fame, even when we receive all that we desire, leaves people cold.
We become simply a piece of utility for others.

My students, for example, look at me with dead eyes when I mention the musical heroes of my youth.
And even when they do recognize the names of some of the supposedly timeless legends, I reflect on how the popularity they received gave them nothing but grief when they were alive, and nothing at all now that they are dead.

When I see someone parading for attention, I don't get easily jealous or resentful anymore.
I calm any of those feelings by simply remembering that soon enough we will both be under the earth, and death plays no favorites.
I don't consider that morbid, because it points to a very positive realization.
I am fighting day by day to live with inner strength and joy.
I care nothing for recognition, the pursuit of which will only make me a slave of the passion of others.
So say a quiet prayer for the seeker of fame.
He needs your sympathy, not your jealousy.

❖ ❖ ❖ ❖ ❖

Day 136

Do not expect to enjoin right-doing upon men who are conscious of your own wrong-doing.
—Musonius Rufus, *Fragments* 32

At one time, I understood teaching to be the transmission of wisdom through the beauty of speech.
But I soon learned that teaching doesn't give wisdom to others at all, but only nurtures what is already within them.
I then also learned that wisdom isn't nurtured merely through words, but most fully through example.

I spent many years trying to teach myself to speak the truth with clarity and eloquence.
I never became a master at it, but I did become passably competent.
I found I had a bit of a knack for explaining difficult questions and arguments in a way the everyman could appreciate, as long as he was open and willing to listen.

But that really never meant much.
The words stayed at the surface of the awareness of others.
I began to see that the only way I could even begin to be a teacher was to be a good man, not simply someone who spoke about being good.
Words flit about, but example shoots to the heart.

This transformation is still very much a work in progress.

❖ ❖ ❖ ❖ ❖

Fear is but a poor safeguard of lasting power; while affection, on the other hand may be trusted to keep it safe forever.

—Cicero, *On duties* 2.6

Machiavelli once famously asked whether it was better for a ruler to be feared or to be loved. Though both would be ideal, he answered, if one had to choose, fear was the more powerful motivator.

This is inherently anti-Stoic, of course, and symptomatic of the politics of modernity, which swaps fear and power for virtue and character.

Cicero's answer depends on a completely different view of human nature, and I think it is difficult for many of us to think outside of our deeply ingrained assumptions about the very purpose of our lives.

I think it boils down to a very simple question:

Were we made to care for one another, or to control one another?

How I answer makes a great difference.

And no, we can't have it both ways.

❖ ❖ ❖ ❖ ❖

When you have such a guide, and your wishes and desires are the same as his, why do you fear disappointment? Surrender your desires to wealth and your aversion to poverty, and you will be disappointed in the one, you will fall into the other. Well, surrender them to health, and you will be unfortunate: surrender them up to magistracies, honors, country, friends, children, in a word to any of the things which are not in man's power.

But give them up to Zeus and to the rest of the gods; surrender them to the gods, let the gods govern, let your desire and aversion be ranged on the side of the gods, and wherein will you be any longer unhappy? But if, lazy wretch, you envy, and complain, and are jealous, and fear, and never cease for a single day complaining both of yourself and of the gods, why do you still speak of being educated?

—Epictetus, *Discourses* 2.17

No amount of insistence that pleasure, honor, power, or wealth won't make you happy will convince you if you wish not to be convinced.
  The theoretical explanation is apparent enough, grounded, as it is, on a consideration of the nature of man within the universe, but simply arguing won't be enough to tip the scales.

Instead, simply put it to the test.
  Practice each model suggested above, and see what happens.
  I warn you, however, that some consequences may be life defining and irrevocable.
  Proceed with caution.

Again, it isn't that the rich, or the popular, or those kissed by fortune can't be happy.
  It's that those who care about being rich, popular, or kissed by fortune can't be happy.

I recently happened upon a photograph of an old friend.
  It was one of those "I am an important person smiling and shaking hands with another important person" sort of moments.
  Journals, newsletters, and websites in the fields of business, law, politics, and academics are full of these pictures.
  They are intended, I believe, to encourage vanity in those featured, and jealousy in those who are not.

On the surface, everything looked just fine.
  He was wearing an expensive suit, grinning from ear to ear, and simply looked pleased as punch to be where he was.
  But the thing is that I knew this man very well, and I could see something.
  His eyes were sad.
  He was beautiful on the outside, empty on the inside.
  I could see it only because we had once been so close.

I fear that too many of us are like that, giving the appearance of happiness, but deeply sad within our souls.

❖ ❖ ❖ ❖ ❖

Day 139

Everything which is in any way beautiful is beautiful in itself, and terminates in itself, not having praise as part of itself. Neither worse then nor better is a thing made by being praised. I affirm this also of the things which are called beautiful by the vulgar, for example, material things and works of art.

That which is really beautiful has no need of anything; not more than law, not more than truth, not more than benevolence or modesty. Which of these things is beautiful because it is praised, or spoiled by being blamed? Is such a thing as an emerald made worse than it was, if it is not praised? Or gold, ivory, purple, a lyre, a little knife, a flower, a shrub?

—Marcus Aurelius, *Meditations* Book 4

They say that beauty is in the eye of the beholder.
 This can be a very helpful phrase, or a very harmful one, depending upon how we understand it.

Beauty is indeed in our act of perceiving, understanding, and appreciating the harmonious relationship within the whole.
 This does not mean that the perception is the cause of the beauty.
 To think that is a symptom of the arrogance and vanity of contemporary subjectivism.

Aesthetics, like morals, hinge upon the basic recognition the beauty and value are already deep within things themselves.
 If I consider another person beautiful or good simply because I appreciate them, then it becomes all about me.
 Another person, or thing, isn't beautiful or good at all, in that case.
 I'm just holding a mirror to my own self and praising my own brilliance.
 There's a perfectly good reason Narcissus perished from his own self-importance.

Everything, simply by being in its own way, is beautiful.

❖ ❖ ❖ ❖ ❖

Day 140

At the morning performances in the arena we often see a battle between a bull and a bear tied together, and when they have harried each other, an appointed slayer awaits them. Their fate is ours; we harass someone bound closely to us, and yet the end, all too soon, threatens the victor and the vanquished. Rather let us spend the little time that is left in repose and peace! Let no man loathe us when we lie a corpse!

A cry of fire in the neighborhood often ends a fight, and the arrival of a wild beast rescues a traveller from the brigand. We have no time to struggle with lesser ills when a more threatening fear appears. Why do we concern ourselves with combat and with snares?

—Seneca the Younger, *On anger* 3.43

I sometimes wonder at the absurd barbarity of the Roman's amusements, and then I remember that our entertainments are just as decadent.

We are far too ready to fill our time with such shallow things, and when look at them from the outside, we immediately recognize their futility.

The measure of our personal and professional lives is often just as petty and weak.

We run after little green pieces of paper and brag, boast, and laugh to impress at dinner parties.

All of this changes, once as we remember the truly important things.

I suppose my own introverted, reflective nature, something that usually seems like a curse, is actually a blessing in this case.

I recall the best party I went to in college.

My friends were eager to drink and pass out after the hard work of a week of skipping most of their classes, and my girlfriend was busy basking in the attention of two fellows who were trying their best to have their way with her.

I stepped out on the back porch, and nearly tripped over a girl sitting there in the dark.

She had been crying.

We had a long conversation about real things, about love, about purpose, about pain, about loneliness.

We both walked away better for it.

I never even really saw her face, didn't know her name, and we never met again.

Indoors, we could hear the bread and circuses of drink and sex, while outside two people were helping one another find peace.

It was the best party I ever went to.

❖ ❖ ❖ ❖ ❖

Day 141

First therefore we must know what it is. Constancy is a right and immovable strength of the mind, neither lifted up nor pressed down with external or casual accidents. By strength I understand a steadfastness not from opinion, but from judgment and sound reason.

For I would in any case exclude obstinacy, which is a certain hardness of a stubborn mind, proceeding from pride or vainglory. And this hardness is only in one respect incident to the obstinate. For they can hardly be pressed down but are lifted up, not unlike to a blown balloon, which you cannot without much ado thrust under water, but is ready to leap upwards of itself without help.

"Even such is the lighthardiness of those men, springing of pride and too much estimation of themselves, and therefore from opinion. But the true mother of constancy is patience, and lowliness of mind, which is a voluntary sufferance without grudging of all things whatsoever can happen to or in a man.

This being regulated by the rule of right reason is the very root whereupon is settled the high and mighty body of that fair oak constancy. Beware here, lest opinion beguile thee, presenting unto you instead of patience a certain abjection and baseness of a dastardly mind. Being a foul vice, proceeding from the vile unworthiness of a man's own person. But virtue keeps the mean, not suffering any excess or defect in her actions, because it weighs all things in the balance of Reason, making it the rule and squire of all her trials.

Therefore we define right reason to be a true sense and judgment of things human and divine (so far as the same pertains to us). But opinion being the contrary to it is defined to be a false and frivolous conjecture of those things.

—Justus Lipsius, *On constancy* 1.4

I often feel that I need to apologize to people for appealing to unpopular and outdated virtues like prudence, temperance, or constancy.
I actually find myself apologizing for even appealing to the word "virtue".
But then I wake up, and realize that I need not define myself by what is popular or fashionable.
I can freely and joyfully choose to live as a man, even if others choose to live like animals.

There is a world of difference between being constant or steadfast, and being obstinate or stubborn.
It parallels the distinction between being brave and being foolhardy.
While the former is commitment grounded in a genuine knowledge of the good, the latter is an insistence built solely on opinion and misleading appearance.
Accordingly, one embraces the humility of seeing the good within things, while another proceeds from the arrogance of imposing our own will.

I have often, in practice, found it difficult to distinguish between the two.
I've been convinced that I'm being constant, when in fact I am being stubborn.
I have discovered that my actions are obstinate when I feel the need to justify myself.
True constancy will flow freely from a commitment to the truth, and requires no twisted excuses to support it.

❖ ❖ ❖ ❖ ❖

Every habit and faculty is maintained and increased by the corresponding actions: the habit of walking by walking, the habit of running by running. If you would be a good reader, read; if a writer, write. But when you shall not have read thirty days in succession, but have done something else, you will know the consequence.

In the same way, if you shall have lain down ten days, get up and attempt to make a long walk, and you will see how your legs are weakened. Generally, then, if you would make anything a habit, do it; if you would not make it a habit, do not do it, but accustom yourself to do something else in place of it.

So it is with respect to the affections of the soul: when you have been angry, you must know that not only has this evil befallen you, but that you have also increased the habit, and in a manner thrown fuel upon fire. When you have been overcome in sexual intercourse with a person, do not reckon this a single defeat only, but reckon that you have also nurtured, increased your incontinence. For it is impossible for habits and faculties, some of them not to be produced, when they did not exist before, and others not be increased and strengthened by corresponding acts.

—Epictetus, *Discourses* 2.18

The Ancients in general understood that character isn't formed merely by knowledge and choice. It is acquired and strengthened through practice and habit.

I often have to bite my tongue in the world of education when the certain social engineers speak of character education as if it were only a set of lesson plans.

At certain schools, for example, it is common to assume that an hour or two of watching videos about sexual abuse will remove the problem from our midst.

And the building of habits, good or bad, is not simply measured by which actions we generally perform more often.

Epictetus reminds us that every single act of anger or intemperance makes us weaker and thereby worsens us.

I once stood slack–jawed when a woman told me that she was faithful to her boyfriend, since she had only cheated on him twice.

I make use of this principle positively when I struggle with "following through".

If I remind myself that every deed, however small or seemingly insignificant, can add to my virtue and happiness, and makes me better and stronger, I am encouraged in the face of what can seem a daunting task.

A single kind word, or a harsh word avoided, is a powerful and transformative step.

Each little step matters very much.

I found this especially helpful when, at some of the lowest points in my life, I have struggled with drinking in the face of despair.

I didn't have to reform my whole life right there and then, or promise to become a teetotaler.

I could simply refuse to grab that one drink that, because of my mood, I don't really need right now.

❖ ❖ ❖ ❖ ❖

Day 143

Every house that mercy enters she will render peaceful and happy, but in the palace she is more wonderful, in that she is rarer. For what is more remarkable than that he whose anger nothing can withstand, to whose sentence, too heavy though it be, even the victims bow the head, whom, if he greatly incensed, no one will venture to gainsay, no, even to entreat—that this man should lay a restraining hand upon himself, and use his power to better and more peaceful ends when he reflects, 'Any one can violate the law to kill, none but I, to save?'

—Seneca the Younger, *On mercy* 1.5,tr Basore

Mercy perfects justice, because it goes beyond what is owed to what can be given. I hope that if you have read this far, you are perhaps beginning to see that Stoicism is hardly a cold philosophy, but an attitude that is charged with compassion and concern.

Though my sensitive temperament has always been so inclined, Stoicism has encouraged me to avoid the cries of "no quarter", or the taking of joy in suffering and punishment.
The good of another, done for the sake of another, must always be the guide.

The true practice or mercy and charity is to be all the more admired in those given power and influence.
As the neighborhood I grew up in slowly went from being solidly middle class to being gentrified, and from gentrified to downright entitled, I was often saddened to see how hard, heartless, and legalistic people seemed to be becoming.

But I need not see this as only negative, because it made those wonderful moments of true human concern, however more rare, all the more beautiful, and therefore all the more a reminder of what I need to become.

Don't just feel sad when you see a cold-hearted person.
Be grateful when you see a kind-hearted one.

❖ ❖ ❖ ❖ ❖

Day 144

Everything harmonizes with me, which is harmonious to you, Oh Universe. Nothing for me is too early nor too late, which is in due time for you. Everything is fruit to me which your seasons bring, O Nature: from you are all things, in you are all things, to you all things return.

—Marcus Aurelius, *Meditations* Book 4

Nature is not merely the laws of the physical universe, or the instincts ruling biology, but refers here more broadly, with Aristotle, to the principles of motion and change inherent in the very being of all things.

And it is right and proper that a part, which I must consider myself to be, exists and acts in balance with the whole.

To recognize this harmony is the attitude of respect and humility shared by every Stoic.

If I were asked to choose my favorite poem, I would choose "God's grandeur" by Gerard Manley Hopkins.

I have felt the toil and smudge he describes, and at times they have nearly made me give up hope.

Then I look to Nature, and to Her Origin, however you may choose to understand what that may be, and I am revived.

The world is charged with the grandeur of God.
It will flame out, like shining from shook foil;
it gathers to a greatness, like the ooze of oil
crushed. Why do men then now not reck his rod?
Generations have trod, have trod, have trod;
and all is seared with trade; bleared, smeared with toil;
and wears man's smudge and shares man's smell: the soil
is bare now, nor can foot feel, being shod.

And for all this, nature is never spent;
there lives the dearest freshness deep down things;
and though the last lights off the black West went
Oh, morning, at the brown brink eastward, springs—
because the Holy Ghost over the bent
world broods with warm breast and with ah! bright wings!

❖ ❖ ❖ ❖ ❖

Day 145

Toward subjects one should strive to be regarded with awe rather than with fear. Reverence attends the one, bitterness the other.

—Musonius Rufus, *Fragments* 33

We saw Cicero say something very similar just a few passages ago.
  A truth is never harmed by being pondered from different perspectives, and is hardly diminished through relation to all of our many and diverse experiences.

I was blessed to have a family that always loved me, was very often firm, but never acted with the threat of force or intimidation.
  This was not always the case in the wider world around me.
  I feared the bullies, both those of body and feelings, at my school when I was younger.
  As I grew older, I feared other sorts of bullies, who traded in power and influence.
  They really weren't all that different.
  The older ones dressed up much fancier and used bigger words.

I have found myself in the rather odd situation of having been called to Jury Duty ten times in the last twenty-eight years.
  I consider it a privilege, not a burden, when I remind myself to value service over convenience.
  Each time, I have observed good cops and bad cops, honest lawyers and rotten scoundrels, wise judges and corrupt power-seekers.
  It has been a wonderful lesson in life.

I once sat on a case where the Assistant DA hounded a witness to tears, constantly threatening legal repercussions if she did not give an answer that he liked.
  The Judge, seemingly bored by the whole affair, brushed aside Objections.
  The trick, of course, was to get what you wanted by any means necessary, including intimidation.

I saw no respect for law that day, no genuine awe for the system, just the look of terror on the face of a shy witness who hadn't had the luxury of three years at a fancy Law School.
  I just remember that all I could do was smile at her kindly, though I don't have a very good smile.
  I hoped that it was just a sliver of decency in a world of too many bullies.

❖ ❖ ❖ ❖ ❖

Day 146

I think, therefore, that kindness to the good is a better investment than kindness to the favorites of fortune. We must, of course, put forth every effort to oblige all sorts and conditions of men, if we can.

But if it comes to a conflict of duty on this point, we must, I should say, follow the advice of Themistocles: when someone asked his advice whether he should give his daughter in marriage to a man who was poor but honest or to one who was rich but less esteemed, he said: 'For my part, I prefer a man without money to money without a man.'

But the moral sense of today is demoralized and depraved by our worship of wealth. Of what concern to any one of us is the size of another man's fortune? It is, perhaps, an advantage to its possessor; but not always even that. But suppose it is; he may, to be sure, have more money to spend; but how is he any the better man for that?

Still, if he is a good man, as well as a rich one, let not his riches be a hindrance to his being aided, if only they are not the motive to it; but in conferring favors our decision should depend entirely upon a man's character, not on his wealth.

—Cicero, *On duties* 2.20

My father and I have long had a friendly argument whenever we enter a church.
He prefers to sit in a pew up front, to be near the holy action, as he says, with a wink.
I prefer to sit as far in the back as possible, so as not to be seen.

Though our bickering is in good fun, my reason is actually a very serious one.
I never wish to tempt myself into doing anything at all so as to be seen doing it, or to receive any praise or reward.
It's for the same reason I prefer having the smallest online footprint possible.

I challenge myself to do much the same when it comes to seeking favor from people with money, power, or influence.
Cicero is, of course, quite right: We should always do good for others, simply because we should always do good.
But I immediately squint at a situation, and look at it from every angle, when the possibility exists that I could be acting simply for favor or benefit.
I prefer to practice charity in private.

Many people I know will grapple to be at the front of line when they see that they may receive a reward for their kindness.
Of course, it is now no longer kindness.
It's greed.

Recently, I was teaching Jane Austen's *Pride and prejudice* to my students, and was offering some background on the world Austen was writing about.
I asked them to consider what defined a gentleman, or a lady.
Was it property and wealth?
Social status? Manners? Perhaps character?

A fine young man immediately suggested that people with character might have money, but having money doesn't make people of character.
This fellow might well be a reincarnation of Themistocles.

❖ ❖ ❖ ❖ ❖

191

What a man applies himself to earnestly, that he naturally loves. Do men then apply themselves earnestly to the things which are bad? By no means. Well, do they apply themselves to things which in no way concern themselves? Not to these either. It remains, then, that they employ themselves earnestly only about things which appear good; and if they are earnestly employed about things, they love such things also.

Whoever, then, understands what is good, can also know how to love; but he who cannot distinguish good from bad, and things which are neither good nor bad from both, can he possess the power of loving? To love, then, is only in the power of the wise.

—Epictetus, *Discourses* 2.22

The Beatles had it right, I think, when they proclaimed that *All you need is love.*
 But they only had it half right, which John Paul II understood when he added:
 There can be no love without the truth.

There's a good reason Nature formed us with both a will and an intellect.
 My will permits me to choose, my intellect directs that choice.
 I cannot choose the good unless I first know what is good.
 And remember that no man deliberately chooses what perceives to be evil.
 In some sense, at least partly, he believes it to be good.

I once made an extremely foolish choice.
 The details are perhaps too personal even for a confessional book of this nature, so I'll leave that part aside.
 It was a life-defining choice, and, as it turned out, a life-defining mistake.

Though I was honestly torn between two options, and my conscience, though incompletely formed, was nudging me away from the wrong choice.
 But I still took the bad turn.
 I did so honestly deciding that the apparent benefit outweighed the harm.
 I was mistaken, and I paid a price.
 Now I know, but back then, I didn't really know at all.

Inform your own understanding, and inspire understanding in others.
 Without it, the ship has no captain to navigate to your destination.

❖ ❖ ❖ ❖ ❖

Day 148

Either it is a well-arranged universe or a chaos huddled together, but still a universe. But can a certain order subsist in you, and disorder in the All? And this, too, when all things are so separated and diffused and sympathetic.

—Marcus Aurelius, *Meditations* Book 4

My now unshakable conviction that the universe is ordered by Providence was quite slow in coming.

The practice took some time to catch up with theory, I imagine, because the Black Dog was trying to keep me from following through.

In my Wilderness Years, I was having a day that was more painful, frustrating, and lonely than usual.

I could feel that I might break.

With what I now see as incredible willpower, I pulled myself together.

I resisted the urge to mope or drink myself into oblivion.

I pulled myself up and forced myself to put one foot in front of the other.

I would go home, have a fine meal, read a good book, say a prayer of gratitude, and have a proper night's sleep for the first time in weeks.

I had a sense that this could be a turning point.

I could feel the hope welling up inside me.

It was already dark, but it was a crisp winter day, and fluffy snow was gently falling.

I saw a man and a boy, who I assumed were father and son, crossing the busy downtown street hand in hand. And everything seemed to slow down as a van not only hit them, but literally ran over them.

Both were killed.

Seeing that made me once again wallow in thinking that the universe was chaotic, unfair, and without purpose.

There could be no God, and there could be no hope.

I wasn't thinking about them, of course, but about my own selfish pride and self-pity.

By all, means let us believe that the universe is without order.

Ironically, I think we tell ourselves this precisely to give ourselves a purpose.

But remember that it is undeniable that there is order within each one of us, and we are a part of the whole.

Does it seem right that there could be purpose in the part, but not in the whole?

As Aristotle asks:

Should we not assume that just as the eye, the hand, the foot, and in general each part of the body clearly has its own proper function, so man too has some function over and above the functions of his parts?

❖ ❖ ❖ ❖ ❖

Day 149

Cruelty is an evil thing befitting least of all a man, and is unworthy of his spirit that is so kindly; for one to take delight in blood and wounds and, throwing off the man, to change into a creature of the woods, is the madness of a wild beast.

—Seneca the Younger, *On mercy* 1.14

People can, and sadly do, choose to be cruel.
  I wonder if this is because hate is easy, but loving is difficult?
  But I must remember that it is our nature, however broken, to love.
  And it's always better to fix something broken than to merely throw it away.

A few years back, I received an e-mail that sent me on what my patient wife calls a hissy-rant.
  The message was from a person well known to me for clouding anything and everything with excuses, and treating other human beings as disposable.
  "Most important of all," she wrote, "I'm just trying to figure out what it means to love."

I shouldn't have lost my temper, but I suppose I did it to let off some steam.
  At least only my patient wife had to hear it.

"Good grief, woman!" I cried out loud, "It's not rocket science.
  All you need to do is think about someone other than yourself for a change.
  Children know how to love.
  You apparently lost that somewhere along the road!"

I admittedly said that in a cruel way, but perhaps there's a lesson here that helps to make the point.
  I have often forgotten my nature as well, and been more of a wild beast than a man.
  And so I remember that I can fix myself, and return to my nature.

I encourage myself with the motto of the Royal Air Force: *Per ardua ad astra*, "Through hardship to the stars."
  It won't help me just to criticize others.
  I need to make myself better.

❖ ❖ ❖ ❖ ❖

No evil is honorable; but death is honorable; therefore death is not evil.

—Zeno of Citium, ex Seneca the Younger,
Moral letters to Lucilius 82

I have often vacillated between fearing death and desiring it.
I've been getting to the point where I don't care either way, and I honestly don't think that's a careless attitude.
The Stoic recognizes that death is our natural end.
That it will occur is a necessary part of life.
How and when it will occur are in so many ways outside of my power, but how I choose to face it is entirely within my power.

Long life or short, rich or poor, healthy or sick, what I can do is use each and every circumstance to become a wiser and more loving person.
That's what matters.

I can die with dignity.
I intend to, and it won't need to be epic or heroic.

I remember with great respect when my grandmother was dying of stomach cancer.
The image of her standing at the top of her stairs, and the look of horror on her face, when we rushed to her house after she learned the diagnosis, is still burned into my brain.

Her body slowly but surely wasted away, and she must have suffered agonizing pain, but her soul became greater.
On what I recall as being the last day I saw her alive, she played me a tape of the song *One day at a time* by Merle Haggard.
Give me the strength to do everyday what I have to do.
There was suffering on her face, but the deepest joy in her eyes.

❖ ❖ ❖ ❖ ❖

Day 151

Appropriate acts are in general measured by the relations they are concerned with. 'He is your father.' This means you are called on to take care of him, give way to him in all things, bear with him if he reviles or strikes you.

'But he is a bad father.'

'Well, have you any natural claim to a good father?'

'No. Only to a father.'

'My brother wrongs me.'

Be careful then to maintain the relation you hold to him, and do not consider what he does, but what you must do if your purpose is to keep in accord with Nature.

For no one shall harm you, without your consent; you will only be harmed, when you think you are harmed. You will only discover what is proper to expect from neighbor, citizen, or praetor, if you get into the habit of looking at the relations implied by each.

—Epictetus, *Enchiridion* 30

I understand that my way of thinking, and therefore the way that I teach, and the way that I live, are hardly in conformity with the norms of the day.
And they are certainly out of line with the trends of academia.
I'm fine with that.
I prefer to do what I estimate to be right, not to be popular.

The first year I ever taught formally, I was doing my best to explain Aristotle's *Nicomachean Ethics*.
A very bright and reflective student expressed her concern that Aristotle had no conception of human rights.
I understood and respected her point: the idea of rights is a largely Enlightenment approach.

I offered the following suggestion. Aristotle doesn't speak of rights as we understand them, but he does speak of justice, and he does speak of responsibilities.
A right refers to what is owed to me; a responsibility is about what I owe to others.
Now, is it better to think of any human relationship in terms of what I deserve, or what others deserve from me?

The Stoic thinks first of what he must do.
He doesn't think of what others should or must do, because this is not within his power.
Rights and responsibilities are two sides of the same coin, but the stress of one or other side makes a real difference.

I owe my family and my friends love and respect.
And that doesn't change if they choose not to show me love and respect.
I owe this to my enemies just as much.

❖ ❖ ❖ ❖ ❖

196

Day 152

Observe constantly that all things take place by change, and accustom yourself to consider that the Nature of the Universe loves nothing so much as to change the things which are and to make new things like them. For everything that exists is in a manner the seed of that which will be. But you are thinking only of seeds which are cast into the earth or into a womb: but this is a very vulgar notion.

—Marcus Aurelius, *Meditations* Book 4

I either suffer from, or I am blessed by, a deep sense of nostalgia.
Which one it is, of course, depends upon my estimation of it.

Because memories, good or bad, have such a powerful effect on my thinking and feeling, I often intensely dislike change.
What I need to remember is the remarkable beauty of growth and alteration, and in the way that the old passes into the new, reflecting and fulfilling itself.
It is an aspect of the "freshness" that Hopkins spoke of in our earlier poem.

I think of this not merely as generation and destruction, but as transformation.
New things are the old rebuilt and restored in a playful dance of infinite combinations.
Though I struggled with translating them when I was learning Latin, Ovid's *Metamorphoses* are a wonderful literary and moral way of appreciating transformation.

❖ ❖ ❖ ❖ ❖

Day 153

Your grief is renewed and grows stronger every day—by lingering it has established its right to stay, and has now reached the point that it is ashamed to make an end, just as all vices become deep-rooted unless they are crushed when they spring up, so, too, such a state of sadness and wretchedness, with its self afflicted torture, feeds at last upon its very bitterness, and the grief of an unhappy mind becomes a morbid pleasure.

And so I should have liked to approach your cure in the first stages of your sorrow. While it was still young, a gentler remedy might have been used to check its violence; against inveterate evils the fight must be more vehement. This is likewise true of wounds—they are easy to heal while they are still fresh and bloody. When they have festered and turned into a wicked sore, then they must be cauterized and, opened up to the very bottom, must submit to probing fingers. As it is, I cannot possibly be a match for such hardened grief by being considerate and gentle; it must be crushed.

—Seneca, *To Marcia on consolation 1.7*, tr Basore

Seneca wrote this letter to a woman who had lost her son, and after three years her grief had only grown worse.

His remedy sounds harsh to some, perhaps even heartless, but while he fully recognizes that sorrow in its early stages must be met with sympathy and gentleness, grief that has lingered for too long can't be cured with mere kindness.

It has become so hardened, so ingrained that it must be met with strength and force.

The analogy of the wound is a fitting one.

I can relate to this all too well. I made the fatal error many years ago of brutally repressing, denying, and ignoring pain.

I didn't manage it with the gentle care I should have back then, and by the time I saw what I had done to myself, gentle care was no longer enough.

Only courage and toughness, being tempered like steel, can now be effective.

I don't think that's heartless at all.

It's tough, but it's still love.

In fact, it would be naive and heartless to think otherwise and to prescribe a weak remedy.

One cannot coddle self-pity.

Never abandon or discard someone who is in sorrow, because no person is ever disposable.

But sometimes the medicine you give, to yourself or another, must taste very bitter.

Love isn't the problem, but the abuse and perversion of love is the problem.

And love often demands radical measures.

Seneca is being truly loving by writing these words to a suffering friend.

This train of thoughts reminds of the wise words of Meša Selimović:

Everyone says love hurts, but that is not true. Loneliness hurts. Rejection hurts. Losing someone hurts. Envy hurts. Everyone gets these things confused with love, but in reality love is the only thing in this world that covers up all pain and makes someone feel wonderful again. Love is the only thing in this world that does not hurt.

❖ ❖ ❖ ❖ ❖

198

Day 154

One might reasonably reflect upon characteristics even of certain animals which are very well calculated to shame us into endurance of hardships. At all events, cocks and quails, although they have no understanding of virtue as man has and know neither the good nor the just and strive for none of these things, nevertheless fight against each other and even when maimed stand up and endure until death so as not to submit the one to the other.

How much more fitting, then, it is that we stand firm and endure, when we know that we are suffering for some good purpose, either to help our friends or to benefit our city, or to defend our wives and children, or, best and most imperative, to become good and just and self-controlled, a state which no man achieves without hardships.

—Musonius Rufus, *Lectures 7*

I believe that suffering can be redemptive, that hardship can offer rewards, that burdens can become blessings.

A dear old friend from years back recently told me that he would be facing yet another heart surgery.

I sent him a copy of this poem, "Invictus" by William Ernest Henley, to lift his spirits, not with sentimentality, but with the inspiration of true endurance.

I hope he understood my intent:

> *Out of the night that covers me,*
> *black as the pit from pole to pole,*
> *I thank whatever gods may be*
> *for my unconquerable soul.*
>
> *In the fell clutch of circumstance*
> *I have not winced nor cried aloud.*
> *Under the bludgeonings of chance*
> *My head is bloody, but unbowed.*
>
> *Beyond this place of wrath and tears*
> *looms but the Horror of the shade,*
> *and yet the menace of the years*
> *finds and shall find me unafraid.*
>
> *It matters not how strait the gate,*
> *how charged with punishments the scroll,*
> *I am the master of my fate,*
> *I am the captain of my soul.*

❖ ❖ ❖ ❖ ❖

What then makes a man beautiful? Is it not the possession of the excellence of a man? And do you, then, if you wish to be beautiful, young man, labor at this, the acquisition of human excellence?

But what is this? Observe whom you yourself praise, when you praise many persons without partiality: do you praise the just or the unjust? 'The just.' Whether do you praise the moderate or the immoderate? 'The moderate.' And the temperate or the intemperate? 'The temperate.'

If, then, you make yourself such a person, you will know that you will make yourself beautiful: but so long as you neglect these things, you must be ugly, even though you contrive all you can to appear beautiful.

—Epictetus, *Discourses* 3.1

Beauty isn't skin deep. Beauty is soul deep.
What makes something beautiful must be a reflection of what it is, that which is intrinsic to its nature, and what is extrinsic is entirely distinct and separate.

When I was in High School, a clever classmate decided to find a nickname for me.
I was always physically awkward, skinny, and pale in complexion.
So she decided I should be called "Sickly".

She found this very amusing, repeated it constantly, and made me feel deeply ashamed.
It caught on, of course.
These were some of the same socially progressive young people who would march against AIDS discrimination, but who were quite ready to ridicule a classmate for looking like an AIDS patient.

Over the years I have learned that so much of what we consider attractive is a measure of custom and fashion, and therefore a completely extrinsic measure built around shallow standards.

Years later, I almost had to cry when I heard one of my students very proudly proclaim that the wife he would one day find would first and foremost have to be "hot".
I am sure he found such a wife, because it was apparent he was headed for big things, and while I hope he is happy, I'm afraid he probably isn't.
I'm not sure how he could be, looking at the world from such a perspective.

Man is measured by the essence of his nature, his willingness, as a being of intellect and will, to know and to love.
It is therefore your character that makes you beautiful.
Remind yourself of this, and save yourself the shame and sadness that comes from listening to those who would tell you otherwise.

❖ ❖ ❖ ❖ ❖

Day 156

All men, brother Gallio, wish to live happily, but are dull at perceiving exactly what it is that makes life happy: and so far is it from being easy to attain the happiness that the more eagerly a man struggles to reach it the further he departs from it, if he takes the wrong road; for, since this leads in the opposite direction, his very swiftness carries him all the further away.

We must therefore first define clearly what it is at which we aim: next we must consider by what path we may most speedily reach it, for on our journey itself, provided it be made in the right direction, we shall learn how much progress we have made each day, and how much nearer we are to the goal towards which our natural desires urge us.

But as long as we wander at random, not following any guide except the shouts and discordant clamors of those who invite us to proceed in different directions, our short life will be wasted in useless roamings, even if we labor both day and night to get a good understanding.

—Seneca the Younger, *On a happy life* 1

I have long thought this is quite simply the most important question, not only of philosophy, but in life itself.

What do you want?

Everything depends upon the answer, because all actions are for the sake of that end.

Call it what you will, happiness, blessedness, joy, enlightenment, salvation.

How we understand what it is, truly and fully, the sum purpose of our lives, and if we understand it only in part, or not at all, we are running blind, because we don't even know what we want.

The glutton or lustful man thinks it is pleasure, the proud or envious man thinks it is honor, the greedy man thinks it is wealth, the angry man thinks it is power.

The Stoic knows it is virtue, a life simply lived well for its own sake and free of impediments, in accord with Nature and the source for the greatest joy.

When I remember that all other things are good for me only as means to this end, I am complete, and I can rest content.

My problems resume when I allow myself, through my own confusion, to seek after lower things for their own sake.

I believe that, in a sense, Nature gives us what we want, in that Nature and Providence reflect back our choices.

If you want wealth or honor, you may or may not end up getting them as you expected, but everything about your life will be defined by those false values.

The trick, of course, is being careful what you wish for, because Nature and Providence will give it to you.

If you truly want a life ruled by things beyond your power, that's exactly what you get.

Let's be careful not to regret deciding what it is that we want.

❖ ❖ ❖ ❖ ❖

If he is a stranger to the universe who does not know what is in it, no less is he a stranger who does not know what is going on in it. He is a runaway, who flies from social reason; he is blind, who shuts the eyes of the understanding; he is poor, who has need of another, and has not from himself all things which are useful for life.

He is an abscess on the universe who withdraws and separates himself from the reason of our common nature through being displeased with the things which happen, for the same Nature produces this, and has produced you too: he is a piece rent asunder from the state, who tears his own soul from that of reasonable animals, which is one.

—Marcus Aurelius, *Meditations* Book 4

Marcus Aurelius once again stresses our social nature.

When we struggle against Nature, selfishly bemoaning our circumstances, we break the bonds we share with our fellows.

I appreciate the image he uses of "tearing away" our souls.

I understand this temptation all too well, and I have often been guilty of it.

I see the same tendency in my children as well, and I am therefore very careful to encourage them against it.

When I am hurt, my instinct is, of course to pull back, or to retreat, or sometimes to fight.

In any case, I am sundering myself from others by running or confronting.

Once I judge by my feeling that I have been wronged, my complaint becomes a barrier to healing or reconciliation.

The silent treatment, or a form of what we sometimes call passive-aggressive behavior, is a prime instance of this.

I can no longer count the times I have seen people compound the hurt ignoring one another.

What we fail to see is that we're one, not just in the sense of politics, but in the sense of Nature.

❖　❖　❖　❖　❖

Day 158

The light of a lamp is eclipsed and overpowered by the rays of the sun; a drop of honey is lost in the vastness of the Aegean Sea; an additional sixpence is nothing amid the wealth of Croesus, or a single step in the journey from here to India.

Similarly if the Stoic definition of the End of Goods be accepted, it follows that all the value you set on bodily advantages must be absolutely eclipsed and annihilated by the brilliance and the majesty of virtue.

And just as opportuneness is not increased by prolongation in time (since things we call opportune have attained their proper measure), so right conduct, I say, and also propriety, and lastly Good itself, which consists in harmony with Nature, are not capable of increase or addition.

For these things that I speak of, like opportuneness before mentioned, are not made greater by prolongation. And on this ground the Stoics do not deem happiness to be any more attractive or desirable if it be lasting than if it be brief.

—Cicero, *On good and evil ends* 3.14, tr Rackham

The fulfillment of man, to act with wisdom and love, to be virtuous, is itself a perfect and complete end.

Nothing can be added to it, and everything else seems meager by comparison.

And to be able to act with virtue and in harmony with Nature is also complete in each moment of time.

As we have already seen, more doesn't necessarily make anything better.

If I feel, for example, that I wasted so many years of my life loving all the wrong things, the number of years need not matter.

I can now begin to love rightly, however late, and that moment will be complete.

The very short time I could love my first child, and not even let him know it, is no less than the two decades of love I have shared with my wife.

I don't know to describe the sense of wholeness that comes with wisdom and love to someone who has never experienced it.

It would be much like trying to describe the pleasures of a fine banquet to someone who had only eaten gruel.

It is only this memory of the times lived well, as rare as they sometimes appear, that can bring me back when I have strayed from the path, when my thinking gets hijacked by my feeling.

❖ ❖ ❖ ❖ ❖

Day 159

Against this kind of thing chiefly a man should exercise himself. As soon as you go out in the morning, examine every man whom you see, every man whom you hear; answer as to a question, 'What have you seen?'

A handsome man or woman? Apply the rule: Is this independent of the will, or dependent? Independent. Take it away.

What have you seen? A man lamenting over the death of a child. Apply the rule. Death is a thing independent of the will. Take it away.

Has the proconsul met you? Apply the rule. What kind of thing is a proconsul's office? Independent of the will, or dependent on it? Independent. Take this away also: it does not stand examination: cast it away: it is nothing to you.

—Epictetus, *Discourses* 3.3

This passage is always like a bucket of ice water for me.
  Shocking, but refreshing.
  If it isn't within what is in your power, it simply doesn't matter one bit for your happiness.

And the way in which Epictetus suggests using this rule as a practical test of value has been very fruitful for me.
  I cannot count the number of times the mantra of "take it away" has saved me from harming myself.

Even something as seemingly insignificant as being caught in traffic can be deeply frustrating.
  So I simply ask myself, is this dependent or independent of me?
  Independent. What can I do?
  I can order my own thoughts, I can say a prayer, I can turn on some music in my car.

The other day, a Bach cantata came on while I was fighting road rage.
  Bestelle dein Haus… Put your house in order, for die you will.
That puts it in perspective, and separates the important from the trivial, the dependent and the independent, quite well.

❖ ❖ ❖ ❖ ❖

Day 160

You are a little soul carrying around a corpse, as Epictetus used to say.
—Marcus Aurelius, *Meditations* Book 4

If you can read this short passage, smile, find it both profound and amusing, without a hint of morbidity, then you are most likely now a card-carrying Stoic.

Huston Smith, the historian of religion, wrote that Judaism has a wonderful counterpoint between the smallness and greatness of man.
They can simultaneously embrace the saying *You are from dust, and to dust you shall return,* while always imagining that walking in front of every man are angels, heralding and proclaiming, *Make way! Make way for the image and likeness of God!*

I read the Stoic passage as having a similar sense.
You are small, you are pulling the weight of dead flesh, but you are still a great soul.

❖ ❖ ❖ ❖ ❖

Day 161

A man thus grounded must, whether he wills or not, necessarily be attended by constant cheerfulness and a joy that is deep and issues from deep within, since he finds delight in his own resources, and desires no joys greater than his inner joys. Should not such joys as these be rightly matched against the paltry and trivial and fleeting sensations of the wretched body?

The day a man becomes superior to pleasure, he will also be superior to pain; but you see in what wretched and baneful bondage he must linger whom pleasures and pains, those most capricious and tyrannical of masters, shall in turn enslave.

—Seneca the Younger, *On a happy life* 1.4

Remember, of course, that Stoicism isn't what people assume it is.
It's not about being tough, distant, and emotionless.
With apologies to *The princess bride:*
You keep using that word. I do not think it means what you think it means.

To be able to rise above circumstance, to conquer both pleasure and pain, is itself joy, which as Seneca recognizes, is one of those moments when you can't even help being happy.
To practice the Stoic turn, to find good in evil and love in hate is a triumph.
And a triumph is to be savored.

I am reminded of the words of Albert Camus from *The stranger:*

> *My dear,*
> *In the midst of hate, I found there was, within me, an invincible love.*
> *In the midst of tears, I found there was, within me, an invincible smile.*
> *In the midst of chaos, I found there was, within me, an invincible calm.*
> *I realized, through it all, that...*
> *In the midst of winter, I found there was, within me, an invincible summer.*
> *And that makes me happy. For it says that no matter how hard the world pushes against me, within me, there's something stronger – something better, pushing right back.*
>
> *Truly yours,*
> *Albert Camus*

❖ ❖ ❖ ❖ ❖

Is it possible for anyone to be a good king unless he is a good man? No, it is not possible. But given a good man, would he not be entitled to be called a philosopher? Most certainly, since philosophy is the pursuit of ideal good. Therefore a good king is found to be forthwith and of necessity a philosopher also.

—Musonius Rufus, *Lectures* 8

We've already considered Plato's suggestion of the Philosopher King, its fittingness to Stoicism, and the fact that we sadly misunderstand what defines the real philosopher.

It is the middle term of "good man" that ties the terms "good king" and "philosopher" together.

Are good rulers perhaps only so rare because it sadly seems so hard to find people that seek the good, who love philosophy?

I don't think that means they are necessarily rare, but rather that they don't immediately attract attention.

After all, it is precisely those who love fortune and power who will draw our eyes toward them.

In a world where loud and boisterous spectacle characterizes those who seek public office, the unassuming becomes invisible.

Humble people slip through the cracks, overlooked and ignored.

We no longer have the eyes to recognize the good, because we have grown so accustomed to illusions and false imaginings.

You can find the good man in any place or position, but it is precisely when he cares for his position that he is no longer good.

I believe most real philosophers, for example, don't get degrees or seek tenure.

Real philosophers could be plumbers, mechanics, salesmen, yes, quite possibly even humble, honest and unassuming bankers or lawyers.

❖ ❖ ❖ ❖ ❖

'What am I to say of power and of the honors of office, which you raise to heaven because you know not true honored power? What fires belched forth from Aetna's flames, what overwhelming flood could deal such ruin as these when they fall into the hands of evil men?

'I am sure you remember how your forefathers wished to do away with the consular power, which had been the very foundation of liberty, because of the overbearing pride of the consuls, just as your ancestors had too in earlier times expunged from the state the name of king on account of the same pride. But if, as rarely happens, places of honor are granted to honest men, what else is delightful in them but the honesty they practice thereby? Wherefore honor comes not to virtue from holding office, but comes to office from virtues there practiced.

'But what is the power which you seek and esteem so highly? O, creatures of the earth, can you not think over whom you are set? If you saw in a community of mice, one mouse asserting his rights and his power over the others, with what mirth you would greet the sight!

'Yet if you consider the body, what can you find weaker than humanity? Cannot a tiny gnat by its bite, or by creeping into the inmost parts, kill that body? How can any exercise right upon any other except upon the body alone, or that which is below the body, whereby I mean the fortunes? Can you ever impose any law upon a free spirit? Can you ever disturb the peculiar restfulness which is the property of a mind that hangs together upon the firm basis of its reason?

'When a certain tyrant thought that by tortures he would compel a free man to betray the conspirators in a plot against his life, the philosopher bit through his tongue and spat it out in the tyrant's face. Thus were the tortures, which the tyrant intended to have cruel results, turned by the philosopher into subjects of high courage. Is there anything that one man can do to another, which he may not suffer from another in his turn?'

—Boethius, *The consolation of Philosophy* Book 2 Prose 6

Power can seem both so enticing and terrifying.

I, for one, have never really had a hankering for it, and I've quite often been scared of it.

Perhaps that has been a blessing, because at the very least I have seen some of the ways we abuse it, and this may help me to avoid wanting to possess it.

On the very few occasions I have been put into a position of authority, I've been more worried about how I am being dragged away from acting with character than I am about finding any pleasure in rule.

Boethius helps me to understand that, just as with wealth, honor, or pleasure, when I seek power for its own sake I have already lost myself.

He repeats the Classical wisdom that honor does not make me good, but the good makes me worthy of honor.

Boethius also reminds me that power is both a petty pursuit, and a fickle one.

I remain just as weak and fragile when I claim to possess it, and it can, and will, bite me back before I even know it.

The amusement we would feel watching a kingdom of mice, or the recognition of the true power of a gnat, reminds me of a proverb my great-grandmother used to tell me:

> *For want of a nail the shoe was lost.*
> *For want of a shoe the horse was lost.*
> *For want of a horse the rider was lost.*
> *For want of a rider the battle was lost.*
> *For want of a battle the kingdom was lost.*
> *And all for the want of a horseshoe nail.*

❖ ❖ ❖ ❖ ❖

Day 164

When some person asked him how it happened that while reason has been more cultivated by the men of the present age, the progress made in former times was greater?

In what respect, he answered, has it been more cultivated now, and in what respect was the progress greater then? For in that in which it has now been more cultivated, in that also the progress will now be found.

At present it has been cultivated for the purpose of resolving syllogisms, and progress is made. But in former times it was cultivated for the purpose of maintaining the governing faculty in a condition conformable to Nature, and progress was made.

Do not, then, mix things which are different and do not expect, when you are laboring at one thing, to make progress in another. But see if any man among us, when he is intent, I see upon this, that keeping himself in a state conformable to Nature and living so always, does not also so make progress. For you will not find such a man.

—Epictetus, *Discourses* 3.6

My own variation on this was when a student asked me why people were better in the old times, but smarter now?
Define your terms, and establish your measure.

Apparently similar questions were asked in the past, just as much as they are in the present.
It's easy to either romanticize or condemn the past or the present, but my sense is that people have always essentially been much the same, even as certain strengths and weaknesses may ebb and flow.

We often think of modernity as scientifically refined, and the past as scientifically ignorant, for example.
We can draw an analogy here to the concept of being "cultivated" that Epictetus speaks of.
We are also conversely tempted to think of people in the past as being wiser and more virtuous, and modernity more being thoughtless and vicious.
We can in like manner parallel this to Seneca's concept of "progress".
In either case, how are we using our terms?

Can we really become more cultivated without making real progress?
What purpose does the cultivation of reason truly serve?
What does it mean to make progress?

Epictetus helps us by clarifying that we may well be using very different standards of judgment.
Perhaps some people mean by cultivation of reason that we value the development of a life virtue according to Nature.
That end will in turn define what progress we seek.
Or perhaps some people mean by cultivation of reason the advancement of logic and calculation.
That end will also, in turn, define what progress we seek.

The former is the development of a moral sense, the latter the pursuit of a technical skill.
I suspect this characterizes, if nothing else, what differentiates the Stoic from the secular materialist.

Ask yourself what you truly care about, and that determines what you consider advancement to be.
Progress isn't just being smarter.
Progress is being better, and no man who loves the good fails to make progress.

❖ ❖ ❖ ❖ ❖

'But even you,' it is retorted, 'cultivate virtue for no other reason than because you hope for some pleasure from it.'

But, in the first place, even though virtue is sure to bestow pleasure, it is not for this reason that virtue is sought; for it is not this, but something more than this that she bestows, nor does she labor for this, but her labor, while directed toward something else, achieves this also.

As in a ploughed field, which has been broken up for corn, some flowers will spring up here and there, yet it was not for these poor little plants, although they may please the eye, that so much toil was expended—the sower had a different purpose, these were superadded -just so pleasure is neither the cause nor the reward of virtue, but its by-product, and we do not accept virtue because she delights us, but if we accept her, she also delights us.

—Seneca the Younger, *On a happy life* 9

The man, the Epicurean, who thinks pleasure can be the only end of all action will assume, by the genetic fallacy, that everyone acts upon this base motive.
It does not occur to him how virtue and pleasure are related, but he believes the first exists for the sake of the second.

The Stoic position has much in common with the distinction made by Aristotle in the *Nicomachean ethics.*
Pleasure does not make all things good, but all good things are pleasurable.
We have our causal wires confused in this matter.

Virtue does indeed give us pleasure, but the pleasure is not the intended goal.
It is a pleasant consequence of having lived rightly.
It's like the cherry on the sundae, the icing on the cake, that cold beer at the end of a hard day, the warmth of the embrace of a loved one after giving anything and everything for their benefit.

A young person is often consumed with the desire for gratification.
I burned with it too, on so many levels, but learned hard and fast that the person who acts rightly will find joy in it, while the person who seeks mere satisfaction will neither be right, not find any joy at all.

❖ ❖ ❖ ❖ ❖

Day 166

Constantly regard the universe as one living being, having one substance and one soul; and observe how all things have reference to one perception, the perception of this one living being; and how all things act with one movement; and how all things are the cooperating causes of all things which exist; observe too the continuous spinning of the thread and the contexture of the web.

—Marcus Aurelius, *Meditations* Book 4

I must once again resist the temptation to go on and on about matters of cosmology and metaphysics, or reflect at length on the distinctions between the subtle concepts of pantheism, panentheism, and causal participation.
It doesn't matter, for our purposes, how you understand the unity of all things.
But know that they are one, and nothing exists in isolation or separation from anything else.

Allow me to once more reference one of my favorite novelists, Dostoyevsky.
In *The brothers Karamazov*, we center our narrative around two brothers, Ivan and Alyosha.
Each holds a very different, and very striking, set of values.
I still recall the first time I was blessed to read of these two approaches with an open mind and heart, because the recognition of their significance was a true epiphany.

Ivan works on the measure that *Everything is permitted.*

Alyosha acts on the standard that *Every one of us is undoubtedly responsible for all men—and everything on earth.*

At first glance, this appears as simple as the contrast between freedom and responsibility.
But please note that both maxims include freedom, and both include responsibility.
It is simply a question of who should be served by that freedom, and to whom we should be responsible.

Likewise, note how radical each statement is.
It isn't simply that choice is good, it's that every choice is good.
It isn't that we are responsible only for what is ours: It's that we are responsible for absolutely everything.

We would like a bit of each, of course, but we can't have it both ways.
As soon as we remove ourselves from one responsibility and relation, we remove ourselves from all responsibilities and relations.
If all is one, we all share in responsibility, directly or indirectly.
But once I fragment or fracture myself from others and the world, I have broken myself off completely.

I don't know if it was Stoicism or Dostoyevsky that taught me this, but I now find insight in seeing any right or a wrong, and knowing that in some way, however small, I have participated in it.
Though I am but a minute part of a glorious whole, the Universe and I are mirrors to one another, and I find that responsibility truly liberating.

❖ ❖ ❖ ❖ ❖

Day 167

If you think that by killing men you can avoid the accuser censoring your lives, you are mistaken; that is not a way of escape which is either possible or honorable; the easiest and the noblest way is not to be crushing others, but to be improving yourselves.

—Socrates , ex Plato, *Apology* 39d

Marcus Aurelius just reminded us never to seek division between things in a universe that is naturally one, and Socrates, with his life on the line, is proving that this principle can be lived fully with character and grace.

I have felt that many things have dragged me down over many years, and they often feel like terrible weights or burdens.
The heavy load of estranged friends, pointless aggressions, and indignant snubbing seems to have taken its toll on me.
What I fail to remember is that none of us need to live this way, and that even if others feel they do, I don't have to play that game.

I was once, in my younger years, having a quarrel with someone.
It wasn't my closest friend, or a romantic love, but just someone I went to class with regularly.
Yet we always very much enjoyed one another's company, and our disagreement was petty.

I was the one that played the offended victim, and looked the other way when she entered the room, while at the same time trying to seem casual.
Don't laugh. You've done it as well.

After about two weeks of this, she walked straight up to me, poked me in the ribs, and said, just like a modern Anne Shirley: "You and I are friends. This is stupid. I'm sorry I was the way I was, and I hope you are, too. Let's be real friends again."

We had a good hug, and resumed where we had left off, two people who cared for one another.
I should have proposed to that girl on the spot, but that would be a story for another time.

Now only if we were all that decent.
She had it right: I never need to fight anyone for the purpose of being better than them, or proving my point.
Ernest Hemingway was himself a man of great struggle and confrontation, but he hit this on the nose:

> *There is nothing noble in being superior to your fellow man; true nobility is being superior to your former self.*

❖ ❖ ❖ ❖ ❖

Day 168

Lay down for yourself from the first a definite stamp and style of conduct, which you will maintain when you are alone and also in the society of men. Be silent for the most part, or, if you speak, say only what is necessary and in a few words.

Talk, but rarely, if occasion calls you, but do not talk of ordinary thing—of gladiators, or horse races, or athletes, or of meats or drink-these are topics that arise everywhere—but above all do not talk about men in blame or compliment or comparison. If you can, turn the conversation of your company by your talk to some fitting subject; but if you should chance to be isolated among strangers, be silent. Do not laugh much, nor at many things, nor without restraint.

—Epictetus, *Enchiridion* 33

I don't think Epictetus is telling us to be gruff, dismissive, or socially withdrawn; that would be yet another aspect of the misguided view of Stoicism.

I suggest, rather, that the Stoic can be sociable, cheerful, and friendly, but what will distinguish him from others will be that he picks his words wisely.

It's as simple as that.

I have often made the mistake of speaking before thinking, and this has often caused great harm.

As the years have passed, and especially when I began to take Stoicism very seriously, I developed the habit of running a routine through my head almost constantly, almost like a little mantra: "How are my words going to do good?"

Will what I am about to say cause benefit or harm?

If I there is any doubt, I try to clam up.

It has made me a much quieter person than I used to be, and I suspect some people worry that my more frequent long pauses during a conversation are the slow creep of senility.

They don't need to know that I'm just trying to be careful.

Observe how most of our conversations are inane, empty chatter.

They are not only hollow, they are downright harmful and hurtful, because empty words make things trivial.

Again, the abuse of words offends truth.

When I first met my wife, and I slowly opened up to her, we were out shopping together, and walked by an old Orthodox Jewish couple calmly sitting on a park bench.

Not a word passed between them, but their eyes sparkled.

My future wife and I looked at one another, and we both immediately knew that we were thinking exactly the same thing.

If we could ever be like that, so happy in silence, we would be blessed.

❖ ❖ ❖ ❖ ❖

215

Day 169

For your body take just so much as your bare need requires, such as food, drink, clothing, house, servants, but cut down all that tends to luxury and outward show.

— Epictetus, *Enchiridion* 33

I laugh at the reference to servants, of course, but that is rather important in the context.
Epictetus is here appealing not only to the everyman, but also to the wealthy gentleman, the patrician who had great social influence and responsibilities.
Such people may have wealth, they may need servants to fulfill their obligations, but they must still be humble and simple.

We don't come across too many humble and unassuming celebrities, politicians, or giants of industry.
They are the exception, not the rule.
It seems they can't help but build up elaborate backdrops of opulence and ostentation to feed their self-love, or perhaps to compensate for their self-loathing.

When I was a teenager, there was a television show called *Lifestyles of the rich and famous.*
It seemed hugely popular, what we now call a water-cooler show.
I absolutely loathed it, because it seemed to canonize decadence.

What we each may need to fulfill our different responsibilities may demand a range of means, it is imprudent and intemperate to add any more.

Instead of saying that I am a teacher who deserves far more than I am given, can I not instead say that I am teacher, and I am grateful that I need very little?

❖ ❖ ❖ ❖ ❖

Day 170

Avoid impurity to the utmost of your power before marriage, but if you must indulge your passion, let it be done lawfully.

But do not be offensive or censorious to those who indulge it, and do not be always bringing up your own chastity. If someone tells you that 'so and so' speaks ill of you, do not defend yourself against what he says, but answer, 'He did not know my other faults, or he would not have mentioned these alone.'

— Epictetus, *Enchiridion* 33

I am far from being a prudish or uptight person about sex, but those who do not understand my thinking often laugh at what appear to be old-fashioned sensibilities.
It isn't that sex is evil or dirty; quite the contrary, it is natural and beautiful.
Sexuality, as one of the deepest expression of human love, is right and good.

Sex becomes a means of doing harm when we abuse it to serve only our own gratification.
We may or not be aware that we do the harm, but we reduce another to a mere object for ourselves.
Even if the objectification is mutual, we simply compound the hurt.
Now we have two objects.

Though promiscuity is one expression of this abuse, one can be just as unchaste in monogamy.
What defines the value is how and why we join desire and love.

And while the word chastity seems so outdated, this is only because we have become a society fueled by selfish pleasure, and this applies to sex as much as it does to business, entertainment, or politics.
We have removed love from the equation, and this leaves us cold and uncaring.

Epictetus understands this, because he reminds us that being chaste is not about boasting of our virtues, or condemning others.
The thoughtful and sympathetic man understands how easy it is to fail.
There is hardly any point in stressing that all things must be done with love, and then not showing hate in my judgment.

I have seen far too often how carelessness, thoughtlessness, and lack of charity in matters of the heart cause deep pain, whether in the offender or the victim.
Seeing these abuses doesn't simply make me angry: It makes me deeply sad.

❖   ❖   ❖   ❖   ❖

Day 171

In your conversation avoid frequent and disproportionate mention of your own doings or adventures; for other people do not take the same pleasure in hearing what has happened to you as you take in recounting your adventures.

— Epictetus, *Enchiridion* 33

This book almost didn't get written because of this passage.

I am always very conscious that pride goes before the fall, and that vainly referring to myself is an obstacle to humility.

I thought for a time that the reflections could be general, with no reference to my own experiences at all, only to realize I couldn't separate my thinking from my living.

I asked myself if the problem was writing about myself, or my motivation in writing about myself.

Accordingly, this isn't a hagiography.

You get the warts and all.

I intend it as an object lesson, and I apologize if it ever comes across as self-serving.

It is intended to humbly serve you, and to help me put myself in my place.

I often meet people who open up to me about themselves.

I suspect that a certain sort of person perceives me as having a sympathetic ear.

It's the reason I spent many parties during my college days listening to girls complaining about their boyfriends, telling me they wished they could date someone like me, but meaning, obviously, not me.

I shamefully admit I am often bored by the monologue, as I may not in the least be interested in their situation.

But I then try to remember that it isn't the story I need to be interested in, it's the actual person, a living, breathing creature, dignified, beautiful, and unique.

I can then listen with genuine attention and honest interest, and be happy to help just by listening.

❖   ❖   ❖   ❖   ❖

Think continually how many physicians are dead after often contracting their eyebrows over the sick; and how many astrologers after predicting with great pretensions the deaths of others; and how many philosophers after endless discourses on death or immortality; how many heroes after killing thousands; and how many tyrants who have used their power over men's lives with terrible insolence as if they were immortal; and how many cities are entirely dead, so to speak, Helice and Pompeii and Herculaneum, and others innumerable. Add to the reckoning all whom thou hast known, one after another. One man after burying another has been laid out dead, and another buries him: and all this in a short time.

To conclude, always observe how ephemeral and worthless human things are, and what was yesterday a little mucus tomorrow will be a mummy or ashes. Pass then through this little space of time conformably to Nature, and end your journey in content, just as an olive falls off when it is ripe, blessing Nature who produced it, and thanking the tree on which it grew.

—Marcus Aurelius, *Meditations* Book 4

I once read this passage to someone, who promptly furrowed his brow, and said, "How dark and depressing!"
My attempts at explanation fell flat, probably because I was a poor champion of the text, or perhaps because the images of weakness and death seemed too much like the cold, uncaring, Gothic Horror world of H.P. Lovecraft.

I understand.
Being reminded about my mortality can seem so depressing.
But Aurelius is making a contrast here, between the ugly and the beautiful, the base and what is noble, the worthless and the priceless.

The vanity, the death, the decay are all images to remind us that our bodies, our reputations, our possessions, and supposed power, are all empty.
But we perhaps overlook the final image.
The ripe olive, falling from the tree, is joyfully content with its Nature and its place within all things.

The frailty of the passing things should redirect us to the great and the noble, the fact that the mind and will can gladly embrace Nature, and be happy in the harmony of the whole.

I often try to practice this as an exercise.
When I find myself in an uncomfortable, frustrating, or tedious situation, I pull back mentally, and search myself for joyful gratitude.
When I can manage it, it's a wonderful relief.

❖   ❖   ❖   ❖   ❖

Day 173

'What then,' you say, 'is the difference between you, the wise man, and me, the fool, if we both wish to have riches?' The very greatest; for in the eyes of a wise man riches are a slave, in the eyes of fool's a master; the wise man grants no importance to riches, to you riches are everything.

You accustom yourself to them and cling to them just as if someone had assured you that they would be a lasting possession; the wise man never reflects so much upon poverty as when he abides in the midst of riches. No general ever trusts so wholly to peace as to fail to make ready for a war that has been declared, even if it is not yet being waged.

As for you, a beautiful house makes you arrogant, just as if it could never be burned or tumble down; you are stupefied by your wealth, just as if it had escaped every risk and had become so great that Fortune had lost all power to destroy it.

Idly you play with your riches, and do not descry the danger they are in—you are like the barbarians who, usually, when they are blockaded, having no knowledge of the engines of war, watch with indifference the effort of the besiegers, and do not surmise the purpose of the constructions that are being erected afar.

So it is with you; you loll in the midst of your possessions, and give no heed to the many disasters that threaten from every side and all too soon will carry off the costly spoils.

But the wise man -whoever steals away his riches will still leave to him all that is his own; for he ever lives happy in the present and unconcerned about the future."

Seneca the Younger, *On a happy life* 15

I have always enjoyed the words of Aeschylus *Ah, lives of men! When prosperous they glitter—like a fair picture; when misfortune comes—a wet sponge at one blow has blurred the painting.*

Recall that the Stoic does not despise wealth, or consider it an evil: He knows that it is indifferent, and that its value depends on our estimation of it.
  The good man can use wealth just as much as the bad man, but what makes all the difference is how he uses it.
  Will I learn how to master it, or will I permit it to master me?
  Will I become its unwitting victim?
  Will I be the deer in headlights?

I note especially Seneca's observation that the lover of wealth and fortune is oblivious to the danger to his soul.
  His ignorance is, however, far from being bliss.
  I have often compared it to the horror of watching the various pieces of an impending traffic accident play themselves out.
  Time slows down, you see each vehicle, each on its own path, and you realize that, however oblivious the drivers or passengers, this will not end well.

I used to think I was unfortunate to grow up among wealthy and fashionable people, while not being at all wealthy or fashionable myself.
  Early on, I was jealous and resented them.
  I sometimes despised them.
  As time passed, I asked myself how I could use that experience to my benefit.

Besides serving as a warning of what not to be, it helped to understand why one could be drawn into false goods, how image and vanity cloud our appreciation of what is truly good about our nature.

The trendy crowds with their platinum cards at the upscale local shopping malls in my old hometown now seemed more like zombies than dastardly villains.

❖ ❖ ❖ ❖ ❖

Day 174

Who of us does not marvel at the action of Lycurgus the Spartan? For when he had been blinded in one eye by one of his fellow-citizens and had received the young man at the hands of the people to punish as he saw fit, he did not choose to do this, but trained him instead and made a good man of him, and afterward escorted him to the public theatre.

And when the Spartans regarded him with amazement, he said: 'This man I received from you an insolent and violent creature; I return him to you a reasonable man and a good citizen.'

—Musonius Rufus, *Fragments* 39

The reader already knows that I am far too sentimental and a hopeless romantic, so it should come as no surprise how this story moves me.
The Spartans were a fascinating bunch.

I still recall one of my favorite high school teachers telling us about the phrase Spartan mothers said to their sons before sending them into battle: *Come home with your shield, or on it.*
Fight with courage, earn victory, or return dead.

This may make them sound heartless.
But Lycurgus, the legendary founder of Spartan law, wasn't just about toughness.
He was about the building of virtue and character, and Musonius' passage reminds us just how deeply a man like Lycurgus cared about others.
He didn't seek vengeance.
He tried to help others become better.
Love is the law.

On a simply instinctive level, I have always been troubled by people who give no heed or concern to the needs, feelings, and wellbeing of others, whether their friends or enemies.

My slow education in Stoicism, in principle and in practice, taught me that one of the essential aspects of the philosophy was its deep commitment to others.
It was not simply self-serving posturing.
It was sincere, humble, heart-felt.
Even the philosophers who expound on all its other characteristics all too often neglect this aspect of Stoicism.

❖ ❖ ❖ ❖ ❖

What is sweeter than to have someone with whom you dare to discuss everything, as if with yourself? How could there be great joy in prosperous things, if you did not have someone who would enjoy them equally much as you yourself? Disasters would be hard indeed to bear without someone who would bear them even more heavily than yourself.

Finally, other things which are sought after are individual advantages for entirely individual things: riches that you may use them, resources that you may be looked after, honors that you may be praised, pleasures that you may enjoy them, health that you may be free from pain and make use of the gifts of the body; friendship contains very many things: wherever you turn, it is present, it is shut out from no place, is never unseasonable, never troublesome; thus we do not use water, we do not use fire, as they put it, in more contexts than friendship.

I am not now talking about the ordinary or regular friendship, although it delights and benefits, but about the true and perfect friendship, of the sort which existed between those few who are famous for this. For friendship both makes favorable things more splendid and disasters lighter, by splitting and sharing them.

—Cicero, *To Laelius on friendship* 22, tr Stout

In the previous passage, I reflected that many sadly ignore the deep sense of caring inherent in Stoicism.
It isn't just a Hallmark card type of sentimentalism: I think it to be a conviction grounded in the deepest character.

Cicero's observations on friendship are yet another instance of this admirable quality.
Though a sense of self-reliance lies at the heart of Stoicism, this does not mean a life of isolation.
The friend becomes a second self, where joys are multiplied by being shared, suffering tempered by being carried together.
It deserves to be repeated that true friendship is the love of others for their sake, not for my sake, and as such it carries no conditions or demands.

For far too long I was too stubborn to grasp that, whatever our differences or disagreements, my family have been true friends.
I often struggled by seeing friendship only by its abuse or absence in others, and it was a hard lesson to discover that people I thought of as friends disappeared when I was no longer convenient.

But this cannot be a matter for resentment, which is a poison to any Stoic peace.
It must be an opportunity for improvement.
I cannot myself give up on friendship because others may have given up on it.
As always, that would be allowing myself to be ruled by my circumstances.
I must forgive the weaknesses of others, but conquer my own.

❖ ❖ ❖ ❖ ❖

Day 176

When you imagine some pleasure, beware that it does not carry you away, like other imaginations. Wait a while, and give yourself pause. Next remember two things: how long you will enjoy the pleasure, and also how long you will afterwards repent and revile yourself? And set on the other side the joy and self-satisfaction you will feel if you refrain. And if the moment seems come to realize it, take heed that you be not overcome by the winning sweetness and attraction of it; set in the other scale the thought how much better is the consciousness of having vanquished it.

—Epictetus, *Enchiridion* 34

Epictetus offers us not only an insight, but also another practical exercise in the practice of Stoicism.
Not only in theory, but also at the very moment, I can think through my choice.

I can take pause, as any hasty decision is intrinsically suspect.
I can then do an ethical version of a cost-benefit analysis.
Can I honestly tell myself that the value of the selfish pleasure will outweigh the moral loss that may follow it?
And how would that temporary satisfaction compare to the joy of having acted with temperance and self-control?

This seems an impossible task in the heat of the moment, but I assure you, from hard experience, that it is far from impossible.
I attempted to follow the advice a number of times, and indeed fell flat.
It seemed like the force of desire was overwhelming.

Then, one day I tried something different.
Instead of thinking about the immediate choice in front of me, I recollected a similar past decision.
With hindsight, I saw how I had allowed myself to be enslaved by passion, not rule myself with reason and love.
I then compared that past situation with the one now in front of me, saw how they were quite alike, and made the right choice with far greater ease.

Desire is indeed powerful, but I can triangulate it, so to speak, by contrasting it to past desires and actions that are now much clearer in my mind.
I suggested this approach once to a friend who was suffering from a painkiller addiction, and while I can certainly not claim to be an expert in the matter, he was kind enough to listen and make an attempt.

One evening, he called me for help.

He was close to having a relapse, and wanted to know if I could come sit with him.

I was glad to do so, but instead of merely preaching at him, or threatening him with dire consequences, we looked at that bag of pills he had in front of him.

He desired them. I asked him to simply wait for a moment, and to remember what happened the last time he fell off the wagon.

Was that a good experience?

Did it even make him feel good?

Did the pleasure then justify the guilt and loss later?

We flushed those pills that very night, and he is still clean after two years.

It wasn't my doing, it was entirely his, and the only thing I brought to the table was stolen fair and square, word for word, from Epictetus.

❖ ❖ ❖ ❖ ❖

Day 177

Always run to the short way; and the short way is the natural: accordingly say and do everything in conformity with the soundest reason. For such a purpose frees a man from trouble, and warfare, and all artifice and ostentatious display.

—Marcus Aurelius, *Meditations* Book 4

When I was a teenager, the phrase "Keep it simple, stupid" was quite popular. No need for the "stupid" part, I think, just to make a clever acronym, but the lesson is a good one.

Why do we choose to make our lives more complex, more winding and indirect, and thereby more burdensome?
Life demands very little for happiness.
I often wonder if we put more obstacles in our way, and take the longer road, as a way to defer our commitment to an authentic life.
The diversions may well be a way to distract ourselves from our inner knowledge that we have put off answering the most basic question: Why am I here?

The shameless practice of self–promotion has much to do with this.
The irony is, I think, that we deliberately wish others to see our outer appearance, all our worldly achievements, while we dance around the true inner self, which is just as scared and uncertain as he was on that first day of school.
We are taking the longer way around, and desperately avoiding the elephant in the room.

My sometimes fiery temperament can get riled up by seeing some of my college and graduate school friends going through complex baroque motions to immortalize their successes, in what Aurelius rightly calls ostentatious display.

These were the same people who would sometimes sit with me and cry, pouring out all their deep existential worries.
They were right to have those worries, and I was glad to sit with them and at least be able to listen, if not help.
But the virtue of charity demands that I learn to see them with compassion, and never with anger.
I must continue to struggle with this habit.

❖ ❖ ❖ ❖ ❖

Day 178

If anyone says that the best life of all is to sail the sea, and then adds that I must not sail upon a sea where shipwrecks are a common occurrence and there are often sudden storms that sweep the helmsman in an adverse direction, I conclude that this man, although he lauds navigation, really forbids me to launch my ship.

—Seneca the Younger, *On leisure* 9, tr Basore

I can't tell you how many times I've been preached to about changing my life.
I've learned to only start listening when I see the preacher actually practicing what he preaches.
We are confidently given the noble principle, only to hear conditions, qualifications, and appeals to being realistic.

One friend, a person I still have deep love and respect for, once advised me to embrace the progressive attitude of going green.
If only I changed my diet and lifestyle by embracing right nutrition, ecological soundness, and bought products that were socially conscious, I would find bliss.

"But you are still a corporate lawyer for Nestlé, right?" I'm reminded of the old *Beyond the fringe* skit, where the hypocritical journalist explains that his excuse for selling out is that he is fighting the system from within.

Another friend, a religious conservative, advised me that I would find happiness if I just submitted my will to the Church, and if I was humble enough to understand that money and power didn't matter.

"Then why do you spend all your time making money from your telecommunications business?"

"Well, that's different. I'm doing that for the Glory of God."

We need to take a rather deep breath and be completely honest with ourselves.
Who we are, what we value, and whether we live with character has nothing to do with our fancy posing for the camera.
Put your money where your mouth is.
Excuses don't cut it.

❖ ❖ ❖ ❖ ❖

'But,' she said, 'do not think that I would urge implacable war upon Fortune. There are times when her deception of men has certain merits: I mean when she discovers herself, unveils her face, and proclaims her ways. Perhaps you do not yet understand what I would say. It is a strange thing that I am trying to say, and for that reason I can scarcely explain myself in words. I think that ill fortune is of greater advantage to men than good fortune.

'Good fortune is ever lying when she seems to favor by an appearance of happiness. Ill fortune is ever true when by her changes she shows herself inconstant. The one deceives; the other edifies. The one by a deceitful appearance of good things enchains the minds of those who enjoy them: the other frees them by the knowledge that happiness is so fragile.

'You see, then, that the one is blown about by winds, is ever moving and ever ignorant of its own self; the other is sober, ever prepared and ever made provident by the undergoing of its very adversities. Lastly, good fortune draws men from the straight path of true good by her fawning: ill fortune draws most men to the true good, and holds them back by her curved staff.

'And do you think that this should be reckoned among the least benefits of this rough, unkind, and terrible ill fortune, that she has discovered to you the minds of your faithful friends?

'Fortune has distinguished for you your sure and your doubtful friends; her departure has taken away her friends and left you yours. At what price could you have bought this benefit if you had been untouched and, as you thought, fortunate? Cease then to seek the wealth you have lost. You have found your friends, and they are the most precious of all riches.'

—Boethius, *The consolation of Philosophy* Book 2 Prose 7

Lady Philosophy reminds us that all fortune can be good fortune, and that what we consider misfortune can actually be the best fortune of all.
 The good luck can all too readily make us dependent and complacent, the bad luck can serve as a means to become responsible and virtuous.
 The beautiful irony, once again, is that suffering evil gives the good man the opportunity to do what is good, while receiving benefits makes the bad man even weaker.
Boethius is offering his own account of the Stoic Turn.
 We must be careful, of course, to not simply swap the terms good fortune and bad fortune.
 Each can be good or bad, and is in itself indifferent, because the value depends upon our judgment and action, but each can be of harm or benefit to the bad or good man in very different ways.

I met a man once, whose name I never learned and who I never saw again, who told me that the
 best thing that ever happened to him was Black Monday, the stock market crash of 1987.
 He lost millions.
 "All that stuff was killing me, making me full of myself, all so sure that they made the world for
 me.
 When I lost it all, I grew up, and started becoming a man."

I hardly know if he was aware of Stoicism, or had read Boethius, but he understood the spirit.
 I laughed at him then, dismissive, as I was prone to be in my youth, but I'm hardly laughing now.

❖ ❖ ❖ ❖ ❖

Day 180

If I had followed the multitude, I should not have studied philosophy.
—Chrysippus ex Diogenes Laertius, *The lives and opinions of eminent philosophers* 7.182

Chrysippus, like Plato, is not being a snob or anti-democratic when he squints at the will of the majority.
He is dubious of it because the desire to conform to what is popular can so readily fly in the face of the truth.

Democracy, the rule, of the many, can be used and abused, just like any other form of rule; but democracy has a particular weakness in that it can mislead us into thinking that something is good simply because it is fashionable.

This is not a just question of theory, but of practical experience.
The appeal to popularity is a deeply powerful one, and the prudent man has often seen evidence, time and time again, of how readily the power of the mob tramples reason and charity.

Any system will only by fair and just where we follow the true and the good, where philosophy is our guide.
But the attraction of mere conformity, being fueled by passion loosed from reason, is in direct contrast to the ability to think for oneself.

In a perfect world, a philosophical multitude would be quite common; in the reality of the world we live in, it is a rarity, because the temptations of honor and power are inherently opposed to a mind that loves the truth.

❖ ❖ ❖ ❖ ❖

Day 181

Every man's body is a measure for his property, as the foot is the measure for his shoe. If you stick to this limit, you will keep the right measure; if you go beyond it, you are bound to be carried away down a precipice in the end; just as with the shoe, if you once go beyond the foot, your shoe puts on gilding, and soon purple, and embroidery. For when once you go beyond the measure there is no limit.

—Epictetus, *Enchiridion* 39

I have referred to the importance of considering a proper measure, or standard of judgment, in other passages, and so I appreciate the treatment Epictetus offers us.
As a shoe is to be measured by the foot, and not beyond it, happiness is to be measured by the man, and never by anything additional or extraneous.

The nature of a foot is to allow a man to walk, and the shoe to assist him in walking.
When the shoe does any more than that, it moves beyond the measure of the foot.

The nature of a man is to know, to love, to act with virtue.
Once we are concerned with any further trappings beyond what assists him in being wise and good, we have moved beyond the measure of a man.

Add all the glitter, glamor, or additions you might like.
They won't make a better shoe, and they won't make a better man.

❖ ❖ ❖ ❖ ❖

Day 182

What we are seeking, therefore, is how the mind may always pursue a steady and favorable course, may be well-disposed towards itself, and may view its condition with joy, and suffer no interruption of this joy, but may abide in a peaceful state, being never uplifted nor ever cast down. This will be tranquility.

—Seneca the Younger, *On tranquility of mind* 2, tr Basore

A state of peace and happiness isn't merely measured by our feelings.
It is guided by our understanding, by our knowledge of our world, and ourselves by an awareness of what is right, true, and good.

I have lately realized that, over the years, I have come to know three things about myself that were not immediately apparent.
Each is, in turn, a necessary tool in my pursuit of joy.
When I forget these things about myself, I end up straying from the path.

First, I am not a person given any extraordinary or exceptional ability or advantage.
There is no special place for me in the halls of honor, wealth, and power.
For that I am grateful, because it reduces the temptation to be enslaved by my circumstances.

Second, there is no "Golden Ticket", no "Get Out of Jail Free Card", no "Instant Happy Ending".
I cannot rest in the assumption that somehow, everything will just work out.
For that I am grateful, because it helps me to be responsible for my own happiness.

Third, the defining pain of my life, the loss of my best friend, can be borne and harnessed through my own thinking.
I was simply one of a string of men she found interesting for a time.
She most likely remembers very little about me.
For that I am grateful, because I should never measure myself through the estimation of another.

These realizations are not themselves the fullness of tranquility, but they are the conditions for it in my own particular situation.

❖ ❖ ❖ ❖ ❖

In the morning when you rise unwillingly, let this thought be present—I am rising to the work of a human being. Why then am I dissatisfied if I am going to do the things for which I exist and for which I was brought into the world?

Or have I been made for this, to lie in the bedclothes and keep myself warm? 'But this is more pleasant.' Do you exist then to take your pleasure, and not at all for action or exertion? Do you not see the little plants, the little birds, the ants, the spiders, the bees working together to put in order their several parts of the universe? And are you unwilling to do the work of a human being, and do you not make haste to do that which is according to your nature?

'But it is necessary to take rest also.' It is necessary: however Nature has fixed bounds to this too: she has fixed bounds both to eating and drinking, and yet you go beyond these bounds, beyond what is sufficient; yet in thy acts it is not so, but you stop short of what you can do.

So you love not yourself, for if you did, you would love your Nature and her will. But those who love their several arts exhaust themselves in working at them unwashed and without food; but you value your own nature less than the turner values the turning art, or the dancer the dancing art, or the lover of money values his money, or the vainglorious man his little glory.

And such men, when they have a violent affection to a thing, choose neither to eat nor to sleep, rather than to perfect the things which they care for. But are the acts which concern society more vile in your eyes and less worthy of your labor?

—Marcus Aurelius, *Meditations* Book 5

I have been a teacher now for a quarter century, and the year does not pass, at any sort of school or in any sort of class, where I don't come across at least one lazy student, and also at least one lazy student who complains incessantly, playing the world's smallest violin, about how learning isn't fun.

I used to make noble attempts to use reason to convince them of the truth.
That I do so less now is not because I've become cynical, but because I know I'm working from an entirely different set of values.
The words of reason will fall flat, because they appeal to nothing the pleasure-seeker cares for.
I prefer to dedicate my efforts to example, and to the school of hard knocks.

But let us find any and every way we can to ask others to consider why they were made as they are.
Can pleasure and gratification, and the sloth and gluttony that go with them, truly be the measure of our existence?
How can it be that all other living things are defines by the excellence of their activities, which bring the deepest satisfaction, but we are to be defined by our passivity?

"But I can be totally happy just having fun."

No you can't, and I know that for two reasons.

First, from reflection, because I can grasp, however poorly, what it means to be human, and it is apparent to me that you don't act with Nature.

The fact that you don't recognize your nature doesn't make you happy; it just makes you ignorant, like a dog drinking anti-freeze.

It tastes real good, but it is deadly.

Second, from experience, you say you are happy, but you do nothing but complain.

If you were happy, you would be content in virtually any circumstance, but you think your circumstances rule you.

You have forgotten who and what you are, so you are not happy.

Aurelius says it even more bluntly: You don't even love yourself, because you don't even know yourself.

To be entirely fair to some of my students, many of whom are still growing into the truth, I see the same things in the wheeler-dealers of our world.

Look at the folks jostling for attention, grappling for scraps of fortune and fame, and tell me that they are happy.

Their frantic anxiety reveals their inner loss.

Even then, let us find ways to help our fellow men, not to condemn them.

❖ ❖ ❖ ❖ ❖

How should exile be an obstacle to the cultivation of the things that are one's own and to the acquisition of virtue, when no one was ever hindered from the knowledge and practice of what is needful because of exile?

May it not even be true that exile contributes to that end, since it furnishes men leisure and a greater opportunity for learning the good and practicing it than formerly, in that they are not forced by what only seems to be their fatherland into performing political duties, and they are not annoyed by their kinsmen nor by men who only seem to be their friends, who are skillful in fettering them and dragging them away from the pursuit of better things?

In fact, there have been cases where exile was an absolute blessing as it was to Diogenes, who by his exile was transformed from an ordinary citizen into a philosopher, and instead of sitting idly in Sinope, he busied himself in Greece, and in the pursuit of virtue came to surpass the philosophers.

—Musonius Rufus, *Lectures* 9

We've already seen observations about exile from Seneca and Boethius.
The concept was an important one for the Ancients, since exile from one's home was considered one of the greatest of punishments and burdens.
Even Socrates was willing to face death over exile, though not because of the pain associated with either, but on account of how they reflected upon his character.

Just as Boethius told us a few passages ago, a misfortune can actually be good fortune.
A hardship can be a blessing in disguise, and a punishment can be a means to redemption.

The fact that I am in "exile" from my old family home isn't anyone else's fault.
There may be thoughtlessness or carelessness on the part of others, but the inability to face this is mine alone:
I haven't built up the good habits necessary to confront it yet.
And that helps me not to resent, but to cope, however slowly, and there we already have an improvement.

Perhaps we might offer an addendum to an earlier rule.
Don't simply meet hate with love, but also meet indifference with love, just as much. I personally find the latter much harder to deal with.
Both are the opposites of love, in different senses; to be exiled from the heart of others need not be your end.
It can be your beginning.

I need not stop loving because I am not loved.
In fact, it wouldn't be love if I did.

❖ ❖ ❖ ❖ ❖

*'But I am rich and I want nothing.' Why, then, do you pretend to be a philosopher? Your
golden and your silver vessels are enough for you. What need have you of principles?*

*'But I am also a judge of the Greeks.' Do you know how to judge? Who taught you to
know? 'Caesar wrote to me a codicil.' Let him write and give you a commission to judge of
music; and what will be the use of it to you? Still how did you become a judge? Whose
hand did you kiss? The hand of Symphorus or Numenius? Before whose bedchamber have
you slept? To whom have you sent gifts? Then do you not see that to be a judge is just of
the same value as Numenius is?*

'But I can throw into prison any man whom I please.' So you can do with a stone.

*'But I can beat with sticks whom I please.' So you may be a jackass. This is not a governing
of men. Govern us as rational animals; show us what is profitable to us, and we will follow
it; show us what is unprofitable, and we will turn away from it.*

*Make us imitators of yourself, as Socrates made men imitators of himself. For he was like a
governor of men, who made subject to him their desires, their aversion, their movements
toward an object and their turning away from it.*

*'Do this: do not do this: if you do not obey, I will throw you into prison.' This is not
governing men like rational animals.*

—Epictetus, *Discourses* 3.7

There was a time, when I was young, where I embraced political ideals.
I honestly believed that party politics could improve things, and that a dedication to social change
and a commitment to political manifestos would make the world a better place.

I do not begrudge anyone such a dedication; after all, I am a student of philosophy, so I cannot
throw stones when it comes to a love of high ideals.
But my own constitution and my own experience tell me that my own efforts are best spent
elsewhere.
This is not because the pursuit of politics is in itself a bad thing at all, but I find it too hard to bear
the politicians who abuse it.

I see far too many people around me in positions of power and authority who are exactly as
Epictetus describes.
Too many of them worship wealth, take pride in their titles, and appeal to their power to coerce
and intimidate.
They too often think they are fine thinkers and judges, but their thinking is base and self-
absorbed.

I once had a very unusual experience.
I had finished playing at a South Boston Irish pub, and sat down for a pint.
A perfectly amiable fellow struck up a conversation with me, and he actually seemed interested in
some things I had to say, which, let me tell you, is quite rare.
I become rather impassioned, and just a bit eloquent, about my commitment to grass-roots
government, as I recall.

"We need young people like you in the party, we need to snag you before the other party does."
I was confused, but I realized later I was supposed to know who he was.
He asked if he could contact me in a week or so. I gave him my number, and thought no more of it.

A week later, his secretary called me, and I found myself in his office on Beacon Hill.
"We can sell this. You're from a working class Boston Irish family, all that meat-and-potatoes bullshit, but you're an egghead doing a doctorate. The quirky music thing is an attention grabber, too, that'll sell some copy.
Teacher-musician-grass-roots man of the people kind of crap, people eat that stuff up.
We'll set you up for a City Council run, which you'll loose, of course.
But your name will be out there, and we'll run you again.
Then we'll have you win.
And then you'll be sitting pretty, my friend.
You'll have to get yourself a wife so they don't think you're queer, because you could come off that way.
We won't play to that demographic…."
He went on like this for a while.

I still have no idea if he actually meant a word he said, or what he really wanted.
It all seemed completely surreal, and in hindsight I still can't explain what had happened.
I was polite, smiled, nodded, and went on my way after having a drink with him at the bar across the street.
I never returned any more of his calls.
Because the entire time he was speaking to me I felt dirty, covered in the filth of manufactured power and self-promotion.
No, just no.

❖ ❖ ❖ ❖ ❖

Day 186

Be not disgusted, nor discouraged, nor dissatisfied, if you do not succeed in doing everything according to right principles; but when you have failed, return back again, and be content if the greater part of what you do is consistent with man's nature, and love this to which you return; and do not return to philosophy as if she were a master, but act like those who have sore eyes and apply a bit of sponge and egg, or as another applies a plaster, or drenching with water. For thus you will not fail to obey reason, and you will repose in it.

—Marcus Aurelius, *Meditations* Book 5

I get easily discouraged, and failure brings me down too easily.
 Part of that is my personality, I think, and another part is that I've developed very bad habits about confidence through my disappointments.
 When I fail, I am too readily tempted to give up.

I know it need not be this way.
 I am finally learning to not only understand, but also to practice, the truth that a failure need not be a discouragement.
 It is an encouragement, a tool for my improvement, if only I choose to make it so.

I can laugh at myself, brush myself off, and do it again.
 There's a fine old truism about this, but I see it as saying something that is actually important:
 Failure isn't about falling down, failure is about staying down.

I am also learning not to treat philosophy as a harsh, judging, and vengeful guide or master, but as a comforter and a soothing panacea for my wounds.
 She is kind and loving, patient and understanding, never dismissive or resentful of me.

Nature herself is also like this, and for all the terrifying force and power with which she acts, she is driven through love.

Finally, Providence, and the Divine, however you choose to understand it, the source and measure of all order and meaning, does not neglect me, for I know I have my place within all things.

❖ ❖ ❖ ❖ ❖

Can anything be sillier than the point of view of certain people—I mean those who boast of their foresight? They keep themselves very busily engaged in order that they may be able to live better; they spend life in making ready to live!

They form their purposes with a view to the distant future; yet postponement is the greatest waste of life; it deprives them of each day as it comes, it snatches from them the present by promising something hereafter. The greatest hindrance to living is expectancy, which depends upon the morrow and wastes today.

—Seneca the Younger, *On the shortness of life* 8, tr Basore

We so easily spend all our time planning to be happy, and then forget about actually being happy.

When I came to college, from a high school that encouraged freedom of thought and expression, I did not quite know what I wanted to do in my future.
I just knew what I wanted to do then and there, to learn, to experience, to understand myself, my world, and my Creator as best I could.
I was, I suppose, already a Stoic at heart, though I did not yet know it.

I was a bit taken aback how so many of my fellow students, at least the serious ones, had their whole lives already planned out.
For many of them, their dedication to the plan was immovable.
The goal, which was a career measured by worldly standards, was all that mattered.
They might let off steam, fall into drink and sex for the weekend, but during the week they were all business.

I do not exaggerate when I say that the lost love of my life already had a house picked out for us in our sophomore year, from which we would proceed to be an environmental law professor and a medieval philosophy professor respectively.
There would be three children, spaced strategically, with private education already planned out.

I never thought like that, and that's probably one of the reasons why I was ultimately not asked to live in that idealized house.

I never thought I would be where I am now, and I'm glad I never thought about it one bit.
Life is to be lived, not categorized, ordered, or reduced to a game of Chutes and Ladders.

❖ ❖ ❖ ❖ ❖

Now they are worthy of friendship who have within their own souls the reason for their being loved. A rare class indeed! And really everything splendid is rare, and nothing is harder to find than something which in all respects is a perfect specimen of its kind.

But the majority of men recognize nothing whatever in human experience as good unless it brings some profit and they regard their friends as they do their cattle, valuing most highly those which give hope of the largest gain.

Thus do they fail to attain that loveliest, most spontaneous friendship, which is desirable in and for itself; and they do not learn from their own experience what the power of such friendship is and are ignorant of its nature and extent.

For everyone loves himself, not with a view of acquiring some profit himself from his self-love, but because he is dear to himself on his own account; and unless this same feeling were transferred to friendship, the real friend would never be found; for he is, as it were, another self.

—Cicero, *To Laelius on friendship* 80

This passage, quite by accident, links nicely to the previous one.

Most of my college peers had the plan, the end of success they desired, and other people either fit into that plan as beneficial, in which case they were maintained, or they did not, in which case they were discarded.

I recently received an e-mail from one such person, after decades, reintroducing himself, and inquiring, in deepest sincerity, about how I was doing. I started the countdown in my head...3...2 ...1, Oh, and by the way, can you do me a professional favor?

I do my best to not feel anger or resentment, but that is very difficult when I realize that, for some people, I am simply a means to an end.

It does not occur to them that they are doing harm, because the only good in their estimation is their own success.

I try to act with respect for their dignity, even as they deny me mine.

A friend, as Cicero, says so beautifully, is to be loved for his own sake, and end in himself, and never for any further profit.

Do not be saddened that the many do not understand this; be gladdened that this makes true friendship all the more precious and joyful.

❖ ❖ ❖ ❖ ❖

As we exercise ourselves against sophistical questions, so we ought to exercise ourselves daily against appearances; for these appearances also propose questions to us.

'A certain person's son is dead.' Answer: the thing is not within the power of the will: it is not an evil.

'A father has disinherited a certain son. What do you think of it?' It is a thing beyond the power of the will, not an evil.

'Caesar has condemned a person.' It is a thing beyond the power of the will, not an evil.

The man is afflicted at this.' Affliction is a thing which depends on the will: it is an evil. ' He has borne the condemnation bravely.

'That is a thing within the power of the will: it is a good. If we train ourselves in this manner, we shall make progress; for we shall never assent to anything of which there is not an appearance capable of being comprehended.

Your son is dead. What has happened? Your son is dead. Nothing more? Nothing. Your ship is lost. What has happened? Your ship is lost. A man has been led to prison. What has happened? He has been led to prison. But that herein he has fared badly, every man adds from his own opinion.

'But Zeus,' you say, 'does not do right in these matters.' Why? Because he has made you capable of endurance? Because he has made you magnanimous? Because he has taken from that which befalls you the power of being evil? Because it is in your power to be happy while you are suffering what you suffer; because he has opened the door to you, when things do not please you? Man, go out and do not complain.

—Epictetus, *Discourses* 3.8

I feel an instinctive resentment when anyone tells me not to complain, but, always one who is seeking reasons, I decide upon gratitude when I am taught why I have no cause to complain.

I am not the sum of my circumstances.
 I am greater than my circumstances.
 You may harm me, cause me pain, trip me in my path, and cripple my body or my emotions.
 Still, I will choose to recognize who and what I am, and the true reason why I am here.

There is no shame in righteous pride, only in self-serving arrogance.
 It is right for each and every one of us to be proud of our nature.
 I have lost a son, been rejected by people I love, been condemned by those in power.
 I once let these things rule me.

They still hurt, sometimes so much that I think I cannot bear them for one more moment.
 Yet hurt can be considered, it can be judged, it can be risen above.
 Hate me or hurt me, and I will do my best not to hate or hurt, but to love.
 That is why I am here.
 That is entirely within my power.

❖ ❖ ❖ ❖ ❖

That which does no harm to the state, does no harm to the citizen. In the case of every appearance of harm apply this rule: if the state is not harmed by this, neither am I harmed. But if the state is harmed, you must not be angry with him who does harm to the state. Show him where his error is.

—Marcus Aurelius, *Meditations* Book 5

That which is not good for the swarm, neither is it good for the bee.

—Marcus Aurelius, *Meditations* Book 6

This last year I have been teaching a Speech and Debate class.
This is something new for me, as I have never really been any good at rhetoric.
I will think a problem through, and I have, most likely to my detriment, far less interest in wrapping it up in an attractive package.
I always look to the content first, the appearance second.
It would seem this probably isn't the best job for someone like me.

But I do very much appreciate one of the three topics we are studying for this round of Lincoln–Douglas debates. "Resolved: When in conflict, the right to individual privacy is more important than national security."

Like Marcus Aurelius, I see here nothing less than a false dichotomy, a seeming contradiction that isn't a contradiction at all.
Why should this be an either/or set of propositions?
Why can't they be entirely compatible?

What is good for the part must be good for the whole, and what is good for the whole must be good for the part, not just some or many of the parts, but all of the parts.
I cannot say that society is served if an individual member of that society is harmed.
As always, the ends do not justify the means.

I offer no apology for my steadfast, Stoic objection to a utilitarian set of ethics.
The steadfastness is not out of stubborn conformity to rules, but out of a deep commitment to offering respect and love to each and every person.
If you harm one, you harm them all.

❖ ❖ ❖ ❖ ❖

Day 191

Life is divided into three periods—that which has been, that which is, that which will be. Of these the present time is short, the future is doubtful, the past is certain.

For the last is the one over which Fortune has lost control, it is the one which cannot be brought back under any man's power. But men who are engrossed lose this; for they have no time to look back upon the past, and even if they should have, it is not pleasant to recall something they must view with regret.

—Seneca the Younger, *On the shortness of life* 10

It should be all too apparent that I am often what Seneca calls "engrossed", and that I have an unhealthy dwelling on the past is in my blood.

This is one of the biggest difficulties I struggle to overcome.

Though I cannot necessarily control my feelings, I can control my thinking about those feelings.

When I was younger I lived for the future, and therefore depended on what was doubtful.

When some things went horribly wrong, I gave up on the future entirely, and brooded on the past, which I could never do anything about.

In my mid-twenties I actually convinced myself, fueled by reading too much romantic poetry, watching too many independent existential films, and listening to too many Marillion songs, that I wouldn't make it past thirty.

I actually felt comfort that I was close to the finish line!

I suspect one reason my Black Dog got worse as I got older was that this illusion of the quick end was shattered.

So now I endeavor to live for the present, and ironically my illness, which actually makes my future deeply uncertain, helps me to not flee to the past as I did before, but embrace the now.

I think that is, at least, an improvement, for which I am grateful.

Giving the wife a kiss, or teaching a single hour of class, or just sitting with the children, takes on a whole new meaning when valuing each and every moment simply for itself.

❖ ❖ ❖ ❖ ❖

Day 192

To share the common notion that we shall be despised by others if in every way we do not strive to harm the first enemies we meet is the mark of mean-minded and ignorant men. For we say that the despicable man is recognized among other things by his inability to harm his enemies, but actually he is much more easily recognized by his inability to help them.

—Musonius Rufus, *Fragments* 41

I was never one to think it good to hurt my enemies, but I recognize that it is a common ideal for many people:

the athlete who takes pride in defeating his opponent, not merely playing a good game;

the policeman who enjoys taking down the criminal, not just protecting the innocent;

the academic who chuckles with glee in insulting his ideological rival, not just loving the truth;

or the lawyer who celebrates winning his case because it has stroked his ego, not just because he has defended the law.

We often admire the wrong sort of toughness, a sense of victory that revolves around destroying another, not doing good for all.

In Plato's *Republic*, the character of Polemarchus defines justice as *doing good for one's friends, and harming one's enemies.*

I truly think that is one of our problems.

As Socrates answers, and as we also see in the Gospels, why should be hate anyone?

I feel anger as much as the next fellow, and my unreliable temper can sometimes run away from me, so I have to consciously remind myself, time and time again, that even someone who has hurt me, or for whom I feel resentment, deserves as much love and assistance as the person who is kind to me.

Perhaps he deserves even more, because he needs it more?

❖ ❖ ❖ ❖ ❖

Day 193

'By Love are peoples too kept bound together by a treaty which they may not break. Love binds with pure affection the sacred tie of wedlock, and speaks its bidding to all trusty friends. O happy race of mortals, if your hearts are ruled as is the universe, by Love!'
—Boethius, *The consolation of Philosophy* Book 2 Meter 8

I was once leaving a college classroom, and overheard two of my students having a very serious conversation as I passed by them.

The young fellow was trying to convince his girlfriend not to leave him, and his face showed sadness and panic.

"I used to love you," she said, "but I don't anymore."

I had to catch myself from laughing out loud, not in mockery or derision of either of them, but out of amazement at the meaning of that phrase.

What she meant, of course, was that she once had affection for him, but that it had faded.

She most certainly did not mean love, rightly understood.

Love is an unbreakable treaty, because it is a choice, a commitment to share in the good of and for another without condition.

Just as the laws of physics bring all matter together and give order universally, the law of love admits of no exceptions.

Aristotle often spoke of all things, both living and non-living, as having a "natural appetite", being drawn, consciously or unconsciously, to where they were supposed to be.

Man is also drawn to where he is supposed to be.

He is meant to know and to love, and to love is to treat others for their own sake, without qualification.

We learn to be human only when we learn to know and love what is true and good.

I hope and pray that the gentleman recovered from his loss, and I hope the lady came to understand the inherent contradiction of what she had said.

If it's love, whether of friendship or of romance, it won't disappear.

It will last.

❖ ❖ ❖ ❖ ❖

When a certain person came to him, who was going up to Rome on account of a lawsuit which had regard to his rank, Epictetus inquired the reason of his going to Rome, and the man then asked what he thought about the matter.

Epictetus replied: If you ask me what you will do in Rome, whether you will succeed or fall, I have no rule about this. But if you ask me how you will fare, I can tell you: if you have right opinions, you will fare well; if they are false, you will fare ill.

For to every man the cause of his acting is opinion. For what is the reason why you desired to be elected governor of the Cnossians? Your opinion. What is the reason that you are now going up to Rome? Your opinion. And going in winter, and with danger and expense. 'I must go.' What tells you this? Your opinion.

Then if opinions are the causes of all actions, and a man has bad opinions, such as the cause may be, such also is the effect. Have we then all sound opinions, both you and your adversary? And how do you differ? But have you sounder opinions than your adversary? Why? You think so. And so does he think that his opinions are better; and so do madmen. This is a bad criterion. But show to me that you have made some inquiry into your opinions and have taken some pains about them.

—Epictetus, *Dialogues* 3.9

Every man has opinions, or makes judgments, or works from a certain standard or measures of true and false, right and wrong.

And every man follows his opinion.

What is more important than having the opinion is that it actually be the right opinion.

If I were to ask, "Will I succeed or will I fail?" the Stoic answer is quite simply, "I don't know, will you?"

The man traveling to Rome is determining his victory or defeat through external conditions.

Epictetus is trying to explain that victory or defeat is determined only through his own attitude.

I wonder if the fellow understood this, or walked away puzzled?

The weight of habit and custom, the steady pressure to measure ourselves by what is outside of us, can be very powerful.

But I can simply remember that I am able, in a single moment, decide what my standards of success will be.

There is no hindrance or necessity in my decision that does not come from my choice.

Knowing it is as simple as that is already half the battle.

❖ ❖ ❖ ❖ ❖

Cities and monuments made of stone, if you compare them with our life, are enduring; if you submit them to the standard of Nature's law they are perishable, since Nature brings all things to destruction and recalls them to the state from which they sprang. For what that mortal hands have made is ever immortal?

The seven wonders of the world and all the works, far more wonderful than these, that the ambition of later years has reared, will some day be seen leveled to the ground. So it is — nothing is everlasting, few things are even long lasting; one thing perishes in one way, another in another, though the manner of their passing varies, yet whatever has beginning has also an end.

—Seneca the Younger, *To Polybius on consolation* 1, tr Basore

Our worldly achievements often seem so grand and imposing, but in the final order of things they are empty and meaningless.

I had a slightly "off" childhood friend who liked to smash anthills, thinking himself some sort of mighty god of destruction for these little creatures.

I prefer to think of myself like the ant.

Remember, I promised no religious preaching or posturing, so I ask that you consider these words from Psalm 49 from the perspective of philosophy, and particularly of Stoicism:

Do not be overawed when others grow rich,
when the splendor of their houses increases;
for they will take nothing with them when they die,
their splendor will not descend with them.
Though while they live they count themselves blessed —
and people praise you when you prosper —
they will join those who have gone before them,
who will never again see the light of life.
People who have wealth but lack understanding
are like the beasts that perish.

❖ ❖ ❖ ❖ ❖

Day 196

The intelligence of the universe is social. Accordingly it has made the inferior things for the sake of the superior, and it has fitted the superior to one another. You see how it has subordinated, coordinated and assigned to everything its proper portion, and has brought together into concord with one another the things which are the best.

—Marcus Aurelius, *Meditations* Book 5

So much of philosophy, especially modern philosophy, seems so deeply subjective, isolating the self from what is around it and turning purely inward.
I picture Rodin's *The Thinker* as a perfect image of this view.
And Stoicism might seem at first glance to be doing much the same.
If happiness is found in our own power, we might think we don't need anything in the world at all.

Aurelius reminds us to avoid this temptation, for all of Nature is, as he says, social.
The fulfillment of our nature is not apart from other things, but with and through other things.
While it was the Epicureans who suggested removing oneself as much as possible from the world, the Stoics encouraged a life of self-sufficiency that is always pointed outwards and in harmony with the world.

While I must rule myself, and not permit myself to be ruled by the world, that is not a rejection of the world, but a freely and gladly given embrace.

❖ ❖ ❖ ❖ ❖

Day 197

Asked where he came from, Diogenes said, 'I am a citizen of the world.'
— Diogenes of Sinope, ex Diogenes Laertius,
Lives and opinions of eminent philosophers 6.63

I regularly keep watch on myself to avoid breeding division.
Even as I write out these reflections, I am deeply conscious that whenever I present a contrast or difference, I should also do my best to point back to something shared and unifying.
For all our differences, our humanity is our common identity, above all else.

I have always felt deeply different from other people.
I was once told that the fact that we all feel so different, alone, and isolated is exactly the one thing we share in common, and while I understand the point entirely, I have great difficulty feeling that way.

I had always assumed that I am less, that I am flawed, that I am not deserving.
Combine this disposition with a few bad turns, and the Black Dog makes perfect sense.
And however much I try to shake off those feelings of exclusion and inadequacy, I have never managed it.

Yet I have started to manage something a bit different, and I think it approximates the desired result.
Instead of worrying about boosting my confidence, and finding my unity and equality with others, I practice simply not thinking of myself at all.
I try to think only of other people, make their thoughts and needs the center of my attention, and then act on those priorities.

What is so odd is that once I stop thinking about myself, I end up having a much better feeling and sense of myself.
After a time of thinking and acting this way, I may catch a reflection of myself, so to speak, and I come back into my own consciousness, and I am happy with what I see.
I don't dwell on it, but I turn away again, back to the task at hand.

I can appreciate my being a citizen of the world precisely when I am acting for others in the world.
I am very much content with that.

❖ ❖ ❖ ❖ ❖

Day 198

Now, if on the stage, I mean on the platform, where there is the greatest opportunity for deception and disguise, truth yet prevails, provided it is made plain and brought into the light of day, what ought to be the case with friendship which is wholly weighed in the scales of truth?

For in friendship, unless, as the saying is, you behold and show an open heart, you can have no loyalty or certainty and not even the satisfaction of loving and of being loved, since you do not know what true love is.

And yet this flattery of which I spoke, however deadly it may be, can harm no one except him who receives it and delights in it. It follows that the man who lends the readiest ear to flatterers is the one who is most given to self-flattery and is most satisfied with himself.

I grant that Virtue loves herself; for she best knows herself and realizes how lovable she is; but it is not virtue I am talking about but a reputation for virtue. For many wish not so much to be, as to seem to be, endowed with real virtue.

Such men delight in flattery, and when a complimentary remark is fashioned to suit their fancy they think the empty phrase is proof of their own merits. There is nothing, therefore, in a friendship in which one of the parties to it does not wish to hear the truth and the other is ready to lie.

—Cicero. *To Laelius on friendship* 97-98

For obvious reasons, I am deeply conscious of the connection between friendship and honesty, and I recognize my prejudice.
But while I may have a personally deep concern for this matter in my own life, I don't think that makes it any less essential for all of us.
There can be no friendship where there is no trust, and there can be no trust where there is deception, manipulation, or flattery.

I keep a pair of rules in mind whenever I am speaking to my friends, or about them to others.

First, if I am speaking about someone, am I saying something I would feel no regret saying directly to that person?
If the answer is no, I do my best to say nothing at all.

Second, if I am speaking to a person, am I telling them the truth, which they deserve, or bending the truth for my convenience?
And if I am indeed telling the truth, am I presenting it in a manner with care and concern for their own good, and their own thoughts and feelings?
Again, if the answer is no, I should remain silent.

Let us please be honest.
We don't tell those lies to protect the feelings of others; we tell them to protect ourselves from anything awkward, painful, or inconvenient.
I owe my friends love and respect, and that is certainly not present when I deceive them in any way.

❖ ❖ ❖ ❖ ❖

Day 199

Solitude is a certain condition of a helpless man. For because a man is alone, he is not for that reason also solitary; just as though a man is among numbers, he is not therefore not solitary.

When then we have lost either a brother, or a son, or a friend on whom we were accustomed to repose, we say that we are left solitary, though we are often in Rome, though such a crowd meet us, though so many live in the same place, and sometimes we have a great number of slaves. For the man who is solitary, as it is conceived, is considered to be a helpless person and exposed to those who wish to harm him.

—Epictetus, *Discourses* 3.13

I have often been alone, but that doesn't mean I am lonely.
 I am quite often deeply content being alone.
 I have also often been desperately lonely in the company of many.
 This is how I relate to Epictetus' distinction between aloneness and solitude.

Using his terms, to be alone is simply to be outside the personal presence of others.
 This is neither good nor bad, but simply indifferent.
 I can use either to my benefit.
 The term is here used in a sense of our external closeness to others.

To be solitary is different, in that it refers to our internal closeness to others.
 I may be in the company of others, but I have no personal connection to them.
 The social bonds of love, respect, or trust are lost, and they are lost because I neglect them myself.
 I have closed myself to a connection with others.

I have regularly confused the distinction between being alone and being solitary, and I have mistaken one for the other to my great harm.
 None of this is about the quantity of people that surround us, or the frequency with which we see them, but the quality of our relationships when we cross paths with others.

❖ ❖ ❖ ❖ ❖

Day 200

The best way of avenging yourself is not to become like the wrong doer.
—Marcus Aurelius, *Meditations* Book 6

The most important day of my life isn't my birthday, or my graduation, the birth of a child, or even my wedding day.
  The most important day of my life is the day I lost my best friend.

This isn't because it was a good day.
  It was the worst day I have ever known, and I never want another one like it, and would not wish it upon my worst enemy.
  It is the most important day, because it formed me to become the man I am now.
  It taught me to respect the lesson Marcus Aurelius offers.

After the shock, I sat down, and realized exactly what was happening.
  I could let my anger and pain kill me.
  I could succumb to despair.
  I had just lost everything that mattered to me.

Or I could take another route. I could take all those feelings of sadness, hate, and anger, and I could do something with them.
  I could learn that I should become the opposite of what I despised.
  I should be better than the offender.

And though I have stumbled and fallen far too often, this became the measure of my life.
  I promised myself I would never treat another human being as a means to an end.
  I would never consider a person as disposable, or subject to my convenience.
  I would never think of love as conditional. I would never say one thing, and then do another.
  I would never lie, cheat, or steal to promote myself at the expense of others.
  I would never be a fraud.

I would never be like that person who hurt me so deeply.
  This now defines my life.
  I struggle every day to do good from evil done.
  I know I will be victorious if I only remember never to hate, but to meet hate with love.

❖ ❖ ❖ ❖ ❖

Day 201

It will also serve as a great relief, if you will often question yourself thus: am I grieving on my own account, or on account of him who has departed? If on my own account, its parade of affection is idle, and my grief, the only excuse for which is that it is honorable, begins to show defection from brotherly love when it looks toward personal advantage; but nothing is less becoming to a good man than to be calculating in his grief for a brother.

If I grieve on his account, I must decide that one or the other of the two following views is true. For, if the dead retain no feeling whatever, my brother has escaped from all the ills of life, and has been restored to that state in which he had been before he was born, and, exempt from every ill, he fears nothing, desires nothing, suffers nothing. What madness this is—that I should never cease to grieve for one who will never grieve any more!

If, however, the dead do retain some feeling, at this moment my brother's soul, released, as it were, from its long imprisonment, exults to be at last its own lord and master, enjoys the spectacle of Nature, and from its higher place looks down upon all human things, while upon things divine, the explanation of which it had so long sought in vain, it gazes with a nearer vision. And so why should I pine away in yearning for him who either is happy or does not exist? But to weep for one who is happy is envy; for one who does not exist, madness.

—Seneca the Younger, *To Polybius on consolation* 8

St Augustine asks himself a very similar question in the *Confessions*.
Was his grief for the loss of a friend really for the friend, or merely for himself?
And if it was really just for himself, wasn't that quite selfish?
The Stoic would also add that the grief, if it is something merely about myself, is something within my power to estimate and consider as I see fit.
Whether I choose to dwell upon what is selfish is entirely up to me.

My own experience tells me that my emotions are not always things I can control, and this is most noticeable with the sadness of the Black Dog.
But what I do with those feelings, how I direct them, channel them, and judge about their meaning and significance is something that I can do.

So there are times when my sadness and grief are extremely intense.
I am just now, as I am writing, recovering from a powerful wave of this sort only a few hours ago, which was so strong I needed to sit down in private for a time to recover myself.

But I have learned to step out of myself, in a sense.
I look at the sadness from a different perspective, from the outside, as objectively as I can, and I consider it from every angle.
From a distance I can make a judgment about it, even as I am feeling it quite intensely.
And more often than not, I can tell that my sadness isn't about the things I have lost, but all about myself.
And I can smile, and say,
"You silly boy. The pain will pass.
It doesn't mean what you think it means."

❖ ❖ ❖ ❖ ❖

Day 202

Thrasea was in the habit of saying, 'I should rather be put to death today than be banished tomorrow.' What then did Rufus say to him? 'If you choose that as the heavier misfortune, what a foolish choice to make! But if as the lighter, who has given you the choice? Are you not willing to train yourself to be satisfied with what has been given you?'

—Musonius Rufus, *Fragments* 43

Over the years, I got very good at bargaining with Providence.

I would try to make deals with the Universe, as if I could even make demands of express my preferences from some menu of cosmic options and side dishes.

The illusion, and the arrogance, is, of course, twofold: the assumption that I am even choosing rightly what I think is best to have happen to me, and the belief that I could even have any control over forces far beyond my power.

The Universe is not going to make deals with me, but I do need to make my peace with the Universe.

To be satisfied with what is given me is not to merely begrudgingly accept whatever scraps may be thrown my way.

It is the understanding that the hand dealt will be what it will be, and that my opportunity is simply to play it well.

Should I be so vain as to expect any more than this gift?

❖　❖　❖　❖　❖

For you see that Caesar appears to furnish us with great peace, that there are no longer enemies nor battles nor great associations of robbers nor of pirates, but we can travel at every hour and sail from east to west.

But can Caesar give us security from fever also, can he from shipwreck, from fire, from earthquake or from lightning? Well, I will say, can he give us security against love? He cannot. From sorrow? He cannot. From envy? He cannot. In a word then he cannot protect us from any of these things.

But the doctrine of philosophers promises to give us security even against these things. And what does it say? 'Men, if you will attend to me, wherever you are, whatever you are doing, you will not feel sorrow, nor anger, nor compulsion, nor hindrance, but you will pass your time without perturbations and free from everything.'

When a man has this peace, not proclaimed by Caesar (for how should he be able to proclaim it?), but by God, through reason, is he not content when he is alone?

—Epictetus, *Discourses* 3.13

The Stoic will be the most political of men in one sense, and the least political of men in another.

He will be political in one sense, because he recognizes his social connection to all persons, and even to all things, and that through his link to what is around him he chooses to live most fully in harmony with Nature.

He will be apolitical in a different sense, because the worldly gains sought by some in politics, wealth, power, and honor, are in and of themselves merely means, things that are completely indifferent, and therefore not sought after by the Stoic.

Think of the things worldly politics says it can offer us: security of the body, of our property, of money, of position.
I am writing this while we are in a presidential election year, and we bicker back and forth about what makes our country great.
Promises are made to defend our jobs, our health care, our borders from our enemies.

But our leaders cannot even assure us those promises, because Nature can sweep all these things away in an instant.
And she often does so.
Even if we were somehow assured of these things, they still not give us the peace we need.
Politics do not give us peace.
Philosophy gives us peace.

❖ ❖ ❖ ❖ ❖

If you had a step-mother and a mother at the same time, you would be dutiful to your step-mother, but still you would constantly return to your mother. Let the court and philosophy now be to you step-mother and mother: return to philosophy frequently and repose in her, through whom what you meet with in the court appears to you to be tolerable, and you appear tolerable in the court.

—Marcus Aurelius, *Meditations* Book 6

Because true happiness arises from the inner workings of the soul, yet we must still live in an external world full of bustle and business, it may seem that our lives will be in conflict, a constant struggle between these two realms of our existence.
Will not the two halves pull us apart with their conflicting demands?

The lower can be, and indeed must be, in harmony with the higher.
I turn to philosophy to discern right from wrong, to find renewal and joy, and I then turn out into the world driven my meaning and sharing that inner joy with others.
Philosophy strengthens me at court, and acting with justice at court serves philosophy.

So the Stoic doesn't need to run away from the world, or face it with resentment, holding his breath until he can breathe clean air again.
When I seem to struggle between philosophy and the court, I must remember that this is only in my perception, and that this error arises only because I am still choosing external goods over internal goods.
If I estimate life correctly, I would always understand that the indifferent can only serve my nature, and my nature can never serve what is indifferent.

I can love both philosophy and the court, but I must always return to my greater love.

❖ ❖ ❖ ❖ ❖

Day 205

Nature requires from us some sorrow, while more than this is the result of vanity.
—Seneca the Younger, *To Polybius on consolation* 18

Again, it isn't the sorrow that's the problem.

My sorrow can serve me.

It's the freely chosen magnification and dwelling upon the sorrow that does me harm.

In reading this book you might think that I must speak quite regularly about my mistakes, my losses, or my disappointments.

In actual life, quite different than the emphasis of this text, I speak of it very little.

Only a very few people close to me even know about my mental and physical health, and even fewer know of my life's baggage.

If someone does pick up a snippet here or there, they are usually quite shocked that I'm still standing.

In fact, for far too long I never expressed my sorrow at all, which ironically is the very thing that compounded it.

My attempts at being brave and silent were really a sort of vanity.

And now I need to make absolutely certain that I don't slip in the other direction.

Everything must be according to its proper measure.

My wife, for example, did not know for many years that I had seen a horrible traffic accident, and that I was still having nightmares about it regularly.

It was good that I finally shared that with her, and it helped me manage the disordered feelings.

Yet now, having addressed it, I found myself gradually dwelling on it again, and it slowly became a hindrance once more.

So I had to turn the appearances again and reset them once more.

Stoic thinking does require, in my experience, a regular readjustment to keep things in order.

I use the image of trimming a tree to help me with this.

Let the branches grow wild, or trim too closely, and the tree will grow too unruly or it will whither.

Accept the emotions, work with them, and put them in their rightful place.

But do not let them move about unchecked, because before I am aware, they have become too strong and wild to tame.

❖ ❖ ❖ ❖ ❖

'There is then no doubt that these roads to happiness are no roads, and they cannot lead any man to any end whither they profess to take him. I would show you shortly with what great evils they are bound up.

'Would you heap up money? You will need to tear it from its owner. Would you seem brilliant by the glory of great honors? You must kneel before their dispenser, and in your desire to surpass other men in honor, you must debase yourself by setting aside all pride.

'Do you long for power? You will be subject to the wiles of all over whom you have power, you will be at the mercy of many dangers. You seek fame? You will be drawn to and fro among rough paths, and lose all freedom from care. Would you spend a life of pleasure? Who would not despise and cast off such servitude to so vile and brittle a thing as your body? How petty are all the aims of those who put before themselves the pleasures of the body, how uncertain is the possession of such? In bodily size will you ever surpass the elephant? In strength will you ever lead the bull, or in speed the tiger?

'Look upon the expanse of heaven, the strength with which it stands, the rapidity with which it moves, and cease for a while to wonder at base things. This heaven is not more wonderful for those things than for the design which guides it. How sweeping is the brightness of outward form, how swift its movement, yet more fleeting than the passing of the flowers of spring.'

—Boethius, *The consolation of Philosophy* Book 3 Prose 8

You may find that even as the habits of your thinking become more and more Stoic, you will still need quite regular reminders of the very particular ways of how and why we should avoid the false road away from happiness.

This passage by Boethius is one of my favorite ways of achieving this.

When are the specific times I have seen how money, honor, power, fame, or pleasure have destroyed myself or others?

This book, for example, repeats a small number of basic principles over and over, often in different language or from a different perspective, but nevertheless still the same guiding rules.

I honestly don't consider that a weakness, but rather a strength of such a text.

Virtue comes through habit, habit comes through practice, and practice comes through constant repetition.

In this way the habits of the heart and mind are much like physical exercise.

I read the above passage and I attach my own memories to each step, which in turn condition and reinforce my conviction.

I vividly recall being invited to the house of an old colleague for dinner.

I'm not much a social butterfly, but I pushed myself to attend.

He's a good fellow at heart, but he's gone down a path I can't follow.

I can still see in my mind's eye items in his house, each of which seemed to me symbols of the above distractions, things I wish to avoid.

I don't think of them as a criticism of him, but as a reminder to myself.

The baroque ornateness of the doorknocker, almost too heavy to lift, reminds me of the vanity of wealth.

The diploma posted over the mantle, complete with special lighting, keeps me away from the love of honor.

The futuristic security system he couldn't work properly was like the trappings of power.

The silverware given to him by a celebrity, mentioned repeatedly that night, was everything wrong with fame.

 And the black and white, professionally done, series of semi-nude photographs of his wife, for all to see on his living room wall, became my image to not fall into pleasure.

This may seem a silly visualization tool, but it helps me make things concrete.

❖ ❖ ❖ ❖ ❖

We must mention the higher, nobler wealth, which does not belong to all, but to truly noble and divinely gifted men. This wealth is bestowed by wisdom through the doctrines and principles of ethics, logic and physics, and from these spring the virtues, which rid the soul of its proneness to extravagance, and engender the love of contentment and frugality, which will assimilate it to God.

For God has no wants, He needs nothing, being in Himself all-sufficient to Himself, while the fool has many wants, ever thirsting for what is not there, longing to gratify his greedy and insatiable desire, which he fans into a blaze like a fire and brings both great and small within its reach. But the man of worth has few wants, standing midway between mortality and immortality.

—Philo of Alexandria, *On the virtues* 167-169, tr Colson

While I have suggested that philosophy of Stoicism can be practiced without any direct religious reference to God, I also believe that the two principles are wonderfully complementary.

I avoid teaching Stoicism from a religious perspective, because while reason and faith can be harmonious, the two are still distinct, and should not be confused.

When a Stoic thinker mentions the philosophy of God, or gods, or the Divine, or the Intelligence, do not assume a particular religious assumption, but do understand that such perspectives can be deeply compatible.

Whatever we consider to be true riches or wealth tells us exactly what sort of things we care for most.

For the Stoic, the true wealth is the riches of character, the life lived through wisdom and virtue, and this means seeking happiness that is as dependent upon oneself as possible.

If a man is happiest when he is most self-sufficient, why would he have any relation to God?

Remember that self-sufficiency is not isolation from the world, but a self-driven relationship to all things.

Philo makes a wonderful observation about such a relationship.

God, as perfect being, is pure sufficiency.

Therefore, by becoming more self-sufficient in degree ourselves, we participate more fully in the Divine.

To be a good person is then, quite literally, to be more God–like.

It might be helpful to remember that acting in conformity to Nature can also be seen acting in harmony with God.

❖ ❖ ❖ ❖ ❖

Day 208

'I am superior to you, for my father is a man of consular rank.' Another says, 'I have been a tribune, but you have not.' If we were horses, would you say, 'My father was swifter?' ' I have much barley and fodder, or elegant neck ornaments.' If, then, while you were saying this, I said, 'Be it so: let us run then.'

Well, is there nothing in a man such as running in a horse, by which it will be known which is superior and inferior? Is there not modesty, fidelity, justice? Show yourself superior in these, that you may be superior as a man. If you tell me that you can kick violently, I also will say to you that you are proud of that which is the act of an ass.

—Epictetus, *Discourses* 3.14

In classic Stoic style, Epictetus reminds us that a thing is perfected through its nature, and never by anything additional or extraneous to it.

How foolish we actually look when we forget this, but how easily we are caught up in the illusion.

Even a horse or an ass know to live better.

I unexpectedly ran into a former graduate school classmate at one of those dreary but obligatory cocktail sessions after a conference.

I hardly remember what we were meeting about.

Our conversation was perfectly friendly, but entirely empty.

I know we've all had these conversations, but I simply wonder why we continue them.

"So what have you been up to?"

I know I am supposed to brag yet seem humble, but I simply can't bring myself to do it.

"Family? Well, that would be nice, but the career just never gives me a moment's rest!"

See, she just made a boast sound like a complaint.

"So where are you working now?"

I respond by indicating some small, Classical and Liberal Arts school working out of creaky old farm buildings far in the countryside.

There was a pause, and a sympathetic tilt of the head.

"But you could be so much more!"

It was meant kindly, I'm sure, but it struck to the bone.

I jokingly mumbled something about how that depended on the true definition of "more", and politely made my excuses.

I was sad because we were running two very different kinds of races.

❖ ❖ ❖ ❖ ❖

Day 209

We are born under conditions that would be favorable if only we did not abandon them. Nature intended that we should need no great equipment for living happily; each one of us is able to make his own happiness. External things are of slight importance, and can have no great influence in either direction. Prosperity does not exalt the wise man, nor does adversity cast him down; for he has always endeavored to rely entirely upon himself, to derive all of his joy from himself.

—Seneca the Younger, *To Helvia on consolation* 4, tr Basore

If you have read this far, you will notice that my reflections are hardly up to the depth and quality of the original sources.

I hope you didn't think they were supposed to be, since my intent has been not to add to or improve classic Stoicism, but to encourage you to reflect upon and apply their original meaning.

I offer my own thoughts not for their sake, but to motivate you do something similar for yourself, for your sake.

I also think our original writers, elevated as they have been in esteem over the centuries, would tell you the same thing.

Don't be impressed or inspired by what others tell you to do, or when they leave you in awe at their seeming wisdom and fine words.

By all means use such externals to assist you, both the good and the bad, and the mediocre in between, but don't depend on them.

Depend on your own thinking, your own judgment, and your own exercise of virtue.

So when Seneca says to treat prosperity and adversity the same, to practice self-reliance, and to depend on very little from our circumstances, don't just take his word for it, simply because he's an esteemed philosopher.

Use his suggestions to understand those truths and work through these questions for yourself.

Then go out and help others do the same.

And certainly don't do any of this because I suggested it.

❖ ❖ ❖ ❖ ❖

Day 210

How strangely men act. They will not praise those who are living at the same time and living with themselves; but to be themselves praised by posterity, by those whom they have never seen or ever will see, this they set much value on. But this is very much the same as if you should be grieved because those who have lived before you did not praise you.
—Marcus Aurelius, *Meditations*, Book 6

I'm not sure I understand the psychology of this phenomenon.
We ignore or even discredit people while they are alive, and praise them when they are dead.
Perhaps the latter is a result of the shame in failing to express respect when we could?

When comic actor Robin Williams died, there was quite the outpouring of public grief.
A colleague described it as a moment where his universe was knocked off its axis, and how he would do anything to bring that man back.
I replied that he couldn't bring him back, but he could still do real work to honor him.
He looked back at me slightly confused.

"Williams was a genius, but also a man who suffered throughout his life, with great bravery," I said.
"Now go out and seek out others who have been forgotten and brushed aside because they suffer from depression.
Help them, tell them what you would have said to Robin Williams, and I think he would be proud."
My colleague didn't seem to like that.

To be completely fair, I have fallen for this same trap on two occasions.
I knew a girl in high school, and though we were like water and oil and often bickered, we strangely became good friends.
I think we both saw that both of us didn't quite feel right in our skins.
When we went off to college, we drifted apart.
I would think of her often, but never reach out.

In the fall of my junior year, I learned that she had taken her own life.
I went to her funeral, and everyone praised her.
I recall someone laughing at me because my hands shook trying to light a cigarette on the way out.
My nerves stemmed from my guilt, and I recognized that while I could never save another person, I could have been there for her, and I hadn't been.
Posterity is too late to show love.

Years later, I received a long letter, the old hand-written sort, from another old friend, never forgotten, but also someone I drifted away from.
He was a jovial redheaded bartender, and we immediately hit it off, had many adventures, but slowly went our own ways when our worlds changed.

263

He wrote about how he missed me, he apologized for having done something behind my back long ago, and he wanted to pick up our friendship where we left off.
I already knew about his confession, since the same girl who broke my heart had also broken his.
He seemed as despondent as I did, and I should have reached out.
I didn't, not out of neglect or malice, but out of fear.
Though I still don't know how it happened, he died a few years later.
I can't even find any of his family members to send my condolences.

Fame and praise are pipe dreams, doubly so when they mean nothing once we are gone.
That, in turn, taught me not to heap praise onto others, but to love them here and now, while I can, and it was part of what inspired me to contact all the people I'd hurt when my own time began running short.

❖ ❖ ❖ ❖ ❖

But to accept injury not in a spirit of savage resentment and to show ourselves not implacable toward those who wrong us, but rather to be a source of good hope to them is characteristic of a benevolent and civilized way of life.

How much better a figure does the philosopher make so conducting himself as to deem worthy of forgiveness anyone who wrongs him, than to behave as if ready to defend himself with legal procedure and indictments, while in reality he is behaving in an unseemly manner and acting quite contrary to his own teaching.

To be sure he says that a good man can never be wronged by a bad man; but nevertheless he draws up an indictment as having been wronged by bad men, while claiming to be accounted a good man himself.

—Musonius Rufus, *Lectures* 10

Though my emotional responses have gradually over time tended more to sadness than anger, I can still succumb to the weakness of rage.

My poor wife can attest to this, as must the occasionally baffled student who expects me to be a kind old hippie to a fault.

I don't wish to embarrass her, but my wife's example has been a great help to me.

She, too, can be quite fiery in her temper, such that I sometimes fear her power.

I suppose that is as it should be for any good husband.

But far more often than not, she meets my own frustrations and complaints with kindness, patience, and concern.

She is able to listen silently while I rant and rave over all that's wrong with the world, or with her.

She will rarely hold a grudge, and if she does it is because I have been more brutally offensive than usual and it doesn't last longer than the night.

She will take my hand, and simply say "I love you, silly man."

That's my concrete example of what I think Musonius means.

I am inspired when he quotes Socrates that a good man can't be harmed by a bad man.

That may seem extraordinary, but we understand it fully when we truly grasp what the human good actually is.

Why do I grow angry when someone treats me poorly?

The harm is on them, and not upon myself, because I may choose to use anything and everything to my benefit.

Again, I can become better as he becomes worse.

No need for anger, just love.

❖ ❖ ❖ ❖ ❖

The husband and wife, he used to say, should come together for the purpose of making a life in common and of procreating children, and furthermore of regarding all things in common between them, and nothing peculiar or private to one or the other, not even their own bodies.

The birth of a human being which results from such a union is to be sure something marvelous, but it is not yet enough for the relation of husband and wife, inasmuch as quite apart from marriage it could result from any other sexual union, just as in the case of animals.

But in marriage there must be above all perfect companionship and mutual love of husband and wife, both in health and in sickness and under all conditions, since it was with desire for this as well as for having children that both entered upon marriage. Where, then, this love for each other is perfect and the two share it completely, each striving to outdo the other in devotion, the marriage is ideal and worthy of envy, for such a union is beautiful.

But where each looks only to his own interests and neglects the other, or, what is worse, when one is so minded and lives in the same house but fixes his attention elsewhere and is not willing to pull together with his yoke-mate nor to agree, then the union is doomed to disaster and though they live together, yet their common interests fare badly.

—Musonius Rufus, *Lectures* 13

I knew instinctively from my earliest memory that all I really wanted was to love and to be loved.
I also knew instinctively, though the words came later, that love was about giving, about self–giving, and that by giving oneself one makes oneself whole.
I also felt that if it was something so important, it didn't just whither and die and pass away.
I also learned fairly quickly that to love, to put oneself out there, to invite rejection, could bring great pain.

I am so deeply moved by Musonius' passage, precisely because he sees this very truth in the example of the beauty of marriage.
He reflects the Classical understanding of marriage, which exists by Nature for mutual dedication and the raising of children, in such a positive and encouraging way.
By giving ourselves fully to each other, Nature magnifies it, creates through it, and gives us the gift of our children.
They, in turn, become yet another channel of our devotion.

There is no love, no friendship, no marriage, where people use one another, or where our children are simply expressions of serving ourselves.
To love is never to look into a mirror.
It is to cast one's own light to warm others.
That love makes us vulnerable is not a weakness, but a sign of our own strength.

I always think of this passage from C.S. Lewis when I ponder the delicacy of love:

> *To love at all is to be vulnerable. Love anything and your heart will be wrung and possibly broken. If you want to make sure of keeping it intact you must give it to no one, not even an animal. Wrap it carefully round with hobbies and little luxuries; avoid all entanglements. Lock it up safe in the casket or coffin of your selfishness. But in that casket, safe, dark, motionless, airless, it will change. It will not be broken; it will become unbreakable, impenetrable, irredeemable. To love is to be vulnerable.*

And this fine one from E.M. Forster:

> *It isn't possible to love and part. You will wish that it was. You can transmute love, ignore it, muddle it, but you can never pull it out of you. I know by experience that the poets are right: love is eternal.*

Day 213

How cruel it is not to allow men to strive after the things which appear to them to be suitable to their nature, and profitable! And yet in a manner you do not allow them to do this, when you are vexed because they do wrong. For they are certainly moved towards things because they suppose them to be suitable to their nature and profitable to Óthem.
'But they are mistaken!'
'Teach them then, and show them without being angry.'

—Marcus Aurelius, *Meditations* Book 6

I used to worry about complex assignments, grades, lesson plans, and learning outcomes quite a bit when I started teaching over two decades ago.
I don't worry about them that much anymore.
I embrace the Classical model of education from the Greeks and Romans, who, despite all their flaws, understood that teaching and learning are not about force and artificially imposed order.
Teaching and learning are about building character, and the best way to build character is simply to practice it.

I'm not going to make a student better or wiser by cramming facts and figures and demanding that he regurgitate them.
The progressive testing model of education follows this, and it really becomes a game of power and resentment.

Instead, I am now happy if a class merely involves a decent discussion or writing exercise, where all we do is practice prudence, justice, temperance, and fortitude.
The student need not even be told what we are doing, or be aware of the goal.
Simply by practicing the virtues he will become better at them.

I am currently teaching a rather lively bunch of younger students.
They seem happiest in class when we tell one another narratives.
So we tell narratives quite a bit, and the entire time they have no clue that the way I am steering them to tell a story, to respond to someone else's story, and to reflect on the meaning of any story is to help them become more thoughtful and more loving.
I still have to curb the cross–talking and goofy behavior, but I'm trying to work with their natures, not against them.

I need to remember, following Aurelius, that I do no service by simply telling a student he is wrong.
He wants what he thinks is good, however foolish he may be, and by pushing against him I will only make the matter worse.
The stick may be there to guide, certainly, but it is never there to intimidate.

Instead, I can try to set an example, not with force but with patience and love, and I can encourage without confrontation.
Stoic wisdom can permeate and inform all levels and aspects of life.

❖   ❖   ❖   ❖   ❖

Day 214

What then is a benefit? It is the act of a well-wisher who bestows joy and derives joy from the bestowal of it, and is inclined to do what he does from the prompting of his own will. And so what counts is, not what is done or what is given, but the spirit of the action, because a benefit consists, not in what is done or given, but in the intention of the giver or doer.

—Seneca the Younger, *On benefits* 1.6, tr Basore

I currently teach at a school that has a wonderful turn back to the times of old, the House System. Students of all ages are members of a particular House, and this helps them see their world vertically, and not just horizontally.

It shares the same merits as the forgotten one room schoolhouse.

We have a model in place where students may earn House Points, not for their own benefit, but for the entire group.

The Faculty is asked to give House Points to students for acts of extraordinary kindness or brilliance.

I imagine I'm not doing it the way I'm expected to, but I will never give House Points to a student who asks for them or seems to expect them.

When I do give House Points, I never tell the student who earned them.

I make the whole thing entirely anonymous.

I do not consider that cruel or mean.

I believe it encourages the virtues expressed by Seneca.

❖ ❖ ❖ ❖ ❖

Day 215

Even when I was rather young, quite probably an indication that I was destined to be a student of philosophy, I wondered about the question of fate.

If there is a God, who is all-powerful and all-knowing, how can I have any free will?
And if there is no God, allowing me my complete freedom, how can there be any purpose or meaning to anything besides my own selfish ego?

All of this is a false dichotomy.
God may be perfect power, perfect knowledge, perfect love.
And within this knowledge and power it is within his power to permit our freedom.
Providence may indeed be the order by which all things are ruled, but the lower causes of our own choices can exist in harmony with the higher causes, and need not be in conflict with them.

An everyday example can perhaps help illustrate the point.
My children were once arguing over an electronic device, and who had the right to use it.
They were both grabbing and tugging at it, becoming louder and increasingly agitated.
At that moment, I could already see what was going to happen, and I had the power to stop it.
But I chose to make it a teaching moment they wouldn't forget.
The grappling continued, and, as I suspected, the device went flying from their hands, crashed to the ground, and the screen shattered.

"And now," I said, "because you were both greedy, neither of you have it."
They needed to replace it with their own money.

I'm hardly God, but I am a father.
I knew what would happen, and could have directly controlled the situation, but I allowed them their own choices.
And though my parental wisdom is hardly Providence, their freedom and my authority worked together for them to learn an important lesson.

I'd like to think it is that way with me and Providence as well, though its workings may be mysterious at the time.
Out of every choice I make, Nature reacts appropriately, all for a higher good.

❖ ❖ ❖ ❖ ❖

From these two roots do spring four principal affections which do greatly disquiet the life of man: desire and pleasure, fear and sorrow. The first two have respect to some supposed or imagined good, the two latter unto some supposed or imagined evil. All of them do hurt and distemper the mind, and without timely prevention do bring it out of all order, yet not each of them in like way.

For whereas the quietness and constancy of the mind rests, as it were, in an even balance, these affections do hinder this upright poise and evenness; some of them by puffing up the mind, others by pressing it down too much.

—Justus Lipsius, *On constancy* 1.7

When we make ourselves miserable we are driven by our emotions, and do not allow our reason to rule our emotions.

Lipsius proposes an interesting pattern of the passions whereby we are drawn toward or draw away from apparent goods and evils.

The good and the evil are, of course, within the perceiving of it.

When we cannot rise above the appearance, we are tossed about by it.

I find that this helps me understand my relations to other people, and helps me to understand how and why these relationships have been healthy or harmful.

It isn't even a matter of whether the other person is good or bad: I can, after all, love a bad person.

If my attraction, or revulsion, centers on a perceived quality, I let myself act under the influence of my feelings about that quality.

If, on the other hand, I look beyond the appearance to what lies behind it, my reason takes over the reins.

I have, for example, desperately missed people, and that feeling can be deeply intense.

Yet it may not be the person I miss at all.

The desire is for the appearance, and the pleasure that would come from possessing it.

If I understand this, the desire is turned, and under my judgment.

On a very few occasions, someone has told me that they love me.

I brought myself to grief because I assumed this meant the person loved me for my sake, not that they enjoyed some perceived quality of me.

When I met my wife, I at first resisted an interest in her, not just because I was afraid of pain, but also far more consciously because I wished to be certain I was not being ruled by passions about appearances.

Was it her I wished to care for, or was it her kindness, her innocence, her gentleness, her convictions?

And I think there's a good reason I am happy together with her.

I was practicing constancy, something I had not done before.

❖ ❖ ❖ ❖ ❖

If a man has frequent intercourse with others, either for talk, or drinking together, or generally for social purposes, he must either become like them, or change them to his own fashion.

For if a man places a piece of quenched charcoal close to a piece that is burning, either the quenched charcoal will quench the other, or the burning charcoal will light that which is quenched.

Since, then, the danger is so great, we must cautiously enter into such intimacies with those of the common sort, and remember that it is impossible that a man can keep company with one who is covered with soot without being partaker of the soot himself.

—Epictetus, *Discourses* 3.16

Understood correctly, bad things don't happen to me.
I permit things to be bad for me.
Nowhere has that been clearer than in my choice of the company I have kept.

I am an introvert, I face any social relations with a certain anxiety, and I am prone to social exhaustion.
This does not mean that I dislike people.
Quite the contrary: I am glad to share in the fellowship of a good and noble soul.
I just need to pace myself.
But whether I am outgoing or inward looking, I have noticed how, over the years, my choice of companions and my own character deeply reflect one another.

Whether or not I deliberately choose it, I usually become better around better people, worse around worse people.
Even as a child, wise or foolish choices of friends changed my behavior quite radically.
My own son is going through this very struggle right now.
He should be civil and decent to all, but stay clear of the malicious, the arrogant, the cynical folks.

I once chose a very cold, self-absorbed, and calculating person as my best friend, and my life spiraled downwards.
More specifically, I permitted myself to be chosen by that friend, because I let myself be ruled by inclinations.

I recently chose new work using these as two highest measures: can I do good for others, and will the people around me help me build my character?
It's been the toughest work I've done in years, but it has so far been fruitful.
I'm the happiest I've been in a long time.

There are all sorts of clever phrases that help us to understand who we are, but in this context, there is indeed truth to saying that we are the company we keep.

❖ ❖ ❖ ❖ ❖

Once when many gifts were being presented to Socrates by his pupils, each one bringing according to his means, Aeschines, who was poor, said to him: 'Nothing that I am able to give to you do I find worthy of you, and only in this way do I discover that am a poor man. And so I give to you the only thing that I possess—myself. This gift, such as it is, I beg you to take in good part, and bear in mind that the others, though they gave to you much, have left more for themselves.'

—Seneca the Younger, *On benefits* 1.8

Aeschines, of course, wasn't poor at all.

He was rich in his soul, because he understood such a beautiful truth, that the giving of oneself, with all sincerity, is the only gift that really matters.

I do think that genuine sincerity is important here.

How often do we give, under the appearance of generosity, and realize we are losing nothing, or very little, only for the reward of only appearing to be good, or receiving benefits, or for self-promotion?

To avoid the temptation of living this way, I've actually started an impish and humorous custom of leaving kind notes, a candy bar, or a cup of coffee on a desk for someone to find, completely anonymously.

I know, that is a very small thing, but I can't handle the big things if I can't manage the little ones.

I was raised with an old-fashioned sense of gift giving, for which I do not apologize, and for which I am grateful.

The price of a gift, even what the gift was, or whether the recipient wanted it or not, didn't really matter.

What mattered was that you thought of him, and that it came from you.

I see little point to gift cards.

Give me something from you, not money so I can buy something for me.

I was once given a little glass bird figurine by a student, a very shy but fine young lady, who wanted to thank me for helping her be more confident in class.

She walked up to me quickly, smiling but with her eyes turned down, handed me a wonderfully wrapped box, promptly turned heel, and rushed off.

I don't much like the look of the figurine, to be honest, and I find it a little tacky.

But it has been sitting on my shelf, right next to my desk, for many years, where I can see it every day, because I am grateful for her kind thoughts.

It's one of the best gifts I ever received.

❖ ❖ ❖ ❖ ❖

Day 219

It is a shame for the soul to be first to give way in this life, when your body does not give way.

—Marcus Aurelius, *Meditations* Book 6

When we seek the good, we must first know the good, and we must be careful in doing so.
What defines my highest and ultimate fulfillment?
The Stoic argues that this lies at the very core of our being, our character.
I must be willing to sacrifice any and all things lower than the goods of the soul.
I must only use the goods of my body only insofar as they help to live with wisdom and virtue.
And this includes even offering my very life.

Something radical changed in my life when I was introduced to the story of Franz Jägerstätter.
A man I never knew became like a close friend.
He was an Austrian farmer, a bit of troubled fellow when younger, but marriage, family, and a deep inner spiritual conversion to his Catholic faith changed him at the core.

When the Nazis stormed into Austria, he was the only villager to vote against them.
When finally called to serve in their army, he refused, on the grounds of conscience.
Even his bishop told him he needed to submit, for the security of his family.
He answered that it made little difference if he gave them security, but then offered his family a life model of cowardice and injustice.
The best thing he could give his children was his moral example, and that he did.

The Germans beheaded him in 1943 for his refusal to serve evil.
He was a simple man, with very little education, but he was a prime example of what Stoicism teaches us.
What is truly yours is your conscience and your own convictions.
Everything else is negotiable.
Never sell the higher for the lower. I think of Jägerstätter's words often:

Everyone tells me, of course, that I should not do what I am doing because of the danger of death. I believe it is better to sacrifice one's life right away than to place oneself in the grave danger of committing sin and then dying.

❖ ❖ ❖ ❖ ❖

Day 220

The first difference between a common person and a philosopher is this: the common person says, 'Woe to me for my little child, for my brother, for my father.' The philosopher, if he shall ever be compelled to say, 'Woe to me,' stops and says, 'but for myself.'

—Epictetus, *Discourses* 3.19

You have noticed, of course, that my own approach to Stoicism is not merely to think it through in theory, but to find little ways to help me in practice.

I admit that some of these may seem silly to the reader, and perhaps they are only useful for me, in my own situation.

But I do suggest that you find your own small habits, however quirky, to engrain your values.

Eastern Orthodox Christians have a wonderful tradition, of saying a short and simple prayer, oftentimes over and over, to cement their faith:
Lord Jesus Christ, Son of God, have mercy on me, a sinner.

My Stoic parallel to this is to repeat to myself, as often as I need to, these words:
Woe to me, but for myself.
Blame and resentment drag me deeper into the pit of sorrow.
When I suffer, I am the one that chooses to succumb to suffering.
I may make of the circumstances of my life something beautiful, or something ugly.
I am the only hindrance to my happiness.

There is no one else to blame when I mess things up.

❖ ❖ ❖ ❖ ❖

D a y   2 2 1

This, in my opinion, is the least surprising or least incredible of the paradoxes of the Stoic school: that he who receives a benefit gladly has already returned it. For, since we Stoics refer every action to the mind, a man acts only as he wills; and, since devotion, good faith, justice, since, in short, every virtue is complete within itself even if it has not been permitted to put out a hand, a man can also have gratitude by the mere act of will.

Again, whenever anyone attains what he aimed at, he receives the reward of his effort. When a man bestows a benefit, what does he aim at? To be of service and to give pleasure to the one to whom he gives.

—Seneca the Younger, *On benefits* 2.30

The flip side of understanding that good action is itself its own reward, regardless of whether we are praised, recognized, or otherwise compensated, is that the mere act of being grateful is already all that must be given in response to the kindness of another.

Let's not confuse the internal act of gratitude with the external expression of gratitude.
It is the former, simply for its own sake, that is required, while the latter can be desirable, but is not a necessary consequence.
In other words, thinking "Thank you" is much more important than saying "Thank you."
Good manners are not an end in themselves, and I should hardly demand them, as much as I may appreciate them.
There is certainly little point in mouthing the words when we don't mean them.

While obviously a very weak analogy, I think of two of the cats that have brightened my life over the years.
I cared greatly for both of them, but Mandy was the feline equivalent of being obsequious.
Any treat, petting, or playtime was met with impressive purring and ornate displays of affection.

Emma was a feral cat that took a cold sort of liking to me, but refused to come into the house.
She was wild, short-tempered and gruff.
She wouldn't meow, she would croak.
She never purred for me, and rarely even let me touch her.
But I knew she felt affection for me, even if she didn't show it, and quite honestly, I had more of a thing for Emma, because she was just honest, with no trimmings or fancy posing.

My grandmother once gave me a gift when I was a child, and I rushed off to play with it.
My mother called me right back, and asked me where my manners were. "Thank your Grandma."

My grandmother, just smiled, and said, "No need. I'm just glad he's happy."
I sheepishly said my thanks.
But she didn't need it one bit.

I of course enjoy and respect when a person expresses his gratitude.
But I don't need that at all. I need only to help them be happy.
That is more than enough.

❖ ❖ ❖ ❖ ❖

Day 222

He who loves fame considers another man's activity to be his own good; and he who loves pleasure, his own sensations; but he who has understanding, considers his own acts to be his own good.

—Marcus Aurelius, *Meditations* Book 6

We often say that fortune seekers and pleasure seekers are self-centered, and that it's all about them.
That is, of course, quite true, in one sense, since they see their own benefit as being primary.
But in another sense, it's quite mistaken.
It actually isn't about them at all, because it's about everything but them.
They define themselves by the opinions of others, or slavery to objects of desire, everything outside of themselves.

I don't think it simplistic pop psychology to observe that we seek to fill the emptiness within from things without.
But the things outside don't fit our inner nature, and we feel uneasy and restless.
Square peg, round hole.

We may wonder why things aren't going quite right, especially in those moments when we are alone, with nothing to distract us.
The temptation is, of course, understandable, because we've been told our whole lives that success is in the world, and we must go out and take it.

We don't go out to find success.
We return back within to rediscover it.
Like one of those muscles that has become weakened from disuse, it will take some effort to get our souls back in order.

❖ ❖ ❖ ❖ ❖

Day 223

How few philosophers are to be found who are such in character, so ordered in soul and in life, as reason demands; who regard their teaching not as a display of knowledge, but as the rule of life; who obey themselves, and submit to their own decrees!
—Cicero, *Tusculan disputations* 2.4, tr Peabody

I was amused recently, and slightly pleased, when someone offered a description of me, not thinking I would hear of it myself.
"He's deeply kind, but firm."
I understand firmness not to be any sort of coldness, meanness, or heartlessness.
I understand it to be the long neglected virtue of constancy.
I embrace this as a form of fortitude, of moral courage.

An ordered mind is one thing, an ordered life quite another.
Plato distinguishes three powers of the soul: the intellectual, the spirited, and the appetitive.
I usually explain these through the analogy of the head, the heart, and the gut.
Prudence is the virtue of the mind.
Fortitude or courage is the virtue of the spirited.
Temperance is the virtue of the passions.
Justice is the virtue that balances all the parts in harmony.

In our world, many of us have big heads.
We are learned, refined, and full of ideas.
We also have big guts.
Our passions are constantly moving us to acquire and consume.
But we have sadly neglected the center of our being, the heart.
Without the drive to act with moral courage, to resist the temptations of ease and complacency, our minds become subject to our passions.
Without the bravery of the heart, we may think all the right things, but we end up not living them.

A man with a big head and a big gut, but no heart, is a monstrosity.
His fancy intellect is simply an efficient slave to his bloated desires:
What he knows is right cannot rule over his passions, because there is no heart to enforce it.
C.S. Lewis described such people as men without chests:

> *In a sort of ghastly simplicity we remove the organ and demand the function. We make men without chests and expect of them virtue and enterprise. We laugh at honor and are shocked to find traitors in our midst. We castrate and bid the geldings be fruitful.*

It is the essential ingredient of fortitude and constancy that will distinguish the man who is a philosopher in the way he lives, not merely in the way he thinks.

❖ ❖ ❖ ❖ ❖

'Can advantage then be derived from these things?' From all of them, and from him who abuses you. Wherein does the man who exercises before the combat profit the athlete? Very greatly. This man becomes my exerciser before the combat: he exercises me in endurance, in keeping my temper, in mildness.

You say no: but he, who lays hold of my neck and disciplines my loins and shoulders, does me good; and the exercise master does right when he says: 'Raise him up with both hands, and the heavier he is, so much the more is my advantage.' But if a man exercises me in keeping my temper, does he not do good?

This is not knowing how to gain an advantage from men. 'Is my neighbor bad?' Bad to himself, but good to me: he exercises my good disposition, my moderation. 'Is my father bad?' Bad to himself, but to me good. This is the Staff of Hermes: 'Touch with it what you please,' as the saying is. 'And it will be of gold.' I say not so: but bring what you please, and I will make it good.

Bring disease, bring death, bring poverty, bring abuse, bring trial on capital charges: all these things through the rod of Hermes shall be made profitable.

—Epictetus, *Discourses* 3.20

There can be no half measures in Stoicism; there is no "kinda" or "sorta".

If I am to understand the basic principles clearly, the commitment must simply be complete.

That commitment must tell me that each and every circumstance and experience can be completely good for me, if I but choose to make it so.

My difficulty has been that I wish to add some sort of addendum to the rule, a condition, or an exception.

It still feels right to cast blame, to think of something as unfair, to complain about the state of the world.

The Stoic can have none of that.

Anything and everything must be an opportunity to think rightly and to act upon the good.

I taught for many years at a college where I at first assumed that the sad state of affairs was due to simple incompetence.

Gradually, I came to realize that it was due to a deeply rooted evil.

Students who felt they could trust me would come to express their frustrations about the emotional and sexual abuse of young ladies at the hands of two men, a campus minister and a monk on the faculty.

I struggled for years with finding a way to handle the situation.

The students would refuse to officially report the matter, because they had been brainwashed to think that they would suffer the fires of Hell if they criticized anyone working for the Church.

My own reports to our administration were ignored.

I was told that I was imagining it all, that this was all a set of lies manufactured by our enemies.

The Abbot of our monastery, the Provost, the President, and our Board of Directors simply looked the other way.

It was only when I finally found hard evidence of the abuses that I could act with confidence.

After making one last official complaint, I blew the whistle.

I publicly called out the offenders, and exposed their actions.

This doesn't have a classic happy ending.

I, of course, had to leave the job.

No one likes a snitch.

Some people were shuffled around, but not a single person was ever punished or prosecuted.

The enabling *status quo* remained.

Many who knew of the abuses, but who remained silent to protect their own security, ended up gaining in power.

And I regularly torture myself about how there was anything good in all of this.

I lost a job, the abused students were never vindicated, and evil people remained in their positions of control.

I was even told by my Archdiocese that I was not welcome to speak in public at Church events because of what I had done.

The whole affair seemed to be one evil followed by another, and by another, and by another.

I cannot fix the world. I can only fix myself.

And that is something I did, at great loss to my circumstances, but with infinite benefit for my soul.

There are no half measures here.

I did what I knew to be right.

I chose to confront something evil and to act for the good.

How, you may ask, can we make the whole world better, if all we can do is make ourselves better?

The answer is simply that if each and every one of us acted rightly, the world would become right. One person at a time.

Every wrong you see around you is a chance to do good yourself, to touch the world with the Staff of Hermes.

❖ ❖ ❖ ❖ ❖

The idle business of show, plays on the stage, flocks of sheep, herds, exercises with spears, a bone cast to little dogs, a bit of bread into fish-ponds, laborings of ants and burden-carrying, running about of frightened little mice, puppets pulled by strings—all alike.

It is your duty then in the midst of such things to show good humor and not a proud air; to understand however that every man is worth just so much as the things are worth about which he busies himself.

—Marcus Aurelius, *Meditations* Book 7

The draw of distraction and diversion is mighty.

I may feel empty, lacking, and incomplete within myself, and I glance around frantically for other things to occupy me.

The solution seems so easy and simple, yet it is so self-destructive.

I will allow myself to be filled with outside things, with petty and shallow things.

They will keep me from what I must truly be, whether I know it or not, simply by keeping me blinded to my true nature.

The noise, the static, and the obsession with things below myself will distract me, if but for a time.

Who am I?

I am now the sum total of my many and diverse follies.

They mean nothing, but they keep me constantly busy, so that I do not remember who I truly am.

Blaise Pascal observed this very nicely:

> *Anyone who does not see the vanity of the world is very vain himself. So who does not see it, apart from young people whose lives are all noise, diversions, and thoughts for the future? But take away their diversion and you will see them bored to extinction. Then they feel their nullity without recognizing it, for nothing could be more wretched than to be intolerably depressed as soon as one is reduced to introspection with no means of diversion.*

I need not be diverted if I know myself, and the innate dignity that Nature has always given me.

No more illusions, no more lies, no more convenient distractions.

❖ ❖ ❖ ❖ ❖

But he who is happy in having received a benefit tastes a constant and unfailing pleasure, and rejoices in viewing, not the gift, but the intention of him from whom he received it. The grateful man delights in a benefit over and over, the ungrateful man but once.

But is it possible to compare the lives of these two? For the one, as a disclaimer of debts and a cheat are apt to be, is downcast and worried, he denies to his parents, to his protector, to his teachers, the consideration that is their due, while the other is joyous, cheerful, and, watching for an opportunity to repay his gratitude, derives great joy from this very sentiment, and seeks, not how he may default in his obligations, but how he may make very full and rich return, not only to his parents and friends, but also to persons of lower station.

For, even if he has received a benefit from his slave, he considers, not from whom it came, but what he received.

—Seneca the Younger , *On benefits* 3.42

My gratitude towards others must rest in an appreciation of their willingness to give, not for the content of what is given.

It's a shame that I can't say "The thought is what counts" without it sounding hackneyed and banal, but I'll say it anyways.

This causes me to consider the larger point of how giving is more valuable than receiving, and how the Stoic once again turns values on their heads.

I must learn to humbly expect nothing, and to gladly give everything.

This isn't about a traditional balance sheet of credits and debits.

It is a Stoic calculus, the recognition that the more I demand, the less I become, and the more I offer without demand, the greater I become.

It's all about the debits.

This is because while the debits are within my power, the credits are not.

On a few occasions, I have had the blessing of running into a certain type of inspiring person.

I have at times been in great need, whether it be financial, professional, or emotional.

Someone may with genuine concern offer assistance, but I am often apprehensive to accept, since I fear I will be unable to repay the money, time, or effort they will spend.

I am always in wonder and admiration for the person who then says, without any hesitation, that I owe them nothing, and should simply "pay it forward" when I can.

Such a willingness to give is not begrudging:

It doesn't drain our vitality, nor does it weaken our condition.

It actually gives us the strength and the joy that go along with virtue simply for its own sake, the fulfillment of our nature.

❖ ❖ ❖ ❖ ❖

Day 227

For in truth what one can get from himself, it is superfluous and foolish as well to get from someone else.

—Musonius Rufus, *Fragments* 45

I have always been, and always will be, a great fan of The Style Council, Paul Weller's project between his time in The Jam and his becoming "The Modfather," a legendary icon of British music.

For some followers, this period was so uncool, that it is now circling around to become ironically cool.

Along with Marillion, Howard Jones, and Talk Talk, this was the music of my best days.

Their greatest achievement, I think, was the album *Our Favourite Shop*.

On that album, the most powerful song for me was called "Homebreakers".

It described the horrors of a Britain suffering from high unemployment.

A young man from a working class family, willing and able, cannot find work in his hometown.

He bemoans the government policy that tells him he must move to find a job.

His angry father, now also unemployed, and his weeping mother wish him well as he walks to his train.

These lyrics are burned into my brain:

Good morning Day, now how do you do?
I wonder what will you do for me?
I should be on my way, I should be earning pay,
I should be all the things that I'm not.

I understand, I sympathize, I am angry at the injustice of a family broken apart by the politicians and the businessmen who make themselves fatter by the day.

When I was younger, this song was an anthem for all that was wrong with our world.

Now that I am older, I still see that just as much, if not even more, and I hope I never loose those values.

Yet now I also see the other side.

I know to say good morning, and be thankful for the day.

I also know not to ask the day what it will do for me.

I try to ask myself, instead, what can I do for the day.

I also know that what I should do has very little to do with what I am expected to do.

I also know that who I am is not something defined by those people who would wish to define me.

❖　❖　❖　❖　❖

Day 228

I have often argued to students that, broadly speaking, the Ancients tended to have a proper sense of the balance within the human person.

They understood that man had a range of aspects and powers within his nature, and that the harmony of these powers defined his purpose and happiness.

In contrast, modernity and post–modernity seem to be dominated by shifts and struggles between extremes, between the dominance of reason and the dominance of the emotions.

A tired old classroom trick I have is to ask students "Is man rational, or is he passionate?"

Kant and Descartes say we are essentially rational.

Hume and Freud say we are essentially passionate.

Aristotle simple says "Yes."

Even when we understand that the question is a false dichotomy, we must be careful about understanding how the intellect and the emotions are rightly related.

We might define a good thought as one that is true.

But what defines a good emotion?

The easiest answer is that a good feeling is one that is pleasant, a bad feeling one that is unpleasant.

This, of course, falls to pieces as soon as we realize that not all pleasurable feelings are good feelings.

I have all to often felt pleasure that was all too far from being good.

I have also felt pain that was all to far from being bad.

The question is resolved if we understand that the value feeling is measured by our judgment.

Pleasure and pain can be good or bad, depending upon my estimation, and how I choose to make use of that feeling to act in accord with the purpose given me by Nature.

A bad feeling isn't an unpleasant one, a bad feeling is one that is not understood rightly.

❖ ❖ ❖ ❖ ❖

Day 229

Do not yourself bring disgrace on philosophy through your own acts, and be not one of those who load it with a bad reputation. But if theorems please you, sit still and turn them over by yourself; but never say that you are a philosopher, nor allow another to say it; but say: 'He is mistaken, for neither are my desires different from what they were before, nor is my activity directed to other objects, nor do I assent to other things, nor in the use of appearances have I altered at all from my former condition.'

—Epictetus, *Discourses* 3.21

By all means, take joy in a life of refined reflection and profound research.

This is the noble appeal of the intellectual life, and the world could use more good, reflective thinkers.

For the Stoic, however, that isn't the fullness of being a philosopher.
  How have I molded my desires?
  How have I improved my actions?
  How have I ordered my choices in a new way?
  How am I seeing through the world as it merely appears, down to my true nature, and thereby made myself better?

Being of a deeply bookish slant, I am often tempted to judge myself only through my thinking.
  I need the sound thinking, of course, but the fruits are in the living and the doing, in the attitude I bring to my daily circumstances.

I often need to hit the reset button.
  The old habits will return if I don't consciously remind myself of the new values I should really be practicing.
  I try to avoid ever introducing or advertising myself as a philosopher.
  I say rather that I am a student of philosophy, because I am still too far from being the good man a true philosopher would be.

❖ ❖ ❖ ❖ ❖

Day 230

We are universally ungrateful. Let each one question himself—everyone will find someone to complain of for being ungrateful. But it is impossible that all men should complain, unless all men gave cause for complaint—all men, therefore, are ungrateful. Are they ungrateful only? They are also covetous and spiteful and cowardly—especially those who appear to be bold. Besides, all are self-seeking, all are ungodly. But you have no need to be angry with them; pardon them—they are all mad.

—Seneca the Younger, *On benefits* 5.17

Seneca isn't just on an angry rant here, exaggerating his frustrations to extreme levels.
As beings of choice, we all make mistakes.
Not a single one of us has avoided being ungrateful, self-seeking, or ungodly.
We are, all of us, each and every one of us, guilty of these sins.
A day does not pass where I not have failed in the virtues.

The question, however, is not whether all of us, without exception, fail.
The question is how I will now estimate and judge that universal failure.
There is the Stoic Turn, and the virtue of following through. I need not be angry with myself or with others.
I need to love myself, love others, and forgive the whole bunch.
What I have then done is wiped that slate clean, removed the resentments that hinder me, and I can now make a new attempt to live the moment well.

Weakness, illness, failure, or vice demand sympathy, not anger.
It does not matter one bit if I am loved and appreciated.
I must simply love and appreciate.
Not only if, but when, I mess all this all up, I dust myself off and start again.
There is nothing tedious in that process, because doing any little thing with hope and joy itself brings us more hope and joy.

❖ ❖ ❖ ❖ ❖

Day 231

Happiness is a good spirit, or a good thing. What then are you doing here, Oh imagination? Go away, I entreat you by the gods, as you did come, for I want you not. But you have come according to your old fashion. I am not angry with you: Only go away.

—Marcus Aurelius, *Meditations* Book 7

We need to understand this, of course, in the right context.
Marcus Aurelius isn't telling us not to be imaginative, to be creative, or to be dreamers.
He is referring to the way our imagination, literally our handling of images, can so easily draw us away from happiness.

I have always liked the phrase "dark imaginings", because I know exactly what it means, and I think that is what Aurelius means.
When I became a cuckold, and the Black Dog started nipping at me, I would lie awake for hours.
Where is she?
What is she doing?
Who is she with?

When I lost my son, I would lie awake for hours.
What would he have looked like if he had grown up?
What sort of person would he have become?
What would the scene have been like when his mother and I were at his graduation or his wedding?

I had made a bit of a start at fixing these flights of fancy, of being ruled by my imagination, years later.
I will always vividly remember the details of my visit to a cardiologist who told me I was dying.
I was now enough of a Stoic to feel calm, and not panic.

But when I lay down that night, my imagination started to do what it does so well.
When will I die?
What will it feel like, and how much will it hurt?
Would anyone care when I was gone?

That is the time to ask your imagination, politely, to excuse itself.
I must rule over the images, and not be ruled by them.
Good day, sir... I said 'Good day!'

❖ ❖ ❖ ❖ ❖

Then, from the other point of view of the good, see what a punishment ever goes with the wicked. You have learnt a little while past that all that exists is one, and that the good itself is one; it follows therefrom that all that exists must appear to be good.

In this way, therefore, all that falls away from the good, ceases also to exist, wherefore evil men cease to be what they were. The form of their human bodies still proves that they have been men; wherefore they must have lost their human nature when they turned to evil-doing. But as goodness alone can lead men forward beyond their humanity, so evil of necessity will thrust down below the honorable estate of humanity those whom it casts down from their first position.

The result is that you cannot hold him to be a man who has been, so to say, transformed by his vices.

If a violent man and a robber burns with greed of other men's possessions, you say he is like a wolf.

Another fierce man is always working his restless tongue at lawsuits, and you will compare him to a hound.

Does another delight to spring upon men from ambushes with hidden guile? He is as a fox.

Does one man roar and not restrain his rage? He would be reckoned as having the heart of a lion.

Does another flee and tremble in terror where there is no cause of fear? He would be held to be as deer.

If another is dull and lazy, does he not live the life of an ass?

One whose aims are inconstant and ever changed at his whims, is in no wise different from the birds.

If another is in a slough of foul and filthy lusts, he is kept down by the lusts of an unclean swine.

Thus then a man who loses his goodness, ceases to be a man, and since he cannot change his condition for that of a god, he turns into a beast.

—Boethius, *The consolation of Philosophy* Book 4 Prose 3

Boethius is here presenting classic Stoicism, with a good pinch of St Augustine on the nature of good and evil, and of being and nothingness.

All things are good, simply by the fact that they exist.
St Thomas Aquinas, for example, says that goodness is the same as being, only insofar as it is desirable.
If goodness is being, then evil is the absence of being, nothingness.

What a remarkable realization that is.
When we experience evil, we are not experiencing a thing at all: We are experiencing the absence of something that is missing, of something that should be present.
When a man is evil, for example, it is not his being that is evil.
It is the absence of virtue, what should be present, according to his nature, which is evil.

So when I look at myself, and I say that I am not good, all I am really doing is pointing out what is missing.

I actually transform myself, my very being, by hacking off those bits that should be there. I become the pieces of a man, but not a man at all.

❖ ❖ ❖ ❖ ❖

Day 233

As a field, though fertile, cannot yield a harvest without cultivation, no more can the mind without learning; thus each is feeble without the other.

But philosophy is the cultivation of the soul. It draws out vices by the root, prepares the mind to receive seed, and commits to it, and, so to speak, sows in it what, when grown, may bear the most abundant fruit.

—Cicero, *Tusculan disputations* 2.5

I love gardens, and I can sit in one and appreciate it for hours, but I am sadly a horrible gardener.
The wife is more committed, but we seem to kill anything we touch.
My mother is quite the opposite: Her garden at the old family home is one of the most beautiful things I have ever seen, and I miss it so much, each and every day.

I think the images of the gardener and cultivation are very fitting.
The true gardeners I know, like my mother, are people who love the beauty of Nature for its own sake.
They take joy merely in the care and attention they give, and the appreciation of having not created anything at all, but rather in having aided their plants to be healthy and robust.
I have never heard my mother ask for compliments, or expect the neighbors to admire her work.
She does what she does because she loves participating in Nature.

I am a great admirer of Peter Sellers' last film, *Being there*.
A simple-minded but good-hearted man, Chance, isolated from the wide world for his whole life, is thrust into the ridiculous game that is modern society.

He expresses simple advice on gardening, and everyone thinks he is a deep thinker.
I suspect part of the point is that yes, he is, but not in the way people think he is.

> *As long as the roots are not severed, all is well. And all will be well in the garden.*

The fancy folks believe he is talking about economics and politics.

❖ ❖ ❖ ❖ ❖

Day 234

Does a philosopher invite people to hear him? As the sun himself draws men to him, or as food does, does not the philosopher also draw to him those who will receive benefit?

What physician invites a man to be treated by him? Indeed I now hear that even the physicians in Rome do invite patients, but when I lived there, the physicians were invited.

'I invite you to come and hear that things are in a bad way for you, and that you are taking care of everything except that of which you ought to take care, and that you are ignorant of the good and the bad and are unfortunate and unhappy.' A fine kind of invitation: and yet if the words of the philosopher do not produce this effect on you, he is dead, and so is the speaker.

—Epictetus, *Discourses* 3.23

It is a dictate of Stoicism to never draw attention to oneself.

It should be sufficient to be as we are, and if anyone who sees us as we are is willing to observe, to listen, and to follow, that is indeed right and good.

Yet never ask someone to observe, listen, or follow you.

Your living should be your model, not your words.

On particularly bad days, when I am tempted to make myself important, I play a little game.

I make myself as invisible as possible.

I will deliberately put myself off the radar, and go into what I call "Stealth Mode".

Don't speak just to be heard.

Don't stand in order to be seen.

Don't do anything to be recognized.

Let your humble deeds be their own message.

I can barely watch traditional television in this country anymore, because it seems that a third of what I see is someone trying to convince me to buy something.

Produce a good product, show me that it is useful, and I will indeed buy it.

Do not try to entrap me in images and false appearances.

I already do not trust you, simply because you are promoting yourself.

What is truly profitable for a man isn't what he sells, but how well he lives.

❖ ❖ ❖ ❖ ❖

Day 235

About pain: The pain which is intolerable carries us off; but that which lasts a long time is tolerable; and the mind maintains its own tranquility by retiring into itself, and the ruling faculty is not made worse. But the parts which are harmed by pain, let them, if they can, give their opinion about it.

—Marcus Aurelius, *Meditations* Book 7

When younger, I would never have expected my older years to be defined by how I face and manage my pain.
That is, however, what it has become. I walk through each and every day with a heart broken, both figuratively and literally.
I can barely distinguish between my psychological and physical symptoms, because they are so closely knotted together.
I have been learning to think myself right, but that doesn't dispose of the pain.

The Black Dog doesn't go away if I ignore him, but he becomes more manageable if I start to tame him.
It has taken me many years to come to a very basic realization: If the pain is too great, it will kill me.
If it does not kill me, I can, and if I only choose to do so, I will, consider it rightly, and I can be happy.

Only the other day, I was leading Lauds at my school, and I found myself overwhelmed by chest pains.
I should have expected them, given the state of my feelings, since bad feelings raise my blood pressure, and the raised blood pressure leads to quite a bit of physical pain.
The problem was that I was on show in public, leading a prayer.

I tried to tough it out, to push back, simply to grin and bear it.
This was deeply unsuccessful.
I could tell that others were beginning to notice my distress.
I changed my tactic quickly, and I took the pain and used it to my advantage.
I had to slow down the words, but each word was fueled by my own feelings.
Instead of keeping it in, I pushed it out, and I transformed it.

I made it through, and lived to see another day, satisfied and deeply content that I had done right.
I had not ignored or looked away from my pain, but I had properly listened to it, and then I made good of it.

❖ ❖ ❖ ❖ ❖

'Yet,' you say, 'many sorrows, things dreadful and hard to bear, do befall us.'

Yes, because I could not withdraw you from their path, I have armed your minds to withstand them all; endure with fortitude. In this you may outstrip God; he is exempt from enduring evil, while you are superior to it.

Scorn poverty; no one lives as poor as he was born. Scorn pain; it will either be relieved or relieve you. Scorn death, which either ends you or transfers you. Scorn Fortune; I have given her no weapon with which she may strike your soul.

Above all, I have taken pains that nothing should keep you here against your will; the way out lies open. If you do not choose to fight, you may run away.

Therefore of all things that I have deemed necessary for you, I have made nothing easier than dying. I have set life on a downward slope: if it is prolonged, only observe and you will see what a short and easy path leads to liberty.

—Seneca the Younger, *On providence* 6

Since starting this little project, I have wanted nothing more than to offer a reflection of a single word:

'Yes.'

Being a verbose and melodramatic Irishman, I, of course, need to say more, with as much treacle as possible.

Dying is easy.

Living is hard, but I have everything I need to do it, and to do it well.

I must turn everything to my benefit, and realize that my suffering, whatever Providence chooses it to be, can make me better, freer, and stronger.

I don't need to do anything I don't choose to do.

❖ ❖ ❖ ❖ ❖

Day 237

For my part I consider the man most enviable who lives amid a number of like-minded brothers, and I consider most beloved of the gods the man who has these blessings at home. Therefore I believe that each one of us ought to try to leave brothers rather than money to our children so as to leave greater assurances of blessings.

—Musonius Rufus, *Lectures* 15

I sadly have no siblings, not from my parents' choice, but from circumstance.
I suppose that explains quite a bit about my personality, and I often envy those who have larger families, with brothers and sisters.

Even if we cannot offer that gift to our children, I think Musonius means that the benefit of friendship and fellowship is far greater than the benefit of wealth.

I have lost count of the couples I know that design their families based on their careers and income. I have suggested to many of them that they design their careers and income based on their families, but I am usually met with a blank stare.

There is nothing at all that a credit card, or any sort of worldly wealth, will give you that is priceless.
Love and fellowship are priceless.
Change the parameters of your life, and you will manage to change the benefits.

❖ ❖ ❖ ❖ ❖

Let not that which in another is contrary to Nature be an evil to you: for you are not formed by Nature to be depressed with others nor to be unhappy with others, but to be happy with them.

If a man is unhappy, remember that his unhappiness is his own fault; for God has made all men to be happy, to be free from perturbations.

For this purpose he has given means to them, some things to each person as his own, and other things not as his own; some things subject to hindrance and compulsion and deprivation; and these things are not a man's own; but the things which are not subject to hindrances are his own; and the nature of good and evil, as it was fit to be done by him who takes care of us and protects us like a father, he has made our own.

But,' you say, 'I have parted from a certain person, and he is grieved.' Why did he consider as his own that which belongs to another? Why, when he looked on you and was rejoiced, did he not also reckon that you are mortal, that it is natural for you to part from him for a foreign country? Therefore he suffers the consequences of his own folly.

—Epictetus, *Discourses* 3.24

I love this passage, and at the same time I despise it.
 I love it because I know every word of it to be true.
 I despise it because it makes it all too clear that the things that drag me down have always been of my own making.
 That makes me feel the deepest shame.
 My intellect tells me it is right, and my vanity pushes right back.

I once heard a popular and learned scholar tell an enraptured audience that Stoicism means recognizing that all the things that hurt us come from outside of us.

No. All the things that hurt us come from our estimation about the things outside of us.
 The things that hurt us come from us.
 This is simply another example of why giving someone a title or fame does not make him reliable or trustworthy.

The things I suffer now, and the things I have suffered for decades, have absolutely nothing to do with my circumstances.
 They are about my unwillingness to properly cope with my circumstances.

Has something been taken from me?
 It was never mine.
 Has love been denied?
 That does not mean I can't still love.
 Has the world been unjust?
 Good. I can still be just.

Long ago, I discovered that the girl I was falling in love with was still dating an old boyfriend back home.
 She saw no problem with this.
 I simply told her she needed to choose one of us.
 She chose me, and I felt vindicated.

That was an incredibly foolish, arrogant, and sadly life–defining, choice on my part.
  I should have graciously walked away, because it was apparent that she was untrustworthy and disloyal.

She had already treated both of us poorly.
  I now made the matter worse by asking her to discard him.
  Many years later, she did exactly the same thing to me that I had once asked her to do to someone else.

I was the only one to blame for that.
  She was what she was, but I should have known better, and I suffered the consequences of my own folly.
  I deserved everything I got, in a true form of poetic justice.
  I reaped what I sowed.
  It hurts when you realize that your problems are of your own making, but it's a necessary lesson.

This recognition need not involve all the shame, self-loathing, or crippling regret I had felt for years and years.
  It could now be a simple awareness of complete responsibility for myself.

❖ ❖ ❖ ❖ ❖

But what folly it is, when the beginnings of certain things are situated outside our control, to believe that their endings are within our control! How have I the power to bring something to a close, when I have not had the power to check it at the beginning?
—Seneca the Younger, *Moral letters to Lucilius* 85

A tough phrase spoken by confident young men in my youth was that "I'll never start a fight, but I'll always finish one."
I found this odd, since everyone seemed to claim it, yet someone must still have started the fights, and then they very rarely ever seemed to finish.

So it is also with the conditions of our lives of our lives as a whole.
We may say that we had no control over the lives we were born into, or even that we were born at all.
As younger children we are ruled by our parents.
We somehow think, however, that as we get older, we gain more and more control over our lives, and that our own dedication and hard work will make us masters of our domain.

This is only true in a specific sense.
We can indeed, with dedication and hard work become free to master ourselves.
What we can barely ever have any control over is our circumstances.
I should not even wish it, and I should be wary of the illusion that it might appear to be true.
That would only divert me from my real responsibility.

In my own case, I have actually found that I am far less in control of my external conditions than when I was a child.
Childhood was the closest I came to living in a free world.
In adulthood I have had to find that freedom within, and not without.

❖ ❖ ❖ ❖ ❖

Day 240

You have lost the leisure or ability to read? But you have leisure or ability to check arrogance: you have leisure to be superior to pleasure and pain: you have leisure to be superior to love of fame, and not to be vexed at stupid and ungrateful people, but even to care for them.

—Marcus Aurelius, *Meditations* Book 8

I find it difficult to imagine a world where I could not enjoy books.
At times, however, I have simply felt too busy to read, and in later years my eyes simply aren't what they used to be.
As with so many things in life, I can then take opportunity to complain about unfair it all is, and I somehow think this makes it better.

I may not have the leisure to read, and I may be loosing the eyesight I need to pursue my love of books, but as with all things, as long as I live I have the opportunity to practice goodness.
I don't merely need to read about it.

Books have moved my imagination, taught me about the truth, helped me to appreciate what is beautiful, and given me the example of virtuous character.
I may not have the opportunity for the book, but I can still appreciate and practice those things.

So I remind myself that the living isn't there for the sake of the books.
The books are there to help me with the living.

❖ ❖ ❖ ❖ ❖

Day 241

If I knew that it was fated for me to be sick, I would even wish for it; for the foot also, if it had intelligence, would volunteer to get muddy.

—Chrysippus, ex Epictetus, *Discourses* 2.6

A quirk, and an annoying one at that for the few who love me, is my attachment to building collections of things I enjoy.

It started with books, moved to music and musical instruments, then fedora hats, smoking pipes and fancy pipe tobacco, walking sticks, die-cast airplanes, and pocket knives.

I had to rein myself in with spectacles and pocket watches.

I suppose there's certain snobbery to some of it, but I mainly just appreciate these things for their own sake.

The problem becomes that I appreciate these things so much, that I sometimes hesitate to use them, to get them dirty, to wear them in.

A dent, or a scratch, or a smudge can cause me worry.

I need not be told how ridiculous this tendency is.

After all, the things we enjoy are meant to be used, not coddled or hidden away.

A smoking pipe must be broken in to shine, a hat must be worn to bind its shape to my head, and musicians even say an instrument improves in tone the more it is played.

I have a beautiful Swedish hunting knife with a fine carbon steel blade.

Unlike stainless steel, carbon will not stay shiny, but through use will take on an increasingly beautiful patina.

Add to that a handle that has been slightly worn away, and repeated sharpening has scuffed the grind.

It is my favorite knife to use, mainly, I think, because it has been so used.

Wear and tear has made it an extension of me.

Now if I can understand and something becomes better when it is used, that should also be true of my own nature.

My feet were made to walk, so they should get dirty.

I was made to live well, so I should not fear living.

Even pain and illness are part of that existence, so I should welcome them, like the wear and tear on my knife.

❖ ❖ ❖ ❖ ❖

Day 242

There is no cause to hate bad men. Vice is as a disease of the mind, just as feebleness shows
ill health in the body. As, then, we should never think that those, who are sick in the body,
deserve hatred, so are those, whose minds are oppressed by a fiercer disease than feebleness,
namely wickedness, much more worthy of pity than of persecution.
—Boethius. *The consolation of Philosophy* Book 4 Prose 4

Boethius understands something that many of us, in our supposedly advanced age, still don't really understand.
Sicknesses of the soul deserve our understanding, compassion, and assistance just as much as diseases of the body.

We see a body ravaged by cancer, and we feel pity, yet when we see a vicious or greedy man, we lash out in anger.
The vicious man, you may say, is different, because he chose to be the way he is.
I don't know the root cause of his condition, whether voluntary or involuntary, just as I don't if the cancer patient made good or bad life choices.

That should hardly matter in either case, as we still owe our compassion for any and every person who suffers.

Even when it comes to diseases such as depression or anxiety, which are both of the body and mind, but hardly voluntary, I often see people blaming and condemning the person who suffers.
I have repeatedly heard educated and thoughtful people suggest, for example, that the victim of clinical depression, anxiety, or PTSD simply "get over it".

Wherever the disease and the suffering, in the physical organs, in the emotions, or in the height of the intellect and will, this asks less for blame than for helping provide comfort and healing.
If you see a wicked person, ask yourself how you can help him heal himself before you dismiss him out of hand.

❖ ❖ ❖ ❖ ❖

Day 243

Well then, even if we have renounced the contest in this matter, no man hinders us from renewing the combat again, and we are not compelled to wait for another four years that the games at Olympia may come again; but as soon as you have recovered and restored yourself, and employ the same zeal, you may renew the combat again; and if again you renounce it, you may again renew it; and if you once gain the victory, you are like him who has never renounced the combat.

—Epictetus, *Discourses* 3.25

Besides the preferences of my personality, I'm not a fan of the usual sort of dinner party, because on at least one instance during the evening, and most likely on a number of instances, the person next to me will cup his hand around his mouth to make some sort of dismissive remark about a guest further down the table.

Someone I hardly remember once kept telling me that a woman a few seats down had failed the Bar Exam, not once, not twice, but three times.
I asked if she passed on the fourth.
"Yeah, but can you imagine?
Would you hire her as your lawyer?"

I tried to be civil, though with great effort.
"Quite possibly, yes, assuming I actually needed one.
I admire someone who fights the good fight."

"But she failed three times!"

"And passed the fourth. That shows character."

I understand that I'm working from a totally different moral map than this sort of fellow, so I try my best to understand.
She was trying to pass the Bar, I was trying not to be snarky with the fellow next to me, and if any of us fail in life, we win the victory through trying again.

❖ ❖ ❖ ❖ ❖

Repentance is a kind of self-reproof for having neglected something useful; but that which is useful must be something good, and the perfect good man should look after it. But no such man would ever repent of having refused any sensual pleasure. Pleasure then is neither good nor useful.

—Marcus Aurelius, *Meditations* Book 8

There's nothing like some clear definitions and a nice chain of syllogisms to make a philosopher smile.

There's simply the joy of the form of the logic itself, of course, but then there is also the appreciation of the content, and how this conclusion can help us to live better.

We have here a variation on Musonius Rufus' and Seneca's insight on pleasure and the good.

Contemporary life tries to convince us that if feels good, it is good.

If a nuanced discussion of the useful, the good, and the pleasing are a bit much, then just think of it in this restructured way.

Have you ever repented of a pleasure?

There's the answer.

I have never been a hedonist or even an Epicurean, but more often than I care to admit sloppy thinking has led me to pursue the pleasant and avoid the painful.

Most, if not all, of my regrets began this way, fueled further by pride and stubbornness.

I have reproved myself for seeking gratification many a time, but I have never reproved myself for a virtuous disposition.

"But hasn't doing the right thing ever gotten you in trouble?"

If you mean by trouble, the presence of pain and dishonor, or the loss of gratification and possessions, then yes, quite a bit.

Those things are not the good, however, because they are indifferent.

Nor should think of real trouble as that which comes from hiding a vice in the appearance of a virtue.

❖ ❖ ❖ ❖ ❖

Day 245

I suppose you call a man rich just because his gold plate goes with him even on his travels, because he farms land in all the provinces, because he unrolls a large account-book, because he owns estates near the city so great that men would grudge his holding them in the waste lands of Apulia.

But after you have mentioned all these facts, he is poor. And why? He is in debt. 'To what extent?' you ask. For all that he has. Or perhaps you think it matters whether one has borrowed from another man or from Fortune?

—Seneca the Younger, *Moral letters to Lucilius* 87

Though I am hardly one who travels in the higher circles of the fancy folks, I have run across my share of rich people.

Even at a financial level, their wealth is often hardly their own, tied up as it is in the red tape of investment and borrowing.

On the even more basic level of the true wealth of character, this is all the more true.

Even if he holds the deeds to all his possessions, and no one is fighting with him to seize his money, he's still entirely in debt.

He may owe nothing to his banker, but he owes everything to Fortune.

All that he defines himself by does not belong to him at all, and Fortune is a much more fickle mistress than any bank.

I've learned to not merely say it begrudgingly, but to appreciate on its own merits: I'm glad the world gave me little, because now I owe the world very little.

Since some missteps in my youth, I have avoided financial debt wherever possible, despite what the bankers would like to tell me, just as I avoid being indebted to anything outside of me.

❖ ❖ ❖ ❖ ❖

Day 246

It is not easy to produce an effect upon soft characters any more than it is to pick up a soft cheese with a hook, but young men of sound nature, even if you turn them away, hold to philosophy all the more.

For that reason Rufus frequently discouraged pupils, using this as a means of testing the superior and inferior ones. For he used to say, 'Just as a stone, even if you throw it upwards, will fall downwards because of its Nature, so the superior man, the more one repels him, the more he inclines toward his own natural direction.'

—Musonius Rufus , Fragments 46

I started doing something similar, long before I read the story about Musonius Rufus, out of the same sort of motive.

When I have taught at the college level, I will occasionally come across the star philosophy student, one who has a talent and love of the craft.

I wait for the inevitable question: "Should I apply to graduate school in Philosophy?"

"Most definitely not. They'll chew you up and spit you out, or they will brainwash you.

Either they'll put you down, leaving you a crippled and disappointed soul, or you'll get sucked into their lies.

And you'll sell out philosophy for your own vanity."

"But—"

"No buts. Don't do it."

Now I am well aware that this seems unnecessarily harsh.

It's only if they keep coming back, making their case over and over, that I know I will write that letter of recommendation, and I will actually mean what I wrote.

They've proven to me, and more importantly to themselves, that they are in this for the right reason, and they have the fortitude to face the temptations.

I once saw a young lady do much the same to a fellow that fancied her.

She resisted, he proved himself, and he won her heart.

The struggle reveals the true character.

❖ ❖ ❖ ❖ ❖

Day 247

Diseases of the mind are more common and more pernicious than diseases of the body.
—Cicero, *Tusculan disputations* 3.3

We only just saw Boethius explaining how both diseases of the mind and of the body are worthy of our love, not our condemnation.
Cicero now adds that diseases of the mind are also more prevalent, and far more dangerous.

I think this is true both of what we narrowly would call mental illness according to modern psychology, as well as moral and intellectual illness.
We are quite ready to assume that others are all right in the head, even while we all know about one another's aches and pains.
Our feelings and our judgments are often glossed over.

I can only speak anecdotally, of course, and not from any academic research or out of deeper human insight, but the more I come to know people, the more I begin to see how deeply many of us suffer in our hearts and minds.
I often bemoan how I am broken down psychologically and philosophically.
My feelings are constantly playing tricks on me, and reacting in ways I simply can't understand.
My thinking, in turn gets garbled and confused by misleading judgments and poor decisions.

When I am given the gift of getting to know someone, to see them, if but for a moment, as they truly are, I wonder if we aren't all like that in differing ways and degrees.
We all feel suffering we don't understand, we all have thoughts and feelings that terrify us, and we are all, in the end, lonely and uncertain.

These need not be seen as a universal burden:
It can be taken as a means for our solidarity, to recognize ourselves in others, and to learn thereby that by helping others we help ourselves.

❖ ❖ ❖ ❖ ❖

'What, then, if I shall be sick?' You will be sick in such the way that you ought to be.

'Who will take care of me?' God, your friends.

'I shall lie down on a hard bed.' But you will lie down like a man.

'I shall not have a convenient chamber.' You will be sick in an inconvenient chamber.

'Who will provide for me the necessary food?' Those who provide for others, also. You will be sick like Manes.

'And what, also, will be the end of the sickness? Any other than death?'

Do you then consider that this the chief of all evils to man and the chief mark of mean spirit and of cowardice is not death, but rather the fear of death? Against this fear then I advise you to exercise yourself: to this let all your reasoning tend, your exercises, and reading; and you will know that thus only are men made free.

—Epictetus, *Discourses* 3.26

The things beyond my control will happen as they will happen, regardless of whether I worry about them.

Some of these things will happen inevitably, so I can't even imagine that the worrying will change the fate.

That I will be sick, and that I will die, sooner or later, is something that must be.

That it is something that must be means it is a part of what Nature intends.

Sickness and death are not evils.

The fear of them is evil.

To know this is freedom.

The story has it that the Manes whom Epictetus refers to was a slave of Diogenes the Cynic.

Manes ran away from his master's rule, but Diogenes refused to bring him back: After all, if his slave could live alone without his master, then the master should be able to live alone without the slave.

So, like Manes, you may die alone, and you still, even then, need not fear death.

I have seen enough people prepare for their futures, for being secure and cared for, only to find that Fortune shuffled the deck, and made those preparations meaningless.

I have also seen many a dramatic and stirring novel, film or television series where the characters go through struggles and hardship, sometimes acting with cowardice and greed, sometimes with courage and justice.

Sometimes the world goes with their desires and sometimes the world goes against their desires. Either way, they must meet their end in the narrative, sometimes alone and unsung.

So too, must life be, but that hardly makes it a bad story.

❖ ❖ ❖ ❖ ❖

'But what,' asks our adversary, 'is there to hinder virtue and pleasure being combined together, and a highest good being thus formed, so that honor and pleasure may be the same thing?'

Because nothing except what is honorable can form a part of honor, and the highest good would lose its purity if it were to see within itself anything unlike its own better part.

Even the joy which arises from virtue, although it be a good thing, yet is not a part of absolute good, any more than cheerfulness or peace of mind, which are indeed good things, but which merely follow the highest good, and do not contribute to its perfection, although they are generated by the noblest causes.

Whoever on the other hand forms an alliance, and that, too, a one-sided one, between virtue and pleasure, clogs whatever strength the one may possess by the weakness of the other, and sends liberty under the yoke, for liberty can only remain unconquered as long as she knows nothing more valuable than herself: for he begins to need the help of Fortune, which is the most utter slavery: his life becomes anxious, full of suspicion, timorous, fearful of accidents, waiting in agony for critical moments of time.

You do not afford virtue a solid immoveable base if you bid it stand on what is unsteady: and what can be so unsteady as dependence on mere chance, and the vicissitudes of the body and of those things which act on the body? How can such a man obey God and receive everything which comes to pass in a cheerful spirit, never complaining of fate, and putting a good construction upon everything that befalls him, if he be agitated by the petty pin-pricks of pleasures and pains?

—Seneca the Younger, *On a happy life* 15

As part of our repeated problem of wanting it both ways, there's also that desire to cover all the bases.

Why can't that morally good life also happen to be the one that's the most fun, and that makes me the richest and most popular?

Why can't all these good things just be the same?

At the most basic level, let us be honest with ourselves.

We would like pleasure as a first principle, but under the appearance of virtue.

This appearance of virtue is in turn, of course, simply another expression of honor.

So if I say that I'd like to feel good and look good to others doing it, character has not even entered into the picture.

Seneca's argument is a typical example of how the Ancients could think clearly and concisely, with their attention always directed toward the essential principles.

I sum up this argument for myself, not as a simplification, but as a sort of shorthand to help me remember:

Goods are all good because they are united, not divided, and a highest good must be totally one.

It can't admit of divisions.

Can virtue go together with joy?

Yes, but the pleasure is not the cause of the virtue: the virtue is the cause of the pleasure.

If you spread your loyalties over many goals, you will inevitably compromise one for the others, and the greater for the lesser, selling your freedom back to your circumstances.

As soon as you wish to move virtue to accommodate lesser things, you no longer appreciate the higher things.
The very fact that you would compromise one for the other, freedom for slavery, already reveals what you really care for.

The Stoic takes joy in living well for the sake of living well, and every pleasure, honor, or worldly benefit can only be measured through that highest end.

❖ ❖ ❖ ❖ ❖

Day 250

You suffer this justly: for you choose rather to become good tomorrow than to be good today.
—Marcus Aurelius, *Meditations* Book 8

This is another one of the short Stoic phrases I have memorized, and repeat to myself regularly when I am beginning to feel resentment.

I suffer things justly not because someone else has acted unjustly.
That has made them suffer from their own actions.
Rather, I suffer something justly because I am continuing to allow it to determine my happiness.
The punishment comes not from outside of me, but from inside of me.

As soon as I change my judgment, I will change the nature of the punishment.
Putting off until tomorrow what I can do today is a consequence of my own lack of commitment, and is not the fault of the wrongdoer.

Do not believe that the Stoic thinks that others do not do wrong to us.
They do, in spades, but that is entirely on them.
When I fail to react rightly to a wrong, I have now added a second wrong.
We know have an unjust act by one, and an unjust resentment by another.

It would be all too easy to cast blame before accepting it, but when I do that, I am also the cause of my own blame.
Beyond amusing and cautionary tales intended to help my students make sense of ideas and values, I very rarely mention the landmark moments of my life to others.
When I do, I'm often given the rote answer: "Don't let the past get you down."
I respect their good intentions.

I know that all too well. I need to distinguish that it isn't the past that is getting me down at all.
After all, it doesn't even exist.
What's getting me down is my struggle to come to terms with these things for myself, to actually be good today.
I view the fact that I struggle, and that I don't simply lay down, as an encouragement, not a discouragement.

Day 251

Diogenes lit a lamp in broad daylight and said, as he was walking about, 'I am looking for an honest man.'

—Diogenes of Sinope, ex Diogenes Laertius,
Lives and opinions of eminent philosophers 6.41

Diogenes of Sinope was in many ways the Ancient version of a performance artist, whose words and actions were intended to engage and challenge the norms and standards of the world around him, often in extreme and absurd ways.
Let me assure you, this is one of his milder ones!

A few passages ago we saw Seneca insisting that we're all ungrateful, all self-seeking, all ungodly.
Understand rightly, that is completely correct.
With our failings, we will regularly stumble and fall.
We differ from one another, sometimes vastly, in the degree of our vices, but never in kind, in the fact that we are subject to error.

I am a far more honest man than I was years ago.
I shamefully admit that in my early youth I would sometimes exaggerate and inflate, only for the purpose of gaining respect.
Having then had the blessing of being on the receiving end of deception quite a few times, I started to consciously build a habit in the opposite direction.

Over thirty years later, I'm much better at it, but there are still gaping holes in the edifice of my honesty.
Instead of deliberately telling a falsehood, I'm now still easily tempted to use silence as a means to deceive.
I'm a man fighting to be honest, but I'm not fully honest.

I don't see Diogenes as offering a condemnation here.
I see him as reminding us that we are all in the same boat, and we all need to bail water together before we all sink together.
Don't damn others for the very same things that we all do.

❖ ❖ ❖ ❖ ❖

Day 252

When a man speaks evil or does evil to you, remember that he does or says it because he thinks it is fitting for him. It is not possible for him to follow what seems good to you, but only what seems good to him, so that, if his opinion is wrong, he suffers, in that he is the victim of deception.

—Epictetus, *Enchiridion* 42

This fundamental Stoic wisdom does not mean, I think, that we are to simply make excuses for evil, or brush off the root causes of our sins.
It is not intended to remove personal responsibility, or use ignorance as a justification.
This isn't about erasing any real balance sheet.

I have seen too often in others, and too often in myself, the temptation to reject and dismiss others because we perceive them as having wronged us, whether that perception is true or false.
Remember, you have only been truly wronged, in your soul, when you permit something to wrong you.

Remember also that the reason why a person acts as he does is that he genuinely thinks that he is doing good.
If he does wrong, don't hate, condemn, or cast him out. Love and correct instead.
Once you truly know why a man behaves as he does, the nature of the disease, you can discern the nature of the cure.

I have slowly figured out that the good people I know, and who have helped me the most, aren't just blindly forgiving me.
They understand me, at the root, and in a certain sense, they don't even need to forgive, as there was never really any offense.
Instead of turning their backs on me, they choose to embrace me.

This is a reason why I have stressed, from the beginning of this project, that Stoicism must, of necessity, show compassion and concern.
I worry that some theorists and practitioners of the school overlook this important point.
A love for others follows directly from all the basic first principles.

❖ ❖ ❖ ❖ ❖

Day 253

There are three relations between you and other things: the one to the body which surrounds you; the second to the divine cause from which all things come to all; and the third to those who live with you.

—Marcus Aurelius, *Meditations* Book 8

As a Department Chairman at a college, I was once given the unenviable task of writing out a Department Mission Statement.

These have become all the rage in the last two decades, along with Learning Outcomes, Objectives, and Goals, because, I would argue, we have become increasingly obsessed with the appearance over the reality.

We want fine and pretty words, and we think we've finished the job.

This is hardly Stoic, or in accord with any sort of common sense.

I dreaded the chore, and passed it on to a colleague who was more politically correct.

I honestly expected him, in accord with the Outcome Model, to write out two or three pages of empty platitudes. I already saw where the trends were taking us, and I had resigned myself to the state of affairs.

Quite to my joy and surprise, he returned the following, in a matter of minutes:

"The Department seeks to assist our students, through the tools of both reason and of faith, to come to know themselves, their world, and their Creator."

The struggle to actually adopt this statement over many years is a soap opera in itself, and for another time.

Needless to say, it was considered too brief, too direct, and not nearly ambiguous enough.

Its merits, however unpopular, were completely in line with Stoicism, and with the words of Marcus Aurelius.

Stoicism does not breed isolation, but rather asks us to understand ourselves in proper relation to all other things.

Know yourself.

Know who you are at your core, and then grasp how that relates to the body that carries you.

Know where you came from, and where you are going.

Seek to see yourself on a vertical plane, how you relate to the ultimate causes above you.

Know others around you.

Strive to live on a horizontal plane with your equals, and how to relate with justice and compassion to your neighbors.

The fundamental question of life and its relations are really that simple.

Don't be discouraged by the clouds of ambiguity, which are, in the end, excuses for non-commitment.

❖　❖　❖　❖　❖

Everything is estimated by the standard of its own good. The vine is valued for its productiveness and the flavor of its wine, the stag for his speed. We ask, with regard to beasts of burden, how sturdy of back they are; for their only use is to bear burdens.

If a dog is to find the trail of a wild beast, keenness of scent is of first importance; if to catch his quarry, swiftness of foot; if to attack and harry it, courage, In which thing that quality should be best for which the thing is brought into being and by which it is judged.

And what quality is best in man? It is reason; by virtue of reason he surpasses the animals, and is surpassed only by the gods. Perfect reason is therefore the good peculiar to man; all other qualities he shares in some degree with animals and plants. Man is strong; so is the lion. Man is comely; so is the peacock. Man is swift; so is the horse. I do not say that man is surpassed in all these qualities.

I am not seeking to find that which is greatest in him, but that which is peculiarly his own. Man has body; so also have trees. Man has the power to act and to move at will; so have beasts and worms. Man has a voice; but how much louder is the voice of the dog, how much shriller that of the eagle, how much deeper that of the bull, how much sweeter and more melodious that of the nightingale! What then is peculiar to man? Reason.

—Seneca the Younger , *Moral letters to Lucilius 76*

Things do not merely share in existence, which simply affirms *that* it is.
Each also has its own essence or form, which defines *what* it is.
Consider not only the vast breadth of existence, but also the incredible depth of diversity in the forms of things, all types with their distinct nature and purpose.

The form of anything is not a mysterious, cryptic concept.
What something is becomes evident directly by what it does, and how it acts.
By being conscious of things we see into them.

The reader is familiar with the Stoic notion that while man has many aspects, including his physical body, instincts, and passions, he is essentially a being of reason.
My very awareness, which guides and directs all my actions, is the obvious proof of this.

Man shares in many qualities, but his mind and will are at his core.
How odd that we constantly draw our attention away from this core, and point rather to all his accidents, qualities he shares with other beings.

We define ourselves by our feelings, our ability to feel pleasure, the strength and beauty of our bodies, our clothing and possessions, our money, our jobs, and our power.
All these things are a part of my existence, but they are not at the heart of my existence.

When was the last time you saw a television advertisement that stressed that you were first and foremost a creature made to know and to love?
You won't, because these are qualities that can't be bought and sold.
To look to all the outside things is perhaps easier for us, because it allows us to be diverted from our true selves.
This may at first make us uncomfortable, because we know we have wrongly neglected ourselves.

❖ ❖ ❖ ❖ ❖

Rufus used to say, 'If you have time to waste praising me, I am conscious that what I say is worth nothing.'

So far from applause on our part, he spoke in such a way that each of us sitting there felt that someone had gone to him and told him our faults, so accurately he touched upon our true characters, so effectively he placed each one's faults before his eyes.

—Musonius Rufus, *Fragments* 48

I never like being praised, and always have to look away if I am, not out of any nobility, but because it embarrasses me.
Musonius gives us a much better reason to turn our backs on praise.
If I'm just getting the fancy words, I may well be doing something wrong.
If I see a genuine effect on others, no words are really necessary.

I made a mistake in one of my classes recently, by mentioning that I had finished the first draft of this book.
I have used the experience of writing these reflections as a pool of examples in my teaching, although it might not be best if they read it at their age.
They erupted into loud applause, and I blushed.
That's all nice and well, but I didn't want to just get praise, and I felt like I was just manipulating them for my pride.
Quite fittingly, that experience became part of the second draft.

It is better to do something else that I can occasionally manage, which is to calmly and thoroughly teach a lesson, without drawing any attention to myself.
Every so often, I will have this wonderful moment.
When I am finished, the room will be completely silent.
No, they aren't asleep, though that happens quite often for different reasons.
No, their faces are fully attentive, and I can almost see those gears turning in their heads.

It doesn't happen too often, but when it does, I know I've done my job.
No words or honors are necessary.

❖ ❖ ❖ ❖ ❖

Wherefore high Providence has thus often shown her strange wonder, namely, that bad men should make other bad men good. For some find themselves suffering injustice at the hands of evil men, and, burning with hatred of those who have injured them, they have returned to cultivate the fruits of virtue, because their aim is to be unlike those whom they hate.

To divine power, and to that alone, are evil things good, when it uses them suitably so as to draw good results from them. For a definite order embraces all things, so that even when some subject leaves the true place assigned to it in the order, it returns to an order, though another, it may be, lest something in the realm of Providence be left to random chance.

—Boethius, *The consolation of Philosophy* Book 4 Prose 6

Providence and Nature will always be victorious.
 The more I fight against it, the more it reacts with meaning and purpose.
 When a will turns to evil here, Providence uses it for good there.

I had a "Eureka!" moment upon first reading this passage in college.
 I still remember exactly where I was, on a sunny spring day, sitting on the grass behind our library, and going back and forth from practicing reels and jigs on my mandolin to reading Boethius.
 It just all came together.

What a joyous revelation!
 Nothing happens in vain.
 When any man does evil, I now have been given an opportunity, to make my world and myself brighter and better.
 Change the measure of success, and you suddenly see the pattern.
 This isn't lowering the bar of my expectations, it's actually raising it to a level that cannot be assaulted by any circumstances, however severe or brutal.

It has taken me many years to even begin to practice this rightly, but that was the moment I first understood.

❖ ❖ ❖ ❖ ❖

Further, then, answer me this question also: Does freedom seem to you to be something great and noble and valuable? 'How should it not seem so?'

Is it possible, then, when a man obtains anything, so great and valuable and noble to be mean? 'It is not possible.'

When, then, you see any man subject to another, or flattering him contrary to his own opinion, confidently affirm that this man also is not free; and not only if he does this for a bit of supper, but also if he does it for a government or a consulship: and call these men 'little slaves' who for the sake of little matters do these things, and those who do so for the sake of great things call 'great slaves,' as they deserve to be. 'This is admitted also.'

Do you think that freedom is a thing independent and self-governing? 'Certainly.'

Whomsoever, then, it is in the power of another to hinder and compel, declare that he is not free.

—Epictetus, *Discourses* 4.1

Here is another reason to be wary of praise, for it may be nothing more than flattery, and succumbing to flattery is like a chain that binds the will.

When others try to move and manipulate me one way or another with their words, and I then permit myself to be so moved, I am like a slave to them.

I am not a free man.

My wife and I have a long-standing and affectionate joke.

She may not ask me for any favor when she has just fed me one of her fine meals, and I may not ask a favor of her for a week after I have given her a spontaneous gift.

Be wary of the Right Hand of Fellowship.

It may be holding a knife.

The restraints that bind us are not merely of the body, of our property, or in the world of business and politics.

We make ourselves unfree the moment we allow our own judgment, and our ability to govern ourselves, be tossed and turned by flattery and manipulation.

❖ ❖ ❖ ❖ ❖

You have been wishing to know my views with regard to the Liberal Arts. My answer is this: I respect no study, and deem no study good, which results in moneymaking. Such studies are profit-bringing occupations, useful only in so far as they give the mind a preparation and do not engage it permanently.

One should linger upon them only so long as the mind can occupy itself with nothing greater; they are our apprenticeship, not our real work. Hence you see why 'liberal studies' are so called; it is because they are studies worthy of a freeborn gentleman. But there is only one really liberal study — that which gives a man his liberty. It is the study of wisdom, and that is lofty, brave, and great souled. All other studies are puny and puerile.

—Seneca the Younger, *Moral letters to Lucilius* 88

This passage raises my spirits, and gives me strength to continue each and every day in my vocation as a teacher.

I will try to resist the temptation to reflect at too great a length on the matter, because I know I could probably fill a whole book on Seneca's Letter 88 alone.

My wife is telling you to not give me any ideas.

There is a fundamental difference between training and education.

Both are about learning, in the broadest sense, but while the former teaches you skills, the latter teaches you to think, learn, and act for yourself.

Even an animal can be trained, however less perfectly, but only a human being can be truly educated.

It is a reflection of the sad state of affairs in modern education, and in our world as a whole, when we insist that school is there to give us good jobs.

Good jobs matter, but they are a means, never the end.

The purpose of education, Classically understood, is to help you be able to rule yourself, to teach you how to teach yourself, to inspire the very core of your being, to encourage you in the practice of wisdom and virtue.

Everything else comes a distant second.

Once we alter, however implicitly, the nature of a human being, from a thinking animal to a merely working animal, from *homo sapiens* to *homo faber*, we are already making a tragic mistake.

Make the Stoic Turn.

Once you recognize yourself through Nature, and not through mere appearance, you will see what education is all about.

If you define yourself by the externals, by all means, pursue only training, but if you rightly understand yourself as a creature made to know and to love above all else, and to act accordingly, seek an education.

The Ancients and the Medievals embraced the model of the Liberal Arts.

That is a topic for another time, but I encourage you to read a short essay by Dorothy Sayers, "The Lost Tools of Learning," if the issue interests you.

It turns everything we think education is about on its head, and all of it is grounded in the wisdom of the Greeks and the Romans.

Yet even those who would champion the cause of the Liberal Arts often get it quite wrong.

I suspect many of them are enamored of all the fancy old books, the tweed jackets, the images of the pompous Professor making snide, self-serving comments, rather than the impassioned love of the true, the good, and the beautiful.

I once suffered through the Chairman of the Board of Directors at my college giving a Commencement Speech.

"You are students from a school that prides itself on its Liberal Arts tradition," he confidently told us.

"The world *liberal* comes from the Latin word for 'book', and you have learned from those Great Books."

I hung my head in shame.

I'm not sure how many of our graduates learned anything from the Great Books of the Classics at all, but *liberal* most certainly doesn't come from the Latin word for 'book'. It comes from the Latin word for 'free'. A Liberal Arts education is one suitable for a free man, one who may govern himself, and thereby has the wisdom and character to govern others.

It isn't about reading books.

The genius that spoke those words thinks he will one day become a Bishop.

Jesus wept.

❖ ❖ ❖ ❖ ❖

Day 259

Pain is either an evil to the body—then let the body say what it thinks of it—or to the soul;
but it is in the power of the soul to maintain its own serenity and tranquility, and not to
think that pain is an evil.

For every judgment and movement and desire and aversion is within, and no evil ascends
so high.

Wipe out your imaginations by often saying to yourself: now it is in my power to let no
badness be in this soul, nor desire nor any perturbation at all; but looking at all things I
see what is their nature, and I use each according to its value.- Remember this power
which you have from nature.

—Marcus Aurelius, *Meditations* Book 8

I do not resent the person who does not quite understand how deeply a soul can feel pain; quite the contrary: I am happy that he has not had to suffer it in order to understand it.

But even knowing and accepting its reality is hardly enough.
I need to remember, at each and every moment, that it is within the power of my nature, through my judgment and the direction of my imagination, to turn my pain into something good.
I can, through my effort, find serenity.

This does not come easy, as is the case with all good things, and it requires fortitude to not surrender and succumb.
That effort to embrace joy is nobly and well spent, because the alternative is a living death.

In an appendix to his classic work, *The problem of pain*, C.S. Lewis cites R. Havard's reflections from his experiences as a medical doctor.
This passage has stuck with me for many years, because I can immediately relate to each of these steps:

> *Mental pain is less dramatic than physical pain, but it is more common and also more*
> *hard to bear. The frequent attempt to conceal mental pain increases the burden: it is*
> *easier to say 'My tooth is aching' than to say 'My heart is broken.'*
> *Yet if the cause is accepted and faced, the conflict will strengthen and purify the*
> *character and in time the pain will usually pass.*
> *Sometimes, however, it persists and the effect is devastating; if the cause is not faced or*
> *not recognized, it produces the dreary state of the chronic neurotic.*
> *But some by heroism overcome even chronic mental pain. They often produce brilliant*
> *work and strengthen, harden, and sharpen their characters till they become like*
> *tempered steel.*

I wish to be like tempered steel.

❖ ❖ ❖ ❖ ❖

Day 260

Philosophy is certainly the medicine of the soul. Its aid is to be sought not from without, as in diseases of the body; and we must labor with all our resources and with all our strength to cure ourselves.

—Cicero, Tusculan disputations 3.3

I do my best to avoid describing too many of the details of my illness, both mental and physical, as I feel it sounds too much like the litany of aches and pains we receive from some of our elders.
I have, however, been told repeatedly that my depression is treatment-resistant, and this means I need to rely all the more on philosophical tools to keep me going.

Make no mistake, just as medicine can help heal both the body and the mind from without, so the power of our thinking can help heal us from within.
Philosophy is not simply something to pass the time, or a mere diversion.
The only reason I don't use the term "philosophical therapy" regularly is that I don't wish to make it appear as a substitute for medicine and psychiatry.

With reason at the core of our nature, it only makes sense that, as the ruling power, it can, with an inward strength deeply improve our attitudes, habits, and actions.
Remember that philosophy need not be a mere abstract exercise, but can be radically life changing.

❖ ❖ ❖ ❖ ❖

Day 261

To this matter before all you must attend: that you be never so closely connected with any of your former intimates or friends as to come down to the same acts as he does. If you do not observe this rule, you will ruin yourself.

But if the thought arises in your mind. 'I shall seem disobliging to him, and he will not have the same feeling toward me,' remember that nothing is done without cost, nor is it possible for a man if he does not do the same to be the same man that he was.

Choose, then, which of the two you will have, to be equally loved by those by whom you were formerly loved, being the same with your former self; or, being superior, not to obtain from your friends the same that you did before.

—Epictetus, *Discourses* 4.2

I have on occasion misunderstood and misused such warnings as advocating a cold withdrawal from those around us.

It is tempting for example, to simply cast away and reject a person who does me harm.

Once I have begun to change my thinking and embrace a new kind of life, I must, however, be wary of how I continue to relate to others who have not moved along with me.

I may, and rightly should, still love them, because love is not negotiable or conditional.

But it may also mean that, if I no longer wish to live as my friends still do, they may not feel for me as they once did.

They may no longer show me love and respect, because I am no longer like them.

If I were to still value the way of living I may have enjoyed with them, then my internal change of character would have to be abandoned.

There are people I still love very deeply, and sometimes miss dreadfully, but I know that I can no longer live with them as I once did.

In many cases this is not even a matter of being undesirable, but of actually being impossible if I wish to strive for wisdom and virtue.

❖ ❖ ❖ ❖ ❖

Day 262

If you ever see a hand cut off, or a foot, or a head, lying anywhere apart from the rest of the body, such does a man make himself, as far as he can, who is not content with what happens, and separates himself from others, or does anything unsocial. Suppose that you have detached yourself from the natural unity- for you were made by Nature a part, but now you have cut yourself off—yet here there is this beautiful provision, that it is in thy power again to unite yourself.

God has allowed this to no other part, after it has been separated and cut asunder, to come together again. But consider the kindness by which he has distinguished man, for he has put it in his power not to be separated at all from the universal; and when he has been separated, he has allowed him to return and to be united and to resume his place as a part.

—Marcus Aurelius, *Meditations* Book 8

To separate myself from Nature, as I do when I live a life dependent upon Fortune, is as disturbing as a severed limb or head.
 Aurelius observes, however, the beauty of the fact that because we are creatures of choice, we can of our own free will always return to Nature at any time, if only we so desire.

It is important to remember that the only thing hindering our choice is our choice.
 All other burdens and obstacles can be dismissed, because they are not the actual hindrance.
 Only our thinking and willing hinders itself.
 If I want the good life of peace, it is right there within me for the taking.

Let us be careful, however, not to paint too simple a picture.
 I know full well this may not mean that my circumstances, my feelings, my inclinations, or my imagination will all magically right themselves as soon as I alter my thinking.
 The whole point, however, is to understand that these things aren't even what define my happiness to begin with.

It may take some getting used to, but once I actually embrace Stoic values, this involves a whole transformation of expectations and hopes.
 I will no longer seek after all the things I used to desire, because I see that they contain nothing that I truly need.
 So the true Stoic won't just make a few external adjustments.
 The true Stoic will be completely rejoined and reborn into Nature.

❖ ❖ ❖ ❖ ❖

In the first place, therefore, if you approve, I shall draw the distinction between wisdom and philosophy. Wisdom is the perfect good of the human mind; philosophy is the love of wisdom, and the endeavor to attain it. The latter strives toward the goal which the former has already reached.

—Seneca the Younger, *Moral letters to Lucilius* 89

Using Seneca's distinction philosophy, or the act of philosophizing, is not the end, but the means by which we may become wise.
The question may only be specific to those, like myself, who chose a life of learning as a vocation, but I believe the same pattern can be applied to most any art or discipline.

The arts of medicine, or law, or economics, or war are not simply ends in themselves.
The doctor isn't a good doctor simply by learning his craft, but by healing others.
The lawyer must not only know the law, but practice it to defend justice.
Economics and business aren't just about rules and regulations, but about the fair growth of wealth.
War isn't merely about the skill of combat, but about achieving victory and peace.

To say "I am a philosopher, so I practice philosophy" is as incomplete as saying I'm a soldier so I'm good at fighting, or a doctor, so I know how the human body works.

Always keep in the very real purpose of employing our minds.
They aren't there to make us richer, to gain respect, or even just to make us look and sound smart.
Our minds are there to make us wiser, and thereby better in how we live.
How has whatever wisdom I may have attained given myself and others the opportunity to choose to be happy?

❖ ❖ ❖ ❖ ❖

Day 264

'When a philosopher,' he said, 'is exhorting, persuading, rebuking, or discussing some aspect of philosophy, if the audience pour forth trite and commonplace words of praise in their enthusiasm and unrestraint, if they even shout, if they gesticulate, if they are moved and aroused, and swayed by the charm of his words, by the rhythm of his phrases, and by certain rhetorical repetitions, then you may know that both the speaker and his audience are wasting their time, and that they are not hearing a philosopher speaking but a flute player performing.'

—Musonius Rufus, *Fragments* 49

So many of our human endeavors have been overtaken by so many of the qualities of theater and performance; Musonius reminds us that this is really nothing new.

We can certainly discern it in politics, in business, in law, yes, most certainly even in academics and in philosophy.

This happens, of course, because we neglect reality at the expense of appearance, which is, in turn a reflection of our weakness for Fortune over Nature.

It is more than enough, we think, to simply appear to be playing the part, not actually doing the part.

I wonder whether we all really know this is a ruse, but we simply must all pretend to be falling for the ruse, and we can then remain in our comfort zones.

Fine words, refined phrases, and noble gestures may indeed have their place; we're in trouble when they are all we have to offer, when form smothers content.

A simple rule to follow might go something like this:

A man is not wise if he sounds or looks good, he is wise if he is good.

We can discern the difference if we are simply honest.

Like the boy calling out the Emperor's new clothes, it really takes only one voice to cause the bubble to burst.

❖ ❖ ❖ ❖ ❖

Day 265

That which exercises reason is more excellent than that which does not exercise reason;
there is nothing more excellent than the universe, therefore the universe exercises reason.
—Zeno of Citium, ex Cicero, *On the Nature of the Gods* 2.8

If reason is to be our guide, we should surely apply it with consistency, and avoid leaving empty
  places where our preference wishes to ignore the precepts of our understanding.
  The laws of Nature admit of order, which in turn requires purpose.
  Things act for the sake of an end, each according to its specific nature.

Now why would we admit order and purpose of the parts, but not of the whole?
  And why do we find it so hard to accept that purpose implies design and intelligence, acting in
  both the part and the whole?

Speaking only for myself, I find that I question or doubt the reason in the universe simply because
  this would conflict with my reduction of all meaning and value to my own desires.
  Even then, I might be willing to accept a reason and an order that conveniently acts in harmony
  with my passions and good fortune.
  It's when Nature reveals itself to be greater than myself that I will selfishly be all too glad to brush
  aside reason for skepticism.

That the universe itself exercises reason need not be frightening.
  Understand it to be liberating, to be fulfilling, to be comforting.
  You are not the whole, but you most certainly matter within the whole, and nothing that happens
  or confronts us is in vain.
  Design and purpose give meaning, and are expressed in the dignity and beauty of everything
  around you.

❖ ❖ ❖ ❖ ❖

Everything has two handles, one by which you can carry it, the other by which you cannot. If your brother wrongs you, do not take it by that handle, the handle of his wrong, for you cannot carry it by that, but rather by the other handle—that he is a brother, brought up with you, and then you will take it by the handle that you can carry by.

—Epictetus, *Enchiridion* 43

I'm not entirely sure why, but I just love that image.

I imagine that awkward moment when I'm all befuddled, not sure how to pick up an oversized box or a piece of ungainly luggage.

The "handle" that can make it possible for me to bear, carry, or help another is charity, not resentment.

I think the idea of carrying in the sense of "bearing" another is deeply helpful; this does not mean mere toleration, or indignant suffering, but to bear in the sense of assisting another through the hard times, through the conflict, through the struggles we all have.

Yes, I can bear it, and yes, I can do this with joy, because the handle by which I can lift another is not indifference or mere begrudging acceptance.

There are many ways for us to come to learn about someone else's character, but I suggest the most telling one is to observe what happens when the situation starts to go poorly.

Will you fight the circumstances, and overcome the troubles for the sake of another, or will you abandon another, for the sake of convenience?

I can distinguish the few true friends I have had from the many freeloaders, simply by this measure.

As corny as it seems, the old Boys Town phrase "He ain't heavy, Father, he's my brother" still rings true to my admittedly hopeful ears.

❖ ❖ ❖ ❖ ❖

Day 267

'What then?' you say; 'will there be no one who will attempt to do the wise man injury?'
Yes, the attempt will be made, but the injury will not reach him. For the distance which
separates him from contact with his inferiors is so great that no baneful force can extend its
power all the way to him.

Even when the mighty, exalted by authority and powerful in the support of their servitors,
strive to injure him, all their assaults on wisdom will fall as short of their mark as do the
missiles shot on high by bowstring or catapult, which though they leap beyond our vision,
yet curve downwards this side of heaven.

—Seneca the Younger, *On firmness* 4, tr Basore

A Stoic life will make deep and lasting demands of you, and I do not suggest that it will come easy.
The reward, however, will far outweigh the effort invested.
If you think of this like investing in the stock market, and replace wealth with character, you will immediately see the profit.

Surely, other people can hurt me?
Distinguish.
Once I understand my inner nature as a person, what can be taken from me are things such as my property, my reputation, my hurt feelings, my bodily health, my worldly freedom, or even my very existence itself.

Yet not a single one of those things will do true harm to me.
Once I recognize myself for what I really am, these things can all fall away, and fall down where they belong.

I have a very distinct memory, one that is also a rather frightful one.
A few of the fine fellows in my fifth grade elementary school class had figured I was a perfect victim for their bullying.
Make no mistake, bullying is not a new problem, despite what the media may tell you.

Their plan was to corner me during lunch break, and all four of them would force me to confess, "A kindergartner could beat me up."
It was very amusing for them.

I simply refused to leave the school during recess, knowing well where this would go.
My very liberally enlightened teacher, when she asked me why I would not leave the building, assured me I would be fine.
Decent children didn't do that to one another, she said, and we were in the one of the most highly regarded and accredited public schools in the state.

It still is, I'm told, and I'm sure the same things still go on.
They will all get into the finest colleges, but many of them will still be monsters.
The teachers often find it easier to look the other way.

I was, of course, promptly dragged into the woods by the playground, and beaten, over and over.
My teacher stood on the field with her favorite whistle the whole time, oblivious to reality.

327

For the first time in my life, I refused to give in.

I said "No."

I was pushed around, punched, and kicked for a full twenty minutes.

Sand and dirt were pushed down my pants, and my face was repeatedly smashed into the ground.

I still remember how that soil tasted.

I didn't cry out, and I didn't submit.

A boy I thought was my best friend just stood by, and he laughed.

When I cam back into class, I was criticized by my progressive teacher for having bruised my face and gotten too dirty.

The class laughed at me.

I never said a word.

I already knew that nothing I could say would change black hearts, or alter ignorant minds.

That was the first time in my life where I started to learn to be the better fellow.

If I had regularly done the same over the years, I'd be a much better man than I am now.

❖ ❖ ❖ ❖ ❖

Day 268

A cucumber is bitter. Throw it away. There are briars in the road. Turn aside from them. This is enough.

Do not add, 'And why were such things made in the world?' For you would be ridiculed by a man who is acquainted with Nature, as you would be ridiculed by a carpenter and shoemaker if you found fault because you see in their workshop shavings and cuttings from the things which they make.

And yet they have places into which they can throw these shavings and cuttings, and the universal Nature has no external space; but the wondrous part of her art is that though she has circumscribed herself, everything within her which appears to decay and to grow old and to be useless she changes into herself, and again makes other new things from these very same, so that she requires neither substance from without nor wants a place into which she may cast that which decays.

She is content then with her own space, and her own matter and her own art.

—Marcus Aurelius, *Meditations* Book 8

We all like to pretty it up.
We like to ignore the things we find ugly, inconvenient, or undesirable, the things we would rather dispose of.

Observe how our celebrities, no more or no less physically beautiful than you and I, make themselves far more attractive through their lies, their literal and figurative make-up, and their false imaginings.
This often makes them far more morally ugly.
Yet the rest are cast aside as unimportant, irrelevant.

There is nothing disposable in Nature.
All of it serves a purpose.
Even the things discarded by the proud and privileged are there for a very good reason.
The shavings and cuttings exist for a purpose.

I once went to a job interview at my *alma mater*, knowing full well that I had only been offered the interview as a family favor.
I did the best I could, but I could tell immediately that the Assistant Dean had no interest in me.
I remained polite, and as kind as I was able, but walked away knowing I didn't have the job.

I received the obligatory rejection letter a few weeks later, of course.
"We appreciate your interest...very well qualified...we made another choice ...we wish you the best of luck."

A month or so later, a former teacher gave me the dirt.
"We don't need anymore of those types around here," is what that Dean actually said.
I understand not getting a job.
I don't quite understand someone considering or treating people that way.

329

But none of that was within my power.

I use that experience to remind myself that I was not disposable, whatever the gentleman thought or said.

In the grand scheme of things, I am certainly a shaving or a cutting.

I still matter.

All of us matter.

❖ ❖ ❖ ❖ ❖

Day 269

'All fortune, whether pleasant or difficult, is due to this cause; it is for the sake of rewarding the good, or exercising their virtue, and of punishing and correcting bad men; therefore it is plain that all this fortune which is allowed to be just or expedient, must be good.'
—Boethius, *The consolation of Philosophy* Book 4 Prose 6

If life is run rightly, there are no losses, only gains.
 Anything and everything that may happen to me is an opportunity for living with truth and love.

Consider the radical claim Boethius is making, and how he makes it like a true Stoic.

Has Fortune given me any external benefit?
 It may be a reward, it may be a challenge to improve myself, or it may be a punishment.
 All three are merited and just.

Has Fortune given me any external suffering?
 It may be a reward, it may a challenge to improve myself, or it may be a punishment.
 All three are merited and just.

As soon as I think there is a difference between the two situations, I have strayed from Nature.

I once foolishly thought that earning a Doctorate would make a better man of me.
 I spent some time thinking, quite wrongly, that this would make me worth something.
 In the end, it made me worth no more than I already was.
 It gave me a title, and nothing else.
 It gave me the trappings of achievement, but the whole affair seduced me into believing that status equals merit.

Everything, each and every thing, that happens to me is intended by Nature, and can serve me for the better.
 I need simply choose to make it so.

❖ ❖ ❖ ❖ ❖

Day 270

And it needs only a few things for the loss and overturning of all, namely a small deviation from reason. For the steerer of a ship to upset it, he has no need of the same means as he has need of for saving it: but if he turns it a little to the wind, it is lost; and if he does not do this purposely, but has been neglecting his duty a little, the ship is lost.

Something of the kind happens in this case also: if you only fall to nodding a little, all that you have up to this time collected is gone. Attend therefore to the appearances of things, and watch over them; for that which you have to preserve is no small matter, but it is modesty and fidelity and constancy, freedom from the affects, a state of mind undisturbed, freedom from fear, tranquility, in a word, 'liberty'.

—Epictetus, *Discourses* 4.3

It is always encouraging when the Stoic reminds us that the now can be lived for the now, and life renewed again at any given moment.
If I have failed, I can, without resentment or despair, learn from my mistakes and carry on, revived and strengthened.

I must, however, not take this gift of opportunity as an excuse for carelessness.
Nature may give me every possible opportunity to live rightly, but this still means doing it rightly.
It does not mean half-heartedly going through the motions, acting with mediocrity, or judging hastily and sloppily.
Understand that you may fail, and that you can grow from this failure, but do not think that this justifies such failure.

I was always impressed as a child by the account of how a space capsule must re-enter the atmosphere in the smallest of windows or either burn up or bounce off the atmosphere, or how a single misplaced decimal place will collapse a building or bridge.
I also remember this in Scouts when I had to learn compass navigation, or in the stories of the High Seas about the measurement of latitude and longitude.
The details do matter, aim matters, the dedication matters.
A ship without a good helmsman and navigator to steer and guide her will soon be lost on the rocks.

❖ ❖ ❖ ❖ ❖

Day 271

Suppose that men kill you, cut you in pieces, curse you. What then can these things do to prevent your mind from remaining pure, wise, sober, just?

For instance, if a man should stand by a limpid pure spring, and curse it, the spring never ceases sending up potable water; and if he should cast clay into it or filth, it will speedily disperse them and wash them out, and will not be at all polluted.

How then shall you possess a perpetual fountain and not a mere well? By forming yourself hourly to freedom conjoined with contentment, simplicity and modesty.

—Marcus Aurelius, *Meditations* Book 8

It's one thing to remind us that the things outside of us can't really do us harm, and that we have it within our power to remain happy and good in the face of them.

This may seem hopelessly naïve, of course, if we also don't explain how and why this is so.

It's quite another thing, therefore, to understand in what way such a goal can be achieved.

The analogy of the spring, and the natural flow of water, as something man cannot tame or destroy, is a wonderful one.

In our modern times one should think also, perhaps even more broadly, of the power of Nature itself, and of the way in which man, in his selfishness and carelessness, batters and scars the natural world.

But I would lay bets that in the face of the worst that man can do, the natural order will always adapt, react, and thrive.

He cannot annihilate Nature itself, being fully subject to its very laws.

Remember that the human mind is like such an endless spring, a source of profound and subtle power able to withstand anything cast against it.

Don't assume the mind confronts its worldly circumstances in a match of equals; truly aware of itself, it rises far above lesser things.

The image of a spring can be employed as it is in Taoism, where water represents something that bends and flows around everything solid, but with its slow power can grind down all things.

The subtlety and the strength of the mind are akin to this natural power.

❖ ❖ ❖ ❖ ❖

Injury has as its aim to visit evil upon a person. But wisdom leaves no room for evil, for the only evil it knows is baseness, which cannot enter where virtue and uprightness already abide.

Consequently, if there can be no injury without evil, no evil without baseness, and if, moreover, baseness cannot reach a man already possessed by uprightness, then injury does not reach the wise man. For if injury is the experiencing of some evil, if, moreover, the wise man can experience no evil, no injury affects a wise man.

—Seneca the Younger, *On firmness 5*

The only thing that really harms the interior person is a poor moral character, and a poor character, much like the vampires in all those fine stories, is only able to enter inside when freely invited.

Another one of Frank Darabont's masterpiece films, *The Shawshank Redemption*, has convict Andy Dufresne say very similar words, speaking of the inspiration that art and music can offer us:

You need it so you don't forget. Forget that there are places in the world that aren't made out of stone. That there's a – there's a – there's something inside that's yours, that they can't touch.

Again, I have often wondered whether one could make the serious case that so many great films, like so many great novels, implicitly or explicitly, reflect the deepest Stoic values.

You may recall that my time working in Prison Ministry was not at all pleasant for me, but I learned many a powerful lesson about the value of life, of human dignity, and the power of good in the face of the darkest evil.

Though he was hardly an Andy Dufresne, we had one fellow who was ten years into a thirty years sentence.

He seemed terribly calm, cheerful, and almost indifferent to the state–sanctioned horrors around him.

His version of the Stoic motto?

"What I have in me is all I've got."

He would occasionally then sing a few satirically inflected and deeply off-tune lines of Sinead O'Connor's "I do not want what I haven't got."

I think this helped him not appear as serious as he really was:

So I'm walking through the desert
And I am not frightened although it's hot
I have all that I requested
and I do not want what I haven't got.

He only smiled and shrugged when we encouraged him to think of the distinct possibility of parole and early release.

"It'll be how it's gonna be.", he would say. "No use worrying."

I'm fairly certain this man, who was a convicted violent criminal, was not simply this way because of his innate gentle disposition.

I'm convinced he had, in some way or another, made a choice to thrive, not merely to survive.

❖ ❖ ❖ ❖ ❖

Day 273

At another time when an old man asked him what was the best viaticum for old age, he said, the very one that is best for youth too, namely to live by method and in accord with Nature. You would best understand what this means if you would realize that mankind was not created for pleasure. For that matter, neither was the horse or dog or cow created for pleasure, and all of these creatures are much less valuable than man.

Certainly a horse would not be considered to have fulfilled its purpose by eating and drinking and mating at will, and doing none of the things which are the proper work of a horse; no more would a dog if it simply enjoyed all kinds of pleasures like the horse and did none of the things for which dogs are considered good.

—Musonius Rufus, *Lectures* 17

Old men and young men, horses and dogs, and all things existing in Nature, are made to fulfill the excellence of their function and purpose.
Do not reduce their meaning to gratification alone.
This is not the removal of pleasure from life, but rather the clear insistence that nothing was made merely for my pleasure.

Pleasure, let us recall, need not appear crude, or brutal, or base.
It can come across as refined, educated, and cultured.
I very rarely fall for the obviously barbaric variety, as it is obvious to be me that I am facing nothing but selfish desire.
But the hedonism wrapped in finery has often had its toll on me.
You need to simply show how a Romantic poet would do it, and you have me half convinced.
I'm too readily fooled by the illusion.

Only recently, while watching a baseball game with a handful of friends at our local VFW, a woman I had never met walked up to me, put her arms around me, and whispered one of the crudest, and most creative, propositions I've ever heard.
Don't worry; I haven't suddenly become handsome or charming, as I think she did something similar to every third fellow in the place.
I assume she needed money, or a place to sleep.

And while these were a touch and words that could probably tempt the strongest man, I laughed it off in an instant.
This was not because I am a paragon of virtue, but because I was honestly disgusted by the thought of reducing myself, and another person, to an object to be used.
In this case, the appearance matched the reality.

Years earlier, a young lady I knew in graduate school, and had also studied philosophy with in college, met me at a party.
We had a good conversation, and decided to ditch all the fellows who were trying to get her into bed.
Again, I can always see the abusiveness in their eyes.
We went into town, ate fine Korean food, and somehow ended up at the ritziest jazz club in Boston.

Maybe it was the music, the fancy lighting, the beautiful people, or the very expensive martini I was drinking, but suddenly I felt drawn to her, which I had never felt with her before.
We spent the next tune in silence, looking into each other's eyes, and at some point started holding hands.

Now if this sounds like the beginning of a romantic story, it most certainly isn't.
Nor does it end up as a raunchy story.
This girl and I would never have been right.
I wanted a soul mate, and she wanted to just have fun.
It would have ended very poorly.
I managed to be the gentleman, and never did anything improper.

What had happened was that I had fallen, however briefly, for selfish greed and base desire under the appearance of class and style.
It took me longer than usual to recognize this, because the illusion so fully clouded the reality.
It made no difference what she may or may not have wanted.
I will always strive to refuse the temptation to treat another human being as a means for my gratification.
There's no love, and there's no justice in it.

❖ ❖ ❖ ❖ ❖

Day 274

Consider, likewise, that the Gods go by what names we give them. Now, in the first place, they have as many names as men have languages; for Vulcan is not called Vulcan in Italy, Africa, or Spain, as you are called Velleius in all countries. Besides, the Gods are innumerable, though the list of their names is of no great length even in the records of our priests. Have they no names? You must necessarily confess, indeed, they have none; for what occasion is there for different names if their persons are alike?

—Cicero, *On the nature of the gods* 1.30, tr Yonge

I'm somewhat proficient in the history of philosophy, and hardly at all in the history of theology, but almost every time I teach philosophy of religion to students, of whatever age or background they may be, I inevitably end up being asked this question:

"Wait, if the Christian have one God, and the Jews have another, and the Muslims have a third, which one is the real God?
I mean, if there's only one God, which one am I supposed to pick?"

"Let's step back for a moment.
Are you saying you agree with the argument that the Divine, being perfect, absolute, and infinite, can by definition be only one?"

"Yeah, I guess so!"

"So if we accept that argument, that perfection must be unity and never division, then there is only one God.
Do the different names matter more than that one reality?"

"Yeah, I get that, but which one is the real one?"

"OK, let's do this one over from the top…"

It is precisely these frustrations that make me love teaching so!

Stoicism always recognized that unity was a mark of perfection, and division a sign of imperfection.
The Divine, however you choose to understand it, must be one, however many ways to wish to perceive it, or give it certain names.

❖ ❖ ❖ ❖ ❖

Day 275

Remember that not only the desire of power and of riches makes us mean and subject to others, but even the desire of tranquility, and of leisure. and of traveling abroad, and of learning. For, to speak plainly, whatever the external thing may be, the value which we set upon it places us in subjection to others.

—Epictetus, *Discourses* 4.4

A few passages earlier, I was wondering out loud whether the base desire for pleasure became more acceptable to us if we made it appear more refined.
I wonder if the same may be true when it comes to our influence and wealth.

It's one thing, of course, to condemn the tyrant and robber baron for their dastardly ways, but surely the refined lady or gentleman, the reader of the *Sunday New York Times*, resident of the beautiful and prosperous suburb, proud owners of the vacation home in Maine or on Cape Cod, and member of the local Squash Club, can hardly be accused of being mean-spirited?

I hardly think what newspaper you choose to read, where you live, where you go on vacation, or what social sport you engage defines your character.
These things are indifferent, but if we desire them for their own sake, we are still slaves to our circumstances.
It might not look ugly, but its still ugly, because of why we choose to want these things.
It never makes you any better to look good or depend upon your standing.
Depend upon your character.

❖ ❖ ❖ ❖ ❖

Day 276

> *We should therefore praise, and number in the company of the blessed, that man who has invested well the portion of time, however little, that has been allotted to him; for such a one has seen the true light.*
>
> *He has not been one of the common herd. He has not only lived, but flourished. Sometimes he enjoyed fair skies; sometimes, as often happens, it was only through the clouds that there flashed to him the radiance of the mighty star.*
>
> —Seneca the Younger, *Moral letters to Lucilius* 93

Being both melancholic and nostalgic, I find it hard to avoid looking back to my past, sometimes with bursts of joy, often with gasps of horror.

Though I can hardly know what will befall me, my health gives me a sense that I'm in my twilight years, even as I'm middle-aged.

That may or may not be the case, but my experiences have finally taught me to be willing to accept any time, whatever time it may be, that I have left.

My father, long a student of Russian culture, has always liked to tell the following intellectual joke, steeped in the rich tradition of Dostoevsky and Tolstoy:

> "What is the definition of happiness?"

> "A pause between two unhappinesses."

My own version of this, inspired by the first time I taught Dostoevsky, is the difference between Western European Romanticism and Russian Romanticism:

> "In the first, we all die alone and heartbroken.
> In the second, we all die alone and heartbroken.
> In the snow."

All snobbish guffawing aside, there's a serious point here.

It so often seems that our lives are long spreads of misery, interrupted only with brief escapes of joy, only to be returned back to be the dreariness of misery.

I imagine the proportions of good and bad fortune, of pain and pleasure, of fame or infamy, of wealth and poverty, of health and sickness, are perhaps different for all of us.

I know some people who have never seemed to suffer much misfortune at all, though perhaps that is only from my limited perspective.

I think what matters more, whatever the proportion may be, is what Seneca suggests: sometimes there will be fair skies, and sometimes there will be clouds, perhaps even raging storm clouds at that.

Neither really matters, in the end.

Are you keeping your eye on the star?

It may be blurred to us, but it is never entirely obscured.

I fail when I don't look at the ever-visible bright light, but instead stare at my shoes.

I can choose to be happy on a sunny day, or on a cloudy day, and yes, even on a stormy day.

Let's not confuse the measure of true happiness and unhappiness.

❖ ❖ ❖ ❖ ❖

Day 277

In one way an arrow moves, in another way the mind. The mind indeed, both when it exercises caution and when it is employed about inquiry, moves straight onward nonetheless, and to its object.

—Marcus Aurelius, *Meditations* Book 8

A number of years back, I happened across a copy of the organizational chart at a large State University where I had been an Adjunct Professor.
I found it disturbing for the simple reason that I could find no direction or purpose in any of it all.
Boxes were connected to other boxes, in no discernible pattern, and there were many hundreds of boxes.
Many seemed to circle back upon themselves, in a beauty that even Escher could not have managed.

I finally, by the way, found myself, as faculty member, down on the far right, lowest of all, removed from all the other important boxes.

I would even have preferred a simple hierarchy, to be honest, as much as I argue for solidarity and cooperation.
Board tells President what to do, President tells Provost what to do, Provost tells all the Deans what to do, and so on, until we hit the people doing the real work, the teachers and the maintenance staff.

There was no direction, order, or purpose.
The object or end was not clearly identified.
I've seen it in the business of modern education, and I've seen it in the waste and corruption that is modern government.
All the academic deans and the government bureaucrats frown when I say such things, because they don't appreciate the consideration of a purpose beyond their own profit.

Why can we not be direct, straightforward, ordered completely to the object of our aim?
Why must everything move sideways?
The only reason I can think of is that we allow our own pride to get in the way of our true goals.

❖ ❖ ❖ ❖ ❖

Therefore, these calamities are good in respect of their beginning; and likewise in regard of their end, because they are ever directed to good and safety in good men. You will object and say, how can this be? Is it not evident that these wars and slaughters are committed with intent to harm and hurt?

It is true so, in respect of men, but not in respect of God; which that you may more plainly and fully conceive I must apply the light of a distinction. There are two sorts of calamities sent from God, some simple, some mixed. The first I call those which proceed purely from God without any interposition of man's policy or force, the second, which are of God yet wrought by the ministry of men.

Of the former kind are famine, dearth, earthquakes, openings of the earth, overflowing of waters, sickness, death. Of the latter are tyranny, war, oppression, and slaughters. In those first all things are pure and without spot, as springing from a most pure fountain. In the latter I deny not but there is some filth and mixed, because they are conveyed and derived through the foul conducts of men.

Is man a means for effecting them? What marvel then is it if there be a fault and offense committed in accomplishing them? Marvel more at the provident goodness of God who converts that fault to our furtherance and the offense to our good. Do you see a tyrant breaking out threats and murders, whose delight is in doing harm? Who could be content to perish himself so that he may persecute others? Let him alone; he strays from his right mind.

And God, as it were, by an invisible string leads him to his destruction. As an arrow comes to the mark without any feeling of him that shot it; so do these wicked ones. For that supreme power bridles and keeps under control all men's power, and directs their straying course to the happy haven.

—Justus Lipsius, *On constancy* 2.7

Whether the evils we perceive ourselves as suffering come from the natural world or with the participation of human choice, Providence makes it possible for each and every one of them to bring us back to what is good and right.
This is somewhat like the Stoic Turn on a cosmic scale.

Say another man does evil to me, in whatever degree.
He already does his own nature deep harm by his vice and ignorance.
This is just and fair, for he punishes himself.

He may continue to pursue evil, in which case he will perish in misery, or he can use his error to learn to improve himself.
Again, either possibility is just and fair.
Good has resulted from every case.

What about the suffering he has inflicted on me?
It indeed hurts me in the lesser things external to my soul, but not the greater things within my soul, unless I so choose.

Hence, I may choose to react to his evil with evil, or to use his actions to make myself better, to do what is good in the face of evil.

Again, either possibility is just and fair.

If the true human good is rightly understood, everything, even every aberration and corruption will always lead to a higher good, and will always be just according to balance of merit and responsibility.

This is why I must have pity and understanding for the vicious man, and never hatred.

If I choose hatred, I choose to drag myself down with him, and I do not give him the chance to become better.

❖   ❖   ❖   ❖   ❖

If a man washes quickly, do not say that he washes badly, but that he washes quickly. If a man drinks much wine, do not say that he drinks badly, but that he drinks much. For till you have decided what judgment prompts him, how do you know that he acts badly? If you do as I say, you will assent to your apprehensive impressions and to none other.

—Epictetus, *Enchiridion* 45

To say that we should not be quick to judge does not mean that we shouldn't make sound judgments at all.

That is the excuse of the relativist who dislikes commitment to truth.

It means rather that we should not be too quick to judge the character of others, but rather limit our scope to judgment to the facts, not our imaginings.

I cannot fully know why a man acts as he does, so let me judge only what I can truly know.

I have myself often had an opposing tendency, and I don't know how common this may be, to assume that I am the one who is to blame, and that others have acted with good intentions.

This, of course, is just as unhealthy as always assuming malice in others.

I'm best served if I don't assume either one or the other.

I simply torture myself if I try to understand someone else's thinking from inside, as I should worry first and foremost what I can clearly know, and, more importantly, what I myself can do.

I always laugh at how we are so quick to condemn people who enjoy their wine to be drunks, or people who refrain from wine as uptight teetotalers.

Our judgment of their character usually has very little to support it, and perhaps has more to do with ourselves than with them.

❖ ❖ ❖ ❖ ❖

It would be a man's happiest lot to depart from mankind without having had any taste of lying and hypocrisy and luxury and pride. However to breathe out one's life when a man has had enough of these things is the next best voyage, as the saying goes. Have you determined to abide with vice, and has not experience yet induced you to fly from this pestilence?

For the destruction of the understanding is a pestilence, much more so indeed than any such corruption and change of this atmosphere which surrounds us. For this corruption is a pestilence of animals so far as they are animals; but the other is a pestilence of men so far as they are men.

—Marcus Aurelius, *Meditations* Book 9

I admire, and admittedly feel jealous of, those who seem to have managed their whole lives having avoided vice to the best of their abilities.
That most certainly isn't me, but I'm working on taking that next best voyage.

The danger is, I think, that I am not only drawn to obsession with my past circumstances, but I am also drawn to obsession with my past mistakes.
I often wonder how I could have done something better, more lovingly, more patiently in the past.

What I may well be failing to recognize is that, for me, that mistake perhaps had to happen so that I could even come to be aware that it was even a mistake, and thereby learn from it as I needed to.
I wouldn't be able to critique myself now without that lesson.
There's really no point in considering how life could have been different, because it has already happened.

Spilt milk.
That doesn't mean, of course, that I shouldn't clean up my mess.
I'm especially sensitive to the fact that while the past cannot be changed, we can certainly address the current consequences.
Too many of us walk away from wrecks.

Here's the thin line I challenge myself to walk: I should remember my past failings to make be a better man now, but I should never remember them in such a way that they still drag me down.
Regret, in this sense, can be a double-edged blade.
Let it assist me, but don't let it hamper me.

Far worse than a disease of the body is a disease of the soul.
I may not be able to avoid the former, but I most certainly avoid the latter, even, and perhaps especially, after I've let myself suffer.

❖　❖　❖　❖　❖

Men say: 'The happy life consists in upright conduct; precepts guide one to upright conduct; therefore precepts are sufficient for attaining the happy life.' But they do not always guide us to upright conduct; this occurs only when the will is receptive; and sometimes they are applied in vain, when wrong opinions obsess the soul.

Furthermore, a man may act rightly without knowing that he is acting rightly. For nobody, except he be trained from the start and equipped with complete reason, can develop to perfect proportions, understanding when he should do certain things, and to what extent, and in whose company, and how, and why.

Without such training a man cannot strive with all his heart after that which is honorable, or even with steadiness or gladness, but will ever be looking back and wavering.

—Seneca the Younger, *Moral letters to Lucilius* 95

We can have right principle and wrong action, as well as wrong principle and right action.
The fullness of a moral life lies in the presence of wisdom and good will as the guide to our deeds.
These two cannot, in practice, rightly be separated.

I have at times thought good thoughts, and done bad deeds, just as I have managed to do quite the right thing, but either entirely by accident, or without good intent.
Neither is worthy of praise, for the fullness of our lives must follow a proper development and process, from a knowledge of the good, and a will open to that knowledge, within me, to my actions that proceed to what is outside of me.
Like a good story, from beginning, to middle, to end, a good life perfects all the stages.

I once knew I needed offer an apology to someone I had hurt very deeply, but I did not have the good will to connect what I knew to what I should do.

I once stumbled across a brilliant solution to a friend's personal problem, but it happened because I was frustrated with the conversation, and I simply blurted out random ideas, just to have the whole thing done with.
I did not have the good will to connect what I knew to what I should do.

Someone I care for very much once asked me to stop smoking cigarettes for my health, and at the same time she actually started up smoking when I wasn't around.
The advice was good action, without wisdom or good will.

The same person knew quite well, and expressed quite regularly, that friendship was the highest good there could ever be, never to be compromised, and then promptly ignored friendship when things became inconvenient.
This was good knowledge, without good will or action.

I have spoken of the Stoic need "Follow through", to bring all things that are intended by Nature, in harmony with Providence, to their right completion.
Leave nothing unfinished or incomplete.
Whether we neglect the beginning, or the middle, or the end of the chain, we break apart the links of the chain whenever we do so.

❖ ❖ ❖ ❖ ❖

I notice that the majority of people strive to obtain these same foods when they are not available and when they are at hand are unable to refrain from them, and they use them so lavishly when they have them that they make for the detriment of their health.

And yet what else is gluttony but intemperance in the matter of nourishment, causing men to prefer what is pleasant in food to that which is beneficial?

—Musonius Rufus, *Lectures* 18

I have always appreciated the subtle, but deeply important, distinction between the gourmet and the gourmand.

It is the difference between eating for the love of beauty, and eating for pleasure.

One feeds the mind and the heart, the other feeds the gut, and the intent makes all the difference.

I will refrain from a rant on the recent media term "foodie".

As I see it, a foodie is not only a gourmand, but also an unrefined one at that.

But your mileage may vary, and I admit my own bias in the matter.

One must eat for the nourishment of the body, but I suggest one may also eat for the nourishment of the soul, insofar as the cooking, presentation, and appreciation of a fine meal can be a true work of art.

A meal that is simply to stuff the face, as my mother used to say, is, however, an aberration.

It is simply pleasure for the sake of brute and self-serving pleasure.

Eating for benefit, whether of the body or of the soul, is good and noble.

Eating simply for the gratification, the stuffing of the face and the gut, is a monstrosity.

What Musonius is doing, of course, is relating the love, or lust, for food to the most basic of human problems: Is a thing good because it is desired, or should it be desired because it is good?

The truths of Stoicism, and of philosophy in general, apply to most every aspect of everyday life.

❖ ❖ ❖ ❖ ❖

Day 283

The wise and good man neither himself fights with any person, nor does he allow another, so far as he can prevent it. And an example of this as well as of all other things is proposed to us in the life of Socrates, who not only himself on all occasions avoided fights, but would not allow even others to quarrel.

See in Xenophon's Symposium *how many quarrels he settled; how further he endured Thrasymachus and Polus and Callicles; how he tolerated his wife, and how he tolerated his son who attempted to confute him and to cavil with him.*

—Epictetus, *Discourses* 4.5

I must wryly laugh at the statement that Socrates tolerated his wife.
 As deeply politically incorrect as that seems, the deeper meaning is, I believe, that we must learn to all bear one another, to carry one another's burdens, not with resentment, but with love.
 I know full well that this includes those closest and dearest to us.
 It also includes those who hate me, or are indifferent to me.

I observe that a certain sort of person actually enjoys conflict, and finds satisfaction from being in opposition to others.
 Perhaps this gives them a sense of value and importance?
 I do not know, and I cannot say.
 What I do know is that I long ago gave up fighting as an end in itself.

This doesn't mean we shouldn't fight in any sense at all.
 First, of course, we fight ourselves, to master ourselves, to rule our own lives with wisdom, and with virtue.
 Then we are free of all bonds.

Must we fight others?
 We most certainly should never fight a person, but can we fight the evil they may do?
 Virtue demands that we work, and sacrifice, for justice.
 Stoicism demands a deep concern and love for each and every person.
 What am I to do when I see those people abused, trampled, or neglected?

Yes, I will fight, at the sacrifice of everything Fortune has given me, even my own existence.
 The virtue of fortitude demands no less.
 But this sort of fighting is not one of hate, vengeance, or malice.
 It is borne of love.
 One does not oppose the person, but one opposes the wrongdoing.
 There is a world of difference.

I have yet another one of my silly phrases, that helps me to understand the distinction between a just and an unjust battle.
 "Go with the grain, and never against it."

To oppose an action that does harm is to work with Nature.
 Do so proudly with the knowledge that you are righting a wrong, and balancing the scales.

To oppose another for your own gratification is the work of evil.
 Hang your head in shame when you act against another person for your own pleasure or profit.

❖ ❖ ❖ ❖ ❖

In spite of all do you still chafe and complain, not understanding that, in all the evils to which you refer, there is really only one—the fact that you do chafe and complain? If you ask me, I think that for a man there is no misery unless there be something in the universe which he thinks miserable. I shall not endure myself on that day when I find anything unendurable.

I am ill; but that is a part of my lot. My slaves have fallen sick, my income has gone off, my house is rickety, I have been assailed by losses, accidents, toil, and fear; this is a common thing. No, that was an understatement; it was an inevitable thing. Such affairs come by order, and not by accident.

—Seneca the Younger, *Moral letters to Lucilius* 96

As I mentioned a few passages ago, I often wonder why some seem to go through life with ease, while others suffer so greatly and deeply. It sadly breeds resentment in me.

I may well need to reconsider that, and then practice the Stoic Turn.
 Why should I assume others have it any better or worse than myself?
 We all suffer, all in our own way, but we all suffer.
 Some of us just hide it better than others.

It is part of my lot, and part of everyone's lot.
 The only difference will be if we meet our sorrow with hatred or with love.

Serve Nature, serve Providence, and serve your neighbors.
 Do all of that until it hurts.
 You may not know how and why it will play itself out, but you will know that you have played your part.

I was raised as a good Irish and Austrian Roman Catholic, by decent people who practiced that faith with love, and who did not abuse it for their own vanity.
 They never allowed their charity to succumb to mindless rules.
 I do not expect you to embrace that tradition of faith, but I do believe that one of my heroes, Cardinal John Henry Newman, expressed these Stoic values so well:

God has created me to do Him some definite service.
He has committed some work to me, which He has not committed to another.
I have my mission. I may never know it in this life, but I shall be told it in the next.
I am a link in a chain, a bond of connection between persons. He has not created me for naught. I shall do good; I shall do His work.
I shall be an angel of peace, a preacher of truth in my own place, while not intending it, if I do but keep His commandments.
Therefore, I will trust Him, whatever I am, I can never be thrown away. If I am in sickness, my sickness may serve Him, in perplexity, my perplexity may serve Him.
If I am in sorrow, my sorrow may serve Him. He does nothing in vain.
He knows what He is about. He may take away my friends. He may throw me among strangers. He may make me feel desolate, make my spirits sink, hide my future from me.
Still, He knows what He is about.

❖ ❖ ❖ ❖ ❖

Day 285

Not in passivity, but in activity lie the evil and the good of the rational social animal, just as his virtue and his vice lie not in passivity, but in activity.

—Marcus Aurelius, *Meditations* Book 9

For a society that has achieved so much in science, technology, or business, we are a remarkably passive set of folks when it comes to understanding ourselves.

We are full of our awareness of what happens to us, of all the circumstances and conditions of the world around us, and how that world moves and shapes us.

We even define ourselves through those externals.

Most tellingly, we understand happiness, for example, to simply be pleasure, a feeling that comes from a thing or an action.

There is a reason the Classical model calls them passions, because feelings are passive reactions to stimulation.

In contrast, the Stoics, like Aristotle, understood happiness rested not simply in what we passively feel, but what we actively do.

More specifically, happiness was considered to be virtuous activity, which relies upon the understanding, and not just the emotions, as its standard and measure.

I rarely find a student who has a sense, at first, what this means, because they are so used to thinking of the good life as defined by pleasure.

It is always one of my favorite class discussions when I throw a monkey wrench into this assumption.

In the simplest sense, Aurelius is reminding us that we are what we do, and not what happens to us.

Yet we remain convinced that the world makes and directs us, and we become passive pieces being pushed around on a game board.

We become powerless and ineffective, victims of our circumstance.

We think that nothing we can do or say will change the way things are, and we silently accept our fate.

Dietrich Bonhöffer saw the grave moral danger in this, and gave his life to show that we must always be actively responsible, not passively submissive:

> *Silence in the face of evil is itself evil: God will not hold us guiltless.*
> *Not to speak is to speak.*
> *Not to act is to act.*

❖ ❖ ❖ ❖ ❖

Day 286

You are mistaken, my dear Lucilius, if you think that luxury, neglect of good manners, and other vices of which each man accuses the age in which he lives, are especially characteristic of our own epoch; no, they are the vices of mankind and not of the times. No era in history has ever been free from blame.

—Seneca the Younger, *Moral letters to Lucilius* 97

Each time and place always has its own characteristics, of course, but it would be foolish to look at the past with rose–colored glasses.

However varied the circumstances, human nature remains human nature, and this includes all our strengths and virtues, as well as all our weaknesses and vices.

I must admit I have fallen for the sentimental trap of thinking that I would be much happier living in a different time and place.

I once, only half in jest, decided I would have been more content as a brooding and introspective romantic poet or philosopher wandering through the Lake District in the 1800s.

I'm sure, however, that if I were magically transported to this role, I would find just as many things to complain about, and just as many ways to sabotage myself.

The danger, of course, of romanticizing the past and demonizing the present rests in yet another instance of assuming that our circumstances make all the difference.

I begin to think that if I changed, one, or two, or a dozen things, my life might be better.

Why not go all out, and just modify my whole identity and environment?

Then everything would be just fine.

No, it won't be just fine, because the value of my living depends only on my own judgments and choices, let the circumstances be what they may.

I can be that brooding and introspective romantic poet and philosopher in rural Oklahoma as much as I can be him in the Lake District, whether now or two hundred years ago.

We must shift our burden of happiness from what is outside, to what is inside.

❖ ❖ ❖ ❖ ❖

Wretched man, will you not see what you are saying about yourself? What do you appear to yourself to be? In your opinions, in your desires, in your aversions from things, in your movements, in your preparation, in your designs, and in other acts suitable to a man? But do you trouble yourself about this, whether others pity you?

—Epictetus, *Discourses* 4.6

Should I care what others think or feel about me?

Should it matter whether others have any concern for me? As always, the philosopher must distinguish in what sense we speak of caring.

I should most certainly care, in the sense that I should have love for others, and a respect for their own thoughts and feelings.

My neighbor may be of great assistance to me with his insights, and I should have the decency to listen to him, consider what he may have to say, and join together with him in solidarity and cooperation.

As a rational animal, the Stoic must also be a social animal, always working for the good with others.

But I should certainly not care, in quite another sense.

I should not define myself, or allow my merit and value to be ruled or determined by the opinions of others.

I can appreciate, understand, and respect if another person thinks well or poorly of me, respects or disrespects me, shows pity or indifference, but I should hardly measure myself through them.

I can measure myself only through myself, and not from without.

To reduce our value to the opinion of others is an offense against the founding Stoic principle that our happiness can never rest in that which is beyond our power.

To care and love for others for their sake is also a founding Stoic principle, as it is a reflection of what is within our power, our virtue and character.

❖ ❖ ❖ ❖ ❖

Day 288

It is your duty to leave another man's wrongful act there where it is.
—Marcus Aurelius, *Meditations* Book 9

Evil, like all corruption and rot, has a way of easily spreading, just as the single piece of spoiled fruit ruins the whole basket.

I think this is more than merely a symbolic expression, but rather a very specific characteristic of evil, that it has a way of becoming infectious when we are too close to it for too long.

The infection, of course, is not the harm forcing its way into the mind or heart, but rather the mind and heart slowly but surely opening itself to allow the harm to enter.

I suggest that this is because when we allow ourselves to be in the face of evil, we become accustomed to it, its presence becomes almost habitual, and we then lower our guard.

It is therefore wise to stay clear and far away from people who are grasping, devious, arrogant, or selfish.

Having them near will do no good for us.

Most importantly, if a man does you harm, treat that act like a hot potato.

Drop it, leave it where it is, and walk away.

He may have acted poorly, but you will allow that rot to spread if you respond in kind, and you will become exactly like him.

One bad piece of fruit…

I am reminded of an old Hindu proverb I heard many years ago, and which I keep ready at hand:

> *Keep five yards from a carriage, ten yards from a horse, and a hundred yards from an elephant; but the distance one should keep from a wicked man cannot be measured.*

You need never believe that anyone who depends upon happiness is happy! It is a fragile support—this delight in adventitious things; the joy, which entered from without, will some day depart.

But that joy which springs wholly from oneself is real and sound; it increases and attends us to the last; while all other things which provoke the admiration of the crowd are but temporary goods.

—Seneca the Younger, *Moral letters to Lucilius* 98

Seneca sees the two very different ways people approach happiness; the happiness that we think comes from the outside, shallow and unreliable, and the happiness that truly comes from within, fulfilling and constant.

Don't be fooled by the first, but deeply embrace the second.

I make note how the passage speaks of those who "depend" on happiness as being very different than those who choose to live well, and therefore in joy.

Though I can admittedly be a bit of a curmudgeon, that isn't why I am immediately wary of people who speak of themselves as being so happy, because everything in their world is in its right place, all nice and cozy.

I wonder whether some of these people are trying to fool us, or even themselves, into a false sense of security, or even if they are being totally honest, whether they are oblivious to how easily those things can and will fail them?

I have known too many people, in so many ways perfectly decent and kind people, who spent years of their lives telling the world how blessed they are to have the things that life has given them.

The passage of time will sadly often reveal the false edifice.

Only recently, I was heartbroken to see not one, but two couples, both with many children, and who had always seemed so safe, secure, and content, unexpectedly separate because of deeply rooted conflicts at the heart of their relationships.

The outside always looked so wonderful, but there was something tragically wrong on the inside.

It gives me no joy to observe this, and I very much hope these folks can find the truly inner healing they need.

❖　❖　❖　❖　❖

If chance is defined as an outcome of random influence, produced by no sequence of causes, I am sure that there is no such thing as chance, and I consider that it is but an empty word, beyond showing the meaning of the matter which we have in hand. For what place can be left for anything happening at random, so long as God controls everything in order?

'It is a true saying that nothing can come out of nothing. None of the old philosophers has denied that, though they did not apply it to the effective principle, but to the matter operated upon—that is to say, to Nature; and this was the foundation upon which they built all their reasoning. If anything arises from no causes, it will appear to have risen out of nothing. But if this is impossible, then chance also cannot be anything of that sort, which is stated in the definition which we mentioned.

—Boethius, *The consolation of Philosophy* Book 5 Prose 1

Boethius offers a fine summation of the Classical argument on causality and chance.
It is a contradiction to say that something can come from nothing, or that an effect has no cause.
Everything happens for a very specific reason, even if we might not ourselves see that reason.
All this is ordered through Providence.
This means that chance is not in things themselves, but only in our perception of those things.

My own impressions will still, quite often, lead me to feel that certain things have been lucky, and other things have been unlucky.
As easily as I can be tempted to feel sorry for myself, I assume that the balance is far more in favor of the latter.
This is my feelings and imaginings playing tricks on me, and the clarity of reason is the cure.

I will start to brood on the idea that it was unlucky that I happened to sit next to someone at a party, and that brought me twenty–five years of pain.
I think it was unlucky that I was hit by a truck, stumbled into some horrible places to work, lost a son, or ended up being cursed by the Black Dog.

None of that was luck, good or bad.
Every one of those things had a reason, and as I learn more and more to pull back and see the bigger picture over the years, those reasons become slightly more apparent.
Each event, each occurrence, has been an opportunity for good in me.
Sometimes I have chosen to take it, sometimes I have dropped the ball.
That's my responsibility, not luck.

❖ ❖ ❖ ❖ ❖

When you behold a large and beautiful house, surely no one can persuade you it was built for mice and weasels, though you do not see the master; and would it not, therefore, be most manifest folly to imagine that a world so magnificently adorned, with such an immense variety of celestial bodies of such exquisite beauty, and that the vast sizes and magnitude of the sea and land were intended as the abode of man, and not as the mansion of the immortal Gods?

—Cicero, *On the nature of the gods* 2.6

Though I can certainly speculate on how and why other people think as they do, I do my best to speak from the perspective of my own knowledge of myself.
There are simply times I don't want to accept that the Universe, the beautiful house in which I live, is so ordered, so full of meaning and purpose, so inspiring, so touched by the Divine.
I'd rather be miserable, so I think the Universe isn't a Universe at all, but just a jumbled mess of chaos, conflict, and randomness.

As is so often the case, I am allowing my impressions to run away from me.
I often try to distinguish between reasoning and rationalizing:
The first is true understanding of why something is; the second is making excuses for why things should be the way my feelings want them to be.

We need not condemn, but can rather understand with sympathy, how easily imaginings can placate our feelings, and how easily we re-write our own history to fit our inclinations.
This has been incredibly difficult for me over the years.

Though I will certainly not understand its full and vast workings, I can know that there must be order and meaning in all things.
I may not know the master of the house, but I am aware of his presence.
There is something so much more than myself, the mouse in the house, and that is a great comfort.

❖ ❖ ❖ ❖ ❖

On no occasion call yourself a philosopher, nor talk at large of your principles among the multitude, but act on your principles. For instance, at a banquet do not say how one ought to eat, but eat as you ought.

Remember that Socrates had so completely got rid of the thought of display that when men came and wanted an introduction to philosophers, he took them to be introduced, so patient of neglect was he.

And if a discussion arise among the multitude on some principle, keep silent for the most part; for you are in great danger of blurting out some undigested thought. And when some one says to you, 'You know nothing', and you do not let it provoke you, then know that you are really on the right road.

For sheep do not bring grass to their shepherds and show them how much they have eaten, but they digest their fodder and then produce it in the form of wool and milk. Do the same yourself; instead of displaying your principles to the multitude, show them the results of the principles you have digested.

—Epictetus, *Enchiridion* 46

I recently suggested to my son, who is facing all the joys and pains of adolescence, that when one is in doubt, it is best to say little or nothing at all, and to let one's actions speak louder than mere words.

My daughter is not far behind.

I hope, of course, that he understands, and I hope just as much that I can understand, and live accordingly.

What makes me laugh at myself quite often is the fact that I have always known quite well that I was never made to be one of the special folks, the ones who draw attention to themselves by doing all those things society tells us are great.

Even if I had those gifts and dispositions, my values simply do not allow me to care for such things.

Yet somehow my impressions manage to deceive me from time to time.

I had a bad Black Dog day very recently.

I was sitting in my office, and having a powerful bout of severely crippling depression, mixed with a frantic anxiety attack, despair and panic all rolled together.

For those of you who are not cursed to know, it is a horrifying combination.

Knowing the pain all too well myself, I have incredible admiration for those that survive such assaults.

For some reason, I was obsessing about the fact that I was not as good as others, that I had wasted my talents, and that I had failed to become a valuable person.

My mind told me this was wrong, but my passions were in revolt.

All of it simply boils down to my caring more how I appear than what I actually am, and the love of appearance over reality is itself an expression of a sick vanity.

As is wisely said in the very cheesy movie *Meatballs*, "It just doesn't matter!"

I earn barely enough to support my family, I am entirely anonymous, no one will remember me, and I have not changed the big picture of the wide world one tiny bit.

This isn't a complaint, but rather the recognition of a blessing.

It gives me the chance to remember that what I do, fighting in the trenches to help just a handful of students in very small ways to start thinking about what really does matter, is what needs to matter to me.

Actions are what matter, not words, or images, or posturing.

I matter, precisely because that clever world tells me that I don't matter.

❖ ❖ ❖ ❖ ❖

Day 293

But many men fail to count up how manifold their gains have been, how great their rejoicings. Grief like yours has this among other evils: it is not only useless, but thankless.
—Seneca the Younger, *Moral letters to Lucilius* 99

Here is yet another of those truisms or platitudes, when we are told to count our blessings.
I took that statement very poorly for too long, though I suspect many people who said it to me also understood it very poorly.

To count one's blessings is not to simply ignore pain and loss, and only dwell on the benefits given by our circumstances.
Even that is a dependence upon Fortune, as it's all about the balance of external credits and debits.
I would both laugh and cringe when I heard people tell me, "Well, at least you have your health."
I actually don't have my health, but even if I did, I'm not sure it would have anything to do with my happiness.

My blessings come not from my circumstances, but from my own willingness to know and to love.
That's all it takes.
My gains or losses are entirely up to me.

Grief is a double curse.
First is the pain felt by suffering, and then there is the pain felt by dwelling upon the suffering.
I must transform the first, and avoid the second.
Self-pity gives no reward.

❖ ❖ ❖ ❖ ❖

Day 294

When you are offended with any man's shameless conduct, immediately ask yourself, Is it possible, then, that shameless men should not be in the world? It is not possible.

Do not, then, require what is impossible. For this man also is one of those shameless men who must of necessity be in the world. Let the same considerations be present to your mind in the case of the knave, and the faithless man, and of every man who does wrong in any way.

For at the same time that you remind thyself that it is impossible that such kind of men should not exist, you will become more kindly disposed towards every one individually.

It is useful to perceive this, too, immediately when the occasion arises, what virtue Nature has given to man to oppose to every wrongful act. For she has given to man, as an antidote against the stupid man, mildness, and against another kind of man some other power.

And in all cases it is possible for you to correct by teaching the man who is gone astray; for every man who errs misses his object and is gone astray.

Besides, how have you been injured? For you will find that no one among those against whom you are irritated has done anything by which your mind could be made worse; but that which is evil to you and harmful has its foundation only in the mind.

—Marcus Aurelius, *Meditations* Book 9

It is part of the temptation of playing God, of being oneself the center and measure, that we think we can rearrange the world to our desires.
What we are in fact asked to do is to rearrange our desires to fit those in the world.

That there are shameless, devious, violent, or greedy people in the world is hardly up to us.
They are as they are, and are so for a reason, and everyone and everything is there to play a part within the whole.
This is by no means a way to excuse wrongdoing, but to understand it, and to show compassion instead of condemnation.

Most importantly, remember that Nature has given us the means to bear and to overcome evil, and the opportunity to transform wrongdoing into good.
I can improve myself, and encourage others to improve themselves.

It is far too selfish to simply wish to remove the inconvenient, the burdensome, and the painful from our sight.
Again, learn to fix the world, not throw it away.
We see here yet another of the many ways we can understand, apply, and express the change of estimation and perspective that Stoicism requires.

I know I'm still not doing it right, or fully enough, if I harbor resentment and disgust, and simply wish to remove people or things from my sight.

❖ ❖ ❖ ❖ ❖

Day 295

What good are courtyards surrounded by colonnades? What good are all kinds of colored paints? What good are gold-decked rooms? What good are expensive stones, some fitted together on the floor, others inlaid in the walls, some brought from a great distance, and at the greatest expense?

Are not all these things superfluous and unnecessary, without which it is possible not only to live but also to be healthy? Are they not the source of constant trouble, and do they not cost great sums of money from which many people might have benefited by public and private charity?

How much more commendable than living a life of luxury it is to help many people. How much nobler than spending money for sticks and stones to spend it on men. How much more profitable than surrounding oneself with a great house to make many friends, the natural result of cheerfully doing good. What would one gain from a large and beautiful house comparable to what he would gain by conferring the benefits of his wealth upon the city and his fellow-citizens?

—Musonius Rufus, *Lectures* 19

Musonius Rufus is, of course, speaking here of financial wealth, but the analogy applies just as well to the spending of anything that is good and valuable, including, our time and efforts, our interest and concern.

Observing how a man of riches manages his wealth, tells us quite a bit about his character, and what it is that he truly values in his heart.
Recall that it is not wealth itself, which is indifferent, that is an evil, but rather the easy temptation to abuse wealth as a false end, or ordered toward some other false end such as reputation, luxury, or power.

The dignity of each and every person comes first, not what they wear, where they live, what luxuries and conveniences they have acquired, or how impressed anyone is with their fine status.
Show that you care about what is truly good for their souls, not just adding to all the extraneous things we possess.

I've always enjoyed a brief passage attributed to the Dalai Lama, *The paradox of our age*.
It reminds me to always ask myself what I truly value and in what I must truly invest:

We have bigger houses but smaller families; more conveniences, but less time.

We have more degrees but less sense; more knowledge but less judgment; more experts, but more problems; more medicines but less healthiness.

We've been all the way to the moon and back, but have trouble in crossing the street to meet our new neighbor.

We built more computers to hold more copies than ever, but have less real communication; we have become long on quantity, but short on quality.

These are times of fast foods but slow digestion; tall men but short characters; steep profits but shallow relationships.

It's a time when there is much in the window but nothing in the room.

❖ ❖ ❖ ❖ ❖

What makes the tyrant formidable?

'The guards,' you say, 'and their swords, and the men of the bedchamber and those who exclude them who would enter.'

Why, then, if you bring a boy to the tyrant when he is with his guards, is he not afraid; or is it because the child does not understand these things?

If, then, any man does understand what guards are and that they have swords, and comes to the tyrant for this very purpose because he wishes to die on account of some circumstance and seeks to die easily by the hand of another, is he afraid of the guards?

'No, for he wishes for the thing which makes the guards formidable.'

If, then, neither any man wishing to die nor to live by all means, but only as it may be permitted, approaches the tyrant, what hinders him from approaching the tyrant without fear?

'Nothing.'

—Epictetus, *Discourses* 4.7

There can be no doubt that fear has an incredible power, often seeming to be far beyond the ability of choice.

To be able to put the power of fear in the right perspective, to be able to understand it, may be the beginning of becoming a master over fear.

First, if I know what it is that I fear, it is no longer hidden from me: I can see it and observe it.

Second, once I understand what I fear, I can begin to harmonize this with the things I should truly value.

In other words, a man may threaten torture and death.

I understand that it is the pain I fear, or the end of my existence.

Then, I ask myself if these are even things I should have care and concern for?

Both pleasure and pain, long or short life, are things that are indifferent, and never desired for their own sake.

If I then know what I truly want, a life lived in wisdom and with virtue, do the lesser things now seem quite as frightening?

Can I now put that fear in its place, thanks to my grasp of what is right and good?

Considered a great masterpiece by some, and a bloated pomposity by others, Frank Herbert's *Dune* did have a great influence on me when I first read it in early adolescence.

I certainly didn't quite understand all of it, but I do remember being deeply impressed with the "Litany Against Fear" which Paul Atreides recites to himself as he faces the horror of pain and death:

> *I must not fear.*
> *Fear is the mind-killer.*
> *Fear is the little-death that brings total obliteration.*
> *I will face my fear.*
> *I will permit it to pass over me and through me.*
> *And when it has gone past I will turn the inner eye to see its path.*
> *Where the fear has gone there will be nothing. Only I will remain.*

❖ ❖ ❖ ❖ ❖

Imagine every man who is grieved at anything or discontented to be like a pig which is sacrificed and kicks and screams.

Like this pig also is he who on his bed in silence laments the bonds in which we are held. And consider that only to the rational animal is it given to follow voluntarily what happens; but simply to follow is a necessity imposed on all.

—Marcus Aurelius, *Meditations* Book 10

If someone is not within our power, no amount of grumbling, complaining, or squealing, will have any effect, except so as to breed further anxiety and despair.
While the conditions remain the same, we merely make ourselves worse.

The image of the squealing pig is both amusing and deeply horrifying.
We may laugh when we see the hopelessness of the struggle, but we should rightly be disturbed when we turn the mirror upon ourselves, and discern the same responses in our own actions.
We need not say any words at all, or resist in any physical way, but our own internal dissatisfaction is far worse than any external circumstance we may suffer.

Half way into my Wilderness Years, in trying to grapple out of the hole I had dug for myself, I started thinking that things might improve if I tried to be more deliberate and confident.
The problem was that I was trying to be deliberate about controlling circumstances, and not ordering myself.

Needless to say, the impact with that big brick wall was going to happen, sooner or later, and when it did, I had my first full-fledged anxiety attack, the first of very many.
At the time, I had not learned the tricks of calming myself, and the resulting monstrosity I briefly became was indeed much like a pig kicking and screaming.
If I could have looked at myself from the outside at the time, I would have been able to repeat Aurelius' observation.

A thoughtful student once gave me a Buddhist prayer card, with a quote attributed to Shantideva, because she recognized how similar an idea she had grown up with was to Stoic and Classical thinking:

If there is a remedy when trouble strikes,
what reason is there for dejection?
And if there is no help for it,
what use is there in being gloomy?

❖ ❖ ❖ ❖ ❖

Begin at once to live, and count each separate day as a separate life. He who has thus prepared himself, he whose daily life has been a rounded whole, is easy in his mind; but those who live for hope alone find that the immediate future always slips from their grasp and that greed steals along in its place, and the fear of death, a curse which lays a curse upon everything else.

—Seneca the Younger, *Moral letters to Lucilius* 101

The well-known 12–Step saying,
One day at a time, enjoying one moment at a time, accepting hardship as a pathway to peace
is once again taken from Niebuhr's Serenity Prayer.
But you need not be in recovery from any particular addiction, compulsion, or malady to understand its universal meaning.
You can just as easily think of it as a part of the recovery of your humanity and its harmony with Nature.

Just as the addict knows he should manage what he can manage, and never to make promises he can't keep, so too any and all of us can not allow ourselves to be haunted by the past, or troubled by the future, but to simply rule ourselves and finds balance and contentment right now.

For me, sometimes even a day seems too big to handle, because I start to worry about the afternoon or evening in the morning.
On a crippling Black Dog Day, I am often reduced to thinking about the hour, or even the minute.
I once survived a moment of dread by promising myself to make it to the other end of the room.
During an attack of intense chest pains, I sometimes manage this by the breath.
This very practical tool of focusing specifically on present choices and actions can be remarkably effective.

I was once helping out a local narcotics support group by doing something as simple but important as making good coffee.
I overheard a phrase spoken by an old veteran that has stayed with me for many years:
"The fellow who got up earliest this morning is the one who's been clean and sober the longest."
Wonderful!
I think Seneca also understands, and agrees completely.

By limiting myself to what is and can be now, I bracket the anxiety and worry over all the things I have no power or choice over, and I need not use my circumstances as a yardstick for myself.

❖ ❖ ❖ ❖ ❖

The health of the soul is to have its faculties, reason, high spirit and desire happily tempered, with the reason in command and reining in the other two, like restive horses. The special name of this health is temperance, or 'thought-preserving,' for it creates a preservation of one of our powers, namely that of wise-thinking.

—Philo of Alexandria, *On the virtues* 171

We must resist to the temptation of thinking that Stoicism opposes reason and passion. Reason should rule and order our passions, but not be an enemy to them.

Philo here employs the three powers of the soul from Plato, and considers the appetitive and spirited like two horses under the reins of the chariot driver, himself representing the intellect.

I had only learned to ride in the most cursory way, and I have never been fully at ease on a horse: It is my wife and daughter who are the inspired equestrians.
There are indeed few things more beautiful and more harmonious, than to see the cooperation of horse and rider joined together, and the bond of companionship that grows from this shared action.
But do not think for a moment that the horse can be the master.
So too, it is with the mind in relationship to the spirited and the passionate.

We acquire the necessary virtue of temperance when our drive and our feelings can shine forth in all their beauty, but only under the guidance of wisdom and sound thinking.
Each plays its part, each in its own distinct way, but always with the higher ruling the lower.

❖ ❖ ❖ ❖ ❖

'There is free will,' she answered. 'Nor could there be any reasoning nature without freedom of judgment. For any being that can use its reason by nature, has a power of judgment by which it can without further aid decide each point, and so distinguish between objects to be desired and objects to be shunned.

'Each therefore seeks what it deems desirable, and flies from what it considers should be shunned. Wherefore all who have reason have also freedom of desiring and refusing in themselves.

'But I do not lay down that this is equal in all beings. Heavenly and divine beings have with them a judgment of great insight, an imperturbable will, and a power which can effect their desires.

'But human spirits must be more free when they keep themselves safe in the contemplation of the mind of God; but less free when they sink into bodies, and less still when they are bound by their earthly members. The last stage is mere slavery, when the spirit is given over to vices and has fallen away from the possession of its reason.

'For when the mind turns its eyes from the light of truth on high to lower darkness, soon it is dimmed by the clouds of ignorance, and become turbid through ruinous passions; by yielding to these passions and consenting to them, men increase the slavery which they have brought upon themselves, and their true liberty is lost in captivity.

'But God, looking upon all out of the infinite, perceives the views of Providence, and disposes each as its destiny has already fated for it according to its merit.'

—Boethius, *The consolation of Philosophy* Book 5 Prose 2

The Stoic understands that free will, the ability to decide for ourselves, is necessarily joined to reason, the power to understand what we should seek and what we should avoid.

Freedom rises above the more determined level of instinct, and can order and direct our passionate inclinations.

That freedom, however, is not equal in all of us, not because we have been gifted with more or less intelligence or power, but by the beautiful order whereby the way we use our freedom itself determines how much of it we possess.

If I decide to love things lower than myself, then I have freely chosen to become more enslaved to them; if I decide to love more perfect things, then I have freely chosen to liberate myself even more fully.

The argument revolves around the very core of Stoicism, the distinction between what is within and not within my power, and I see it around me all the time.

When I care about the pettiness of the externals, I depend on them, but when I care about the things that are untouched by outward necessity, I maintain and strengthen my independence.

A man in prison is only as chained as much as he cares about the bars and the jailer.

Boethius knew this first-hand.

❖   ❖   ❖   ❖   ❖

When you see another man in the possession of power, set against this the fact that you have not the want of power; when you see another rich, see what you possess in place of riches: for if you possess nothing in place of them, you are miserable; but if you have not the want of riches, know that you possess more than this man possesses and what is worth much more.

Another man possesses a handsome woman: you have the satisfaction of not desiring a handsome wife. Do these things appear to you to be small? And how much would these persons give, these very men who are rich and in possession of power, and live with handsome women, to be able to despise riches and power and these very women whom they love and enjoy?

Do you not know, then, what is the thirst of a man who has a fever? He possesses that which is in no degree like the thirst of a man who is in health: for the man who is in health ceases to be thirsty after he has drunk; but the sick man, being pleased for a short time, has a nausea; he converts the drink into bile, vomits, is griped, and more thirsty.

It is such a thing to have desire of riches and to possess riches, desire of power and to possess power, desire of a beautiful woman and to sleep with her: to this is added jealousy, fear of being deprived of the thing which you love, indecent words, indecent thoughts, unseemly acts.

—Epictetus, *Discourses* 4.9

It's never advisable to argue with an ignorant man, but if you must, by no means argue at his level. He will tell you that the power, pleasure, and popularity he desires and possesses are what you really want, and that he is superior to you because he desires and possesses them.

Clearly, you must be miserable, because you don't have what he has.

The Stoic will differ essentially on two crucial points here.

First, the Stoic will never define any man by what he has or does not have: He will define a man by who he is.

Second, the Stoic is able to say, with humility, charity, and the utmost confidence, that he does not even desire the things the world tries to sell him.

You can rightly be proud if you can honestly say that you wish him well, but you have no interest in any of those trappings.

He may be selling, but you are not buying.

Power, wealth, and sex aren't even on the radar as ends.

I admit there have been times I have wanted to have it both ways, but that was only because I was still listening to the wrong measures, even if only in part.

If what I truly want and need does not include what is base and vulgar, I have so much more in my life when I lack those things.

How could I have more, one may ask, if I have less?

It's a question of what one has more or less of, might or right?

I adore the image of thirst here, because it clarifies the point wonderfully: a healthy man has more, because he drinks only what he needs, but the sick man has less, because he cannot control what he desires.

❖   ❖   ❖   ❖   ❖

"There is, in my opinion, this difference between renown and glory — the latter depends upon the judgments of the many; but renown on the judgments of good men.
—Seneca the Younger, *Moral letters to Lucilius* 102

Remember that Stoicism seeks the balance of the mean, and also remember that yours truly has long been absolutely terrible at striking that mean.
 I often swing wildly back and forth, because all too often, when I aim at the center, I overreach.

It's very easy to get trapped up in fame, only to realize that it offers no true rewards.
 Then it might seem that one should deny and forgo all recognition, and seek to avoid it all cost.

Neither is right, of course.
 Fame is indifferent.
 Both to seek and to reject fame, simply for its own sake, is misguided.
 What measure, then, could I use to distinguish how honor could help me, and how it could harm me?

How might it be a means for me to make myself better?
 The respect of the right people can remind me what is right, and the respect of the wrong people can remind me of what is wrong.
 Cicero, therefore, distinguishes between renown and glory.
 The respect of another can be a great blessing or curse, depending upon who it may be coming from, and toward what end I wish to use it.

Neither sell yourself to fame, nor reject it outright.
 Discernment makes all the difference.

❖ ❖ ❖ ❖ ❖

When you are offended at any man's fault, immediately turn to yourself and reflect in what like manner you err yourself; for example, in thinking that money is a good thing, or pleasure, or a bit of reputation, and the like. For by attending to this you will quickly forget your anger.

If this consideration also is added, that the man is compelled: for what else could he do? Or, if you are able, take away from him the compulsion.

—Marcus Aurelius, *Meditations* Book 10

To look at another with anger or condemnation is the gravest arrogance.
  I compare myself to another, find myself entirely fitting, and find the other wanting.
  I raise myself, and lower another.
  The resentment and diminishing of his value offers me a sort of sick comfort.

I can do better, and turn the attention around, and look at myself in the mirror.
  I am the one I can change, I am the one for whom I am responsible.
  I can compare myself to another in a very different sort of way.
  I need not differentiate myself from him at all, but ask what it is we share in common.

Have I been greedy, lustful, or arrogant, just like him?
  The answer must, of course, be yes, and now I can give my attention and energy where it belongs, to improving myself.

At the same time I can understand another through my own failings, I can show compassion, and perhaps help to understand.
  If I have shown love, but been hurt in return, I recognize that I too have caused hurt, and I offer the same patience and care I would expect for myself.

I often used to dabble in a sort of moral balance sheet, trying to calculate the order of credits and debits.
  I loved someone, but they didn't love me, so I don't owe them love anymore, and I have a right to complain about it.

Ridiculous. I love someone, whether or not they love me, whether or not they have done right or wrong, because we are both really the same in dignity, and both worthy of that love.
  When I recognize myself in another, I truly can't go wrong.

❖ ❖ ❖ ❖ ❖

For my part, then, I would choose sickness rather than luxury, for sickness harms only the body, but luxury destroys both body and soul, causing weakness and impotence in the body and lack of self-control and cowardice in the soul. Furthermore, luxury begets injustice because it also begets covetousness.

For no man of extravagant tastes can avoid being lavish in expenditure, nor being lavish can he wish to spend little; but in his desire for many things he cannot refrain from acquiring them, nor again in his effort to acquire can he fail to be grasping and unjust; for no man would succeed in acquiring much by just methods.

In still another way the man of luxurious habits would be unjust, for he would hesitate to undertake the necessary burdens for his city without abandoning his extravagant life, and if it seemed necessary to suffer deprivation on behalf of his friends or relatives he would not submit to it, for his love of luxury would not permit it.

—Musonius Rufus, *Lectures* 20

Musonius, as always, pulls out all the stops.

Though wealth is, like all externals, indifferent, prudence warns us nevertheless to always avoid using wealth for luxury, which is in itself the goal of a disordered desire.

I can't seek extravagance without being greedy and grasping, and I can't practice justice if I am grasping.

Only a merely personal level, and avoiding putting aside the bigger question of social and political theory, I have often wondered if a rich man can be a truly fair man.

Though this indeed may be very difficult, I have certainly seen people, however rare, who manage their great wealth in a noble way, for the service of others: Aristotle calls this the virtue of *magnificence*, excellence in the giving and receiving of great things.

But can a virtuous man be luxurious and opulent?

With, Musonius, I think this involves an inherent conflict.

As soon as I desire things simply for pleasure or status, and even greater and more extravagant things because they give me greater pleasure and status, I am already driven by selfish greed.

It's one thing to enjoy fine things, quite another to allow oneself to be consumed by a desire for them.

And when I acquire what is excessive for myself, this must in the end be at the expense of others, of those in need, of my community.

I don't squint at a man just because he's rich, but I will question his merits if he has much and flaunts what he has, while others have too little.

This need not be any kind of political "–ism".

It's just a plain and simple question of justice and mercy.

❖ ❖ ❖ ❖ ❖

Nature has treated man less like a mother, than a step-mother. She has cast him into mortal life with a body naked, fragile, and infirm; and with a mind agitated by troubles, depressed by fears, broken by labors, and exposed to passions.

In this mind, however, there lies hid, and as it were buried, a certain divine spark of genius and intellect; and the soul should impute much of its present infirmity to the dullness contracted from its earthly vehicle.

—Cicero, *Of the republic* 3

The Stoic life is a bit like coming in from the cold.

The world we are thrown into can be lonely, uncaring, brutal, and threatening.

This realization isn't cynical or pessimistic at all, because I need only look out my window to see so many people in pain and in need of comfort.

What would be pessimistic is assuming there is no cure.

The warmth and comfort that we need, however, is already within us, and must simply be discovered.

I can learn that I have dignity if only I use my understanding to rule myself, to act with justice and kindness when I am confronted with indifference or hatred, to always live by choosing to act well and right, regardless of what the world throws at me.

I sometimes joke that I didn't adopt Stoicism, Stoicism adopted me, and like a good parent, or step-parent, taught me what was good in me.

❖　❖　❖　❖　❖

But that this may be done, a man must receive no small things, nor are the things small which he must lose. You cannot both wish to be a consul and to have these things, and to be eager to have lands and these things also; and to be solicitous about slaves and about yourself.

But if you wish for anything which belongs to another, that which is your own is lost. This is the nature of the thing: nothing is given or had for nothing. And where is the wonder?

If you wish to be a consul, you must keep awake, run about, kiss hands, waste yourself with exhaustion at other men's doors, say and do many things unworthy of a free man, send gifts to many, daily presents to some. And what is the thing that is got? Twelve bundles of rods, to sit three or four times on the tribunal, to exhibit the games in the Circus and to give suppers in small baskets.

—Epictetus, *Discourses* 4.10

We have already seen that we can't have it both ways, if the two things jostling for our attentions are at odds with one another.

I just might be a good man who is rich and famous, but I'm not good because I'm rich and famous, and we now add, I can't be good and ever want to be rich and famous.

In my own experience and practice I think of this in terms of what I focus on, very much like the idea of how clear or blurry something is in my vision, and where the rays of light converge.

I cast my eye clearly directly on my daily goal of thinking and acting with wisdom and virtue, and while that is the point of my attention, I am also quite aware of other things hovering around, things like wealth, honor, or pleasure.

I certainly see them, but they are blurry, or at the edge of my vision, and I do not focus upon them.

In fact, a practical exercise is to deliberately make them blurry again if they should happen to become clear, in an act of deliberate choice.

I must be aware of them, but I let them be in the background, so to speak.

I'm hardly an expert on film, but I believe the term for changing the focus between something further and closer is called *racking focus*.

I've always liked it when a director uses it, and it provides an image that is helpful in practicing this deliberate focus of attention.

❖ ❖ ❖ ❖ ❖

The healthy eye ought to see all visible things and not to say, I wish for green things; for this is the condition of a diseased eye. And the healthy hearing and smelling ought to be ready to perceive all that can be heard and smelled. And the healthy stomach ought to be with respect to all food just as the mill with respect to all things which it is formed to grind.

And accordingly the healthy understanding ought to be prepared for everything which happens; but that which says, Let my dear children live, and let all men praise whatever I may do, is an eye which seeks for green things, or teeth which seek for soft things.

—Marcus Aurelius, *Meditations* Book 10

Just as I shouldn't just simply see or hear what I prefer, selectively ignoring the rest, my thinking should be open to things as they are. I shouldn't try to force things to fit my thinking.
A mind willing to be open to anything and everything the world presents to it is the only kind of mind that can ever be sane.

The analogy of the eye's openness to light as akin to the mind's openness to truth is a recurring theme in Ancient and Medieval philosophy.
Plato employs it with the Allegory of the Sun and the Allegory of the Cave in the Republic, while in the Middle Ages the Gothic Cathedrals were designed to be flooded with light, a symbol of Divine illumination.
Just as the eye can see by means of light, so the mind can know by means of truth.

If my eye is open only to one or another appealing color, my ears to only soft sounds, or my stomach to only certain foods, none of these organs are acting fully and completely.
So too, my mind is diseased if it only recognizes those things that are convenient or pleasing.

Over the last two decades, I have coped with the deeply ridiculous, but also deeply saddening, situation of someone who chooses to ignore me, and quite literally looks the other way, if I walk by.
I can't speak for the person's inner motives, but I imagine, because of some perceived slight, I am considered unpleasant.
So I am ignored.
It's very childish, but also very common even in the arrogance of adulthood.
To pick and choose what I see or hear, to pick and choose the people whose existence we acknowledge, is much like picking and choosing the truths we prefer, cafeteria style.

❖ ❖ ❖ ❖ ❖

Day 308

Suppose that you hold wealth to be a good: poverty will then distress you, and—which is most pitiable—it will be an imaginary poverty. For you may be rich, and nevertheless, because your neighbor is richer, you suppose yourself to be poor exactly by the same amount in which you fall short of your neighbor.

You may deem official position a good; you will be vexed at another's appointment or re-appointment to the consulship; you will be jealous whenever you see a name several times in the state records.

Your ambition will be so frenzied that you will regard yourself last in the race if there is anyone in front of you. Or you may rate death as the worst of evils, although there is really no evil therein except that which precedes death's coming fear.

You will be frightened out of your wits, not only by real, but by fancied dangers, and will be tossed for ever on the sea of illusion.

—Seneca the Younger, *Moral letters to Lucilius* 104

The dependence upon the things of fortune has a frustrating and life-sapping quality, which is that nothing is ever enough.

If I choose to find joy in my own nature, that joy can be total and complete, because I want nothing more than what is already within me.

Yet if I choose to seek satisfaction in what is outside of me, I require sustenance and support from things that are external, and this must be renewed constantly.

This means, therefore, that no amount of wealth, honor, or pleasure will ever really be enough, because I constantly need and desire more.

I will never be completely satisfied, because what I have must always be added to, supplemented, and augmented in order to remain satisfying.

Once I have wealth, honor, or pleasure, I will crave more, much like an addict, and I will build a tolerance to the lesser dose that once was enough.

If I see a man who is richer, or someone who is more famous, or a friend with a more attractive wife, I will be jealous, and I will actually become impoverished through this jealousy and grasping need.

I have often wondered, for example, why a man who has already made millions, needs to make millions more?

Why the politician who has been elected to office at the very least needs to re-elected, or must seek ever-higher office?

Why the man who has seduced one woman, tries to seduce another dozen?

We have our answer above.

❖ ❖ ❖ ❖ ❖

Day 309

The universe itself is God and the universal outpouring of its soul.

—Chrysippus ex Cicero, *On the nature of the gods* 1.15

As we have already seen, Stoics usually stressed the immanence, not just the transcendence, of the Divine, and some, like Chrysippus, seemed to embrace downright pantheism, literally identifying the Divine with the Universe itself.

I have my own views on this matter, but that is best left for a discussion on metaphysics and religion.

What I offer for our purposes touches on a more personal angle.

When you look for what is Divine, sacred, or eternal, you need not gaze far up or far away, but you can simply look at what is right in front of you.

Something that is perfect and infinite can be both here and there, close and far, above me and next to me.

Some may take this figuratively, and some may take this literally, but the Divine is "in" you, is "in" your neighbor, whether friend or enemy, is "in" every little thing in your world.

It can be seen simply in the fact that all things have being, that they are good in their own way, that they are beautiful.

If you seek God, don't look around wondering where He is.

Mother Teresa once said:

> *Seeking the face of God in everything, everyone, all the time, and His hand in every happening; this is what it means to be contemplative in the heart of the world.*

❖ ❖ ❖ ❖ ❖

Day 310

When my sons are grown up, I would ask you, O my friends, to punish them; and I would have you to trouble them, as I have troubled you, if they seem to care about riches, or anything, more than about virtue; or if they pretend to be something when they are really nothing — then reprove them, as I have reproved you, for not caring about that for which they ought to care, and thinking that they are something when they are really nothing. And if you do this, I and my sons will have received justice at your hands.

—Socrates ex Plato, *Apology* 41e-42a

Socrates has just been convicted of impiety and corrupting the youth, and has been sentenced to death.

He doesn't cry out in despair, or go into a fit of rage, or beg the court for mercy.

No, instead he asks the Athenians for a favor.

Please keep and eye on my boys, and don't take it easy on them.

Please be a gadfly to them, as I have been to you.

Remind them about what really matters in life.

Seek virtue over riches, and hate hypocrisy and pride.

It's moments like this when you see exactly why the Stoics invariably admired Socrates as their inspiration.

We do so many things, and go through such convoluted procedures, to apparently raise our children well.

The right schools, the right activities, the right social circles, and all so they can get a good job and then become respectable and successful.

By all means, appreciate these things if you must, but only if they help our children become what they really need to be.

They don't necessarily need to be successful in the way the world tells us.

They need to be wise, they need to be virtuous, and this will lead them to happiness, whatever their circumstances.

Care about the important things.

❖ ❖ ❖ ❖ ❖

Day 311

When then? Does any man require you to ornament yourself? Far from it; except to ornament that which we really are by Nature, the rational faculty, the opinions, the actions; but as to the body only so far as purity, only so far as not to give offense.

But if you are told that you ought not to wear garments dyed with purple, go and daub your cloak with muck or tear it. 'But how shall I have a neat cloak?' Man, you have water: Wash it.

—Epictetus, *Discourses* 4.11

I have been reflecting on all the things that we use to ornament ourselves and our lives, and the way that we put things on the outside to hide what is inside, to replace what matters with what is vain, or to fill an emptiness in our souls with the diversion of pretty pictures.

The business suit, bought at the finest boutique, that proves you have arrived.
That fancy car, the one where you are certain that all eyes turn as you drive by.
The perfect family photograph, where everyone is smiling, but has spent hours before and after bickering.
Social media profiles.
Professional resumes.
A perfectly green and weedless lawn.
An article published in a reputable journal, complete with an intense but casual photograph.
That little self-depreciatory comment, seemingly so innocent, dropped in company to draw praise.
Laughing at your boss' bad jokes.

I no longer have the inclination to care for any of that.
A Stoic will be one of the most tolerant and caring people you will ever meet, so don't think he's condemning you.
He has simply learned to care for other things.
He has no real interest in impressing you or anyone else, or appearing to be handsome, or successful, or well liked.
He wants nothing more than to be a good man.
There are certain blemishes even the best make-up won't hide.

❖ ❖ ❖ ❖ ❖

Day 312

You will escape envy if you do not force yourself upon the public view, if you do not boast your possessions, if you understand how to enjoy things privately.
—Seneca the Younger, *Moral letters to Lucilius* 105

If I can't live well, and be completely happy, in complete privacy, I'm not doing it right.

As soon as I begin to be concerned about how I am perceived, or how my actions affect my position in life, I am no longer acting according to Nature.

For someone like myself to be jealous, or to be tempted by self-promotion, what I consider to be one the gravest sins of our modern world, may seem rather odd.

I have always been an introvert, deeply counter–cultural, and quite out of tune with the trends of the times.

I still wear a vintage fedora in honor of one of my heroes, Jimmy Stewart, and I now refuse to wear a tie, as a protest against lawyers, businessmen, and politicians.

I am an eccentric, and I am proud of that.

Yet there are always times when I feel this tugging, this powerful pull, a beckoning from the world of Fortune.

Maybe, just maybe, I could be someone who really matters.

I could, perhaps, be admired and respected, and people would feel honored to meet me.

I could still try to be a decent human being, but that struggle might make me loved.

I have those desires, or feel envy for others, only because I am letting my feelings rule my thinking.

I need not care at all, not one tiny little bit, whether others admire me, or whether others have more or less of the random rewards of worldly success.

For myself, I need to look away from those temptations.

❖ ❖ ❖ ❖ ❖

Day 313

Men despise one another and flatter one another; and men wish to raise themselves above one another, and crouch before one another.

—Marcus Aurelius, *Meditations*, Book 11

The draw of power, whether it is through politics, money, reputation, sexual dominance, or simple brute physical force, can be enticing and devastating.

I've seen all of the above variations, I've seen them all too frequently, and I've seen the suffering and shattered lives that follow.

What I thought was friendship, collegiality, kindness, or romance has sometimes turned out to be the flattery and control Aurelius describes.

I know very well the pain when you recognize that you have been duped and played for a fool.

It does not need to be this way.

The games, the manipulations, or the long knives in the dark are wholly unnecessary.

But surely, you may say, my enemy, the one who wishes to dominate or destroy me, will use these tools?

He may well do so.

But you do not, and you are better, and stronger than all the harm that can be done to you by all the power plays in the world.

The dignity that is truly within you cannot be taken from you, as long as you don't surrender by becoming a player in the game.

In *The Mission*, one of the first films to really get me thinking when I was a teenager, Fr Gabriel says:

If might is right, then love has no place in the world. It may be so, it may be so.

But I don't have the strength to live in a world like that.

But it isn't so.

Might does not make right.

You do have the strength, and might can have no power over you unless you yourself surrender your own ability to love.

❖ ❖ ❖ ❖ ❖

378

Day 314

A cheeky monkey, that Musonius.

The foolish man assumes money is always a gift, a blessing, and a lucky catch.

The Stoic knows that money will always be a curse to the rascal, and if the man who pretends to be noble seems to get a reward when he becomes rich and famous, he's actually being punished and corrected by Nature.

Because he doesn't know the good, wealth will drag him down.

Understood with the right qualifications, I think it entirely correct to say that we get what we deserve.

I do not mean this in the simple sense of receiving good or bad fortune because we have been good or bad.

I mean rather that Nature gives us exactly what we need, in each and every case offering us the opportunity to honestly reflect and to choose.

Will I live to pull myself up, or will I wallow in my own filth?

The British progressive rock band, Marillion, have, for over thirty years, been one of my greatest pleasures, old friends, in a way, though I have only spoken to the lads twice.

In their song "Deserve," I think they consider a similar point:

> We get the toys that we deserve,
> the quiet and the noise that we deserve,
> the girls and the boys that we deserve.
>
> We get what we want if we really want it,
> we get what we want if we're really honest.
> You know what you are,
> you know what you want,
> you know what you deserve.

❖ ❖ ❖ ❖ ❖

Day 315

When you have adopted the simple life, do not pride yourself upon it, and if you are a water-drinker do not say on every occasion, 'I am a water-drinker.' And if you ever want to train laboriously, keep it to yourself and do not make a show of it. Do not embrace statues.

If you are very thirsty take a good draught of cold water, and rinse your mouth and tell no one.

—Epictetus, *Enchiridion* 47

I often feel like I fail in most of my outside endeavors, and as a result I have an unhealthy tendency to automatically assume that I have done something wrong.

If I am corrected by another, for example, by a person who intends to be helpful and kind, I feel deeply wounded, and consider myself a failure.

I know full well that this is toxic thinking, and I combat it each and every day.

I'm a blemished and broken mess, thanks to my poor decisions, but I'm working to fix all of that, day-by-day.

The vast majority of people in this world lead simple and ordinary lives.

They are not special, or important, or influential, according to the measures of the very people who think that they are precisely the ones who are special, important, or influential.

We need to stop listening to that very small clique of important people.

They are not important at all: They are vain and self-serving.

I suspect that my own weakness, in being tempted by worldly success, comes from having grown up at the fringes of the important crowd.

I went to school with many of them, and academia as a whole is a breeding spot for the pursuit of fame.

I have a very bad habit of sometimes feeling that merit is measured by recognition.

It isn't.

Merit is simply measured by merit.

The last time I was in Austria, over twenty years ago, the country of my birth and so important in my early years, I took a bus from the Hauptbahnhof in Graz to Gösting, in order to visit the ruins of a medieval castle.

Being the annoyingly precise fellow that I am, I arrived ten minutes before the bus departed.

I had a truly wonderful conversation with the bus driver before the other passengers arrived.

He was the son of a shopkeeper.

Though he was only sixteen years old at the end of the Second World War, he was drafted by the Wehrmacht to fight the Russians.

He deserted from his unit, and made his way back to Graz to care for his parents and his brothers and sisters.

He expected to be caught and shot by the Germans, but he made it back, and after the war, got a job driving busses for Graz public transport.

380

He was a few months from retirement.

I asked him if he felt that he had a good life, and if what he did had made a difference.

"Of course," he said with a good, hearty Austrian laugh.

"I've spent forty years of my life helping people get to where they need to go. I take pride in that."

This was a man who lived a simple life, a life with no bells and whistles.

I will remember him to the end, because he cared nothing for ostentation or display.

I think of him often, and he inspires me.

❖ ❖ ❖ ❖ ❖

Day 316

How unsound and insincere is he who says, 'I have determined to deal with you in a fair way'. —What are you doing, man? There is no occasion to give this notice. It will soon show itself by acts. The voice ought to be plainly written on the forehead. Such as a man's character is, he immediately shows it in his eyes, just as he who is beloved forthwith reads everything in the eyes of lovers.

The man who is honest and good ought to be exactly like a man who smells strong, so that the bystander as soon as he comes near him must smell whether he choose or not. But the affectation of simplicity is like a crooked stick. Nothing is more disgraceful than a wolfish, false friendship. Avoid this most of all. The good and simple and benevolent show all these things in the eyes, and there is no mistaking.

—Marcus Aurelius, *Meditations* Book 11

I am immediately suspicious of the man who tells me he is going to do right by me, or insists that he has my best interests at heart.
I don't just mean condescending lawyers or smarmy used-car salesmen, but any sort of fellow who sounds too good to be true.

I am much more impressed by the sorts of people who don't insist on their reliability, but are simply reliable, or brag of their fairness, but just act fairly.
Such folks are recognized easily by their deeds.

I am comforted that I'm not alone in thinking that false friendship is one of the lowest things, and if Marcus Aurelius confirms this, I can be a bit more confident that my own estimation isn't simply colored by the weight of my emotional baggage.

I am also intrigued by Aurelius' observation about how the eyes show character.
It seems so trite to say such a thing, yet I believe it in some sense to be true.
Perhaps it is the fullness of a person's demeanor, but the eyes seem to be at the center.
I'm not sure how it could be explained, but that sense of the measure of personality and character I get from the expression of someone's eyes is almost always borne out by longer experience of the person.
I have done myself great harm on a few occasions when I have ignored such signs.

❖　❖　❖　❖　❖

Day 317

Life is not a dainty business. You have started on a long journey you are bound to slip, collide, fall, become weary, and cry out: 'O, for Death!' or in other words, tell lies.

At one stage you will leave a comrade behind you, at another you will bury someone, at another you will be apprehensive. It is amid the stumblings of this sort that you must travel out this rugged journey. Does one wish to die? Let the mind be prepared to meet everything; let it know that it has reached the heights around which the thunder plays.

—Seneca the Younger, *Moral letters to Lucilius* 107

Stoicism certainly has a very tough component, and I suspect that this is what has stood out to many at first glance, and perhaps has been the reason it gets its reputation for unflinching strength.

The sensitivity and compassion that go alongside this toughness are often overlooked.

Yet the toughness is not cold or hard, it is not heartless, it is not dismissive.

When some people say that one should toughen up, or get over it, they are actually being very demeaning, because they don't affirm the reality of a person's sincere thoughts and feelings.

A passage like Seneca's does not intend to intimidate or shame us, it intends to encourage us, to remind us that, yes, life is hard, and can be very ugly, but there is within us the ability to rise above, to be both strong and to be good.

It's much like the difference between the coach who yells at his athletes, "What are you, some kind of wimps?" as opposed to the coach who yells at his athletes, "Get back up, dust yourself off. You can do this!"

❖ ❖ ❖ ❖ ❖

Day 318

Of all the questions which are ever the subject of discussion among learned men, there is none which is more important to thoroughly understand than this, that man is born for justice, and that law and equity have not been established by opinion, but by Nature.

—Cicero, *On the laws* 1.10

I recognize my own bias, but I have grown deeply tired of the escapades of those who think of themselves as learned.
Academics and scholars debate obscure minutiae, and claim that they are somehow helping the world.
They are sadly helping nothing but their own sense of self-esteem.

That world tried to suck me in, but somehow I managed to resist, and I am deeply grateful that I did not become that person.
I even have an alternate image of myself, which I employ as an everyday warning, of what I could so easily have turned into.
I have very many flaws, but I am not vain, I am not obsessed with my reputation, and I don't see philosophy as a means for my worldly gain.

The things academics should really worry about are the same questions that haunt the everyman, each and every day.
How should I live?
How can I figure out what really matters in my life?
How can I decide on the best way to relate to others?

And sadly the answers that most academics have to offer are the furthest removed from Nature.
We quote what one person said about another person, and we call it scholarship.
We reduce wisdom to citations and name-dropping, and insist the work is of quality because it has been peer–reviewed.

When we contemplate justice, we see it as an artificial creation, the result of man's conventions and preferences.
We fall into the academic love of self-reference.
Justice, however, is not something we have made, and no amount of citing authorities gives it any weight.
Justice is granted by Nature, because she has made all things with their own dignity and merit, and the respect we owe one another is innate to our very being.

Academics should, I think, spend far more time pointing to the Natural Law, and far less of their time looking into mirrors.

❖ ❖ ❖ ❖ ❖

Just as foreknowledge of present things brings no necessity to bear upon them as they come to pass, so also foreknowledge of future things brings no necessity to bear upon things which are to come.

—Boethius, *The consolation of Philosophy* Book 5 Prose 4

I must recognize at all times that the free will which defines me does not exist outside of the order of Nature and Providence: It functions within it, and in harmony with the balance of all other things.

This is one of the most beautiful and amazing aspects of our world, that freedom and necessity work with one another.

Boethius offers a wonderful observation.

Simply because I know that something is happening now, my knowledge does not cause that event to occur.

Likewise, if God knows that something will occur in the future, his knowledge does not cause that event to occur.

Providence is so broad, and so wide, that it already knows what we will choose, without making us choose it, and orders all things accordingly.

From our perspective, as beings that undergo change, and therefore exist in time, there is a present, a past, and a future.

From the perspective of the Divine, which transcends all change, there is only an eternal present.

All things are now, and all things that have been, or will be, are, in a sense, always real.

That worst moment of my life, when I lost all that I loved, was always going to happen.

But it did not happen because of fate, it happened because of my choices.

I know this is some high–octane metaphysics, but it really does help us to know that what will be will most certainly be, and what will be also involves how I choose to live.

❖ ❖ ❖ ❖ ❖

Day 320

When you have remitted your attention for a short time, do not imagine this, that you will recover it when you choose; but let this thought be present to you, that in consequence of the fault committed today, your affairs must be in a worse condition for all that follows.

For first, and what causes most trouble, a habit of not attending is formed in you; then a habit of deferring your attention. And continually from time to time you drive away, by deferring it, the happiness of life, proper behavior, the being and living conformably to Nature.

If, then, the procrastination of attention is profitable, the complete omission of attention is more profitable; but if it is not profitable, why do you not maintain your attention constantly? 'Today I choose to play.' Well then, ought you not to play with attention? 'I choose to sing.' What, then, hinders you from doing so with attention?

Is there any part of life excepted, to which attention does not extend? For will you do it worse by using attention, and better by not attending at all?

—Epictetus, *Discourses* 4.12

Stoicism always reminds us that we can begin again.
But it most certainly does not encourage us to let down our guard, or to assume that there are no consequences for our wrongdoing.

I must remind myself that my actions have very real consequences, both for others and for myself.
All too often I have seen how we hurt one another and damage ourselves in dramatic and lasting ways.
My own poor choices, often hinging upon a single action, have affected me for decades, and I can list to myself all the ways, even a few words misspoken or the smallest deeds have greatly altered the state of my character.

In my early years of teaching, a college freshman excitedly told me about a new fellow she had just met, and how he was going to take her skiing for the weekend.
I smelled a rat and told her as politely as I could that she might want to rethink the arrangement.

She brushed off my suggestion, of course.
I still speak with her all these years later, and she confessed to me recently how that single misguided event snowballed into a series of poor choices that steered her away from a good life for many years.
I understood completely, because I'd done much the same thing myself.

By all means learn from your mistakes, but that doesn't mean you should be deliberately making them.

❖　❖　❖　❖　❖

Day 321

We have withdrawn the soul from the divine contemplation and dragged it into mean and lowly tasks, so that it might be a slave to greed, so that it might forsake the Universe and its confines, and, under the command of masters who try all possible schemes, pry beneath the earth and seek what evil it can dig up therefrom—discontented with that which was freely offered to it.

Now God, who is the Father of us all, has placed ready to our hands those things which he intended for our own good; he did not wait for any search on our part, and he gave them to us voluntarily. But that which would be injurious, he buried deep in the earth.

We can complain of nothing but ourselves; for we have brought to light the materials for our destruction, against the will of Nature, who hid them from us. We have bound over our souls to pleasure, whose service is the source of all evil; we have surrendered ourselves to self-seeking and reputation, and to other aims which are equally idle and useless.

—Seneca the Younger, *Moral letters to Lucilius* 110

I enjoy the imagery here.

We were made to soar in the bright heavens, but instead we grovel and dig deep under the dark earth.

We ignore the higher things and dedicate ourselves to the lower, even as Nature has given us easy access to what is good, but has purposefully hidden away what is evil.

It is always helpful for me to catalog the amount of time and effort that we expend on all the least important things, the trinkets, and how little time we dedicate to the real riches.

When I visualize this to myself, it takes on an absurd and ridiculous character.

Out of a waking day of sixteen hours, how many of those hours are spent on career, gaining social status, or satisfying the desire for pleasure?

And how much time and effort goes into improving my soul by pursuing the true, the good, and the beautiful?

For many people, the greater may be completely lacking, and for even those who understand the nature of life, the proportions will still be wide of the mark.

I prefer to avoid laughing at others, so I just laugh at myself, at how even I, the insane student of philosophy, live a life that is grossly out of proportion.

❖ ❖ ❖ ❖ ❖

Day 322

If any have offended against you, consider first:

What is my relation to men, and that we are made for one another; and in another respect, I was made to be set over them, as a ram over the flock or a bull over the herd. But examine the matter from first principles, from this: If all things are not mere atoms, it is nature which orders all things: if this is so, the inferior things exist for the sake of the superior, and these for the sake of one another.

Second, consider what kind of men they are at table, in bed, and so forth: and particularly, under what compulsions in respect of opinions they are; and as to their acts, consider with what pride they do what they do.

Third, that if men do rightly what they do, we ought not to be displeased; but if they do not right, it is plain that they do so involuntarily and in ignorance. For as every soul is unwillingly deprived of the truth, so also is it unwillingly deprived of the power of behaving to each man according to his deserts.

Accordingly men are pained when they are called unjust, ungrateful, and greedy, and in a word wrongdoers to their neighbors.

Fourth, consider that you also do many things wrong, and that you are a man like others; and even if you do abstain from certain faults, still you have the disposition to commit them, though either through cowardice, or concern about reputation, or some such mean motive, you abstain from such faults.

Fifth, consider that you do not even understand whether men are doing wrong or not, for many things are done with a certain reference to circumstances. And in short, a man must learn a great deal to enable him to pass a correct judgment on another man's acts.

Sixth, consider when you are much vexed or grieved, that man's life is only a moment, and after a short time we are all laid out dead.

Seventh, that it is not men's acts which disturb us, for those acts have their foundation in men's ruling principles, but it is our own opinions that which disturb us. Take away these opinions then, and resolve to dismiss thy judgment about an act as if it were, something grievous, and thy anger is gone.

How then shall I take away these opinions? By reflecting that no wrongful act of another brings shame on you: for unless that which is shameful is alone bad, thou also must of necessity do many things wrong, and become a robber and everything else.

Eighth, consider how much more pain is brought on us by the anger and vexation caused by such acts than by the acts themselves, at which we are angry and vexed.

Ninth, consider that a good disposition is invincible, if it be genuine, and not an affected smile and acting a part. For what will the most violent man do to thee, if you continue to be of a kind disposition towards him, and if, as opportunity offers, you gently admonish him and calmly correct his errors at the very time when he is trying to do thee harm, saying, Not so, my child: we are constituted by nature for something else: I shall certainly not be injured, but thou art injuring thyself, my child.- And show him with gentle tact and by general principles that this is so, and that even bees do not do as he does, nor any animals which are formed by nature to be gregarious. And you must do this neither with any double meaning nor in the way of reproach, but affectionately and without any rancor in thy soul; and not as if you were lecturing him, nor yet that any bystander may admire, but either when he is alone, and if others are present.

Remember these nine rules, as if you have received them as a gift from the Muses, and begin at last to be a man while you live. But you must equally avoid flattering men and being vexed by them, for both are unsocial and lead to harm.

And let this truth be present to you in the excitement of anger, that to be moved by passion is not manly, but that mildness and gentleness, as they are more agreeable to human nature, so also are they more manly; and he who possesses these qualities possesses strength, nerves and courage, and not the man who is subject to fits of passion and discontent.

For in the same degree in which a man's mind is nearer to freedom from all passion, in the same degree also is it nearer to strength: and as the sense of pain is a characteristic of weakness, so also is anger. For he who yields to pain and he who yields to anger, both are wounded and both submit.

But if you will, receive also a tenth present from the Apollo, leader of the Muses, and it is this—that to expect bad men not to do wrong is madness, for he who expects this desires an impossibility. But to allow men to behave so to others, and to expect them not to do you any wrong, is irrational and tyrannical.

—Marcus Aurelius, *Meditations* Book 11

There are, throughout human history, all sorts of ways to classify and categorize moral precepts. Don't worry so much about the letter of the law, as you do the spirit of the law.

I am sorry that this is a very long passage. When I first confronted it, I actually broke it into ten parts, and considered it over ten days.

I'll simply give my own very brief version, summarizing the passages for my own thinking.

• How should I approach some one who does me wrong?

• Nature has made us for one another, not to use one another.

• Always consider not only how people act, but also why they act as they do.

• Even when acting unjustly, a man acts for what he perceives to be good, however ignorant.

• I also do wrong, and I must recognize my own weakness.

• Do not be quick to judge, because we do not understand all the circumstances.

• Do not overestimate the severity of an evil suffered, because in the end it is trivial.

• The action is not bad for us, but our own judgment about the action is what is bad for us.

• Our own frustration hurts us more than the action.

• Meet the harm with good will, and you defeat the harm.

Do not expect people to do good for you, and you will never be disappointed. Do good yourself.

This is all simple, common sense, and shows how grounded Stoicism really is. It's a shame it is so apparent that we overlook it, and instead of making evil good, we simply mix in more evil from our own misguided thinking.

❖ ❖ ❖ ❖ ❖

If one accomplishes some good though with toil, the toil passes, but the good remains; if one does something dishonorable with pleasure, the pleasure passes, but the dishonor remains.
—Musonius Rufus, *Fragments* 51

Remember what is lasting, and what is fleeting, and that when we have our house out of order, it is the fleeting things are the ones we want, and the lasting things the ones that we would give anything to cast away.

I think it entirely fair and accurate to say that the vicious things I have done have almost always involved a quick burst of pleasure, followed by the glacial slowness of regret.
And while the virtuous acts I've managed have often pained me in the short run, they are now my refuge in the long run.

I've heard many an addict describe his life in this way, and I've also seen it in all aspects of our lives, where we tell that little lie to get out of trouble, or swindle a business partner for a bigger cut of the pie, slander a colleague to move on up, or throw away the people who really loved us for some instant gratification.

Once I've sold my character for immediate convenience, I gain nothing and lose everything.

❖   ❖   ❖   ❖   ❖

If melodiously piping flutes sprang from the olive, would you doubt that a knowledge of flute-playing resided in the olive? And what if plane trees bore harps which gave forth rhythmical sounds? Clearly you would think in the same way that the art of music was possessed by plane trees. Why, then, seeing that the universe gives birth to beings that are animate and wise, should it not be considered animate and wise itself?

—Zeno of Citium ex Cicero, *On the nature of the gods* 2.8

We don't even need to bring religion and the supernatural into this issue, because the beauty and order of Nature should be enough to convince us; there is nothing in the effect that is not within the cause, and the more perfect cannot be caused by the less perfect.
Anything less is a logical contradiction.

Though I have never seemed to have the necessary gifts to be any good at the work of physics, chemistry, or biology, I have always admired the fact that the natural sciences reveal a universe that operates through laws, with order, and with an overwhelming beauty.
I have also been inspired by the natural scientists who themselves observe quite the same awe and amazement, and who tell us that this sense of wonder at the universal laws of nature was the very reason they were drawn into such study.

I wonder also, then, why so many of these brilliant people, influenced perhaps by the gloomy materialism and nihilism of the modern world, don't seem willing to make the obvious connection between a universe that produces life and wisdom, and a universe that already contains within its very self the principles of life and wisdom?

Where there is truth, it proceeds from what is ultimately true; where there is beauty, it proceeds from what is supremely beautiful; where there is goodness, it flows from the highest of goods.
I cannot attribute order and purpose to effects, and deny there are not equally ordered and purposeful causes.

I admittedly cannot explain why the relationship between laws of classical and quantum physics, for example, may seem so confusing and confounding to us, but this does not mean I will automatically assume the universe is random and chaotic, because reason itself tells me that randomness and chaos are not at all what they seem.

I don't insist there is no solution to a crossword puzzle because I can't find the words, and I certainly shouldn't deny causality in the natural sciences because my perception and judgment are not yet fully formed.
It took at least two millennia for philosophers and scientists to flesh out a workable description of gravity, but no one in his right mind ever denied the existence of gravity.

❖ ❖ ❖ ❖ ❖

What then? Is it possible to be free from faults? It is not possible; but this is possible, to direct your efforts incessantly to being faultless. For we must be content if by never remitting this attention we shall escape at least a few errors. But now when you have said, 'Tomorrow I will begin to attend,' you must be told that you are saying this, 'Today I will be shameless, disregardful of time and place, mean; it will be in the power of others to give me pain; today I will be passionate and envious.'

See how many evil things you are permitting yourself to do. If it is good to use attention tomorrow, how much better is it to do so today? If tomorrow it is in your interest to attend, much more is it today, that you may be able to do so tomorrow also, and may not defer it again to the third day.

—Epictetus, *Discourses* 4.12

I must often perform the now ubiquitous "facepalm" whenever I hear someone, faced with the struggle between striving for achievement and settling for failure, by saying "Well, nobody's perfect!"

One must distinguish.

No man, who is a creature and a part of the whole of the Universe, can be absolutely perfect, because no man is everything.

Man is not God, and our greatest vices, driven by pride, result if we think that we are.

Yet simply because I am not the sum of all perfection, does not mean I cannot participate in it most fully, and strive to serve it.

I may not be the Absolute, but I can share in its fullness.

Just as putting off until tomorrow what can be done today is often an excuse for our own moral cowardice, so too justifying failure because I'm not God can be a symptom of moral laziness.

By all means, let us admit our failings, but let not this admission compound our failings even further.

❖ ❖ ❖ ❖ ❖

Day 326

Socrates used to say: 'What do you want? Souls of rational or irrational men?'
'Souls of rational men.'
'Of what rational men? Sound or unsound?'
'Sound.'
'Why then do you not seek for them?'
'Because we have them.'
'Why then do you fight and quarrel?'

—Marcus Aurelius, *Meditations* Book 11

I hear many things, each and every day that I consider to be nonsense, and I most likely say far many more things, each and every day, which are actually nonsense.
If I cannot be, even in part, as patient as others are with me, the bickering of the world would be unbearable.

Reasonable people don't quarrel with one another.
A fool may quarrel with a wise man, and the wise man will respond with patience and kindness, or disengage, or at the very most simply hold the line.
And when two fools quarrel, the feathers will fly.

This is because reason and harmony are necessary for one another, each being a property of the other.
A man cannot be reasonable and respond to his neighbor with deliberate anger or hatred, and nothing can be harmonious which is not guided by the order and purpose of reason.

A disagreement may be charitable, because both parties are still united in their love for what is right and good, even as their estimation of it may differ.
A quarrel is always personal, however.
We no longer only differ in our opinions, but we differ because we now no longer even love what is true, but love only ourselves.

❖ ❖ ❖ ❖ ❖

Day 327

Let each man convince himself of this before all else—'I must be just without reward.' And that is not enough; let him convince himself also of this: 'May I take pleasure in devoting myself of my own free will to uphold this noblest of virtues.' Let all his thoughts be turned as far as possible from personal interests.

You need not look about for the reward of a just deed; a just deed in itself offers a still greater return. Fasten deep in your mind that which I remarked a short space above: that it makes no difference how many persons are acquainted with your uprightness. Those who wish their virtue to be advertised are not striving for virtue but for renown.

—Seneca the Younger, *Moral letters to Lucilius* 113

The more that there is of value within me, the less I need to seek distraction by what is outside of me.

The weaker I am in my soul, the more the world will end up ruling my soul.

Stoics repeat this point not to fill copy, but because it is so deeply important.

My own experience tells me that once I think I have understood Stoic values, the only thing keeping me from practicing them is my weakness in listening to my passions over my thinking.

This means that, for whatever reason, I didn't really fully know those values to begin with.

Perhaps constant habit will strengthen my wisdom, and not merely the sudden brute force of will.

There is a perfectly good reason that prayers, moral habits, memorization, or any exercise, physical, mental, or moral, are strengthened by repetition and slow, but sure, commitment.

The only reason I would ever think that the value of thoughts, intention, and actions is measured by the respect they receive would be if I quite simply did not understand the value of those actions for their own sake.

My opinion is at fault.

If I fix this, then I fix myself, and I will care absolutely nothing about defining myself by what others think.

Since I have been very young, I've been drawn to the ideal of a simple, reclusive life, with little to worry me from things outside.

In these last few years, I have come closer to that than I ever have, yet I still sometimes struggle to find the fullness of such joy.

I live in a quiet, rural area, full of wildlife, livestock, and the sweet smell of hay, but sometimes my vanity will tug at me.

There are far more animals than people running around my little homestead, I can see the stars more clearly than I ever have, and I can even leave my front door unlocked with little fear of burglary.

Why might I still feel troubled?

Why do I care if I am not recognized?

Because my judgment, and therefore my habits and actions, are not yet quite right.

I continue the path of improvement, however hard or steep.

I will get up again and climb some more, even as I fall again.

I have been using a rather simple, but deeply effective, means of avoiding the temptation of renown.

I simply don't listen to the noise and mania of the world.

I severely limit what I watch on television, and when I do, I mute or fast-forward through the crippling advertisements.

I don't get involved in social media debates.

I keep my access to politics at a minimum.

I spend any time I have only with people that I can truly love, and who help me to become better.

❖ ❖ ❖ ❖ ❖

Day 328

The hour of departure has arrived, and we go our ways—I to die and you to live. Which is the better, only God knows.

—Socrates ex Plato, *Apology* 42a

If I love what is right and fair, how much am I willing to give for it?

If I say I care about wisdom and virtue above all else, will I sacrifice anything else for its achievement?

Some say that every man has his price.

Do I have a price, where my commitment to character stops, and I'm willing to sell it for worldly gain?

Socrates didn't have such a price, because he had a very different sense of wealth.

Don't believe those who think you have a price, because all they are really describing isn't you, but rather themselves.

Figuring out if people have a price isn't hard.

You just need to observe them whenever they face a conflict between their moral worth and their worldly gain. Even a small situation will usually do.

At what point do they stop making excuses for doing what is right, excuses they themselves might even believe?

Socrates may seem like a stubborn and prideful man to some, but I think again, that says more about us than it does about him.

❖ ❖ ❖ ❖ ❖

Day 329

Nature made us just that we might share our goods with each other, and supply each other's wants.

You observe in this discussion, whenever I speak of Nature, I mean Nature in its genuine purity, but that there is, in fact, such corruption engendered by evil customs, that the sparks, as it were, of virtue which have been given by nature are extinguished, and that antagonist vices arise around it and become strengthened.

—Cicero, *On the laws* 1.12

I smile when I hear people tell me that religion, race, or creed have destroyed the world.
None of those things has ever rightly destroyed anything.
The abuse of them, however, might wrongly destroy some things.

If you have a respect for Nature, you will have a respect for your fellow man.
If you love a God, any God, you will respect Creation, and all that is within it.
If you respect your origins and heritage, you will recognize the dignity of everyone's heritage.
If you have certain habits and beliefs, you will respect why others have their own habits and beliefs.

Yet if you are so quick to judge, to condemn, or to kill, you are not embracing Nature.
You are embracing your own vanity, and all those good and wonderful things become corrupted tools for your own selfishness.

I was raised to believe that cops were decent people, and there was a bunch of them in my father's family.
I've seen many good cops.
One drove me all the way home, ten miles away, after I got stuck at a party, when my ride had a fight with his girlfriend.

I've also seen bad cops.
One drew her gun on my wife simply for stepping out of her car to help me when my own car had broken down.
Until one of those other good cops intervened, I was pretty sure it would end very poorly.

Don't condemn law enforcement itself because you've seen it abused.
Praise or blame an individual for upholding or corrupting his vocation.

It's not being a policeman that is good or bad.
It's not being a priest, teacher, lawyer, or doctor that is good of bad.
What is good or bad is what you choose to make of those conditions.

Here's my version of self-reflection:
Nature is never corrupt.
I'm corrupt, however, whenever I hijack Nature.

❖ ❖ ❖ ❖ ❖

Day 330

The ignorant man's position and character is that he never looks to himself for benefit or harm, but to the world outside him.

The philosopher's position and character is that he always looks to himself for benefit and harm.

—Epictetus, *Enchiridion* 48

I had the lovely privilege of administering final exams just the other week, as I have had now for well over twenty years.
Few things will reveal the content of character as the giving, and the receiving, of those dreaded tests.

I'm not sure why we need this foolish construct, but I bend and conform to those who apparently know better.
The Stoic solution is not to complain, but to make something of the things we dislike.
I end up writing exams that are not exams at all, but exercises in learning to think for oneself.

About ten minutes before our exam began, a young lady was quite insistent:
"This is so unfair. I don't need to do any of this. It's so unfair!"

Quite to my surprise, one of the quietest and most humble fellows in the class interjected.
"It's only as fair as you think of it."

Good grief, I thought, have I inspired an actual Stoic?

"Go to hell," she said, but in terms a bit cruder than that. "It's not fair!"

His response was calm and clear.
"They're not the problem. You're the problem."

There's the rub.
As soon as we blame others for our grief, we've already lost ourselves.
When I am unhappy, I have learned not to blame another.
I am still working on the recognition that blame at all is unnecessary. Only responsibility is necessary.
Knowledge and love will remove the burden of both guilt and resentment.

❖ ❖ ❖ ❖ ❖

D a y   3 3 1

When prosperity has spread luxury far and wide, men begin by paying closer attention to their personal appearance. Then they go crazy over furniture. Next, they devote attention to their houses —how to take up more space with them, as if they were country-houses, how to make the walls glitter with marble that has been imported over seas, how to adorn a roof with gold, so that it may match the brightness of the inlaid floors.

—Seneca the Younger, *Moral letters to Lucilius* 114)

By all means, make yourself pretty.
I'd probably do the same myself, but I'm afraid there's little I can do to live up the acceptable standards.

I'm not a good-looking fellow, and I've learned to be content with that.
Some accounts have it that Socrates looked hideous, but he had the soul of a great man.
In High School a cruel few told me I looked like an AIDS patient, and in College I was simply ignored by most everyone because I faded into the background.
I was not interesting by the standards of the world.
I wasted far too much of my time trying to convince folks that I was worthy of their attention.

I sometimes truly wonder whether many of us go through the steps in our lives not because we freely choose them for their own sake, but because we are expected, for the sake of appearance, to do so?
We may not even be directly aware this is what's happening.
Again, I don't exclude myself from this, because I know that I have done this at times.

So we attend to our physical beauty, because it attracts and pleases other people.
We buy nice things, and nice houses, and fineries, because it attracts and pleases other people.
We get good jobs, because it attracts and pleases other people.
I think we sometimes even get married and have children, not because of genuine self-giving love or true commitment, but because, you guessed it, it attracts and pleases other people.
We are told we must do it, so we do it, as a necessary step in our social advancement, to follow the herd.
There are indeed trophy wives, trophy husbands, and trophy children.

❖ ❖ ❖ ❖ ❖

Day 332

I have often wondered how it is that every man loves himself more than all the rest of men, but yet sets less value on his own opinion of himself than on the opinion of others. If then a god or a wise teacher should present himself to a man and bid him to think of nothing and to design nothing which he would not express as soon as he conceived it, he could not endure it even for a single day. So much more respect have we to what our neighbors shall think of us than to what we shall think of ourselves.

—Marcus Aurelius, *Meditations* Book 12

It certainly seems rather odd that we think so much of ourselves precisely by depending on how much others think of us.

And I have suspected that those who seem to be so full of themselves are actually not vain at all, but simply sad and empty.

I believe that all of this hinges on what we actually mean by loving ourselves.

We ought to love ourselves, as we ought to love all people and things in their own way, simply for existing within Nature.

We can truly love ourselves when we act as our own nature intends, to give our love simply for its own sake.

But we fail in this endeavor when we go against our nature, and define ourselves by what we receive, and not by what we give.

That is the deceiving self-love.

I think it fair to say that most all of the pain in my life has been the result of my failing to see this, and defining myself by what is given, or not given, to me, and not by what I give.

It is my responsibility, and no one else's.

False pride always moves from the inside depending upon the outside.

Righteous pride always moves from the outside depending upon the inside.

It is certainly ironic, because it depends on what we mean by depending!

❖ ❖ ❖ ❖ ❖

But, speaking generally, if one devotes himself to the life of philosophy and tills the land at the same time, I should not compare any other way of life to his nor prefer any other means of livelihood.

For is it not living more in accord with nature to draw one's sustenance directly from the earth, which is the nurse and mother of us all, rather than from some other source? Is it not more like the life of a man to live in the country than to sit idly in the city, like the Sophists?

—Musonius Rufus, *Lectures* 11

I mentioned a few passages ago that I have always been drawn to a country life.
Having spent so much time in rural Austria during my formative years surely led to this preference, but I am beginning to also see the reasons why there is also such a wonderful sort of person, the Philosopher-Farmer, who could give the Philosopher-King a run for his money.

The reason for this is neither a Jeffersonian political romanticism, nor any sort of Norman Rockwell populist sentimentalism, not that I disapprove of either.
The reason is simply that a man close to Nature in one way is more likely to be close to Nature in others.
There's no guarantee, of course, but it certainly helps.

I have worked, day by day, for over two decades, in education and social services.
I have great respect for so many of the caring, refined, intellectual folks I have had the pleasure of knowing.

But when push comes to shove, during my social leisure time, you will usually find me at the local diner, VFW or Honky-Tonk, and not at a lecture on ontology or metaethics at some university.
This is because I usually prefer my real people to be real.

Show me a man who does real labor, gets his hands dirty, literally or figuratively, and does it with pride and dignity, and you've most likely shown me a man I can trust.
Are there such people in Academia?
Yes, of course, but I find that they are rare.
Many of the best and most caring friends I have ever known often never finished high school.

Neither snobbery, nor reverse snobbery, has any place in Stoicism.
I think you may also, however, find that the people closest to the earth, in whatever manner, are often also the best people you'll ever know.

❖ ❖ ❖ ❖ ❖

If they are unwilling to give, they should at least lend with all readiness and alacrity, not with the prospect of receiving anything back except the principal. . . In place of the interest which they determine not to accept they receive a further bonus of the fairest and the most precious things that human life has to give, mercy neighborliness, charity, magnanimity, a good report and good fame.

And what acquisition can rival these? No, even the great king will appear as the poorest of men if compared with a single virtue. For his wealth is soulless, buried deep in storehouses and recesses of the earth, but the wealth of virtue lies in the sovereign part of the soul, and the purest part of existence.

—Philo of Alexandria, *On the virtues* 213

The Ancients and Medievals were often very serious about the vice of usury, understood in different contexts as either the charging of excessive interest, or even the charging of any interest at all.

The real concern was that the lender could be taking advantage of another's need or misfortune.

As the structure of finance and banking has changed over the centuries, and we live in an economy driven not simply by the trade of goods but by credit, our attitudes towards moneylending have also changed.

But this does not mean that the old moral lesson no longer applies.

If the lender is interested in his own profit at the expense of the borrower, he acts selfishly and unjustly.

The deeper point is really to ask what the true purpose of an economy is.

We now automatically say that the purpose of business is to make a profit, to which the Stoic would ask, what sort of profit?

When we answer that we mean, of course, a financial profit, the Stoic will shake his head.

The highest profit any of us can have is to practice virtue and to live well.

That is happiness.

Men do not exist to serve money, but money exists to serve men.

We confuse the end and the means when we seek only greater wealth.

Consider the sort of society and economy a Stoic would suggest, a community where the service of neighbor, simply for its own sake, would come first, and need would triumph over greed.

Consider also how deeply our society has veered from these Stoic values by embracing a model with the increase of wealth, not of character, at the center.

You might think a Stoic sense of economy and society is a naïve pipe dream.

Such a world, we say, is impossible.

No, it is not impossible.

We only live the way we do by our choice, and we can choose to live differently.

The problem is that many of us don't want to live differently.

Let that be, because I can choose to live that way, whether the mob wishes to or not.

This wouldn't mean that we must abolish wealth, or live in poverty.
Wealth is a tool, but it is not a tool for our greed and vanity, but a tool to improve human living.
Philo is calling us to love humanity over money.
I would even suggest that a truly humane economy would be a far more profitable one, both morally and financially.

Don't listen to the pessimists and doomsayers who roll there eyes and tell you that you must compromise your morals to make the world work.
Doing that is precisely what makes the world not work.
You could choose to do it right, whatever others may do, and maybe it could even catch on.
Like they say, good deeds can be infectious.

❖ ❖ ❖ ❖ ❖

Day 335

What is my object? To understand Nature and to follow Her. I look then for some one who interprets her, and having heard that Chrysippus does I come to him. But I do not understand what is in writings, so I seek an interpreter. So far there is nothing to be proud of.

But when I have found the interpreter it remains for me to act on his precepts; that and that alone is a thing to be proud of. But if I admire the mere power of exposition, it comes to this —that I am turned into a grammarian instead of a philosopher, except that I interpret Chrysippus in place of Homer.

Therefore, when some one says to me, 'Read me Chrysippus', when I cannot point to actions which are in harmony and correspondence with his teaching, I am rather inclined to blush.

—Epictetus, *Enchiridion* 49

This harkens back to our classic Stoic principle, that actions matter more than words, that reality trumps appearance, and practice needs to be added to theory.

I consider in how many ways we can see this reflected in all walks of our life.

In academia, of course, we talk about the ideas, but don't necessarily follow them.

In politics, we say we want to improve people's lives, but we seem so tempted to really just improve our own.

In advertising, we don't sell the product, we sell the image associated with the product.

In business, we speak about serving society, and too often only serve ourselves.

In our personal lives, we speak grand words of love, and then we act with selfishness or indifference.

I am all too aware that I can be a bitter person, so I try very consciously to avoid that in both how I speak and act.

I don't always succeed, of course, but I get better with practice.

The other day, I drove by a truck on the highway, which had a clever sign.

The words "This is our most important asset" were printed in large letters on the trailer, with an arrow pointing to the cab.

I really had to control my cynical and rude response, and it was good daily practice for me.

Yet I still couldn't help thinking whether that was truly meant, or just a set of words that meant little.

If the drivers were the company's greatest asset, that would mean the people were more important than the profit.

Again, I'm resisting a negative attitude and tone here, but do we think the company would do that?

Lower its profits to help its drivers?

I'd be very happy if they did, but I have my doubts.

❖ ❖ ❖ ❖ ❖

Day 336

Does the light of the lamp shine without losing its splendor until it is extinguished, and shall the truth which is in you and justice and temperance be extinguished before your death?

—Marcus Aurelius, *Meditations* Book 12

This makes me think of the Parable of the Wise and Foolish Virgins in the Gospel of Matthew.
It works in a religious sense, of course, but also in a philosophical sense.

Have I prepared myself, and lived in such a way, that I can keep my light burning?
I know I'm mixing metaphors here, but I also think of the example of building a good campfire.
Throw on too little wood, and the flame will go out, throw on too much wood, and the fire will become too hot and flare out too quickly.

I've also had to use this subtle skill when keeping my wood smoker at just the right temperature, for just the right time, to make the perfect low-and-slow brisket or pork shoulder.
A full run from dawn until dusk is about right.

This book is about Stoicism, but I cannot resist reminding all my old Yankee friends, tongue firmly in cheek, that throwing burgers on a gas or charcoal grill is not barbecue.
You are all too hectic, and too busy.
A burger on a smoker, for example, would take about an hour or more, not a few minutes.
Do it slow, and do it right.

I never thought I'd use proper barbecue as an analogy for Stoicism, but it fits.
Use your intellect, will and vitality, but do so thinking slowly and carefully about the final goal, to live with excellence.
Don't burn out.

❖ ❖ ❖ ❖ ❖

You are familiar with the young dandies, natty as to their beards and locks, fresh from the bandbox; you can never expect from them any strength or any soundness. Style is the garb of thought: if it be trimmed, or dyed, or treated, it shows that there are defects and a certain amount of flaws in the mind.

Elaborate elegance is not a manly garb, If we had the privilege of looking into a good man's soul, oh what a fair, holy, magnificent, gracious, and shining face should we behold— radiant on the one side with justice and temperance, on another with bravery and wisdom!

—Seneca the Younger, *Moral letters to Lucilius* 115)

My students will laugh and laugh about the fashions of the past, whether they be codpieces, wigs, top hats, bell-bottoms, or mullets.

I don't blame them at all, because fashion, by its very definition is a ridiculous thing.

We follow things because other people follow them.

The Stoic will not mock, but he may have a wry grin.

What is so ironic and amusing is that students have their own fashions, which they cannot see outside of.

I did as well, when I was their age.

I had a 1980's pompadour that covered half my face, and I thought it was the best thing since sliced bread.

If I could only look like Tom Bailey of the Thompson Twins, my life would be grand.

So much of this is all about diversion, about covering what we really are by nature.

Perhaps we wish only to appear a certain way to others, or perhaps we use our appearances to distract ourselves.

Your character makes you beautiful or ugly.

At my high school we were an eccentric bunch, so we rarely conformed to one or another look, but we all tried to be as different from one another as possible, assembling an elaborate pastiche of clothing, music, and philosophies of life.

As refreshing as it was not to have armies of drones, we were all, in sense, still hiding.

And we substitute those things of youth with adult replacements when we flaunt our degrees, our achievements, or our possessions.

It remains the same game with different pieces.

A friend of mine liked to say that "The difference between men and boys is the price of their toys."

We certainly should look down on young people's fashions if we can't look down on our own.

❖   ❖   ❖   ❖   ❖

Once Diogenes saw the officials of a temple leading away some one who had stolen a bowl belonging to the treasurers, and said, 'The great thieves are leading away the little thief.'
—Diogenes of Sinope ex Diogenes Laertius,
Lives and opinions of eminent philosophers 6.45

Diogenes was always a master of the dramatic turn, but his quip has real bite.
The trappings of human power are such that the veneer or authority and respectability will cover the same vices in men.
The difference is that the vices of the powerful and influential can grow unhindered, and are therefore correspondingly greater.

Who will suffer the greater penalty, a burglar or a corporate swindler?
I was once at a dinner party where an important man was criticizing poor women who were too promiscuous and therefore, he said, had too many children, and I wondered how many of us at the table knew that he regularly cheated on his wife.

This is yet again an example of how we think the outside can cover or hide what is inside, where the appearance tries to mask the reality.
We think the trappings of power can mask, or perhaps even justify a disordered soul, but the harm is now twofold: the moral rot on the inside, and the vanity and presumption to think that power and position makes it any better on the outside.
I also think of the double sin of those Churchmen who condescendingly preach chastity in public while pursuing their abuses in private.

❖ ❖ ❖ ❖ ❖

Day 339

> *There is expiation for the crimes and impieties of men. The guilty therefore must pay the penalty, and bear the punishment; not so much those punishments inflicted by courts of justice, which were not always in being, do not exist at present in many places, and even where established are frequently biased and partial, but those of conscience; while the furies pursue and torment them, not with burning torches, as the poets feign, but with remorse of conscience, and the tortures arising from guilt.*
>
> —Cicero, *On the laws* 1.14

We have now seen, in a number of different ways, how the shift of center embraced by the Stoic, where the highest good shifts from conditions outside of us to the excellence of the actions within, has many radical consequences.

An important one of these consequences has been that we can revaluate the nature of reward and punishment.

Only recently my son and daughter, who appear to have, for good or for ill, inherited their parents' reflective temperament, cooperatively put it something like this:

"A car is supposed to get you from one place to another. If you don't change the oil, and keep all the parts running, it breaks down, and then it's not really a car anymore.

"And even if you put in tinted windows heated seats and those fancy tires and racing stripes and video screens all over the place, it still won't drive."

I decided to push the point, not intending in any way to turn my children into philosophy experiments, of course, but hopeful they were growing in their awareness of life.

"Are people anything like that as well?"

They thought for a few moments, and then simultaneously started giving very similar answers.

"Yes, because if you're not a good person, you won't be happy, and you can add all the fancy things and still won't make you happy!"

Both of them worry, just like their father did, that the world is unfair, that some people were full of vice but somehow got all the heated seats and chrome wheels.

Why were the bad people being rewarded?

Well they weren't being rewarded, the children begin to understand in their own way, because they weren't being good people.

When I first started teaching, a student wrote a reflection that compared Stoic thought to the verse of a then–popular song by Sheryl Crow:

> *If it makes you happy*
> *it can't be that bad.*
> *If it makes you happy*
> *then why the hell are you so sad?*

I've known that terror of the evil inside of me making me miserable, even when I was never caught out.

Don't fail to seek external justice and correction; but all of that exists only as a reflection of that torment within.

Nature never fails to punish and reward in this way.

❖　❖　❖　❖　❖

Whatever principles you put before you, hold fast to them as laws which it will be impious to transgress. But pay no heed to what any one says of you; for this is something beyond your own control.

—Epictetus, *Enchiridion* 50

As a variation of my love of flipping measures, inspired by Plato and the Stoic tradition, I often tell my students, whose first questions often revolve around policies and procedures, that people are not made to serve rules, but rules are made to serve people.

They struggle with this a bit more than I would have suspected.
On the one hand, some of them have just been blindly trained to conform without question.
On the other hand, some are in love with their own desires, and openly deny that there are any rules at all.

I can hardly blame them for their confusion.
The first misunderstanding is that the moral law derives first from external convention.
The second misunderstanding is that a person is defined by passion over reason.
In either case, we fail to see that what is right and good is that which derives from human nature, and that the good of such principles is itself precisely that they aid us in living well.

A deep respect for the principles of the moral law is not, therefore, to be seen as something to which we conform without thought, but rather more fully how we must employ our thought to understand what is innately good for ourselves and for Nature.

❖ ❖ ❖ ❖ ❖

Day 341

Most men admire that which deceives them at a distance, and by the crowd good things are supposed to be big things.

—Seneca the Younger, *Moral letters to Lucilius* 118

They used to sing *The grass is always greener in the other fellow's yard.*
Beyond the fact that we greedily tend to want those things that others possess, simply because they are not ours, our distance from them surely also plays a role.
Seeing something from afar may give it an appearance of beauty and goodness that it hardly has.
Distance of any sort has a way of seeming to remove flaws.

Such a distance need not only be one of physical distance, but also a the larger sense of how far the appearance has been separated from the reality, and how filtered and distorted the image has become.
Products are sold under certain conditions of lighting to make them more appealing, lighter to draw attention to that which glitters, darker to divert attention from what is dull.
One need look no further than to the brightness of a jewelry store or to the dimness of a nightclub.

Another tool that affects perception is magnitude, that what is grand and imposing must be good, that bigger is better.
Corporations and nations compete to build the highest skyscraper, the largest stadium, the most massive ship of war.
Faster, higher, stronger comes to mean better, since, of course, a big thing can be seen by the most people as being the most impressive, and once again the appearance of greatness is compounded by distance.

Do not confuse quantity with quality, the grandiose with dignity, or magnitude and multitude with beauty.
All things that share in nature are good and beautiful simply by being what they are, not by the distortions of my perception and estimation.
They become no better by whoever possesses them, and we are advised not to conform to the dullness of those who only choose to follow the herd.

❖　❖　❖　❖　❖

In everything always observe what the thing is which produces for you an appearance, and resolve it by dividing it into the formal, the material, the purpose, and the time within which it must end.

—Marcus Aurelius, *Meditations* Book 12

Marcus Aurelius here offers a model that shares something in common with Aristotle's Four Causes.

The Peripatetics would say that to understand a thing, one must consider it by breaking it down to its basic principles or causes.

The efficient cause was the mover or agent of action.

The material cause was what something was made out of.

The formal cause was the identity of a thing.

The final cause was a purpose or goal of a thing.

Aurelius is similarly telling us that we only truly know something, and thereby come to see behind the mere appearance to the true nature, when we have divided it into such basic principles.

Three of the four, matter, form, and purpose, are the same.

He also adds duration, which could be understood as an aspect of the formal and final causes.

He does not here directly mention the efficient cause, or the principle of where something comes from, but perhaps he already understands it as implicit that Nature itself is the cause of all motion and change, and that we ourselves participate in this Nature through our judgments and actions.

Whether we consider the question from the perspective of Aristotle or Aurelius, the overall, guiding rule is very much the same.

Do not merely perceive something as a vague, hazy, or undefined whole, but with the power of intellect distinguish all the related parts and principles that compose it.

It is only then that the actions, relations, and purpose of the reality will become clear, and only then can its place in Nature, and in relationship to yourself, be understood.

Many children, and still a good number of adults, have a wonderful instinct to take apart a device to figure out is workings, and respond with awe and wonder when the functions of the parts and their connections with one another gradually become apparent.

I consider what Aurelius discusses, and what is also discussed in the Peripatetic tradition, to be the philosophical equivalent of such mechanical tinkering.

Nothing can be of any real use for a good life if I do not know what it is, what it is made of, and why it is here.

❖ ❖ ❖ ❖ ❖

Day 343

'To relax [remittere] *the mind,' said Musonius, 'is to lose* [amittere] *it.'*

—Musonius Rufus, *Fragments* 52

Even when we have built up good opinions, disposition, and habits, we can't let our guards down. Since life is itself activity and not a mere state, and human life is action grounded in a sound mind, a good life is constant in awareness, good judgment, and ordered deeds.

As a child, I was fascinated by the account that many species of sharks must remain in constant motion so that water passes through their gills.
I think this works as a nice analogy for what Musonius is saying.
Motion need not be busyness or constant distraction, which many of us sadly think it is, but simply attentiveness and awareness.

I have let my guard down often, and sometimes have caught myself in time, though just as often I see the danger too late.
I once ran into some people I knew who had just decided to spontaneously take a road trip to the next state to visit a huge casino.
I was invited along, and trying also to be fun and spontaneous, agreed.

The whole trip is still a good symbol to me of a life lived poorly, and I have this vivid memory of flying down the highway in the back seat, aware just too late that I could no longer ask them to turn around and take me home.
It's also the reason that the cacophony of beeping and ringing slot machines still sends me into a mood of panic and horror.

❖ ❖ ❖ ❖ ❖

Show me the causes, you say, why the vengeance of God skips over some and whips others? Do you seek the causes? I may safely say that I know them not. For the heavenly court never included me, nor do I understand the decrees thereof.

Of this only am I assured, that God's will is a cause above all causes, beyond which, who so seeks another, is ignorant of the efficacy and power of the Divine nature. For it is necessary that every cause be in a sort, before and greater than its effect but nothing is before nor greater than God and his will, therefore there is no cause thereof. God has pardoned; God has punished; What will you have more?

—Justus Lipsius, *On constancy* 2.12

Justus Lipsius had sought to renew the study and practice of Stoicism in the late Renaissance, and as such blended his Stoic principles with Christian thinking.

I always advocate beginning with what is common before discerning the differences, and I see no reason to do any differently here.

Lipsius was a Christian, and Chrysippus was a Pagan.

Consider first what they share, regardless of how they might view the being of the Divine.

If we defer for the moment, the theological context, and the deeper metaphysical question of Divine transcendence, that God is *above* Nature, and of immanence, that God is *in* Nature, such thinking is very much in line with Ancient thinking.

I humbly suggest that this is a false dichotomy.

In either case, what is subject to the order of Nature and Providence is hardly to be measured by the limits of man.

I can perceive that the circumstances of life may appear to be random, and deeply unfair.

Yet I can also know, from reason and the principle of causality alone, that nothing is by chance, and Nature never acts without purpose.

I can also know that I have been made in such a wonderful way that nothing will do me harm unless I choose to permit it.

Finally, I can also know that while the workings of Providence are far beyond my limited understanding, and this need not diminish my reliance on its power.

I fall into vanity and error when I assume that I, a part of the whole, should be able to determine the harmony of the whole.

I also fall into presumption and disorder when I insist that the order of the highest, ultimate causes are subject to the same patterns of lower, proximate causes.

The things that are good for me, and the things that are good for all of Nature, are not in conflict.

Accept their harmony, their deeper wisdom, and do not presume to be God.

Justice will play itself out, in its own wonderful manner and in its own time, regardless of how much I complain and struggle against it.

❖ ❖ ❖ ❖ ❖

Something of this kind happens to us generally. Now as this man has confidently entrusted his affairs to me, shall I also do so to any man whom I meet? For when I have heard, I keep silence, if I am of such a disposition; but he goes forth and tells all men what he has heard. Then if I hear what has been done, if I be a man like him, I resolve to be revenged, I divulge what he has told me; I both disturb others and am disturbed myself.

But if I remember that one man does not injure another, and that every man's acts injure and profit him, I secure this, that I do not anything like him, but still I suffer what I do suffer through my own silly talk.

—Epictetus, *Discourses* 4.13

I have a recent former student, for whom I have the deepest respect.
  Such people are often the ones that help me to continue the thankless job I struggle to do, even as I realize that I should not depend upon such affirmation to follow my vocation.

She recently said something along these lines, not to me personally, but as general observation about life:
  "I'll be your friend, trust you, and do anything for you, but if you're going to be a jerk to me, I'm going to be a jerk to you."

I understand her frustration, and I sympathize.
  Some people are simply so thoughtless, careless, or downright malicious that I wish to pay it back in kind.

Then I remind myself that if someone else is being a jerk, I don't have to be a jerk myself.
  I may learn not to trust your word, I may realize that your intentions are selfish, and I may indeed rightly walk away from the twisted wreck that our relationship has become.
  But I will not cease to love you, because I owe love to all my fellows, and I will never do you harm because you have done harm to me.

They say "Fool me once, shame on you, fool me twice shame on me."
  I will not, however, turn my own shame into anger or hatred for another.
  Let him suffer his vices: I'm certainly not suffering my own because I allow myself to be ruled by his.

❖   ❖   ❖   ❖   ❖

Day 346

The day has already begun to lessen. It has shrunk considerably, but yet will still allow a goodly space of time if one rises, so to speak, with the day itself. We are more industrious, and we are better men if we anticipate the day and welcome the dawn; but we are base churls if we lie dozing when the sun is high in the heavens, or if we wake up only when noon arrives; and even then to many it seems not yet dawn.

Some have reversed the functions of light and darkness; they open eyes sodden with yesterday's debauch only at the approach of night.

—Seneca the Younger, *Moral letters to Lucilius* 122

I often chastise myself for being too lazy, but I see more and more that the problem was never a lack of effort, but of effort directed toward all the wrong things.

I managed to do much that was good when I was younger, and I manage much that is good now that I am older.

I have a gaping hole in the middle of my life, however, where I lived in much the way Seneca condemns.

These were the Wilderness Years, my failed reactions to the Black Dog.

I would do what the world asked of me, and then get pulled in by all the diversions.

I would spend the nights avoiding my pain by ignoring it or numbing it, and then avoiding the tasks I should have embraced with joy.

I knew I had hit the bottom when I slept until noon, only then to go to work looking perfectly like a professional.

My father would tell me when I was younger, quoting St. Paul:

You are the children of light, and the children of the day; we are not of the night, nor of darkness.

He added a lovely, but frustrating, addendum:

"The night is for thieves, prostitutes, and drunkards, all the things that you shouldn't be."

I resented it then, but I embrace it now.

This isn't just about the literal time of day, but the attitudes we have about our day.

Once work is a burden, and selfish gratification is now our goal, we're clearly in the wrong line of work.

❖ ❖ ❖ ❖ ❖

Day 347

Perceive at last that you have in you something better and more Divine than the things which cause the various affects, and, as it were, pull you by strings. What is there now in my mind? Is it fear, or suspicion, or desire, or anything of the kind?

—Marcus Aurelius, *Meditations* Book 12

"Pop psychology" has told you for decades that you are better, brighter, and worth more than what you have received.
That's entirely true, but for the exact opposite reasons why they tell you that it's true.

You aren't better just because you try, or even wish, harder, because what really matters is not what you try or wish for.

You aren't better because you built up your self-esteem, because you really have no true sense of why you should love yourself.

You aren't better because you are richer or more popular, because you have no sense of what to do with those gifts that Nature gave you.

You will be better if you look into yourself, and change the measure of your own thinking.
Redefine who you think you are, recognize the Divine within you, and you will have the opportunity to be happy.

❖ ❖ ❖ ❖ ❖

Day 348

Can we then hold the poverty-in-wealth of the money-grubbing usurers to be of any account? They may seem to be kings with purses full of gold, but they never even in their dreams have had a glimpse of the wealth that has eyes to see.

—Philo of Alexandria, *On the virtues* 215

I used to feel deep anger, even rage, at the self-absorbed folks who made the world a playground for their money, reputation, and pleasure.
It even led me to hate rich people.
I recently apologized to someone I had treated poorly, many years ago, simply because she was wealthy.

There's nothing Stoic about such resentment, of course, because it's not the wealth itself that's the problem.
It's the desire of such things for their own sake that is the problem.
I have come to see that now, and instead of anger, I've learned slowly to feel sympathy.
I must still resist the temptation, however, to only slightly nudge the concern of sympathy into condescending pity.
The exercise of the balance of the mean always requires attentiveness.

The love of neighbor, required by Stoicism as it is by any reasonable way of life, always asks me to seek what is good for others, for their own sake, and never to wish or do them deliberate harm.
When I see someone who desires all the things that I know will hurt them, it does me no good at all to hurt them for hurting themselves.

I need to recognize that they have never experienced the genuine joy of virtue.
Can I give it to them?
They can only give it to themselves, but if I struggle to practice that life myself, perhaps I can learn to be an example of what is right and good.
I can show them the joy of love by loving them.
That is the only way I can help.

❖ ❖ ❖ ❖ ❖

417

Day 349

> *If the will of the people, the decrees of the senate, the adjudications of magistrates, were sufficient to establish rights, then it might become right to rob, right to commit adultery, right to substitute forged wills, if such conduct were sanctioned by the votes or decrees of the multitude.*
>
> *But if the opinions and suffrages of foolish men had sufficient weight to outbalance the nature of things, then why should they not determine among them, that what is essentially bad and pernicious should henceforth pass for good and beneficial? Or why, since law can make right out of injustice, should it not also be able to change evil into good?*
>
> —Cicero, *On the laws* 1.16

Moral relativism is our new religion.
 We assume by default that if something is popular, accepted by the majority, or if it becomes law by custom or legislation, then it must be good.

I say that it takes on the attributes of religion because I observe more and more how any disagreement with this maxim is now treated as heresy.
 The man who speaks against the culture of relativism is anathema.
 He is intolerantly cast out because he is not tolerant in the accepted way.

I am hardly an old man, but in my years on this earth I have seen quite a number of complete flips on what is considered socially, and therefore, morally, acceptable.
 Something I was expected to do forty years ago is now considered a hate crime, and vice-versa.
 The difference is even more pronounced in the span of my parent's generation.

We need not, however, lose faith.
 The sky is not falling.
 The majority need not become a mob, for we can just as easily turn the tables.
 All that would be necessary is for the many to recognize what is truly good, instead of following all the tempting evils.
 But if popular opinion is just opinion, how might we recognize this?
 This can only be achieved if we seek a measure or standard of the good that is above popularity.

Cicero is reminding us that nature, and not convention, is the source of the good.
 Employ reason to grasp the identity of man to know what benefits him, not to the fleeting movements of his passions.
 By all means, let us encourage what is good to be popular.
 I am not so much a pessimist that I do not think this can be done.
 But let us never assume that something is good because it is popular.

❖ ❖ ❖ ❖ ❖

Show yourself to me to be faithful, modest, and steady: show me that you have friendly opinions; show that your cask has no hole in it; and you will see how I shall not wait for you to trust me with your affairs, but I myself shall come to you and ask you to hear mine. For who does not choose to make use of a good vessel? Who does not value a benevolent and faithful adviser? Who will not willingly receive a man who is ready to bear a share, as we may say, of the difficulty of his circumstances, and by this very act to ease the burden, by taking a part of it.

—Epictetus, *Discourses* 4.13

I once knew a fine fellow who, however, had a quality that sometimes frustrated me.
He would usually reduce any and all human questions to matters of astrology, and considered it as if it were the true science of fate.

We were once having a discussion on the nature of friendship, and I expressed my usual rule.
"You will have my complete dedication, and my complete trust, but for that I ask your unconditional loyalty."

"Of course," he said. "I already knew that about you, because you're a Leo."

Now I hardly know if my astrological sign and my views on friendship have anything to do with one another, but I still hold by that rule, learned not from fancy books, but from hard and painful experience.

The Stoic must show justice to all, without exception, but to those who are his personal friends he is a second self.
Find these true friends by looking for those who are faithful, modest and steady.
You are not asking too much for your friends to be loyal to you.
If they are disloyal to you, you must still love them, but they are not your friends.

❖ ❖ ❖ ❖ ❖

Day 351

These three principles you must have in readiness.

In the things which you do, do nothing either inconsiderately or otherwise than as justice herself would act; but with respect to what may happen to you from without, consider that it happens either by chance or according to Providence, and you must neither blame chance nor accuse Providence.

Second, consider what every being is from the seed to the time of its receiving a soul, and from the reception of a soul to the giving back of the same, and of what things every being is compounded and into what things it is resolved.

Third, if you should suddenly be raised up above the earth, and should look down on human things, and observe the variety of them how great it is, and at the same time also should see at a glance how great is the number of beings who dwell around in the air and the aether, consider that as often as you should be raised up, you would see the same things, sameness of form and shortness of duration. Are these things to be proud of?

—Marcus Aurelius, *Meditations* Book 12

Marcus Aurelius likes to put his principles into clearly ordered lists.
The Germanic half of me takes great comfort in this.
In practice, this helps me to quickly memorize them, and then allows me to quickly reference them during the challenges of the day.

As always, these principles follow a causal train of thought.
Begin with the recognition that Nature demands us to always act with consideration and justice from within us, but it is not suitable for us to demand anything from whatever is outside of us.

Continue, then by looking at the larger picture.
Consider all things, each made according to its specific nature and purpose, and understand how all the parts, in their comings and goings, participate in the harmony of all that is.

Finally, complete the exercise by seeing the whole picture, as if one were looking at all of Nature from above.
Consider that all the things we care for and worry so much about, our jobs, our reputations, our possessions, mean absolutely nothing in the grand scheme of things.
And that is a truly comforting thought.

❖ ❖ ❖ ❖ ❖

D a y   3 5 2

Let us retreat from the objects that allure, and rouse ourselves to meet the objects that attack. Do you not see how different is the method of descending a mountain from that employed in climbing upwards? Men coming down a slope bend backwards; men ascending a steep place lean forward.

For, my dear Lucilius, to allow yourself to put your body's weight ahead when coming down, or, when climbing up, to throw it backward is to comply with vice. The pleasures take one down hill but one must work upwards toward that which is rough and hard to climb; in the one case let us throw our bodies forward, in the others let us put the check-rein on them.

—Seneca the Younger, *Moral letters to Lucilius* 123

This is a wonderful analogy.

I am defined by my effort and by my action.

Through inaction, by refusing to think and judge soundly, I allow what is lower in me to topple what is higher in me.

"Go with the flow" can be such an insidious statement, because it does not define going, and it does not define flowing.

Unclear terms make for horrific lives.

Going is not a matter of passive acceptance, but rather one of active engagement.

You are not a piece to be played: You are the player in the game.

Flowing is not a matter of being moved, but of deliberately moving with nature, and never against it.

You are not flotsam and jetsam, but the captain of your own ship.

❖ ❖ ❖ ❖ ❖

Men of Athens, I honor and love you; but I shall obey God rather than you, and while I have life and strength I shall never cease from the practice and teaching of philosophy, exhorting any one whom I meet and saying to him after my manner:

You, my friend—a citizen of the great and mighty and wise city of Athens—are you not ashamed of heaping up the greatest amount of money and honor and reputation, and caring so little about wisdom and truth and the greatest improvement of the soul, which you never regard or heed at all?

And if the person with whom I am arguing, says: Yes, but I do care; then I do not leave him or let him go at once; but I proceed to interrogate and examine and cross-examine him, and if I think that he has no virtue in him, but only says that he has, I reproach him with undervaluing the greater, and overvaluing the less.

And I shall repeat the same words to every one whom I meet, young and old, citizen and alien, but especially to the citizens, inasmuch as they are my brethren. For know that this is the command of God; and I believe that no greater good has ever happened in the state than my service to the God.

For I do nothing but go about persuading you all, old and young alike, not to take thought for your persons or your properties, but first and chiefly to care about the greatest improvement of the soul. I tell you that virtue is not given by money, but that from virtue comes money and every other good of man, public as well as private. This is my teaching, and if this is the doctrine which corrupts the youth, I am a mischievous person.

—Socrates ex Plato, *Apology* 29b-30b

If I had to choose one, and only one, passage from the entire history of philosophy that defines what I value the most, this must be that passage.

It is my "Desert Island quote".

It defines the man I have struggled to be for over twenty years.

I have hung these words in my office and in my classroom whenever and wherever I have taught, because it is, quite simply, my mission statement.

I care very little whether you are a card-carrying Stoic, or which school of thought or religion you subscribe to.

We can hash out all those issues when, and only when, we have agreed that the purpose for our being here on Earth is to pursue the highest function and purpose of our human nature.

Yes, you have a body that asks for sustenance.

Yes, you have emotions that wish to be satisfied.

But at the top, you are a being of intellect and will, and you are made to know the truth and to love what is good.

Let's not just speak those words, and praise them in writing.

Let's live them, as Nature means us to do.

I don't challenge the people I run across in my life to be annoying, though I do often achieve that effect.

I challenge them because I love them, and I wish that they would bridge that divide between what they know and what they do.

I relate very much not only to the universal content of what Socrates has to say, but also to the particulars.

I too live in what defines itself as the greatest nation on Earth, and I see the same arrogance.

You will never be great because you are rich, and you will never be great because you are admired or feared.

A society that bases itself upon such false values is doomed to failure.

You will be great, whether or not it gives you any earthly reward, if you have lived well, and when you have allowed what is higher within you to order what is lower within you.

You will recognize the real philosopher as soon as he calls you out on this very matter.

❖ ❖ ❖ ❖ ❖

Day 354

Someone who was urging me to take heart quoted a saying of Musonius. 'Musonius,' said he, 'wishing to rouse a man who was depressed and weary of life, touched him and asked, 'What are you waiting for, why do you stand gazing? Until God in person shall come and stand by you and utter human speech? Cut off the dead part of your soul and you will recognize the presence of God.'

—Musonius Rufus, *Fragments* 53

I was raised as a Roman Catholic, and I embrace that faith still, with all my heart, despite all the failings and human corruption within my Church.
It's not about those twisted folks at all, but it's about me and my Creator.

I once got myself in trouble in Middle School, not for the first or for the last time, because I questioned the guidance given to me that I should look upwards to the sky when I spoke to God.

"Sister, you say that God is in the Tabernacle, where God is present in body, blood, soul, and divinity, right here in front of us in the church.
Shouldn't I look at something that is right here and now, and not up to the sky?"

"Stop being difficult," was the answer I received.
I had to go see the Headmistress for being disrespectful, and I promised to never do it again.
I lied.

Why look to the sky, why look for your joy and happiness to come from what is physically above?
It is already right there, the Divine is already within you.
You are certainly not God, but the Divine pervades who you are.

I'm as stubborn as a mule, and I still pray to the Tabernacle, not to the sky.
God is not up there.
He is right here.

❖ ❖ ❖ ❖ ❖

D a y   3 5 5

This was how Socrates attained perfection, paying heed to nothing but reason, in all that he encountered. And if you are not yet Socrates, yet ought you to live as one who would wish to be a Socrates.

—Epictetus, *Enchiridion* 51

This book started out simply as a private exercise, a desire to consider Stoic passages in an orderly and disciplined way, to help me with own moral recovery.

It started out paying attention to my own reasoning, and how it could improve my living, and nothing more.

I slowly started sharing some of the passages and comments with others, never to gain their approval, but in the hope I could help in a small way.

I found that others seemed to be suffering like I was, and perhaps they needed a similar prescription.

I was surprised by some of the interest, and turned the practice into a blog.

Soon, I was being advised and encouraged by some to write a book along these lines.

I set out to do so, expecting to simply distribute it privately.

A friend with some connections in the publishing world actually ended up getting me in contact with a company that seemed to show some interest in offering the book professionally.

Intrigued, I actually followed up on the option.

Here was the catch. The fellow I corresponded with wanted me to make changes.

First, he said the book was too bland, and needed more excitement.

"Can you rewrite some of the passages to be about sexual experiences?"

Second, he asked me to name the names of the public figures that occasionally cross into the narrative.

"That way we could promote it with some media attention."

Needless to say, if you have a copy of this book in your hand or on your screen, it has been self-published, on my terms alone.

I was foolish to think, however briefly, that mixing Stoicism with a moneymaking venture, or with any desire for attention, would work.

Stick with the right reason for philosophy, which is the practice and use of Right Reason.

❖ ❖ ❖ ❖ ❖

Day 356

Those who rate pleasure as the supreme ideal hold that the Good is a matter of the senses; but we Stoics maintain that it is a matter of the understanding, and we assign it to the mind. If the senses were to pass judgment on what is good, we should never reject any pleasure; for there is no pleasure that does not attract, no pleasure that does not please. Conversely, we should undergo no pain voluntarily; for there is no pain that does not clash with the senses.

—Seneca the Younger, *Moral letters to Lucilius* 124

Measure yourself by the degrees of your pleasure, and you are nothing but an animal.
  Measure yourself by your merit, and you are now a man.

What I always find so befuddling, and so amusing, is how the finest social scientists and biologists tell us that we are nothing more than beings of instinct.
  We apparently do everything we do in order to survive, and we survive in order to pass our genes to our offspring.

Apparently, I don't love my wife.
  I desire her as a means to have children.
  Nor do I love my children. I desire them to continue my bloodline.

It doesn't take too much sense to see the ridiculousness in all of this.
  The fact is that an intellect is able to rise above those very instincts in order to understand them.
  Therefore that same intellect can choose whether to marry, and whether to have children.

Do not believe the lies.
  Your greatness is not how long you live, or whether you marry a genetically superior spouse, or how many children you may have.
  Your greatness is your character.

Your instincts and feelings do not rule you, whatever the self-important scientists may say.
  Your judgments and choices rule you.
  Pleasure is not the measure you were made for.

❖ ❖ ❖ ❖ ❖

When you are troubled about anything, you have forgotten this, that all things happen according to the universal nature; and forgotten this, that a man's wrongful act is nothing to you; and further you have forgotten this, that everything which happens, always happened so and will happen so, and now happens so everywhere; forgotten this too, how close is the kinship between a man and the whole human race, for it is a community, not of a little blood or seed, but of intelligence.

And you have forgotten this too, that every man's intelligence is a god, and is an efflux of the deity; and forgotten this, that nothing is a man's own, but that his child and his body and his very soul came from the deity; forgotten this, that everything is opinion; and lastly you have forgotten that every man lives the present time only, and loses only this.

—Marcus Aurelius, *Meditations* Book 12

The things I have forgotten far outweigh the things that I have remembered.

What did I learn at a public school?
To obey, to conform to what was considered acceptable, to memorize, and to pass the standardized tests.
That was it.
I originally assumed this was just my own poor and particular experience.
Then I saw my own son and daughter run through exactly the same pathetic race.
They weren't treated as people, they were just statistics.

The real things we should never forget have nothing to do with all of that.
We need to remember who we truly are.

Please do not forget that you truly matter, that your neighbor matters just as much as you, and that all of us are made for the whole, not just for ourselves.

There is no test by which to judge your character, beyond your own informed conscience.
Know yourself, and be truly honest with yourself, even if it must be in complete privacy.
How have you defined your life?
Are you a dependent, or are you dependable?

You and I may have forgotten it, but there is the spark of the Divine within each and every one of us.
Let us not extinguish that with our greed.

❖ ❖ ❖ ❖ ❖

Day 358

Diogenes once begged alms of a statue, and, when asked why he did so, replied, 'To get practice in being refused.'

—Diogenes of Sinope ex Diogenes Laertius,
Lives and opinions of eminent philosophers 6.49

I could have used such practice.
 I wasted too much of my life depending upon those things that were not at all dependable.

I loved someone who did not love me, and I whined and complained about it for years.
 The fault was my own, not that of another, just as Diogenes was refused by the statue.
 When we are hurt, we lash out.
 We are better advised to lash in.
 The casting of blame is not necessary, only the admission of personal responsibility.
 Then even the blame is removed.

I should neither hope for acceptance nor expect rejection.
 I should work on myself, and the rest will manage itself.

❖ ❖ ❖ ❖ ❖

Day 359

In truth all virtuous men love justice and equity for what they are in themselves; nor is it like a good man to make a mistake, and love that which not deserve their affection.

Right, therefore, is desirable and deserving to be cultivated for its own sake; and if this be true of right, it must be true also of justice. What then shall we say of liberality? Is it exercised gratuitously, or does it covet some reward and recompense?

If a man does good without expecting any recompense for his kindness then it is gratuitous; if he does expect recompense, it is a mere matter of traffic. Nor is there any doubt that he who truly deserves the reputation of a generous and kind-hearted man, is thinking of his duty, not of his interest. In the same way the virtue of justice demands neither emolument or salary.

—Cicero, *On the laws* 1.18

Life is not a business transaction.
Do not expect a separate return for your investment, because the reward is itself the investment.
This only makes sense if you understand that the measure of your life is what you give, and not what you receive.
It only makes sense if you embrace a life measured by what is internal, and never judged by what is external.

I may feel I am nothing, because I have not been praised.
I am in fact everything, because I have done right, and still have not been praised.

I admire a man who gives of himself.
I love and respect a man who gives of himself, and never drew attention to himself.
That is virtue.

❖ ❖ ❖ ❖ ❖

We are mad, not only individually, but nationally. We check manslaughter and isolated murders; but what of war and the much-vaunted crime of slaughtering whole peoples? There are no limits to our greed, none to our cruelty.

And as long as such crimes are committed by stealth and by individuals, they are less harmful and less portentous; but cruelties are practiced in accordance with acts of senate and popular assembly, and the public is bidden to do that which is forbidden to the individual.

Deeds that would be punished by loss of life when committed in secret, are praised by us, because uniformed generals have carried them out. Man, naturally the gentlest class of being, is not ashamed to revel in the blood of others, to wage war, and to entrust the waging of war to his sons, when even dumb beasts and wild beasts keep the peace with one another.

Against this overmastering and widespread madness philosophy has become a matter of greater effort, and has taken on strength in proportion to the strength which is gained by the opposition forces.

—Seneca the Younger, *Moral letters to Lucilius* 95

I challenge you to apply Stoicism to modern politics, and I assure you that you will be heartily disappointed with the world.

Whether you lean to right or to the left, whether you are a conservative or a liberal, there is only one thing we all need to remember: the people who say they rule us, apparently with our own consent, are little more than hypocrites and slightly veiled slave-drivers.
They differ from us only in that they are permitted things you and I would never be permitted.

They may wage war, even as we may not.
They may steal, abuse, torture, or oppress, even as we may not.
They are special, and we don't matter.

But don't let that standard get you down.
You and I can be better than that, just by living well ourselves.
You may not be as special as they are, but you can be better than they are.

There could never be a Stoic political party, I think, because Stoicism does not reduce itself to the bickering of politics, or to the thirst for power.
The Stoic will never be a partisan, and he will always care for people over ideology.

❖ ❖ ❖ ❖ ❖

The first and most necessary department of philosophy deals with the application of principles, for instance, 'not to lie'.

The second deals with demonstrations, for instance, 'How comes it that one ought not to lie?'

The third is concerned with establishing and analyzing these processes, for instance, 'How comes it that this is a demonstration? What is demonstration, what is consequence, what is contradiction, what is true, what is false?'

It follows then that the third department is necessary because of the second, and the second because of the first.

The first is the most necessary part, and that in which we must rest. But we reverse the order: we occupy ourselves with the third, and make that our whole concern, and the first we completely neglect.

Therefore we lie, but are ready enough with the demonstration that lying is wrong.

—Epictetus, *Enchiridion* 52

There are the things we should do, there are the reasons we understand why we should do them, and then we have the grasp of the very principles that define our understanding.

The problem is that we spend all our attention in the thinking, and give lesser attention to the doing.

I can no longer keep track of the many noble words and ideas I have heard expounded, sometimes with great insight and eloquence, and then not acted upon in any way.

I have seen many politicians, clergymen, scholars, lawyers, and businessmen explain why we should be good, and I am now no longer under any expectation that they will follow through.

I hope they will, but I don't hold my breath.

I am very pleasantly surprised when they do.

Once again, this is not a ground for resentment or despair.

I cannot determine whether the deeds of another conform to his words, and my estimation must be such that I recognize he does what he thinks is best.

I can only make certain that my thinking and doing go hand in hand, and then my part of the battle is already won.

When I do manage to live rightly in this way, some people look confused, some get angry, some consider me a loose canon or a firebrand.

And a very few will give a nod or a smile of approval.

Those who are of the Stoic mind, and therefore commit Stoic deeds, seem to recognize one another, even without a secret handshake.

❖ ❖ ❖ ❖ ❖

Thus, therefore, mortal men have their freedom of judgment intact. And since their wills are freed from all binding necessity, laws do not set rewards or punishments unjustly.

God is ever the constant foreknowing overseer, and the ever-present eternity of His sight moves in harmony with the future nature of our actions, as it dispenses rewards to the good, and punishments to the bad. Hopes are not vainly put in God, nor prayers in vain offered: if these are right, they cannot but be answered.

Turn therefore from vice; ensue virtue; raise your soul to upright hopes; send up on high your prayers from this earth. If you would be honest, great is the necessity enjoined upon your goodness, since all you do is done before the eyes of an all-seeing Judge.

—Boethius, *The consolation of Philosophy* Book 5 Prose 6

After his long struggle with his own moral doubts, with his confusion on the goods of Nature and the goods of Fortune, and on the harmony of human freedom and Divine Providence, Boethius ends his Consolation with this passage.

In his real life he will go on to meet a brutal execution for a crime he did not commit, a fate he thought was deeply unfair when he started writing.

He now recognizes he need have no fear, and that there is the hope of certain justice in all things.

His happiness is not measured by what happens to him, which is outside of his power, but rather his own thinking and acting, which are always within his power.

The world is never truly unfair if we but choose to understand it rightly.

Have I suffered pain from external things?

It is entirely up to me to choose whether I will make good of evil, or choose evil myself.

And nothing that happens is random or in vain, because all causes and effects are balanced and harmonized under Providence.

If I can choose to truly understand this, and therefore to live it without doubt or hesitation, then I have embraced happiness, and nothing can disturb me.

If I am still failing or struggling, it is because I still have my doubts, and I am still harboring a desire for the wrong things.

The conversion of my character will not be complete until I fully commit and remain always attentive to the path.

The pull of old habits, and the draw of outside diversions is indeed powerful.

This is why I still fail. No matter, use the failure to build more strength.

I imagine that each and every one of us, each in his own way and in his own time, makes the ultimate life choice.

Who am I, and what do I truly want?

How I answer this question determines everything else.

❖   ❖   ❖   ❖   ❖

What is the happy life? It is peace of mind, and lasting tranquility. This will be yours if you possess greatness of soul; it will be yours if you possess the steadfastness that resolutely clings to a good judgment just reached.

How does a man reach this condition? By gaining a complete view of truth, by maintaining, in all that he does, order, measure, fitness, and a will that is inoffensive and kindly, that is intent upon reason and never departs therefrom, that commands at the same time love and admiration.

In short, to give you the principle in brief compass, the wise man's soul ought to be such as would be proper for a god.

—Seneca the Younger, *Moral letters to Lucilius* 92

I have saved this for near the end, because it is something that touches my heart very deeply, and something I remember each and every day. I don't mean this through my feelings alone, but also through my free decision to know and to love.

At one of the darkest moments of my life, I was in an Acid Jazz club in downtown Boston.
I was sitting alone in a corner, and while I was enjoying the music, I felt that this was it.
There was nothing else to do but end it.

The DJ played a track by the Acid Jazz band Mother Earth, called "Look to the Light."
Some completely random and perfectly decent people suddenly pulled me up from my seat to dance with them.
Now please know that I cannot dance, even though I can play a decent funk bass, but that was a decisive moment.
These folks helped me to help myself.

The lyrics were straight from Max Ehrmann's poem, "Desiderata".
This isn't sentimental slop.
It's Stoicism, through and through.
That moment saved me for another day, an opportunity to right all the wrongs:

Go placidly amid the noise and haste,
And remember what peace there may be in silence.
As far as possible without surrender
Be on good terms with all persons.
Speak your truth quietly and clearly;
And listen to others,
Even the dull and the ignorant;
They too have their story.

Avoid loud and aggressive persons,
They are vexations to the spirit.
If you compare yourself with others,
You may become vain and bitter;
For always there will be greater and lesser persons than
* yourself.*
Enjoy your achievements as well as your plans.

Keep interested in your own career, however humble;
It is a real possession in the changing fortunes of time.
Exercise caution in your business affairs;
For the world is full of trickery.
But let this not blind you to what virtue there is;
Many persons strive for high ideals;
And everywhere life is full of heroism.

Be yourself.
Especially, do not feign affection.
Neither be cynical about love;
For in the face of all aridity and disenchantment
It is as perennial as the grass.

Take kindly the counsel of the years,
Gracefully surrendering the things of youth.

Nurture strength of spirit to shield you in sudden
* misfortune.*
But do not distress yourself with dark imaginings.
Many fears are born of fatigue and loneliness.
Beyond a wholesome discipline,
Be gentle with yourself.

You are a child of the universe,
No less than the trees and the stars;
You have a right to be here.
And whether or not it is clear to you,
No doubt the universe is unfolding as it
* should.*

Therefore be at peace with God,
Whatever you conceive Him to be,
And whatever your labors and aspirations,
In the noisy confusion of life keep peace with
* your soul.*

With all its sham, drudgery, and broken
* dreams,*
It is still a beautiful world.
Be cheerful.
Strive to be happy.

Day 364

If it is not right, do not do it: if it is not true, do not say it. Let these be your fixed principles
—Marcus Aurelius, *Meditations* Book 12

Stoicism is not hard to do: Its precepts are easy to practice, and the benefits of this practice are immeasurable.
That is especially true for those of us who have been knocked down, disenfranchised, rejected and betrayed, or those of us on the fringes of the world of important people.

The world may not care, but you need not care for what the world cares about.
That is true freedom.

What is deeply difficult, especially for modern man, is the judgment that must stand behind the doing.
Do not think of this as a burden, but as the greatest of opportunities.
Change your judgment, and you can, and will, change the benefits of your life.

Once you have conquered yourself, by your own efforts, you have conquered anything and everything that matters.
The struggle will never be with what is outside of you.
The struggle is only within yourself.
Do not despair.
The source of you happiness can never be taken away, and it is always right there in front you.

Nature made you to be happy, not to be miserable.
Once you change the settings on your dial, you will be in tune with what is right.
It just takes the courage to change the station.

❖ ❖ ❖ ❖ ❖

On every occasion we must have these thoughts at hand:

Lead me, O Zeus, and lead me, Destiny,
Whither ordained is by your decree.
I'll follow, doubting not, or if with will
Recreant I falter, I shall follow still. —Cleanthes

Who rightly with necessity he complies
 In things divine we count him skilled and wise. —Euripides

Well, Crito, if this be the gods' will, so be it. —Socrates

Anytus and Meletus have power to put me to death, but not to harm me. —Socrates

—Epictetus, *Enchiridion* 53

Epictetus thought that these four quotes, one from the second leader of the Stoic School, one from a great Greek playwright, and two from one of the greatest philosophers of all time, were a perfect way to end his own text. I certainly can't try to outdo a master, so I will simply follow suit.
I offer my own last thoughts to you, inspired by Epictetus' choices.

Whether I choose to embrace or combat the fact, Nature is greater than me, and it rules all things.
If I embrace this in complete freedom, I will be in harmony with all things, depending only upon my own wisdom and virtue in order to live with joy.
If I resist Nature, and fight against the world, that same freedom will still end up serving Nature in its own way, but it will now bring me slavery and misery.

I need to think of more than myself.
I can order myself, but I can only do this rightly in the light of being part of the whole.
I am not the whole, I do not determine the whole, and I am not the measure of all things.
Yet what I can do, with great success, is to choose to participate in that whole, and to find contentment in whatever place or situation I am placed.

What will be is what will be.
I have no real power over any of my circumstances.
What I do have power over is my own thinking, my own willing, and my own actions.
What matters far more than what the world does to me, is what I choose to do with what the world does to me.

There is no need to worry or to fret.
The circumstances of our lives, the actions of others, and the fickle conditions of Fortune cannot truly, at the core of our being, harm us in any way.
Take my money, my reputation, my pleasure, or even my life.
You have not hurt me.
You have given me the chance to be better.

❖   ❖   ❖   ❖   ❖

❖ ❖ ❖ ❖ ❖

Kind reader, I thank you for your consideration, your patience, and your understanding.
I have written this humble text to help myself through my own struggles, and I hope it is possible that perhaps some other person may at least use it to help heal his own wounds.

I will have been a success, a good man, and a happy man, if I only choose to make myself wiser and more loving, and at the same have in some way encouraged others to be wiser and more loving.

Do not be deceived.
All the rest is window dressing.

❖ ❖ ❖ ❖ ❖

If you work at that which is before you, following right reason seriously, vigorously, calmly, without allowing anything else to distract you, but keeping your divine part pure, as if you should be bound to give it back immediately; if you hold to this, expecting nothing, fearing nothing, but satisfied with your present activity according to nature, and with heroic truth in every word and sound which you utter, you will live happy. And there is no man who is able to prevent this.

--Marcus Aurelius, *Meditations*, Book 3

Stoicism is a school of philosophy that flourished in ancient Greece and Rome, yet still remains vital and timeless. It asks us to consider the root of our happiness, and to discover the strength within ourselves to live well depending upon our own character, not merely upon the circumstances of our lives.

The Stoic recognizes that philosophy isn't just about thinking, but how that thinking assists us, day by day, in living.

This book is a breviary in the classical sense, a collection of 365 passages from the great Stoic philosophers, for meditation on each day of the year.

The author offers his own experiences, thoughts, and reflections on the original texts, so as to encourage the reader to apply ancient lessons to modern life.

Stoicism asks us to recognize our true humanity in relation to Nature, to live life with a genuine understanding and love for what is true and good, and to find the deepest joy in measuring our lives by our own excellence.

stoicbreviary.blogspot.com

❖ ❖ ❖ ❖ ❖

Dr Liam Milburn was a teacher of philosophy and the classical liberal arts.
Born in Austria, and then growing up in Boston, Massachusetts,
he, and his family, eventually settled in rural Oklahoma.

Made in the USA
Monee, IL
31 December 2021

87622687R00240